BEFORE MILTON KEYNES

Exploring the District's past

Volume 3

JOHN A. TAYLOR

BEFORE MILTON KEYNES
EXPLORING THE DISTRICT'S PAST
VOLUME 3

Published by Magic Flute Publishing Ltd. 2023
ISBN 978-1-909054-90-5

Magic Flute Publishing Limited

231 Swanwick Lane

Southampton SO31 7GT

www.magicflutepublishing.com

A catalogue description of this book is available from the British Library

INTRODUCTION

This is the third volume in a planned series about the Milton Keynes area before the creation of the new city. In times past this would have been known as North Bucks, South Northants and West Bedfordshire.

Milton Keynes, as a new town, is just over 50 years old and in that half century, what was a rural landscape between a triangle of small towns, has been rapidly transformed. Underlying that fresh development are many, many stories about our forebears, with a written history that goes back a thousand years and an archaeological record that extends into the Stone Age. The stories are worth telling and reading about.

The creation of the new town has provided a central focus for all communities to the north, east, south and west and we have extended our remit to include all communities within about a 12 mile radius. That is almost all of North Bucks, some parts of South Northamptonshire and parts of West Bedfordshire.

John Taylor has been writing about the history of the Milton Keynes area for close to a half century and has established himself as the pre-eminent historian of this part of the world. For many years he contibuted regular articles to the Milton Keynes Citizen and we have gathered these articles in a single volume. As with previous volumes in this series, we have designed this book so that it can be referenced and dipped into and the stories are, for the most part, brief and digestible. These articles have been ordered by community, alphabetically.

To avoid confusion we have called the ancient village of Milton Keynes by its original name of Middleton. Therefore Milton Keynes will refer to the new city that was created in 1967 and Middleton Keynes will refer to the ancient village.

Further volumes in a similar format will follow in due course.

Bryan Dunleavy,

September 2023.

I began writing articles for the local newspapers in the 1970s, variously with the Milton Keynes Mirror, Bletchley Gazette, and Wolverton Express. Applying a totally new approach the Milton Keynes Citizen then came on the scene, and commercially their new methods spelt an eventual end for all of their competitors. Some of the articles written for these past titles probably lurk in local newspaper archives in the local libraries. However I didn't keep any copies, and the only print copies I occasionally put away were some of those published by the Milton Keynes Citizen. These came to the kind attention of Bryan Dunleavy, of Magic Flute Publications, who suggested the content would be of sufficient interest for a book. Hence this publication.

The intent of the articles was to hopefully stimulate casual readers' interest in the local past. Therefore to attract a glance I sometimes began with a brief and definitely non academic introduction! Since the paper was a weekly publication these normally centred on an episode nationally occurring that week. Where available I've included the date of issue, for the curious to perhaps investigate what that might have been! Not least a 'rumble in the jungle' by a 'celebrity' MP, whose definition of 'with immediate effect' seemed to be prolonging the extent of 'immediate.'

John Taylor

September 2023

CONTENTS

ASPLEY GUISE

AERONAUTICS

As a little lad, one of the highlights of the long summer holidays was to cycle over to the aerodrome at Cranfield, peer expectantly over the perimeter hedge, and hope to see a Lancaster bomber run up its engines, taxi out and power majestically into the Bedfordshire skies.

With a large vertical fin attached to the upper fuselage it was engaged in de-icing trials on aerofoil surfaces, but of course with schoolboy imagination it was really embarking on an heroic mission over heavily defended enemy territory.

Perhaps Guy Gibson was at the controls, for he had once been the station commander. But of course he is more famously remembered for the Dambusters, of which the village of Aspley Guise has an association through a grandson of the village rector from 1880 until 1915, the Rev. James Chadwick Maltby.

As for Lancasters, the village has an association with one of the most famous that now survives, 'S for Sugar,' which endured numerous raids over wartime Germany.

Of the wartime crews, Frank Rutt, the rear gunner, later made his home at Mount Pleasant, Aspley Guise, and it would be at the RAF Museum at Hendon, where 'S for Sugar' is on display, that he and the rest of his crew had their first reunion. In fact prior to this the pilot, Jack Colpus, had come from his home at Perth, Australia, to stay with Frank and his wife, and it would be at the Wheatsheaf pub in the village that a reunion with some of the other crew members took place.

However, only when the missing complement came over from Canada was the full crew reunited, to reminisce among other experiences about a raid on Berlin on the night of November 26/27th 1943, when, having dropped the bombs, the aircraft was picked up by searchlights. The pilot took immediate evasive action but in doing so collided with another Lancaster and, with some five feet of the starboard wing sheared off, went into a dive. However, he regained control, and at 10,000 feet flew back to Waddington, only to have to divert to Linton on Ouse due to fog.

Even from the early days of aviation Aspley Guise can claim aeronautical connections, for in 1871 the Aspley Guise and Woburn Sands Gas Works had been asked to supply sufficient gas for a balloon ascent by a Mr. Gaueus.

Following the advent of powered flight, in 1917 having passed low over the area an Army aeroplane landed in a local field, and the pilot and the other occupant gratefully accepted refreshment at a local farm. Soldiers from Bletchley were called to guard the aeroplane and from a suitable distance large numbers of villagers inspected the machine, which then took off the next day.

In the south aisle of Aspley Guise Parish Church is a memorial plaque on which is commemorated Observer Lieutenant Guy Owen-Jones RN whose home was at Aspley Guise.

He was killed aged 25 in 'a naval flying accident' and the memorial is even more poignant since it also commemorates his brother, who, as a midshipman, had drowned at sea in 1924.

Of a more recent tragedy, on Friday 15th,1950, reports began to reach Bletchley Fire Brigade that an RAF jet had exploded at high speed over Brickhill Woods. In the company of three other brigades they immediately rushed to the scene and, having scoured 15 sq miles of heavily wooded terrain, at Aspley Heath found the body of the pilot, 28 year-old Squadron Leader J. Muller Rowland, still strapped into the wrecked cockpit. The aircraft had been a DH108 'flying wing', and the twisted remains lay scattered between Sandy Lane and Woburn Road.

(Milton Keynes Citizen, January 26, 2012)

ASPLEY SCHOOL

The British Museum in London, designed by former Aspley pupil. Robert Smirke.

In the recent Citizen, it was interesting to read the views on the dismal, but predictable, legacy of 'progressive' teaching methods, and, as regards spelling and grammar, it should have been obvious, even to 'trendies,' that conventions and rules are not there to be dictatorial, but to provide a consistency and ease of understanding for the benefit of all.

In fact they would no doubt have also liked to tear up the Highway Code, to promote a similar chaos and anarchy on the roads.

Now to proper schools, and in the words of one ex pupil and head boy 'Rugby was the only school in England, with the exception of Eton and Harrow, which could compete with Aspley.' Founded about 1720 the school, in Aspley Guise, was built in the grounds of Guise House, but at one time appears to have been none too healthy a place, since the master wrote to Richard How, of the village, asking if he could recommend any additional pupils, 'for the smallpox has caused some vacancies.'

However, having once been an errand boy at the school, in 1778 William Wright took over as the master, and the outlook soon improved, for 'sickly half nourished London boys nearly doubled their weight in six months,' with 'fever scarcely ever known.' William died in December 1807, and is duly commemorated in the parish church. Following his death the Reverend Richard Pain took over, but, facing competition from other educational establishments, he closed the 'Classical Academy' in 1844/5.

Nevertheless, he remained at Guise House, and, building a wall down the middle of the property, sold the dormitory, offices, school rooms, and playground to a builder, George Farr Arnold, for £950. (This would later become Powage Press.) Of all the Aspley pupils perhaps the most renowned was Robert Smirke, (1781-1867), who became a celebrated architect. In fact his work included much of the former Mint on Tower Hill, a rebuilding of Covent Garden theatre (which tragically burnt down in 1856) and the restoration of York Minster. He is best remembered, however, for his involvement with the British Museum, and more especially the construction, between 1823 and 1828, of the oldest part of the building, the King's Library, which was designed specifically to house an enormous collection of books, given to the Museum by George IV.

As for modern day education, fortunately I'm too long in the tooth to have experienced the antics of the 'jus spel it ow u fink it sowndes' brigade. Which is just as well, or these articles would no doubt be only intelligible to those well versed in medieval English.

FOOLING HESS

In some firms where I've worked, it's been one of life's imponderables as to why – among a significant profusion – a large number of 'sickies' seem to occur as add ons to either a weekend or national holidays.

Obviously pure coincidence, but somewhat puzzling all the same. Also, why this phenomena appears most prevalent among those outfits whose competence seems negated by the financial blessing of a captive market, or copious amounts of Government money.

But during World War Two the Government positively encouraged 'sickies', although not of course among its own population. Instead, by the covert distribution of a 'malingerer's handbook' it was the intention to encourage foreign slave workers, and no doubt German soldiers who had no wish to be transferred to the Eastern Front, to feign all kinds of ailments by reference to its pages, which suggested all manner of ways to induce the symptoms of illness.

In fact this was just part of an extensive 'black propaganda' operation, the sole intention of which was to deceive the Nazis by the disinformation contained in printed material.

This was either disseminated by secret agents or dropped by air over enemy territory, and during the so called 'phoney war' the main efforts of the department involved were directed to the production of three or four varieties of leaflet.

These were first dropped on the night of November 6/7th 1939 over Hamburg, Bremen and Dusseldorf, with the most prominent being a two page imitation Nazi newspaper entitled 'Wolkiger Beobachter.'

Translating as 'From the Clouds' this was a play on the name of the genuine German newspaper, 'Voelkischer Beobachter' and for the manufacture of such productions within a hanger in the grounds of Woburn Abbey, where the aeroplane of the 'Flying Duchess' had once been housed, two compositors from University Press at Oxford set up a composing room in September 1939.

Here they typeset the propaganda leaflets and, with the early versions being set by hand in old fashioned German Fraktur type, these were then printed by rotary letterpress at HM Stationery Office in Harrow.

The German occupation of most of Western Europe, plus the entry of Italy into the war, then greatly increased the demands for propaganda and accordingly the Woburn print unit was relocated to Marylands, near Woburn. Replacing an earlier centre, this had been built during 1902/3 as a model hospital by the Duchess of Bedford and during the First World War was used as a military hospital.

With Monotype equipment installed in a hut in the grounds, here during the Second World War staff of the composing room were augmented to allow working around the clock and the recruitment of expert typographers and graphic artists caused a consequent improvement in the quality of the work.

The actual printing was carried out by the Sun Engraving Co. at Watford and also Waterlows at Dunstable and when necessary the printing expertise could also be employed for specialised one off requirements.

The defection of Rudolf Hess in May 1941 provided just such an occasion, and produced at Luton News under the tightest security faked versions of Voelkischer Beobachter were planted for him to read.

In fact as an intriguing aside, eight days after his landing two German agents parachuted into England near Luton Hoo, and on being found to be members of the SS were interrogated and executed at a secret establishment, with the nature of their mission never being revealed.

Oh, what a murky world of lies and deceit, much in fact like the realm of illicit 'sickies.' On the subject of which I could do with a couple of days off to finish painting the bathroom. But stuff wasting annual leave. So let's have a think; 'bad back?' Naw, that's more for the long term. 'Flu and sniffles?' Possibly, but best kept for December and Christmas shopping.

Ah, I know, 'gippy tummy,' that always fools them. But then perhaps not. For it could be counter productive, since just the thought of taking a crafty 'sickie' is enough to make my stomach churn.

(Milton Keynes Citizen, September 13, 2012)

OTTO JOHN

The Rookery at Aspley Guise.

Mention in previous articles has been made of the wartime propaganda station at Milton Bryan and also of The Rookery, Aspley Guise, which provided accommodation for the head of the activities, Sefton Delmer.

This was a murky world of intrigue and to become acquainted with both locations would be the only survivor of the 'Generals Conspiracy' (to eliminate Hitler) to escape abroad. He was Otto John, who before the war as a law student had been repulsed by the Nazi excess.

As an avenue to escape from Germany he took an unpaid job at Frankfurt airport and a chance meeting with the head of Lufthansa saw him appointed as a lawyer, supervising Lufthansa's subsidiary companies abroad. Thus he occupied an ideal position by which to establish contact with the Allies and in fact would advise them of the various attempts to assassinate Hitler and of the Peenemunde secret.

Then in the aftermath of D Day the newsroom at Milton Bryan intercepted a report concerning another plot against Hitler. A bomb had exploded at his headquarters but he survived and thereon the revolt was ruthlessly suppressed. Otto's brother was killed in the ensuing purge but Otto escaped the Gestapo by virtue of his Lufthansa employment. He boarded a plane for Madrid and the British Secret Service made arrangements for him to be flown to Britain.

Now with his hair dyed black he eventually arrived at Poole by flying boat, to next be conveyed to London. After two weeks of questioning he was interrogated by Delmer about working for British propaganda and in consequence was driven to Milton Bryan, where he again met Delmer. He was then driven to his accommodation at The Rookery and at Milton Bryan spent his days exploring the station and investigating the files.

At the end of the war Otto remained at The Rookery and having instructions to remain there he countered the inactivity by borrowing a bicycle and exploring the local countryside. Eventually he was summoned to London and being asked to join a German Austrian division of the Foreign Office, regarding the re-education of the population in the British occupied zones, was given the use of an office and very much left to his own devices. In time arrangements were made for him to acquire the status of 'British War Reporter' and he travelled by air to Germany.

Later his duties involved interrogating high ranking German officers and in December 1950 he was appointed Head of the Federal Internal Security Office in West Germany. Working from an office in the ruins of Cologne, the objective was to investigate extremist intrigues against the state. However the timing proved most inopportune for in that very year the Soviets infiltrated a former S.S. officer into German intelligence.

From his information they made plans for a mass arrest of Western agents but to preserve the cover of their source needed a suitable 'incident,' to explain how they obtained the knowledge. That incident would be set up by the K.G.B. and involve the unwitting Otto. In July 1954 he was drugged by a 'trusted friend,' who was in fact a K.G.B. agent, and regained consciousness on the sofa of a K.G.B. house in East Berlin.

Coerced into making a statement over East Berlin radio he was then given instructions to apply for political asylum to the East German Government. After consuming drugged food the next sensation involved him in an anti German performance at a rehearsed press conference, after which he was transferred to a dacha outside Moscow.

During his Soviet stay he then realised the extent of the K.G.B. penetration, when shown copies of recent secret reports from his West German department. Under guard, by 1955 he was back in East Berlin occupying an office but pretending to visit a university professor he managed to shake off his 'minders,' and eventually reached West Berlin in a car driven by a friend.

Yet his reception proved anything but welcome and charged with treason on December 22nd 1956 his trial by the German High Court sentenced him to four years' hard labour. It would not be until July 28th 1958 that he eventually gained his release.

Milton Keynes Citizen, July 5, 2012)

ASTWOOD

THE HISTORY OF DOVECOTES

The Dovecote at Astwood.

Apart from their recent use for providing recreation, or carrying messages, pigeons since Norman times have been kept as a useful source of food, although only as the preserve of the lord of the manor or the parson.

However, eventual improvements in farming enabled cattle to be kept throughout the winter, and the consequent decline in the need for dovecotes was no doubt greatly welcomed, as they were renowned for being unhygienic.

In fact the Rev. Coles, the Bletchley diarist, records in 1760 that, being made of 'mud and plaister and old timber,' a dovecote adjoining the Rectory was so infested with fleas that he had it pulled down, to be replaced by one built of brick, as far away from the Rectory as possible!

Nevertheless, now converted to purposes far removed from their original use, there are still several dovecotes to be seen within our region, including a fine example at Astwood.

An octagonal building, with a pyramidal roof, this is now a private dwelling, and was in fact all that remained of Astwoodbury House. A mansion alleged to once have been 'one of the best old seats in the county.'

For reasons somewhat obscure, the house was pulled down in 1799, but a few years earlier the Olney poet, William Cowper, had noted 'There is a Mr. Towers at a place called Astwoodberry, about seven miles off; but he is a fox-hunter merely.'

Fortunately, the dovecote survived a visit by the Luftwaffe in 1940, when bombs severely damaged the village church. A German bomber also menaced Dovecote Farm at Shenley but fortunately the bomb failed to detonate. As for the dovecote of the name, this had long been demolished, having at one time belonged to the Fenny Stratford Guild of St. Margaret and St. Katherine.

By dint of the same name, at Stewkley, Dovecote Farm, (Dove House), may once have been a building of considerable importance (Queen Elizabeth I is supposed to have stayed there on one occasion) but the dovecote has long since disappeared.

However, more definite is the past importance of nearby Manor Farm, for this is an 18th century conversion of a16th century manor house, which itself was a descendant of a manor house built in the vicinity after the Norman Conquest.

Here, within the confines of a recent business park the previous status is emphasised by the surviving octagonal dovecote, built in 1704 of brick in Flemish bond.

Yet probably even pre-dating this by a few years is the well preserved dovecote at Church Farm, Little Woolstone.

The farmhouse was once the home of William Smith, of agricultural steam ploughing renown, but since the arrival of the New City the surrounding acreage has long been built on.

Also now built over are the agricultural acres that once surrounded the village of Great Linford, although dating from the early 17th century the future of the dovecote of the Old Rectory, having 600 nests, was thankfully more assured when declared a scheduled monument.

BATTLESDEN

A BRIEF HISTORY OF BATTLESDEN

In many of our local villages several interesting features are to be seen, recalling their history and heritage, but some also have associations with people who achieved a national renown. One such community is Battlesden, the lake of which was an early project by Joseph Paxton, who later became Sir Joseph Paxton, of Crystal Palace fame.

The early mansion of Battlesden was built in Tudor times, and during the Civil War became a hiding place for Royalists.

Thus in the wake of Parliament's victory the Duncombes, as lords of the manor, fled to France, but according to the diarist Samuel Pepys, when Sir John Duncombe returned at the Restoration he, despite being made a Knight of the Royal Oak and Chancellor of the Exchequer, was the sole member of the government to offend the King by protesting against his extravagant expenditure.

In a later century Battlesden was sold to Sir Gregory Page, a director of the East India Company, and following the death of his descendant, Sir Gregory Page Turner, the house in the early 19th century remained empty for many years. Yet despite the supposed mysterious appearances of the ghostly 'Sir Griggery', it was looked after by a female caretaker, but on one occasion when she needed a night off two women from the village were called in to take charge.

As the night wore on they eventually retired to bed, but, with the clock in the tower having just struck midnight, suddenly their bedroom door began to slowly creak open and a 'presence', said to be a ghostly grey lady, began to pull at the bedclothes. Having a young baby with her, one of the women then remembered that a ghost would not touch innocent blood, and so she laid the infant upon the bed. Indeed, no harm befell the child.

Another ghostly tale regarding the old mansion was that of a cheating steward, whose apparition was said to appear on certain nights in the dairy. During his lifetime he was said to have deceived the villagers by mixing water with the milk, and as he rattled his ghostly chains he was heard to chant:

> 'Milk and water I sold ever,
>
> Weight and measure I gave never
>
> And I shan't rest, never, never.'

In 1635 Sir Saunders Duncombe, the brother of the lord of Battlesden, obtained the monopoly for the manufacture, sale and hire of sedan chairs in England. As a great traveller he had probably seen this type of conveyance at Sedan, where they were supposedly made, and his patent vested the sole right to himself and his heirs.

As for his other achievements, as inscribed on the memorial above the pulpit in Battlesden church he 'hath bin a gent pentioner in ordinary to King James of blessed meo and also to King Charles about ye space of thirty yeares.'

Another form of transport to which the village could lay claim was 'The Battlesden Car', a type of horse drawn trap. Built by Mr. King, of Linslade, the original model had been made for Mr. David Bromilow, during his tenancy of Battlesden mansion and with the conveyance becoming very popular with all classes, Mr. King's works became known as 'The Battlesden Carriage Works.'

The local community has never been populous, and so the plan of Battlesden church is a simple nave and chancel.

The church at Battlesden.

Appointed in 1219, Robert de Gatesden is recorded as the first rector, although it is from the late 13th century that the earliest structural vestige is now apparent, in the form of the two light window in the south nave wall. The chancel arch dates from the 14th century, and the tower is an addition of the 15th century. In fact a mention in 1551 records that there were 'in the stepull of the church iij bells.'

However, it seems that the tower had been built on insubstantial foundations, and a subsequent tilt had to be arrested by brick buttressing.

Contemporary with the brick battlements, in 1898 the tower underwent repairs, but despite these attentions from 1928 it became necessary to keep the church closed (except for the months of August and September) from 1931 to 1934.

Then in August 1947 a church fete, held in the grounds of Milton Bryan rectory, raised over £100 for the restoration of the local churches, and this would especially please the Reverend Kenyon, who had been appointed to the combined parishes a few months before.

Indeed, his was the ambition to have the church of Battlesden restored, and towards this intent he was greatly aided by a gift of £200 from William Merridale who, having lived for many years in the village, had sung as a youth in the choir. In fact he had spent all his working life on the Woburn estate, and because he lived near the church he tried to maintain it in some sort of order.

Sadly, damage to the organ and pews had been caused during the Second World War and it was by the advice of the famed Professor Richardson that a meeting of the parishioners, held in July, agreed that for a few hundred pounds the church could be made fit for use. In fact during the meeting Mr. Merridale's £200 was substantially increased by other donations, and the much hoped for restoration could now take place.

Thus the church re-opened in 1949, but sadly William Merridale did not live to witness the event.

He died in December 1946, and a plaque to his memory is to be seen on the north wall of the nave.

Following the restoration, the church was open to anyone with an ecclesiastical interest and, with the benefices of Battlesden and Potsgrove having been officially united in 1732, (by the Bishop of Lincoln), an Order in Council by Queen Elizabeth was made in 1971, whereby Battlesden church became denominated to serve the communities of both Battlesden and Potsgrove.

The church of the latter therefore became redundant, while Battlesden church remains in regular use.

At Battlesden once stood the mansion of the Page-Turner family, who were prominent as East India merchants, and several views of the palatial glory were included amongst a magnificent collection of local watercolours, presented by the family to the county of Bedford.

Born in the nearby village of Milton Bryan, during his early career in 1821 Joseph Paxton had been engaged to lay out the gardens of the mansion, and still to be seen is his 13 acre lake, complete with a boathouse and central island. In fact Joseph's uncle kept the pub in the nearby village of Milton Bryan, and was owed money in 1823 by Sir Gregory Page-Turner for supplying beer to the workmen!

Locally the lake became known as 'the new fish pond' - as opposed to an earlier watery expanse lying to the north, which had been dug some 300 years previous but as for Joseph, he would progress to much greater renown, and is today best remembered for his design and construction of the Crystal Palace, built to commemorate the Great Exhibition of 1851.

BLETCHLEY

BANKING IN BLETCHLEY

An early view looking towards the Town Hall from Aylesbury Street, Fenny Stratford.

Except as a Stringfellow's talent scout, career wise I've never had much idea of what I've wanted to do. And so along life's thorny path there have been a number of jobs, from slick and streamlined operations to those which can best be described as a bumble of amusing dysfunction. The latter seem to be either Government funded, or blessed with a captive customer base, whereby a guaranteed income creates such a cushion of complacency that, since the buffoonery are rarely discarded but merely elbowed to one side, the inept not only thrive but multiply. Rewarding failure today is nowhere more apparent than in the world of banking, which until recently seemed a profession of staid and responsible repute. Even towards the end of the 19th century Bletchley and Fenny Stratford did not have a bank and people had to go to Bassetts Son and Harris in Leighton Buzzard. Then in 1887 the firm opened an office each Thursday in a room on the ground floor of the Town Hall, Fenny Stratford, which, as custom grew, was extended to twice a week and eventually every day. In time the bank merged with Barclays Bank, for which a branch (now a dental suite) was built near the Council Offices in 1912, with another at the corner of Park Street and Bletchley Road (now Queensway) around 1921. As for the old accommodation in the Town Hall, here in late June 1916 Thomas Best opened offices for his business as certified accountants and public auditors, having for the past 15 or 16 years been involved in such aspects with his namesake late father. Normally the bank dealt with the usual transactions of the local residents, farmers and traders, but in 1921 they were entrusted with most of the £1,000 'Derby' sweepstake of the National Federation of Discharged Soldiers and Sailors (forerunner of the British Legion) won by 23 year old Bert Garrett. He was the eldest son of Mr. and Mrs. Garrett, with whom he lived in a little cottage in Aylesbury Street. Another who had seen service during World War One, winning the M.C. as a Lieutenant in the South Wales Borderers, was Mr. Hart, a Cambridgeshire man, who in August, 1937, moved with his wife, Jean, from Ampthill to take over from Frank Caton (a native of Shefford) as Barclay's manager at Bletchley. Wisely during World War Two they sent their children to the Isle of Man and on Mr. Hart's eventual retirement in July, 1950, the couple moved to 'The Cheverals', Bow Brickhill, where Mr. Hart died a few years later, leaving a widow, a son and two daughters. With the post war expansion of Bletchley, Frederick Gibberd, the architect of the Metropolitan Cathedral of Christ the King, Liverpool, designed a new Bletchley branch of Barclay's Bank which opened on Monday, November 30th 1964, at 25, Bletchley Road. This was on the site of the old sub branch, with the original main branch, at 259, Bletchley Road, now becoming the sub branch. Apart from Barclays, Lloyds Bank have also been prominent in the town and perhaps some residents still have memories of Terry Harrison. He came from their employment at Market Harborough to be the manager at Bletchley and in his leisure pursuits he was well known as a banjo player, performing not only in local concerts but also in several B.BC. radio broadcasts. Apart from his musical skills he was also an expert model maker and after his death at the early age of 59 in 1945, at his home 'Bowden', in Denbigh Road, his son, John, would complete some of his work for entry at the exhibitions of the Bletchley Model Making Club. In fact he had been a model bank manager, unlike some of the more recent specimens who have reduced their profession to a semblance of the wild west. As for other cowboy outfits, well from my experience they've always been those where the Chiefs outnumber the Indians.

THE BATHING PLACE 1

In days gone by, for those seeking the cure of medicinal bathing, there were at various times several locations where healing waters could be locally sought, including Gayhurst, Flitwick and Winslow.

However, for recreational purposes for centuries the River Ousel remained in favour, until rivalled in the early 19th century by the challenge of the Grand Junction Canal, (known from 1929 as the Grand Union Canal).

Before the advent of the railways, the canals introduced an unparalleled opportunity for commercial success, and, apart from the goods that could now be economically transported from the mining and industrial areas, a lucrative custom also awaited those who were prepared to cater for the needs of initially the navvies, and then the bargees.

Originally a private thatched house at Fenny Stratford, the first mention of the canal side Red Lion is made in 1835. Not surprisingly, the location could often prove hazardous to customers who over-indulged - although it was not only drunken adults who occasionally ended up in the canal but also children, for whom the lock provided an added fascination. In fact, one landlord of the Red Lion would even be recommended for a medal by the Royal Humane Society, for having twice jumped into the lock to rescue small boys. Eventually, so many complaints were being made about children bathing in the canal that, in the words of public opinion, "We sadly want a bathing place where the youngsters may bathe, without being a nuisance."

In 1896 a Mr. Garner and a Mr. Whitney were tasked, on behalf of the council, to find a suitable situation. Adjoining the river, a location 'on the London Road' was deemed ideal, and in consequence correspondence was received from the agent to the Duncombe estate asking if, for the sum of £10 per annum, the council might wish to rent the whole of the field.

With the proposal accepted, it was then decided to spend around £50 on providing sheds for bathers, while for the existing hut £1 would be paid to Alfred Benford, who had been the late occupier of the site. In finalising the arrangements, mention was then made that the gate to the field would need painting, but in the event a new one was provided.

For supplying the sheds, of the two tenders received, that of £42 10s from Rowland Bros, was accepted. As for the grass-keeping - "either mowed or grazed" - that from Mr. H. Wright of £6 10s proved successful.

In order to hide the 'Bathing Place' from view, permission was sought from the agent of the Duncombe trustees to erect two or three posts in the field occupied by Messrs Hammond and Sons, to support a latticework - apparently a necessity, in the light of Mr. G. Cave's letter of July 1, 1897, in which he complained to the council about the nuisance caused by indecent bathing in the canal.

Therefore, to be ordered from Messrs. A. Stilton, a board warning bathers against "indecent exposure of the person", would be placed at the entrance to the site - along with the bathing regulations including that "Every person using the Bath must be provided with bathing drawers".

The bathing committee would recommend that certain hours should be set apart for the exclusive use of those subscribing 1s 6d a year, but nevertheless the facility began to deteriorate, until the council schools were established.

Thus, in a policy of continuing improvements, after a meeting on site in 1919, Lady Leon and the educational representatives decided that if the floor of the shed was concreted, and a partition put in place, the standard for both sexes would prove temporarily adequate for the school swimming classes. The cost of £30 was to be divided between the education authority and the urban council, and in May 1919 it was agreed that the Bathing Place should be reserved for schoolgirls on Mondays and Fridays from 2pm to 4pm.

In the long term, the intention was to raise sufficient funds to provide a proper swimming pool, but in 1921 the clerk of the council reported that the Bathing Place was to be auctioned on July 20, and it was decided to offer £150 by private treaty. If this was not accepted, then the chairman of the council should be authorised to attend the sale and purchase the Bathing Place on behalf of the urban council.

So it was with the council that a deputation of the unemployed met in October 1921 regarding the cleaning out of the facility, as a way of providing work. Completing the change of ownership the following month, the Bathing Place was then conveyed from Sir E. Duncombe to the council, and in July 1925 the surveyor arranged to have certain improvements carried out, including the building of a retaining wall.

Bathing Place. Watling Street, at the bend of the river.

THE BATHING PLACE 2

Last month, we mentioned the 'Bathing Place', situated on the bend of the river alongside Watling Street. The nostalgic photograph above has been kindly supplied by Mrs. E. Corden, who learned to swim there.

She remembers that one of the reasons for the decline in the facility's popularity was the presence of several dead sheep on the adjoining river banks - left behind by the receding waters of an extensive flood.

Apart from the Bathing Place, local swimmers also had the 'pond' at Water Eaton Mill, (although for the unwary this posed a peril, by reason of a deep section towards the middle). Otherwise they could brave the hazards of the Denbigh pits.

Even before the gravel excavations, the site had been greatly favoured for sporting activities, due to being one of the flattest meadows in the county. As implied by the name, 'Flannels Meadow' had on one occasion even hosted a match between the All England cricket team and "the top hatted Gentlemen of Bucks".

With swimming continuing to be a popular local recreation, in 1928 the Fenny Stratford members of the council recommended that, using water from the river, a bathing pool, or swimming bath, should be dug alongside the Bathing Place, but in 1935 plans for a proper swimming pool in the town were proposed.

Despite the resignation that year of the council's surveyor John Chadwick, the council had decided to retain his eminent services as consulting engineer for certain special schemes. Although he received instructions to proceed with the planning of the proposed swimming pool, after several delays the council abandoned the project.

Then, with the prospect of a government grant, they decided to proceed, but appointed the new surveyor as the architect. Not surprisingly, Major Chadwick claimed damages in respect of the old contract and, after considerable negotiations, the matter was settled out of court, with the council agreeing to pay him a sum of £850.

The council now prepared plans to provide a covered swimming pool, designed to have one side open with folding doors, to be financed by a £6,000 grant from the National Advisory Council and Grants Committee for Physical Training and Recreation. Agreement was reached with the education authority for a sum to be paid in return for using the pool, and tenders were invited, with construction due to begin during the summer.

However, the outbreak of war caused the cancellation of the grant - a tender of £12,000 had been accepted the day before hostilities broke out.

The prospect of London being heavily bombed caused the evacuation of children to rural areas, and for those arrivals in Bletchley the countryside would provide a fascinating contrast to their previous urban confinements. Yet although there was less danger from enemy air raids, for those unfamiliar with the countryside there were new hazards to face, as would be tragically proved, especially those posed by the profusion of streams and ponds.

Attending the Ecclesbourne Road School Senior department, (which was accommodated in Bletchley Park pavilion), for the past 18 months, 12 year-old Peter Kelly, an evacuee from Highbury in north London, had been billeted with

Mr. and Mrs. H. Ince of 6, Watling Street Terrace.

One evening in June 1941 he met up with another 12-year-old, Arthur Cox, of Lennox Road and, having decided to go for a swim in the Mill Pond at Water Eaton, the boys got changed and entered the water.

Suddenly Peter got into difficulties and grabbed his friend's bathing costume, but when this tore he began to slip under the water, and tragically drowned. At the inquest, 18-year-old Herbert Smith of 11, Windsor Street, said that he had been near the pond at about 7.30pm on that evening, and when told that a boy was drowning had dived on two occasions into some seven feet of water. Eventually he recovered the body, but despite desperate attempts at artificial respiration by four soldiers plus the attentions of Dr. Dorothy Lufkin, all their efforts proved in vain. A verdict of accidental death was recorded by the Coroner, Mr. E.T. Ray

Another evacuee to fall victim to the watery perils was seven-year-old Frank Tootell, who, whilst playing on the bank, fell into the canal near Hammond's Bridge. With his brother Billy, he had been billeted for the past two and a half years at the home of Mrs. Adelaide Linden, of 19, Church Street, and on Friday, April 3th 1942 the boys had been playing with a dog and other children near the canal when they met 10-year-old Nancy Quinn, of 54 Aylesbury Street.

They all then walked along the towpath towards the bridge. Having told Frank not to play with a stick by the water, when she heard a splash Nancy initially thought that the dog had fallen in. When she realised that it was Frank who had fallen in, Billy immediately raced along the path to tell a woman, who quickly told a soldier of the predicament.

Meanwhile, Nancy ran to the other bank and, despite the water being rough, used a stick to pull Frank to the side of the canal. She then held his head above water until Private Richard Griffiths arrived, with two colleagues, and tried to give artificial respiration. Unfortunately, the boy was already dead and, following an inquest, the funeral was held on Monday in the Salvation Army Hall.

In a letter of March 27th 1944 to the council, Mr. G. Goodwin, of Dropshort Farm, offered a rent of £4 10s per annum for the Bathing Place field and this was accepted, provided he kept the weeds down.

Despite the war, during that year plans were shown for a swimming pool to be constructed at Central Gardens - 35ft x 100ft, enhanced by footpaths, cubicles, dressing rooms, showers, and underwater lighting. Perhaps in anticipation of this, in March 1945 the council announced the sheds at the Bathing Place were to be dismantled, and the fencing removed.

In July they invited tenders for the purchase of the several sheds, plus a quantity of galvanised corrugated iron sheets - and thus the water-filled gravel works in Denbigh Road would gain in favour for both fishing and swimming.

However, in early July 1946 the former pit manager, Fred Carvell, who for many years had occupied a house in Staple Hall Road, died aged 40. He had been living with his wife in Wellingborough Road, Olney, and was soon to have moved to Great Linford, to manage another pit belonging to the same firm, Thomas Roberts (Westminster) Ltd.

In 1947 Mr. Norman Green purchased The Grange, at Far Bletchley - a property with a swimming pool (which had served as a static water tank during the war) - and offered its use to the local schools. He even hoped to open a lido at the premises before the end of the year!

As for a public swimming pool, a proposal to revive the scheme to celebrate the Festival of Britain met with little enthusiasm, and it would not be until the coronation of Queen Elizabeth II that a plan would materialise, with a Town Committee being formed to raise sufficient money.

Unfortunately, the amount proved disappointing, but nevertheless a plastic-lined open air pool, known as 'Queens Pool', opened in June 1958, with Bletchley Swimming Club securing the use for a forthcoming season on Mondays between 6pm and 9pm, for a fee of £25.

In order to allow for shifting and subsidence, the plastic liner had been left deliberately looser and slacker than necessary, and at the end of the season the sheet was sent back to the manufacturers for trimming. However, when duly returned to Bletchley it was found to have hardened in the cold weather, and the subsequent work had to be postponed until the warmer months. Even so, the liner would prove less than adequate and, as a remedial measure, a surface coating of fibreglass had to be applied.

Eventually, enhancements were made to the pool, including the provision of heated water, which could be enjoyed by the public following a re-opening in July 1969. The pool remained as a popular and much-used local amenity until the 1970s, when, together with Central Gardens, the area succumbed to the 'futuristic' Bletchley Leisure Centre.

BLETCHLEY COUNCIL OFFICES

Before the introduction of local councils, public responsibilities had been vested in a variety of different 'Boards' and bodies - the Highways Board, Burial Board, etc - and although worthy in their aspirations, the overall result produced a somewhat wasteful and inefficient system.

On 13 August, 1888, Queen Victoria then set her signature to an Act which would amend the laws relating to local government in England and Wales, and theron 'A council shall be established in every administrative county.'

Following the formation of the County Councils, there came into being the Rural District and Urban District Councils, and, of local relevance, by Local Government Board Order No. 32776, Fenny Stratford and Simpson amalgamated to form an Urban District Council in July, 1895.

By a narrow vote the first Chairman was a local hay and corn dealer, James Baisley, and the new Council held responsibility for such matters as sanitation, water supplies and housing.

The former Bletchley Urban District Council offices.

During the following years the resulting benefits then became increasingly apparent, and directly lead to a consequent decrease in the mortality rate.

In 1898 a formal agreement was reached to transfer Bletchley Parish to the UDC and, agreed by public meeting, this was finalised, except for the name, on 1st April by Government Board Order 37157. However, not until May 16th 1911 did the name formally change to Bletchley, with Water Eaton being included within the Council's jurisdiction in 1934.

Regarding accommodation, in the early years the Council endured a somewhat nomadic existence, and this was evidenced in early January, 1896, by a decision that the premises in the High Street, lately occupied by the Cooperative Society, should be acquired as the Council Offices, at a rent of £25 pa.

A list of the necessary furniture would then be compiled by John Chadwick, the newly appointed Surveyor and Inspector of Nuisances, and at the opening of the tenders that of George Pacey was accepted, at 10s 6d per chair, 1s 6d per square yard for lino, £3 10s for a large table, and £3 for a small table.

Yet when eventually delivered the tables were not accepted, and 'in accordance with the order of his tender' Mr. Pacey would arrange to have new ones manufactured.

As a permanent centre for the Council, the Town Hall and the old Wesleyan Chapel, in the High Street, had both been suggested, and in consequence the Local Government Board Inspector held an enquiry. However, his deliberations duly ruled out the Town Hall as being unsuitable, whilst as for the old chapel, built in 1813, on account of this antiquity no sanction for a loan would be forthcoming.

Plans were therefore proposed for a new building, and in 1903 the Council at last moved into purpose built offices, designed by John Chadwick. At a cost of £2,000 the premises had been constructed by the firm of Tranfield and Co., a family with origins in New Bradwell, and with this being their first major project perhaps the venture proved even more challenging, since the site had allegedly once been a pond! Apart from the usual Council business, by invitation on 14th April 1910, about 50 people attended a meeting at the Council Offices where Dr. C Deyns, presiding, said that 'the time has arrived when a determined effort should be made to establish a horticultural society in the district.' Mr. Leon subsequently gave the use of Bletchley Park and although the idea soon caught on, no shows would be held during World War One, a conflict at the beginning of which not only did Captain John Chadwick, the Surveyor to the Council, enter military service, but also his staff as well. Yet this was excepting the elderly clerk, Thomas Best, who was placed in charge of the Surveyors Department. His namesake son was then appointed as deputy surveyor in 1915, but when on the death of Thomas Best senior he was passed over for the position, with, at a salary of £250 pa, Mr. Charter Wilson appointed instead, he promptly resigned.

Against the possibility of aerial attack, in 1916 the Council applied to insure the Council Offices with the County Fire Office for £2,000, but although the premises would be spared an airborne assault, during the same year came the tragic news that 20 year old Lt. Douglas Chadwick, the son of John Chadwick, had been killed in action.

After the war, in 1921 the Council Offices would accommodate the town's first library, and this was perhaps included amongst the caretaking duties of Annie Mead who, (since the intended applicant, Mrs. Tearle, had proved unable to accept the duties), was appointed to the position of caretaker at the Council Offices in June 1926. The situation paid a wage of 12s 6d a week, with the free provision of a house, gas, and coals.

Born at Leighton Buzzard, Miss Mead was a daughter of the late William Mead, a parcels carrier who had moved to Bletchley over 50 years ago. Being well known as a toffee maker, in his younger days he had been a confectioner, and Miss Mead came to Bletchley to look after him in 1920, when he became ill. Two years later he died, and, living on the premises, Annie and her sister, Edith, would eventually take up the caretaking duties at the Council Offices.

With the outbreak of World War Two there would then be a new and important role for the Council Offices, at the rear of which on Friday, 1st September, 1939, following an appeal for sandbag fillers many volunteers reported for this duty the next morning.

Their efforts then seemed fully justified when at the Bletchley Report Centre, accommodated in the Council Offices, just after 7.30am the first air raid warning in the town was received on Wednesday morning, although the 'All Clear' would sound soon after 9am. With a continuing increase in ARP duties, including having to now clean the Control Room and the Food Control Room, Annie not surprisingly sought an increase in pay, and by the subsequent agreement her weekly wage would be raised from 20s to 30s, payable from 18th November, 1939.

In fact her retirement had been scheduled for 31st December, but after considerations the Council decided to renew the appointment until 31st March, 1940, and this was subsequently extended until 30th September, 1940.

Maintaining a telephone watch for an average of 12 hours a day, seven days a week, as full-time members of the Council staff Mr. W Bradbury and Mrs. Olive Moser, not only carried out all the clerical and administration work of the ARP Department, but also the clerical work of the Fire Brigade and the AFS, and this was all in addition to their normal employment!

At the Report Centre, a full time officer of the Council would generally be on duty from 8.30am until 7pm each day, and volunteers would then attend 7pm until 10pm.

Manning the telephone, to which a loud gong was attached, a night operator then took over, with the provision of a chair bed to sleep on.

In the event of a possible air raid, on receiving a 'yellow alert' the Report Centre would call the fire station, and either from there or the police station the regular fireman would be summoned by a bell system, a bell having been installed in each of the firemen's homes, worked on the Post Office open wire system.

In April 1940 the ARP Committee then announced that in place of the existing 0.9hp siren the Home Office Divisional Officer had suggested installing a 4hp Gent model.

With the original siren being kept in reserve, this, at an estimated cost of around £40, was then fixed on the Council Offices, where in early May perhaps as an omen the Coronation clock suddenly stopped one Tuesday evening, and began to go backwards! During the monthly air raid test, in early June 1940 the new 4hp siren was then heard for the first time, and being found to have a louder note experiments were duly made to increase the sound even more, which was eventually achieved by fixing an upper sounding board.

In the event of an air attack, the Air Raid Casualty Centre for the town was to be located at the Council Offices in the ARP Report Centre, and in other wartime uses the Council Chamber of the Council Offices would be variously rented by the Bletchley Food Control Cornmittee and also HM Office of Works, being sometimes also used for County Court sittings.

As for the Council yard at the rear of the building, here would be established the depot for the Decontamination Squad, consisting of 18 fully trained men led by Mr. J. Thurlby. With the imminent threat of a German invasion, secret plans were made to blow up the Council Offices, and with key areas designated for 'defence to the last', in preparation for a siege tinned rations were stored on site. As winter approached, with the probability of ice and snow attention was then given to finding a means of keeping the air raid siren at the Council Offices operational, and this was resolved by a letter of 18th October, 1940 from the Senior Regional Officer at Aylesbury, which stated 'It is understood that the cost of the heater without a thermostat is £4 10s and the expenditure will rank for grant subject to the terms of the relevant financial regulations'.

No doubt the siren would also help with the heating, by drawing a typical start current of 60amps!

Even in 1942 invasion was still viewed as a very real danger, and at a meeting on Thursday 5th March of the ARP Committee Major General Blount, by a letter dated 24th February, asked permission to use the Council Chamber - 'in case of necessity' - as a local defence battle headquarters. This was duly agreed, but thankfully such measures would not be required. After the end of the European war, in late July, 1945 the Fire Force Commander wrote to the ARP Committee asking if the Council would transfer the use of the air raid siren to the National Fire Service.

This was for the purpose of calling part-time members of the brigade to any fires that occurred between 8am and 10pm and on condition that the NFS saw to the repairs, this request was agreed.

However, with the siren remaining in the present position only the control point would be transferred to the police station.

Despite her earlier contracts, Annie Mead would remain as caretaker at the Council Offices until 1946, and indeed it was only the effects of a road accident, in the autumn of 1945, that hastened her retirement.

On leaving the caretaker's house she would then live with her sister at 11 Abbey Road, a council house in Simpson, and in fact it had been arranged by the Council that the sisters should have the property subject to the tenant's wife undertaking the caretaking duties, for £2 a week, at the Council Offices.

Thereby the tenant, Mr. L Odell, would be granted, rent free, the occupancy of the Council Offices house. As for Annie Mead, aged 78 she died on 6th January 1947.

In 1960, Mrs. D. Ramsbotham would be elected the first woman Chairman of BUDC and this was a responsibility that now seemed to be burgeoning for, due to an increase in staff, plans were being proposed to extend the Council Offices.

Then in another timely move, with the hands on one side of the previous clock having been missing for many months, on Monday July 19th 1965, the new clock on the Council Offices came into operation, at 6.10pm.

Being a 42 inch Smiths English Clock System, the timepiece had cost £250, and in further expense earlier during the year machinery costing £4,000 and weighing 32 cwt, was installed for the Treasurers Department of the Bletchley Council Offices.

This was a replacement for the worn out manual system of book keeping, and the main section of the new apparatus would be a card puncher, verifier and sorter, with most of the equipment located in the former stables at the rear of the building. (Horses had been acquired by the parish in 1888 to pull the dust carts, and, replacing those of the local coal merchants the same horses would

additionally be used to pull the fire engine).

BLETCHLEY GAZETTE

Time travel. Now there's a conundrum.

There is the old chestnut of how could you exist if you travelled back in time and did away with your grandfather before he had a chance to procreate. Personally, I think this approach is quite wrong. All you need to do is reconstitute the exact states of matter that existed at a particular time and you would have the past in the present without altering the future.

Before the men in white coats arrive, how, I hear you ask, would you know what these states of matter were, and their ongoing sequence? Umm, well I'm still working on this, but, in a gross over simplification, perhaps equating the Big Bang to a break of billiard balls comes to mind.

By fundamental laws their path and position can be predicted at any point and so someday perhaps the same will be possible for particles of matter, on a Universal scale. Anyway, I'm just off for a lie down, before beginning this week's piece on a less fanciful means of time travel - reading through the archives of the local newspapers, and more specifically the Bletchley Gazette.

During December 1930, Mr. Harold Price came to Bletchley to look at a small amount of printing equipment that, having belonged to the deceased Mr. Tuckey, was being offered at an 'absurdly cheap' price in a building (not for sale) that many years later would become the Dudeney and Johnston store.

At the time Mr. and Mrs. Price owned a small print business in the Oxfordshire village of Steeple Aston and while Mr. Price purchased and arranged the storage of the equipment, his wife continued the established business. The couple then decided to settle in Bletchley and having purchased 87, Bletchley Road (now Queensway) in a field at the bottom of the back garden Mr. Price built a timber and asbestos printing shed. Born in Oxfordshire of a 'numerous family' he had joined the Army at the age of 16½ but was invalided out due to the effects of a gas attack.

Lacking any specific skills he then returned to civilian life and while being employed as an auxiliary postman he learnt the print trade with a country printer. In Bletchley, as a junior stationery salesman Mr. E. Staniford had often visited Mr. Price for orders and he one day suggested that there seemed a need in the town for a local newspaper.

This met with an enthusiastic response and their first office was in a tackling shed in Mr. Price's back garden, with the actual printing undertaken by the Bedfordshire Times Publishing Co. Despite being busy with his printing business Mr. Price wrote the lead articles and the children's column whilst Mr. Staniford produced the rest.

However, soon the printing costs of the Bedfordshire Times proved too expensive and so they decided to acquire an 'intertype' printing machine and a flat bed machine. As these were too expensive to purchase new they travelled to the headquarters of Intertype and persuaded the managing director to sell them a new machine, with payment over four years.

They then went to a firm in London which had advertised a flat bed machine for sale and this they purchased for £250, to be spread over two years. Thus in June 1934, the first Bletchley Gazette to be printed and published in Bletchley appeared and they now took on a full time operator, working in a derelict shed next to Mr. Price's home.

Despite a fire in May 1948 the paper flourished and with the relaxation of wartime constraints could expand and from January 1949 sell as many copies as it could.

Expansion of the town by the London overspill brought additional readers and in the late 1960s the offices moved from Queensway to Ward Road, Mount Farm. Then came the New City and in September 1974 the name was changed to the Milton Keynes Gazette. This was a time of new printing technology but the proprietors refused to embrace the methods and in 1981 came the challenge from the more forward thinking Citizen.

In 1985 the proprietors then closed the Ward Road premises but under new ownership the paper was produced from the spring of 1986 in small offices in Aylesbury Street, until circumstances forced a final closure in 1993.

BLETCHLEY IN 1926

Continuing our look at Bletchley in 1926, in order to service the increased residential developments, several improvements and expansions were made to the necessary facilities, including the completion of a filtration scheme for the water supply.

As a further advantage, due to the 'very satisfactory expansion of business during the past year', the Fenny Stratford Gas Light and Coke Co. Ltd. even announced a decrease in the cost of gas although it has to be said that, for the moment, they served virtually a captive market.

Yet proposals for an electricity supply by the Northampton Electric Light Company were being recommended by the Highways Committee, with the proviso that across private property the cables ran overhead but not along or across roads or streets.

Many businesses and manufacturing concerns would of course benefit from the introduction of an electricity supply but for the Vulcan Works in Bletchley Road it was the end of the road.

'By Order of the Owners who are retiring' the foundry and the workshops were to be sold although as an ex employee Mr. A. Hurst continued to carry on a part of the business from a 'temporary' workshop in Denmark Street. (This 'temporary workshop' has only recently closed and now gives shelter to a completely different business!)

Another name synonymous for many years with Bletchley business was that of Weatherheads, the electrical retailers and at one stage their empire encompassed 14 branches.

The introduction of electrical superstores spelled their demise, however and only that at Woburn Sands now remains, itself to be closed in a few weeks time.

The Weatherheads business had begun with the approval for two houses in Bletchley Road to be converted into shops, for Mr. E. Weatherhead, who intended to then trade as a florist, fruiterer and seedsman.

With the enticement, "Scotch Seed potatoes at rock bottom prices. Give us a trial", at 73, Bletchley Road the shop duly opened on Friday, March 9th, but sensing the potential popularity, it was Mr. Weatherhead's son who steered the business towards satisfying the public's fascination with the then new tangled wireless sets.

This, throughout many years, proved a lucrative decision.

Amplifying the diverse range of commerce, now being attracted to the town came proposals to site, at a cost of £250,000, a sugar beet factory on land bordering the canal.

This was formerly Scrivens Farm but had been sold at the disposal of Mr. Robert Hammond's estate at the turn of the century.

The factory, which continued until recent years, was supposed to be served by a railway siding but this idea was shelved following concerns about carrying the rail track over or across the A5, then a major arterial road.

The importance of the A5 proved an attractive point of sale when, 'as a going concern', the Fenny Stratford Motor Company, 'occupying a valuable position on the main London to Birmingham Road', was put up auction at the Swan Hotel.

The first bid was only for £2000, against an asking price of £3500 and in the event Mr. E. W. Maclaren, of Croydon, bought the business for £2900, subsequently becoming an agent for Swift cars and Triumph, B.S.A, Douglas and Matchless motorcycles.

BLETCHLEY PAGEANT

With regard to a previous article, in a recent letter Mrs. W. Stanley drew attention to the Bletchley Pageant in which she proudly played a role.

Staged in 1974, the Pageant proved a significant local event and commemorated the point at which the town ceased to be a separate local government unit and instead became a part of the Milton Keynes District.

In this week's article it might therefore be appropriate to briefly recall the origins of the local council, which played such a significant role in the development of the town.

Previously, public responsibilities had been rested in a proliferation of different 'Boards' and bodies - the Highways Board, Burial Board and so on - and although worthy in their aspirations, the overall result produced a somewhat wasteful and inefficient system.

On August 13th 1888, Queen Victoria set her signature to an Act to amend the laws relating to local government in England and Wales, whereby A council shall be established in every administrative county.

Having set up the county councils there then came into being the Rural District and Urban District Councils and of local relevance by Local Government Board Order No. 32776, Fenny Stratford and Simpson amalgamated to form a UDC in July 1895, having responsibility for such matters as sanitation, water supplies and housing.

In the following years the benefits of the new UDC became increasingly apparent with vast improvements made to the water and sanitary facilities, leading to a consequent decrease in the mortality rate.

In 1898 came a formal agreement to transfer Bletchley Parish to the UDC and although a proposal was made to also simultaneously change the name to the Bletchley Urban District Council, not until May 1911 did this actually take place.

Bletchley Urban District Council then remained in existence until 1974, having included Water Eaton within its jurisdiction in 1934.

After World War Two BUDC enthusiastically embraced plans to expand the town and in accordance, having purchased towards this intention the Manor Farm Estate and other land interests, house building began, employing - because of the shortage of manpower - Italian prisoners of war.

At the other end of the town the Saints Estate took shape during 1951 and with provisions now made to accommodate the increased population, the need for their employment became a parallel necessity.

Industrial estates were consequently begun, encouraging many new firms to set up their operations in the town. Since the London overspill formed the basis of the additional population, in January 1956 a delegation from the London County Council arrived in the town to witness for themselves the progress being made.

In the company of members from BUDC they toured the housing estates by coach and visited several homes, to see how the Londoners were settling in - some 162 workers and their families having, by then, been nominated under the council's 'Industrial Selection Scheme' for employment in the new factories.

By the 60s the council realised that a new city would be the ideal means by which all of these expanding activities could be accommodated and administered and of a similar view, in 1967 the Government then announced the beginnings of Milton Keynes New City.

Reflecting the coming needs, on Sunday 31st March, 1974, Bletchley and BUDC became a part of the Milton Keynes District and it was to celebrate this historic event that between March 27th and March 31st the Bletchley Pageant was held at Bletchley Leisure Centre.

With a script written by a local author, Douglas Loak, in a series of '14 vivid episodes, linked by narrations', the Pageant told the story of the district from ancient times to the present day and employed a cast of more than 200 actors. Events were brought to a close by a firework display on the Leon Recreation ground and at midnight many watched the final lowering of the Bletchley Council flag at the council offices.

So came to an end a significant chapter in the town's history but for many people, memories of the Pageant are still alive.

BLETCHLEY PARK PAVILION

In present-day Bletchley, there is possibly no sight so sad as the forlorn and derelict condition of the former cricket pavilion of Bletchley Park. It is perhaps a blessing that such humiliation is now largely screened by some sort of 'fitness facility', which seems to have recently been plonked on the once superb playing field.

During Sir Herbert Leon's ownership of Bletchley Park, many county-class cricket matches were hosted on this ground, which also provided an ideal setting for the annual Bletchley Show.

The story of Sir Herbert and his family belongs to another article, but suffice to say that, primarily as a London financier, he had amassed a fortune, which in 1883 enabled him to purchase Bletchley Park. Soon he began to make enlargements to the existing dwelling, and in 1896 plans were submitted to the council for a cricket pavilion.

As well as being a picturesque backdrop to the annual Bletchley Show, by permission of Sir Herbert Leon the pavilion was often used by local organisations. One such occasion was a concert held by the local Railway Temperance Union.

At the outbreak of the First World War, all entertainments and sports at Bletchley Park were cancelled and, with the country now facing more pressing needs, Sir Herbert Leon offered to lend the pavilion as a convalescent home for wounded soldiers.

With a view towards providing garments for the anticipated inmates, in August 1914, Lady Leon presided at an afternoon meeting of ladies from the town and

district, on the vicarage lawn. The offer of Miss F. Ridgway to act as under-nurse was accepted, and agreement was reached to help with making clothes for soldiers and sailors on foreign service and their dependents.

Mrs. Kirby was unanimously elected as secretary, and it was agreed to appoint a 'cutting out' committee, with any surplus clothing to be sent to central offices.

A representative was appointed from each village, and it was proposed to make a house-to-house collection to raise funds. As a welcome bonus, Lady Leon announced she and Sir Herbert would equip the pavilion at their own expense.

Providing convalescence was an obvious need, but also of national concern was accommodating the increasing influx of Belgian refugees, fleeing from German oppression.

Lady Leon herself provided a home for a Belgian family - mother, father and five children -in one of her cottages on the Bletchley Park estate. When the man eventually found work (at the Diamond Iron Foundry) the family moved to London.

Several Belgian families, however, remained in the district, including one at the pavilion. In early 1915, with the 'stability' afforded by the stalemate of the Western Front, two Belgian ladies accommodated at the pavilion would make a brief trip to Antwerp and return safely to Bletchley.

Also more relaxed now were restrictions regarding the holding of sports events at Bletchley Park. This was due mainly to the need to provide recreational facilities for the troops now being stationed in the area.

Thus one Saturday afternoon in May, the gates of Bletchley Park were opened to the public for a cricket match staged between the Regular Royal Engineers, based at Woburn Sands, and the Southern Army troops, (Signal Company), which had their headquarters in Bletchley.

In late July, however, rain washed out an already postponed cricket match, which should have been played between an 11 drawn from the Signal Company RE (TF), now at Sandy, and a Bletchley XI. But due to advance sales of tickets, the sum of £1 17s 4d was still handed over to the Bucks Territorial Units Comforts Fund.

In late August 1915 there would be a more poignant military presence when 50 wounded soldiers from Northampton General Hospital, and the Weston Home were driven to Bletchley Park for an afternoon outing.

On arrival, the men, many of whom had lost limbs, were shown around the grounds, gardens and conservatories by head gardener Mr. Cooper. Those who were unable to walk were entertained on the grass near the pavilion.

Following an excellent tea served by the Bletchley Park household staff in the pavilion, the men were each presented with a packet of cigarettes by Master Richard Leon, grandson of Sir Herbert and Lady Leon. From the gardens Mr.

Cooper had sent a choice buttonhole, not only for each of the men but, at their earnest request, also for their nurses at the hospital and home. The men were conveyed back to Northampton in cars, all of which had been lent by their owners.

Established in December 1916, War Hospital Work For Women was being regularly undertaken at the pavilion in the Bletchley War Work Rooms, which were open every Wednesday from 10am to 5pm. The articles made would be sent to hospitals at home and abroad, and "Donations and gifts of old linen, wool and other materials will be gladly received by Lady Leon, Bletchley Park, or Mrs. Stockley, Gable Cottage, Far Bletchley".

On a typical day visitors would be able to see 32 energetic ladies busy at their work, as well as not only Lady Leon, industriously engaged at a sewing machine, but also Mrs. Stockley, busy at her desk. In the centre of the large room, a board gave details of subscriptions received, gifts of materials and other donations. These included £1 4s - profits on the sale of cheese made in cheese-making classes at the Rectory.

In November 1917, the committee thought it advisable to become affiliated to the British Red Cross Central Work Rooms, whose headquarters were in London.

Following the end of the war, the work sessions finally closed on Wednesday, February 12th 1919. A total of 2,766 garments had been made, and it was proposed to send the balance of the funds, amounting to £4 7s 9d, to the Star and Garter hospital in Richmond, for the relief of totally disabled soldiers.

With the end of the hostilities, Bletchley Park resumed its recreational roles, and after the death of her husband in 1926 Lady Leon continued the tradition. It was with her permission that the Bletchley Town Cricket Club, founded on February 16th 1928, enjoyed the use of the Bletchley Park ground.

Lady Leon died in 1936, and the entire Bletchley Park estate was put up for sale. Lot 3, the cricket ground and pavilion, was acquired by Bucks Education Department, and this was to soon prove opportune. For, with the influx of evacuees from London at the beginning of the Second World War, Mr. E. C. Cook, headmaster of the Bletchley Road Senior School, received information that the Ecclesbourne Road Senior Boys' School, from Islington, would be accommodated in the Bletchley Park pavilion.

Among the teaching staff was the headmaster, Mr. S. Taylor. Although he qualified for retirement on the very same day, he had chosen to travel to Bletchley with the school, and subsequently became known to all the pupils as 'Dad'. He eventually retired in late August 1944 at the age of 65, and was presented with a cheque by the London teachers.

His place was taken by Mr. Jackson, another teacher who had originally travelled to Bletchley with the boys, and who had been teaching at the Yeomanry Hall since Easter. He retired at the closure of the London Senior Boys' School, in the pavilion, in February 1945 and the occasion was marked by the presentation of a cheque at a social gathering in the Spurgeon Memorial Baptist Church. Letters were read from both the former head, Mr. Taylor, and a former colleague, Mr. Michael, and on behalf of the children and parents a moving tribute was also paid by the headmistress of the Old Bletchley and Yeomanry Hall schools, Mrs. Zilpah Bailey.

The lessened number of pupils now attending the London Senior Boys' School were transferred to St. Martin's Hall, with Mr. W. Davies as the headmaster.

The pavilion continued to play a useful role in the community. At the end of 1946 it would be used as a parcel depot, due to the volume of Christmas mail being sent. The central heating system broke down, but oil stoves were quickly brought in as an alternative.

As for other uses, the Bletchley Town Silver Band was entered for a contest at Reading, on November 14th 1947. Coached by Stanley Bonnington, of the famous Munn and Felton's Band, the members were granted the use of the Bletchley Park pavilion for one evening a week, at a cost of £3 per year.

In 1956/57 Bletchley Grammar School was built, on land which had once formed a part of the Bletchley Park estate.

During the building, the pavilion was employed for temporary classroom accommodation, and it was also used for sports and annual sports days.

In 1964, with finance from county funds, the new North Bucks Music Centre was officially opened at the pavilion in late June by Sir Thomas Armstrong, president of the Royal Academy of Music. One of only two such centres in the country, it was intended for use by North Bucks children, and adults in general.

Yet nowadays there is no music to echo through the decayed architectural elegance, and to judge by the looming structural colossus that masks the previous grandeur, it might be said that, sadly, the building styles of the past seem to be quite literally overshadowed by the current idea of 'progress'.

BLETCHLEY PARK SPIES

HOW THE COMMUNISTS INFILTRATED BLETCHLEY PARK DURING WORLD WAR TWO

Strike a light. Just when you thought things couldn't get sillier, in the realm of interviews up pop 'dinosaur' questions.

In the jargon, apparently a 'curved ball' to test how one thinks on one's feet. But personally it seems pretty obvious that the only dinosaur you'd want to be is one that wasn't extinct.

However, in the wacky world of 'H.R' the ludicrous has long become the norm and nowadays it's always a chuckle when some new broom tries to enthuse a 'team' with the inevitable 'bonding' and 'team building' exercise.

Always good for a giggle although if they think I'm going to 'group hug' with some of the females where I work they can go and whistle.

But perhaps the real motive is for these young dudes to impress an immediate superior who, not infrequently being in an advanced stage of fossilization, and with therefore only the preservation of a pension as the prime concern, is all too happy to nod through any 'trendiness,' at the risk of being otherwise deemed archaic.

Yet regarding interviews, in the realm of national security the vetting has to be thorough although during the desperate days of World War Two it was the view of MI6 that 'Anyone who was not pro-German was all right for us.'

Which was rather alarming because several who were covertly pro Communist would gain access to Bletchley Park, and indeed most of the infamous Cambridge spies would have association with the code breakers in one form or another.

Whilst teaching him at Cambridge University, Anthony Blunt had 'talent spotted' John Cairncross who, due to his fluency in German, having studied modern languages at Trinity College, found work in 1942 at Bletchley Park in Hut 3, dealing with air intelligence intercepts.

Via Blunt he then covertly supplied the Soviets with a mass of deciphered information and MI5 came to harbour few doubts about his guilt.

Another Communist penetration was almost made by Kim Philby. He

Bletchley Park as it is today.

underwent a promising meeting, but his interviewer, Frank Birch, a notable of Bletchley Park, who would head the German naval signals interception centre in Hut 4, turned him down, thinking the position would pay the potential recruit insufficient money!

However, Philby became romantically involved with Aileen Furze, a fiercely patriotic young lady who worked with the Bletchley code breakers.

Another to compromise the security was Leo Long, a Trinity College graduate. Mainly dealing with the assessments of the German army he was an officer in MI14 of the Directorate of Military Intelligence and at his offices, in a bomb proof basement in Central London, teleprinters constantly chattered out information coming from Bletchley. This then formed the basis of the information he passed to Blunt at meetings arranged in snack bars or pubs.

Meanwhile at the offices of MI5 in St. James, London, Herbert Hart sifted through the summaries of Abwehr traffic deciphered at Bletchley, completely unaware of the duplicity of his colleague, Anthony Blunt, who, scribbling down notes based on the documents he had seen, dropped the information at pre-arranged locations for his Soviet controller.

Fortunately MI5 only received summaries of the Bletchley information which, although able to confirm the British ability to read the German signals, gave no indication as to the method.

On a more positive note, throughout the war the Germans believed they had an established network of spies in Britain.

This was basically true but the information they sent was selected by the British, for the spies had been captured and could either co-operate or be shot.

Agent 3719, a parachutist captured in September 1940 near the village of Denton, Northants., chose to co-operate and his subsequent 'interview' revealed a second agent, who was arrested at Yardley Hastings.

But back to the present, and, who knows, in modern interviews there may be something in this dinosaur thing.

So the next time I need an emergency plumber I'll ask if he'd rather be a diplodocus or a brontosaurus. It will be entirely dependent upon the answer as to whether he gets to change my tap washer.

BLETCHLEY ROAD, SOME OBSERVATIONS FROM THE EARLY 20TH CENTURY

Bletchley Road (now Queensway) stretches away towards Fenny Stratford and while new housing has become apparent, previous to this only the Halfway House interrupted the rural isolation that separated Bletchley and Fenny Stratford.

The state of the road leaves much to be desired and becomes 'a genuine muddy slough of despond' in winter and 'as dusty as the Sahara' in summer.

On the left a footpath provides pedestrian access and along its course stand the poles for the telephone service, introduced at the turn of the century.

In a severe winter a heavy fall of snow brings down all but two of these poles and the Royal Engineers, stationed at Staple Hall, are detailed to effect temporary repairs.

These temporary efforts then suffice until the end of the year, when work begins on providing an underground cable.

When the telephone service was introduced to the town the council had wanted the poles to be erected on the other side of the road, so as not to obstruct the footpath.

The Post Office, however, insisted on erecting them on the other side, for the reason that this side was already built up and installing connections would therefore be easier.

As the council curtly pointed out, while it may well have been built up the occupants 'then, and could not ever, require or think of having telephone connections'.

Bletchley Road, now Queensway..

The 'occupants', in fact had only the local choice of using the public call box at Fenny Stratford, although within a few months another call box would be installed at the Bletchley post office, the council having agreed that if the yearly revenue proved insufficient, then they would make up the difference to the Post Office authorities.

BROWNE WILLIS AND EDWARD WELLS

I need a woman. Not permanently of course because they can sometimes be quite annoying. But more for the essential skills which they bring to this planet; primarily sewing buttons on shirts. On which subject there was once a button making factory in Fenny Stratford, where amongst the 200 families in 1685 was that of the Hinchleys.

Within premises that during the 19th century would be converted into three cottages - nos. 22 - 26 Aylesbury Street - they began the production of buttons turned on a simple pole lathe, and as business flourished apprentices from as far away as Buckingham were taken on. Apart from button making, Joseph Hinchley was involved in raising finance for the building of a church in Fenny Stratford, and this was also the passion of the lord of the manor, Browne Willis.

Eventually Joseph sold his property for £66 to Samuel and Thomas Linnell, the father and son bakers of Stony Stratford, and they added new chimneys to the premises, constructed new walls at the back, and built an oven to bake their bread.

However, in more recent years the premises (now demolished) became the shop of the award winning ice cream maker Mr. Golding.

As for Browne Willis and the church, by the beginning of 1727 sufficient monies had been raised to allow the construction of the walls, and the year also witnessed the building of the leaded roof. Browne Willis was also lord of the Bletchley manor, and therefore had the right to appoint the rector of St. Mary's Church.

Not that his judgement centred much upon ecclesiastical prowess for, being always attired in a wig, and suffering no one else to do the same, he selected his former tutor at Oxford, Edward Wells, simply because 'Your wearing your own hair is a circumstance so very agreeable to me, that it has determined me to offer you the living ---.'

However, when Edward suddenly took to wearing a wig the pair very soon fell out, and matters deteriorated further when, on a visit to Edward at his other rectory of Cotesbach, in Leicestershire, Browne Willis was served a dinner of bacon and beans.

This he deemed an unworthy offering, and so the morning after Edward's arrival at Bletchley he sent a messenger to deliver a present of beans to the rectory, a ritual repeated every day thereafter.

Then having been invited to dine with Browne Willis, on making his way home from Whaddon Hall Edward found that on the orders of his host all the fence stiles had been smeared with fresh cow dung!

Thus it was of little surprise that Edward spent most of his time at Cotesbach, where he would end his days.

Regarding Browne Willis, in later life he became slovenly and none too particular about his attire, and even wore an old blue coat that he had purchased in 1705.

Another none too particular about their appearance was 'the Duke of Whaddon,' not the more locally well known second Duke of Buckingham, by whose spendthrift ways the estates had to be sold, but Jonathan Mackerness.

He was known throughout the county as 'The Duke,' and with his chief companion being a cat lived for many years at Whaddon in a wooden hut of his own making.

He was visited out of curiosity by many strangers, and when asked when he would have his hair cut, which he had allowed to grow to an enormous length, he replied, "I always have it cut at Whitsuntide, whether it wants it or not."

Being disappointed in love during his early life was thought to have been the reason for his eccentricity.

But back to the modern day. In consequence of the initial rant on buttons, and with memories still vivid of the wrath that can be incurred in female readers, this piece has of course been penned from a place of suitable refuge.

In fact garbed as a Mongolian yak herder from the remoteness of a hermitage perched high in upper Nepal.

Who knows, here I might even find a nice lady Yeti with needlework skills. Apparently they're big hairy creatures with bulging muscles and a stunted vocabulary.

But hang on, didn't I met some near relations in Milton Keynes. ONLY JOKING!

BURYING HIMMLER

People sometimes ask why, with all the opportunities of 'internet publishing,' I don't aim for megabucks by penning some lascivious 'bonk buster.'

Well, I suppose the short answer is that my knowledge of erotica could be written on the back of a microdot.

But more essentially is the conviction, or perhaps calling, of the need to preserve a few tales of this region's heritage for future generations, and not least because of the concrete changes wrought over the past few decades by the New City.

Another reason is to remember the generations who sacrificed so much to preserve the freedoms that we now enjoy.

In fact in my schooldays nearly every classmate had a grandfather who had fought in the First World War and a father who had fought in the Second, and it seemed that regular ding dongs with the Germans were just an accepted way of life.

But looking back it seems that the persons I knew were unassumingly modest about their wartime feats and always in a typically British understated manner. So it was not until many years after that I discovered that one of my early teachers at the Bletchley Road Schools had been awarded the Distinguished Flying Cross.

He was William Burns, who having joined the RAF in 1941 became a bomber navigator and, mostly on daylight raids, flew 93 missions. Using special radar his role was to pin point targets and he was often responsible for the accuracy of the whole flight.

Making his home at Newton Longville he joined the Bletchley Road School staff in November 1948 and the following year was elected vice president of the Bletchley association of the National Union of Teachers.

He duly progressed to become a headmaster and in 1961 he and his wife moved to Little Brickhill. There he became secretary of the Brickhills Gardeners' Club, indeed winning a cup for the best kept garden in the three Brickhills.

The story of Carl Moser as a wartime prisoner of the Japanese has been recently told and although the treatment of prisoners in German POW camps was more humane, after his fourth escape Lance Corporal Stan Corby, of Oxford Street, Bletchley, was sentenced to be shot on Himmler's orders.

Thus with little to lose just before VE Day he and others hid a revolver and shot their way out, killing a guard. They were then rescued by the Americans and flown home. It was ironic that Himmler would be the one who came to a sticky end, an episode in which the father of one of my classmates was involved.

As a platoon sergeant in the Welch Regiment, one night in May 1945 he was serving in an interrogation centre set up by the special headquarters defence company in a house in Lueneburg, near Hamburg. At about 10pm an officer told him to prepare some provisions as an important prisoner was about to arrive and sometime later a small man was marched in, wearing an army shirt and covered by a blanket.

The sergeant overheard him called Himmler during the interrogation and about 20 minutes later an officer ran out telling him to get a needle and thread. Himmler had taken a cyanide and they needed to pull his tongue from his throat. The sergeant stood outside the door while this was done but after a while he overheard an officer say "The bastard has beaten us."

With the death officially recorded, a couple of days later the body was wrapped in chicken wire camouflage and put on the back of a lorry, to be taken to a spinney a few miles outside Lueneburg.

There the sergeant and another soldier dug a shallow grave and "We tossed him in it and spat on him. We felt no compunction. That man was responsible for the deaths of over six million people."

Both men were then sworn to secrecy, to prevent the location becoming a shrine to fanatical followers.

So penning bonk busters, no thanks. At my time of life the only sheets I'm romping between are the paper ones that form the fascinating pages of history.

CHRISTMAS TRUCE WW1

O'No! Whatever's happened to the magic of Christmas past – when wide eyed tiny tots spent hours lovingly crafting handwritten letters to Santa Claus, hoping for their wishes to be fulfilled? But did my eyes deceive me, has the ageing process kicked in early, is there really an invitation in a local supermarket for kids to now 'text' their wish lists?

To meet emission controls on flatulent reindeer, I suppose Santa's banned from riding his sleigh, and is now banged up in the geriatric ward of some retirement home for faded celebs, emailing CAD programs to 3D printers installed in every kid's bedroom, courtesy of an EU grant.

As for poor Rudolph, well the fate of him and his mates doesn't bear thinking about.

Probably hived off to a local safari park, or served up as burgers in some fast food joint in Lapland. But enough about the material side of Yuletide and so to its true meaning, the season of goodwill to all men. Regarding which the greatest contradiction is undoubtedly the Christmas Truce of 1914 during the First World War when, as a break from killing each other the opposing armies downed tools for a few hours and fraternised in No Man's Land.

One of the soldiers who was there was the grandson of Mrs. T. Holdom, of Bletchley, and of the experience he wrote: "We were in the trenches for Christmas, and had the funniest Christmas I have ever had.

"On Christmas Eve we had orders not to fire until 12 o'clock midnight Christmas Day unless the Germans did, so we shouted across to the Germans that we would not fire unless they did, and they shouted back the same. So the rest of the evening we spent in singing carols, hymns, National Anthems etc. The Germans lighted fires on top of their trenches and sang and danced around them. On Christmas Day they shouted across and wished us a Happy Christmas and, of course, we did the same, and we both got out of our trenches and walked along the top.

"During the morning we went half way across to the German trenches and beckoned to them to come over to us, which, after a little hesitation, they did.

When they arrived we shook hands and exchanged cigarettes, cigars, buttons, money and anything we could get hold of. I got four kinds of cigarettes, two cigars, a button, and I also got two of them to write their names and addresses in my pocket book. One of the two had the Iron Cross, which he showed me. We were surprised to find how many of them could speak English.

"One of them said he knew Clapham Junction well, and another said he used to take the No 87 bus home to Kilburn every night. We found them to be quite a gentlemanly lot of chaps.

"Before we left we said we would not fire until they did.

"They said the same. But early Boxing Day morning we were relieved and are now in the outskirts of a town in reserve and are going into the trenches again on Friday.

"We are going into different trenches this time and I hope they are not so muddy as the ones before." Unbelievable.

But perhaps not surprising, for as with most wars it seems the instigation is usually down to a handful of nutters, who through coercion, mass hysteria and the herd instinct manipulate the majority into becoming their cannon fodder – when at base level all the majority wants is to be left in peace to look after their families.

Rowland Brothers Staff photograph.

So perhaps there is something to be said for Christmas in a high tech age. For at least via social media people across the globe can now express sanity and goodwill to each other in their own voices, and not just a State imposed voice.

Until, of course, the State gains control of the social media.

COMMERCIAL LIFE 1886

With their legacy still to be variously viewed - examples being Ropley House, the memorial home in Denmark Street and cottages in Brooklands Road - for many years the Rowland Brothers, timber merchants, were predominant employers in the locality.

As we begin our voyage into the commercial life of Fenny Stratford, towards the year 1887, it is therefore of little surprise to find the employees of the firm enjoying their annual Christmas Eve supper at the Red Lion, provided by the courtesy of their benevolent employers. (For the daughter of Mr. W. Rowland, the coming year would also bring a cause for celebrations, when she passed the third division of the Cambridge exams.)

In this season of festive feasts the Maltsters, in Aylesbury Street, hosted a similar gathering for the Town Band and much merrymaking was the order of the day. Of more sober pursuits, the proprietor of the 'Fenny Stratford Mineral Water Works' had his thoughts on the profit to be made in the coming months and begged 'to inform his Friends and the Public' that he had recently purchased and fitted up 'a Most Complete Plant of SODA WATER MACHINERY', manufactured by no less than Barnett and Foster, the recipients of many awards and three gold medals at the International Health Exhibition.

Also warming to the coming months were the members of the local co-op who at their quarterly meeting announced a profit of £160 5s 1d. They were thus able to declare a rosy 'divi' of 2s in the pound although on a frostier theme the natives were dismissively short-changed by a lady who, in her quest for a general servant, specifically advertised that 'No one from Fenny or Bletchley need apply'.

No such discriminations were applied by a randy grocer in Aylesbury Street, however, whose frolics with a lady assistant spelled his eventual commercial demise. Yet in his more well behaved moments, for the meanwhile he was able to not only supply the great unwashed with 'Sunlight self washer soap, in 3d Tablets' but also 'Jubilee Drops', at 9d per lb. When finally lust overruled business acumen, inevitably he was obliged to 'do a runner' although before disappearing perhaps had the option to stow a few household effects up the road with the ironmonger George Pacey and his 'house furnishing warehouse', established 1840.

Just in case other ardours were in need of cooling it was just as well the essential question of watering the streets during the summer months had now to be considered. As a primary measure, Mr. Thomas, the Grand Junction Canal Engineer, gave consent for a reduction in the price of water from £10 to £8 and in association, an agreement was reached with Mr. W. E. Clarke to pay him 15s pa, for the right to cart water across his timber yard. For a lump sum of £25 10s, Mr. Rollins eventually gained the watering contract and the terms required his attendance for seven hours a day if necessary.

It was also hoped he would perform his duties rather better than his predecessor, by whom some streets had been watered several times but others not at all. As Mr. Rollins went about his daily business, so others continued theirs, including Mr. H. W. Welsh, builder and contractor, who 'trusts to receive a continuance of a share of the patronage of the public'. Perhaps not from Mr. C. Stuart, of the Bletchley Iron Works, however, for whilst completing some works at Mr. Stuart's foundry, Mr. Welsh had completely forgotten to mention the need for planning permission.

As a result, Mr. Stuart now had to apply to the Parochial Sanitary Committee or else he would have to take his Works elsewhere.

That would certainly have been a pity, depriving Fenny not only of Mr. Stuart's patented 'Pneumatic Boxing Gloves' but also his 17 imp gallon railway milk churns 'Made of Best Bessemer steel. Gauged and Plated, at 27s 6d each. Happily the necessary permission was swiftly granted.

As the New Year approached, dinners were held, toasts proposed and new horizons envisaged although in the toast proposed by Mr. Illing, these extended somewhat beyond the boundaries of Fenny; 'I love the Army,' he enthused, 'and if I were a single, young man I would not hang about Fenny but would go and join up.'

COMMERCIAL LIFE 1891

Pursuing our ongoing theme of historical voyeurism, this week we drop in on the year 1891 and find out what the traders of Fenny Stratford were getting up to.

Strengthening the ties of trade and in a nifty business manoeuvre Mr. Blunt the butcher, of Fenny Market Place, married off his daughter to Mr. Smith the grocer and ensured himself a lifetime's supply of meat and two veg.

Something else to be chewed over were the many bargains at The Peoples Hatter; of London House where - with Tweed suits at 12s 11d - Mr. James Berwick vied to clothe the entire population by his talents as a hosier, glover, clothier and supplier of boots and shoes - in competition with his cheaper rival down the road, The Fenny Stratford Cheap Drapery and Clothing Stores'.

Elsewhere in the town there was discord in the ashpits and closets department, the emptying of which had proved to literally be a one-horse operation. It was widely held that if the present operator had at least two, then the work would have been fairly satisfactory but it was too late. The stable door had been firmly bolted and both he and his horse were put out to grass. Unbeknown to most, the horse-drawn age was now slowly plodding into the sunset but one with an inkling of what the future might hold was Mr. Stuart at the Bletchley Iron Works. Together with Mr. Binney, he had recently been granted a patent for a design of gas engine and suitably encouraged went on to patent several other 'Motor and

Rotary Engines'.

Whilst gas engines may have been in their infancy, the gas industry - especially at Fenny Stratford - was not only fully fledged but also expanding in all directions with a bigger and better works and a bigger and better gas holder.

The reason for this welcome prosperity had been the rapid growth of the town and with trade increasingly vibrant, 'For the purpose of considering a Proposal to Form a Local Trades' Association for Criminal Prosecutions and the Collection of Trade and other Debts', a public meeting to consider this matter was held at The Swan.

Perhaps with Mr. Cheshirc, 'Pastry Cook and Confectioner', supplying the nibbles from his Fenny Stratford Refreshment House, in High Street, amongst those assembled may well have included Mr. Holdom, the brewer, the Rowlands Brothers at their 'steam saw mills', Mr. T. Read at his brick works, Mr. Cook, the brush manufacturer and perhaps a representative from the Bucks Post Office in Aylesbury Street.

For those involved in water-borne trade, however, it was not such plain sailing. Mr. C. Johns, canal carrier at Navigation Wharf managed to keep afloat but William Clarke, with wharves at Fenny Stratford, Simpson and Water Eaton was sinking fast and in fact by the direction of the Official Receiver the sale had to be made of 'the entire stock in trade and plant of a coal and builders merchant and wharfinger', including 30,000 bricks, an Avery's coal machine, two timber carriages and an 8hp engine by Clayton, Shuttleworth and Co.

The Bull and Butcher

Also included were three canal boats, four horses and the Valuable Contents of the Residence; not to mention an Acre of Mangold Wurtzels, at Water Eaton.

Troubled waters indeed but at least the Mangold Wurtzels might have found a ready market with the labourers of Fenny, who had just been given a field in Denbigh Road by Sir Herbert Leon.

This, for their benefit, would be subdivided into allotments at a low cost rent and as we close our look at the year, we therefore find the labourers and Mr. Leon's farm bailiff in amicable negotiations at the Bull and Butcher, discussing the appointment of trustees and the election of a regulating committee.

CONSCIENTIOUS OBJECTORS

As recounted in a previous article, despite the 'tactical' retreat from Dunkirk the contingent of Bletchley men, despatched with the British Expeditionary Force, had acquitted themselves with great courage in the previous fighting.

Indeed, they gained a well-deserved praise from their commanding officer, himself to be soon decorated at Buckingham Palace for bravery but only to later die in a tragic air crash.

With the national situation now bleak and with no immediate hopes of victorious conclusion, able bodied men were facing call up and Bletchley Employment Exchange became the registration centre.

Aged between 20 and 23, 85 men were the largest number to be called so far and most expressed a preference to join the army. A few choose the RAF and two or three opted for the navy.

Yet on the positive side the war was doing wonders for the unemployment figures and from a total of 151, including 13 'casuals from barges', within a couple of months this number had been halved.

In fact by virtue of the increasing male vacancies, opportunities now arose for women to take up employment formerly barred to them and for the first time since World War One they could join the indoor staff of the GPO.

Each military registration invariably threw up a small quota of conscientious objectors, including a young outfitting salesman from the Bletchley Co-op.

He appeared before a tribunal to plead his case, stating that since he had been a member of the Methodist church all his life, he would not serve in the forces or munitions factories.

However he would consider any other non-combatant role and the tribunal agreed with his request.

An officer in the Boys Brigade, another Methodist and a lay preacher, also expressed reluctance for the sharp end. As long as he took up agriculture or forestry work, or full time ambulance duties, this again was agreed by the South

East Tribunal at Southwark.

In a similar instance, the manager of a local bookshop had resigned from this position in January 1939 to become an auxiliary fireman.

He now appeared before the same tribunal as a conscientious objector which was all rather tragic, since he became one of the town's earliest casualties, killed in action whilst serving with the RAMC. He left a wife and young son.

Plans did not go quite according to form when the proprietor of a local newspaper decided he would also like to be a conscientious objector. Undergoing a bit of a grilling, or more diplomatically when 'severely questioned' by Judge David Davies, at the South East Local Tribunal, he then found himself charged with sanctioning articles alleged to be 'intended to produce defeatism and dismay among the public'.

With his application thrown out he then appealed to the Central Conscientious Objectors Appellate Court, which granted exemption from military service on condition he stayed in his present occupation.

A member of the Baptist Church for 12 years, he was also captain of the Bletchley Boys Brigade and at their annual inspection supervised a display of semaphore.

However, to ensure they weren't sending out the wrong signals, the members of the brigade swiftly sent a communication to the local press, stating that in no way were they a pacifist organisation.

Meanwhile, local womenfolk were up in arms about an interview given to a London newspaper by a lady War Office official. Tasked with trying to recruit 6,000 women for the ATS, on visiting the town she apparently gained the impression that most of the girls spent their time in cafes and cinemas.

However one sweet innocent declared that 'if I went into the ATS my husband would have to get someone else in to prepare meals and do the housework and no one would benefit'. Try getting away with that one in today's generation!

COWLISHAW FAMILY

John Cowlishaw was the last headmaster of the old school in the High Street, and at the schoolhouse was born the last of his three sons, Alfred Gervase, who was in due course educated at the school. (Of the other sons, Arthur would eventually make his home in London, and Herbert in Australia.)

After various employments, including a while with Peter Robinson's in London's Regent Street, Alfred was apprenticed to the drapery trade in Bedford. Following his marriage to Natalie Fisher, a court dressmaker, in 1913 he and his wife set up in business in Aylesbury Street as A.G. Cowlishaw.

Apart from his commercial activities, he would also take a keen interest in birds, winning many trophies - he was among the first in the country to keep blue budgies!

During World War I he served with the Royal Garrison Artillery, duties that would sadly inflict deafness and while he was away on military service Mrs. Cowlishaw continued to run the family business.

As for their staff, in 1918 Constance Gore began work as an assistant at 2s 6d a week, and would become one of their longstanding employees.

The Chalet

In 1937 the family took over a site that had formerly accommodated a bakers on the comer of Aylesbury Street and Denmark Street and here, at 'The Chalet', the dressmaking department run by Mrs. Cowlishaw would locally attain a high-class distinction, at one time employing 14 girls.

Meanwhile, Mrs. Cowlishaw's only son, Douglas, who had been educated at Bedford Modem school and then served an apprenticeship with Elliston and Cavell Ltd, began a separate business as an outfitters at 7, Bletchley Road, which would continue until the end of June 1940, when he announced his enlistment in the RAFVR. He would subsequently spend four years in the Middle East as an electrician.

As for his only sister, Audrey, in September 1941 she married a member of the RAMC, Ronald Tew, from Petersfield, at St. Mary's Church.

Sadly, in November of the following year, Alfred's mother, Catherine Amelia, died aged 89, having lived for several years with her son and daughter-in-law.

In 1947, one Saturday towards the end of October at the church of The Holy Child and St. Joseph in Bedford, the wedding took place of Douglas Cowlishaw and Joan Catherine Pincher, the eldest daughter of Mr. and Mrs. H. Pincher, of 3, Clifford Avenue.

Bletchley's first war casualty

Joan had originally been engaged to Peter Eric Meadows, the son of Arthur and Nora Meadows, of 'Bradley', Eaton Avenue. But, having at the age of 22 volunteered for service in the Navy as an Ordinary Signalman in the Royal Naval Patrol Service, he would be the first Bletchley man to be killed in the war when, on May 20 1940, HM Trawler Rifnes, the 431 ton trawler to which he had been posted, received a direct hit.

A tennis player for the St. Martin's club and also a keen stamp collector, Peter had been employed before the war on the Bletchley postal staff, but then moved to the Civil Service Engineering Department at Reading, where he would stay for two years. At Reading, he became involved with Toc H, and following his death it was announced by the organisation that a photograph of him wearing naval uniform would be hung in the clubroom. Today he is commemorated on the Lowestoft Naval Memorial.

Honey for the honeymooners

As for Joan, in married life she would live at the Clock House, Little Brickhill, and on the couple's return from honeymoon they unexpectedly received another wedding gift when, on removing some floorboards to re-house a colony of bees, Douglas obtained around 151b of honey. With the attempt to re-house the colony having failed, the boards were then replaced!

Douglas had how added a footwear department to adjoin his business at 9, Bletchley Road, and extensive new additions were added to the rear of the premises in 1960.

The following November, Alfred Cowlishaw died, aged 74, having carried on the Aylesbury Street drapery business following the incapacitation of his wife by a stroke some seven years before.

With Douglas now managing both the stores, Audrey was responsible for the soft furnishings, curtains, and loose cover-making at the Aylesbury Street premises.

Both businesses have long since closed but, though the Aylesbury Street premises now accommodates a cycle shop, the fading lettering on a doorstep reminds of a not-too-distant past.

DENBIGH HALL INN

According to the local diarist, the Reverend William Cole, before 1700 there were two 'constables houses' on the Watling Street - Willow Hall and Denbigh Hall.

The former was pulled down in 1706 but as 'a reputed Bawdy House' Denbigh Hall 'alas still stands'! In fact at the beginning of the 18th century mention of 'Denby Hall' is made as being situate just south of Rickley Wood in, as oft repeated in most books on local history, an area long associated with nefarious deeds. As an alehouse the inn was supposedly the haunt of highwaymen and in 1725 mention is made of William Norris as an 'ale draper.'

As for the naming of the pub, according to a letter from the contemporary Earl of Denbigh, published in the Rugby Advertiser of June 3rd 1909, he claimed that his great, great grandfather, Basil, the 6th Earl, had been forced to put up at the Marquis of Granby (as the inn was then supposedly known) when a wheel sheared from his carriage. On receiving commendable service he began to regularly patronise the establishment, whereby the name became the Denbigh Hall. However, since the inn is mentioned as Denbigh Hall in 1715, and the 6th Earl wasn't born until 1719, something seems amiss!

Creating further confusion, at the building of the London to Birmingham railway line a rail guide states that the inn had been recently named the Denbigh

Denbigh Hall Inn, now demolished.

Hall by the purchaser, Mr. Calcroft, prior to having been called the Pig and Whistle!

Between Denbigh Hall and Northampton the line had been surveyed by Richard Sheppard and one of the local farmers who hired his carting team to the contractors was Thomas Crane.

Before the completion of the Kilsby tunnel, railway passengers alighted at Denbigh Hall to continue their journey by road to the next completed section of the railway and, in his old age, Thomas could recall the coaches pulling up at this Denbigh Hall 'station,' around which a veritable 'shanty town' had arisen to cater for the travellers' needs.

The arrival of the railway killed off the coaching trade and in 1914 the inn was put up for sale by Mr. W. Villars, who was leaving the district. However, after World War One motor traffic began to increase, bringing a more prosperous custom, and when in 1922 Albert Chambers came to Bletchley he ran a farm of 40 acres whilst his wife, Daisy, ran the Denbigh Hall Inn. However, apart from the railway and road the inn also witnessed another form of transport when a monoplane, piloted by a French woman, made a forced landing in nearby Buttons Field. She had lost her way whilst flying to Northampton and continued her journey by car. Moving to 56, Bletchley Road, Mr. and Mrs. Chambers retired in 1936 but in the early months of World War Two the inn became acquainted with notoriety when the landlord, who had previously been the licensee of the Maltsters Arms, was sent to prison for two months for dealing on the black market in meat.

During the war a soldier was killed under the railway bridge when a lorry ploughed into a column of troops, and with many accidents having occurred here it was a few years after the war that, in the wake of a triple crash, which caused a nose to tail traffic jam in both directions for 1½ miles, a proposal was made for roundabouts to be constructed on either side.

However, in view of proposed new developments the Bletchley Road Safety Association postponed the idea. As for the inn, in 1956 this was temporarily reprieved from closure when, having been given reasons why a water supply had not been laid on, Bletchley magistrates renewed the licence.

This was dependent on attempts being continued to provide a supply, although the whole question was perhaps academic, since with the inn being an old unlicensed house the brewery wondered if the magistrates had any power to withhold a licence! Finally the matter came to a close on April 4th 1957 when the premises were closed by the Aylesbury Brewery Company due to a lack of running water.

The building was then demolished at the end of the year.

DENTISTS OF YESTERDAY

Along with a general grumpiness, another step towards enrolment at the University of the Third Age is having had the last of my teeth extracted. With a complete set of dentures, the only aspect to miss about the dentist's chair is the matronly bosom of the comely dental nurse, comfortingly poised above one's slowly swelling lips as, with practiced nimble fingers, she probes deep within one's inner cheeks with her gurgling suction tube. But that's quite enough of the Mills and Boon, and so to dentistry as it was 'when I were a lad.' A time when fillings were performed without anaesthetic, and extractions were performed under gas, the mere mention of which will no doubt strike terror into those of a certain age, who can remember the nauseous smell of the rubber mask, and the fitful descent into semi oblivion. So to those for whom a visit to the dentist seems traumatic, just be thankful that you didn't live in times gone by. Speaking of which, in April 1914 Mr. J. Austin Bayes transferred his business as a chemist to Mr. F.H. Holyoak, who had come to Bletchley from 'a high class establishment' in Leicester. The business, in Aylesbury Street, would be known as 'The Modern Pharmacy,' and the arrangement for Mr. C. Gaston to operate a dental surgery there, on Thursday afternoons, would continue as before. The following year, anyone in need of a dentist could also visit the 'House of No Pain,' at 15, Bletchley Road, where 'A first class West End London operator will continue to use Mr. Pilcher's Successful Method.' Extracts would cost from 1s, and complete sets from £1 1s. Scrolling forward in time, in 1927 Mr. Ernest Copeland took over the practice of a Mr. Saunders, and although he first operated from premises in Aylesbury Street, he later moved to accommodation above Lloyds Bank in Bletchley Road, and then to 77, Bletchley Road, where, until retiring through ill health, he would continue his dentistry until 1949. (He died in 1952, leaving a daughter who was the wife of Jack Haynes, the landlord of the King's Head, Fenny Stratford.) As for other dentists, for several years Mr. Warren Wise had practised at 'Heytor,' Bletchley Road, until the family moved from the town about 1939. Tragically, the following year his only son, Corporal Jack Wise, aged 21, would be officially posted as missing, whilst in the aftermath of the war, towards the end of August 1946 his daughter, Eleanor, married Peter Lenton, whose parents lived at Park Farm, Brampton, Huntingdonshire. No doubt still remembered by many in the town is Mr. Marshall, who around 1951 began as a dentist in Bletchley Road, where he continued until his short lived retirement in the south of France. Having taken over the dental practice of a Mr. Barnes, he was initially helped by his father, who, born at Paisley, and educated in Ireland, had qualified as a dental surgeon in Glasgow. Being for awhile the President of the West of Scotland branch of the British Dental Association, for many years he would be the dental officer for Renfrewshire, but on giving up his school work he - instead of retiring to Ireland - came to help his son at Bletchley. He died in 1966, aged 78. Now based a little further along Bletchley Road, the former practice of Mr. Marshall continues as C. Vitiello and associates. As for the original premises, this came to accommodate a firm of solicitors, and ironically not only in the same room where the dental surgery had been, but in the very same place that the dentist's chair had been, it was there that I sat with pen eagerly poised to sign my divorce papers. In fact almost deja vue, for there it had been many years before when I thankfully got rid of another pain, in the form of an abscessed molar!

DOCTORS OF THE PAST

Clinical decisions were needed in the Bletchley of 1950, with negotiations being held for a new physiotherapy unit.

Currently situated in Victoria Road, it was hoped that a new location could be found near Wilton Avenue which, as it happened, wasn't far off the mark!

For a much needed headquarters, a lack of finance was hampering the optimism of the Bletchley Nursing Division and Ambulance Brigade although the county council was toying with an idea for building an ambulance station, at the corner of Bletchley Road and Leon Avenue.

One who had long been associated with the Bletchley Nursing Division was Mrs. E. Vaughan, of Bedford Street, who - in recognition of her 20 years as Superintendent - was proudly presented with a miniature insignia of the St. Johns nursing badge.

Sadly, after 25 years of service, Nurse Rawley died aged 71 and the position as district nurse was filled by Nurse Stockham who came from Somerset but her new home was 87, Manor Road.

From nurses to doctors and amongst the several names from the past were those of Dr. Kelland, of 54, High Street, who in the 1920s made over his practice in Bletchley and Fennv Stratford to Dr. Kelman Smith.

Also in the High Street the Red House came up for auction in 1924, having at one time been occupied by Dr. Deyns.

His son, Lt. Col. Deyns, then took over the practice and his partner, Dr. Nicholson, continued at the Red House when the Lt. Col. later moved to The Gables in Bletchley Road.

At the time of the auction, however, the Red House was offered with vacant possession, except the two rooms (with separate entrance) which had been used as the doctor's surgery and subsequently as offices for Mr. E. Thornley and his successor, the solicitor, Mr. Ernest Marchant. As for the Lt. Col., apart from medical duties, he was also active as JP and at one time chairman of Bletchley Gas Company and Bletchley Council. Possibly these proved lucrative positions in view of the £50,115 he left when he died, aged 87, on January 27th.

Another well known doctor in the town was Dr. Edgar Carter, of the Red House. Originally a surgeon at Leeds Women's Hospital, he there met his wife, Kathleen, a nurse and the couple were married in 1913.

After running a practice in Cambridge in 1927, taking over from Dr. Nicholson, Dr. and Mrs. Carter then moved to the Red House in Fenny Stratford where, at the back of the house, Nurse Curtois, who had travelled with them from Cambridge, opened a nursing home. Here, during the war Mrs. Carter played an active role.

Their daughter, Katherine, trained to be a SRN at St. Bartholemews Hospital and during this time she met her future husband, the acting Squadron Leader of an RAF hospital.

The couple were married with a reception at the Red House, in a marquee set up in the grounds. Dr. Carter retired two years later and leaving the practice in the hands of his son, he and his wife then moved back to Cambridge. With distant echoes of Dr. Gent, more than a century before, so continued the long association of the Red House with the medical profession which ended only in recent times, when the practice moved to Bletchley Road.

The years may have rolled on but despite scientific advances - and the ailments of the present health service - the fact remains a doctor with time for his patients and an understanding in his approach, is a tonic still as welcome as any medicines prescribed.

DR. ERNST BLUMENAU

Some readers may recall Dr. Ernst Blumenau who, seeking refuge from Nazi persecution, eventually came to Bletchley on being appointed the schools' dentist.

For a while he lodged with the local headmaster Mr. E. C. Cook in Church Walk.

Still remembered is his kindly disposition which helped calm the fears of those children in need of treatment.

Born in 1890 Ernst Blumenau was the elder of two brothers whose temperaments differed widely.

Serious, reserved and quietly spoken, his natural good looks and refined interests in music, art and architecture ensured he received the amorous attention of women.

Despite a frailty of health and being eventually diagnosed with diabetes his infirmities proved deceptive and for recreation he would canoe the lengths of rivers and lakes in Germany.

After studying medicine he served during the First World War in the German Army Medical Corps and it was at this time he met his future wife, Meta Schlueter, although his parents were not entirely approving of her as a practising Catholic.

In marriage Meta assumed the dominant personality and at her instigation Ernst gave up medicine for her profession of dentistry and the couple established a joint practice in Mainz.

But after Kristallnacht and the beginning of the open persecution of the Jews Ernst sought refuge in England and initially Meta expressed her intention to join him once - so the story went - he had earned enough money 'to keep her in the wines to which she had become accustomed!'

Dr. Ernst Blumenau.

However as the Nazi persecution of the Jews and mixed marriages intensified she, for safety's sake, divorced him causing Ernst obvious distress.

Setting up as a dentist in Portsmouth he employed as receptionist an old friend Lilian Bruckner but when Ernst was interned on the Isle of Man in July 1941 she rejoined her husband in America.

At the end of the war she secured a divorce from him and returned to England where she and Ernst were married in 1945.

At first the couple rented a part the Old Rectory at Wavendon before moving to a little house in Wavendon where socially complementing each other they lived contentedly - 'Lilian being the chatty one while Ernst radiated a benign presence.'

Enjoying a wide circle of friends they especially enhanced the local musical scene and with Ernst playing the viola and Lillian the piano they formed a welcome part of weekly quartets.

EDUCATION 1891

School Boards, elected from local citizens of a suitable standing, pioneered the paths of learning in Fenny Stratford.

However one of the Fenny Stratford members, Mr. Eaton, was soon to leave, having been promoted to a position in connection with the LNWR, at Northampton.

But a goodly number of the pupils hardly bothered to turn up for lessons at all. So much so that the harassed Mr. Thomas, the attendance officer, demanded an increase in his salary, which he swiftly and sympathetically received!

Hopefully the truants would now be hauled in to face the music, possibly played on the new school piano, donated by Mr. H. Leon after a request from the governess to the School Board for a musical instrument had been turned down.

As a measure to help ensure their prosperous future the pupils were provided with a Savings Bank - open every Monday from 5am until 5pm so they could deposit their money with Post Office Savings books supplied free of charge.

This was an age that allowed the meting out of physical punishment by teachers - although not perhaps by horses, as was the unfortunate incidence with one young lad. Leaving school one Friday he was knocked down by a horse which kicked him in the head.

Then established for 10 and a half years, no horsing around was allowed at Dunmore College.

Now plans were in hand for a 'handsome New College' in Bletchley Road. With the plans accepted, construction began. Containing 21 rooms the building was scheduled to open at Christmas.

Nothing as tangible became evident for the proposed Science and Art Institute at Fenny. however, the plans for which never progressed beyond the discussion stage.

Educationally more modest was the school newly established in Bletchley by Mrs. Kemp at which, in varied entertainments, she performed recitations and gave piano recitals.

Recitals were also in mind for the Primitive Methodists, who were hoping to raise enough money to replace their harmonium with a new American organ. There was the slight matter of £63, outstanding on their chapel in Albert Street, and to clear this debt they made preparations to hold a bazaar.

They hoped to build larger premises and this also was the intention of the Baptists who had plans prepared, including a provision for re-burials, since the new building would cover the existing vaults.

With the plans for the chapel approved, the building committee then invited tenders and in reply received bids from as far afield as St. Neots and Grimsby Elsewhere in Fenny the Salvation Army was packing a punch by inviting the converted prizefighter, Billy McLeod, to come and address large numbers at their barracks.

At the Vicarage the 'Society for the Propagation of the Gospel in Foreign Parts' held an open air gathering for the promotion of their cause.

ENTERTAINMENTS IN 1887

Our travels in time for this article take us back to the year 1887 and a look at the entertainments that were then available in the town and the celebrations that were taking place.

For those local residents, or travellers, seeking more general relaxation, formerly the Post Office the new rooms at the Bletchley Station Coffee Tavern were opened in April by the chairman of the LNWR, Richard Moon and thereby, those sympathetic to the ideals and increasing activities of the Temperance Movement (their original hall, built in George Street in 1892 still remains) no doubt found this a welcome balance, to the otherwise lure of the many pubs in the locality.

Fenny Stratford Town Hall, long associated with the varied talents of the singing Walfords, a family whose repertoire included an ability to knock out tunes on semi-filled wine bottles, often provided a venue for indoor entertainments and in May, here was staged the return visit of Mr. E. De Vere and Mr. H.J. Moseleys' especially selected Company of London Artists including, not least, 'the Parisian Danseuse', Miss Blanche.

Elsewhere, perhaps as more of a benefit performance, providing for the 'entertainment of parishioners and observance of Saint Martin's Day the Saint Martin's House charity generated an annual income of £510s 6d, this rental being expended on a dinner, rates, tradesmen's bills, the vicar's fee and bell ringing.

Celebrations of a national importance had also to be considered and in the instance of those celebrating 50 years of Queen Victoria's reign, to locally mark the occasion three schemes vied for acceptance.

At the National School the consequent attendance at a public meeting proved an unfortunate disappointment but it was nevertheless decided to appoint a committee of 20, to consider the relative merits of each scheme; a) to complete a peal of bells for Saint Martin's church, b) to establish a Literary and Scientific Institute or c) to declare a public holiday.

At the conclusion, the idea of the bells appealed.

During the summer, inhabitants of a sporting inclination could enjoy the facilities of a newly formed archery and lawn tennis club while for the masses, on August Bank Holiday, in a field kindly lent by Mr. Makeham, along Bletchley road, the Fenny Stratford Flower Show took place, enlivened by a series of athletic events.

Mr. Harley Gates, of the Bull and Butcher, supplied alcoholic drinks and with a nod towards political correctness, for the first time a tent was provided with special seats for the ladies.

At 3 pm the sports commenced, with matters much enlightened when a hurdler fainted and a wheel fell off one of the bikes.

In an opposite field a steam merry-go-round was set up and many showmen and stall keepers vied for trade until at 9 pm the Fenny Stratford Town Band led proceedings to a field lent by Mr. G. Holdom, where a display of fireworks brought the day to a close.

Yet there were still other festivities on the horizon, especially in December when Mr. George Sanger brought his 'World-famed English and Continental Circus' to town.

Enclosed by a 'Grand Waterproof Pavilion', which could accomodate 20,000 people in seated, draught free comfort (except for lowlife in the 'sixpences') this 'Only Olympia' arrived with 'All and Daring of Ancient Rome', to include the perils of chariot racing!

As if this wasn't enough, an 'Exciting Kangaroo Hunt' then took place with six real kangaroos - the most mirth provoking exhibition ever witnessed'.

Onlookers and possibly kangaroos also jumped for joy when Buffalo Bill Wainer and his Bully Boys took the ring and events were brought to a grand finale by the 'Grand Tableaux', of 50 horses and 100 men.

Ye Gods, it all makes present day life in Fenny seem positively tame by comparison!

ERNEST COOK

Well, bang goes that idea. The New Year's resolution was to dispense with the pantomime of daily employment, and instead belatedly complete a sadly lacking education.

Namely a long contemplated PhD; 'The Considered Opinions of the Working Man on Modern Day Political Correctness, as Debated in the front Bar of the Duck and Ferret.'

Even in these austere times it seemed that finance wasn't a problem, for a website came to light offering students – including presumably mature ones – the necessary readies in exchange for a few 'discrete liaisons' with wealthy clients.

Right on, Pedro. I'm up for that. A doctorate for putting a smile on some matronly lady's face. (Well she'd have a laugh when she saw what's on offer.) But sadly this interesting arrangement came to the notice of Plod, and alas exists no more.

So for the necessary funding I suppose I'll now have to ask my editor if I can do one of the paper rounds.

While on the subject of further education, it was at the opposite end of the age spectrum that Ernest Cook took his first steps into such realms at the age of 12, when he was told by his headmaster, "On Monday you will be a teacher, Cook, and this will be your class."

The son of a county cricketer, Mr. Cook was born at Runswick Bay, Yorks., and three years after becoming a pupil teacher he gained top marks in the teaching candidates exam. He then went on to study at St. John's College, York, and as his first proper teaching position was appointed as headmaster of a village school in North Yorks.

He next obtained a headmastership at a school in the Huddersfield area and there in 1914 he met the girl who would become his wife, Adeline.

Seven years his junior, she was born at Marsden, Huddersfield, and had begun to teach at Mr. Cook's school at the age of 18. At Slaithwaite, Huddersfield, the couple were married six years later, whereupon she then gave up teaching.

In 1924 on Mr. Cook's appointment as the headmaster of the Bletchley Road Senior School the couple came to Bletchley, where in the following year Mr. Cook helped to form the town cricket club. In fact being a keen wicket keeper batsman he kept wicket for Yorkshire against Northants at Dewsbury on the day of George V's coronation. Following the outbreak of WW2, apart from his educational duties Mr. Cook, whose home was at 'Draycot,' Church Walk, would fulfil a number of roles, including that of Chief Evacuation and Reception Officer, deputy to the chairman of the Food Control Committee, and billeting official, whereby under the Emergency Powers Act he was able to requisition any property or billet.

He was also associated with Bletchley Park, and in a clandestine role acted as a messenger, driving a camouflaged car to take secret messages to Bomber Command Headquarters on Salisbury Plain.

At Aylesbury, on February 24th 1945 he attended a conference of head teachers which, with regard to the new Education Act, had been convened to consider the change of status of the school after March 3rd. Thus when the school reopened after the holidays on April 12th it would be as a Modern Secondary School, with the activities of the new order detailed by Mr. Cook in a two column article in the Times Educational Supplement.

With VE Day announced on May 8th the school then closed for two days, and, in the presence of the chairman of the council, on the afternoon of Wednesday, May 16th a special Victory Celebration took place at the Bletchley Park sports ground.

The events commenced with a fancy dress parade, and much amusement was caused by a teachers' race in which the blindfolded masters were lead by the mistresses. Mr. Cook and his partner would be the winners.

Mr. Cook, who was also a lay preacher for over 50 years retired in August 1953 and eventually he and his wife would make their home at Flat 1, Shenley Park, Shenley Church End.

EVACUEES ARRIVE

For most schoolchildren, no doubt a history lesson is a prospect about as welcome as a political correctness advisor in a workingmen's club.

Yet if the subject is perhaps superimposed on a topic that will engage their sympathies, within a familiar environment and presenting an opportunity to relate with people having a first hand experience then - for a while - a flicker of interest might well be kindled, especially should the topic concern the local evacuees of World War Two.

As previously recounted, as international tensions increased, surveys were then undertaken to establish the number of evacuees to be accommodated by each community and with little more than a commendable sense of duty and a letter of thanks, this was duly carried out in Bletchley by the efforts of voluntary enumerators.

Under the Government scheme the distribution of blankets and mattresses had been made and for the storage of their allocation, at an all inclusive fee of 5s, Bletchley Council hired temporary accommodation in a building near the Lantern Cafe, in Bletchley Road.

As the Chief Evacuation Officer for the BUDC scheme the local headmaster, Mr. Cook, gave the Council a full report of the measures in place.

As soon as a crisis arose, the evacuation train was scheduled to arrive from London at 1.43pm each day, with the complement of 822 children being met at Bletchley station by himself and other appointed officials.

On the first day the entire contingent would detrain for local billets but on the second day the batch would be transported to the Winslow Rural Area by road. On the third, 274 would remain in Bletchley with the rest dispersed to Winslow.

At least such was the initial plan but then a Ministry of Health Inspector called on Mr. Sherwood to announce that a further 1500 might have to be catered for. After arriving at Bletchley station, children and their accompanying teachers and helpers would then proceed to Bletchley market for the receipt of their rations, the organisation of which fell to Miss Gascoigne, Mr. Jones, Miss Wing and others.

With war just days away, London was protected by sandbags while evacuation plans were readied.

Filing past long tables, especially set up for the purpose, issued with a carrier bag each child would receive a can of meat, a can of milk, 1lb of biscuits and 1/4lb of chocolate with the adults qualifying for an extra can of meat.

With the town divided into zones, each under the charge of a marshall, after receiving their rations the assembly would then be parted off to their allocated marshalls and marched to the respective zones, where, having handed over their billeting books, they would be escorted to the various houses by helpers.

If for some reason accommodation proved unavailable, then a guide would lead them to the Senior School, for the issue of further instructions.

As a procedure - after an initial settling in period - to deal with any problems, the helpers had organised themselves into a welfare organisation and should extra accommodation become needed then, under the Emergency Powers Act, Mr. Cook was entitled to requisition whatever property he deemed necessary with any objections dealt with at a later date by a tribunal.

In accordance with the Bletchley plans, no buses would be required on the first day of evacuation but on the second, six would be waiting in Oliver Road, to make at least two journeys to the Winslow area.

Everything therefore seemed organised and awaiting the call - except, however, for a slight discrepancy that was encountered when the biscuit rations were first received - a shortfall of 317lb to be precise.

On further investigation it then transpired that some of the tins had been incorrectly marked, which reduced the figures to a more digestible 95lb!

By late August 1939, war was only days away and London had hastily prepared for the onset of bombing.

Bletchley was also prepared, with plans well advanced to receive evacuees from the capital.

EVACUEES WW2

As the result of the upheavals caused by the start of the Second World War, several young evacuee children met their early deaths in Bletchley.

Among the first of these was a seven-year-old boy, who drowned in the disused reservoir at the back of North Street and Western Road.

Evacuated from Essex Road, Islington, he was staying in North Street. Although warned not to go by the water, he went fishing for tadpoles and despite the urgent attentions of a local doctor, could not be revived.

Messing about in the water also claimed the life of another evacuee, a 12 year-old boy who for some 18 months had been staying in Watling Terrace. One evening he accompanied a local boy to the popular swimming venue at the Mill Pond, Water Eaton, but having managed a few strokes, then got into difficulty and tried to hold onto his companion's bathing costume. When this tore, he lost his grip and went under and although an older boy immediately dived to the rescue, the body could not be revived.

Ironically, at one time there had been suggestions that the Council should take over Mill Pond and make it suitable and safe as a public bathing place.

Primarily, this had been in view of a report, by the Medical Officer, expressing concern at the state of the river, and the owner of the pond had even agreed to let in fresh water and allow the dangerously deep hole in the middle to be filled in.

However, due to the wartime conditions, nothing was done and the pond remained in its previous condition, with the only alternative being the even more dangerous Denbigh Road gravel pits, 17 feet deep near the bank and 30 feet deep elsewhere.

Not only children of course were evacuated to the town and from natural causes one elderly gentleman died who, as a coincidence, had been a personal friend of the Rev. C. Spurgeon, after whom the Baptist Church at Fenny had been named.

Another Londoner, now evacuated to Brooklands Road, was Mr. Fred McQuillin who, for his gallantry during the Blitz, received the OBE from the King at Buckingham Palace. As the leader of a rescue party, on being told a family of six were buried under the rubble of their home, despite continued bombing he and his party worked for three hours and eventually saved the occupants, the last two from under 18 feet of earth and rubble in the cellar.

Rather more tragic, during her duties as a night porter at Bletchley Station, a woman evacuated from Islington 12 months earlier was struck by a train and killed, while pulling a truck of mail sacks from no. 7 platform to the general post office.

She left two small children, who had been living with her at Denbigh Road.

In every town there could be found similar tales of heartbreak and misery, but by the measure of the modern yardstick if only we could have been first into the ruins of Berlin and if only Adolf hadn't pulled that trigger, then he could have perhaps looked forward to an intensive treatment of state-funded psychotherapy and the prospect of peacefully ending his days in a cosy twilight home for the criminally deranged.

FENNY STRATFORD BOARD SCHOOL

By the late 19th century the Government had recognised the national need for a formal education, to prepare pupils for those skills born of the Industrial Revolution.

For these proposed board schools, preparations to elect persons for their local administration were made.

Regarding a school board for Fenny Stratford, by November, 1886, the necessary signatures had been obtained and a requisition was made to Mr. Powell, clerk to the Newport Board of Guardians, to call a public meeting.

This was for the purpose of forming a school board for Fenny. In accordance, a meeting of the Church School Managers and Teachers Association (North Bucks Branch) was held in St. Martin's Mission Room on November 27th where the chairman informed the members that the existing Fenny Schools would soon have to come under a school board.

This was mainly due to extra accommodation being needed by the Education Department and since the Railway Company had refused to help them, they preferred a rate supported school, rather than one funded on the voluntary principle.

In due course a meeting was therefore convened in the town hall whereby the ratepayers of the parish would pass a resolution, as to what steps should be taken to form a new school board.

Fifty ratepayers had signed the request but in the event, held 'at the inconvenient hour of 11am' the turnout was poor, since the Education Department had not allowed the expense of advertising the meeting in the local papers.

Nevertheless it was eventually resolved that a school board of not less than seven members should be formed. In January, 1887, a meeting of the local nonconformists was held in the Wesleyan schoolroom to discuss who should be nominated for the board and a similar meeting by the vicar and churchwardens of St. Martin's also took place to consider their moves.

Mr. Rowland suggested that four candidates should be nominated but when one of the hopefuls was rejected, he promptly announced that he would stand as an Independent!

As for the railwaymen of the LNER they held a meeting in the Co-op assembly room, having decided that they should be represented since their children filled the schools. Mr. A. Read, the goods yard Inspector, was eventually chosen. Then, towards the end of the month, a notice to the ratepayers of Fenny Stratford called for them - on January 31st - to elect the seven representatives necessary, to preside over the educational interests, as required by the Elementary Education Act, and in early February the election duly took place.

The church candidates had blue placards, the conformists red and Mr. Rowland, as an independent yellow and the poll, held in the infants' schoolroom closed at 8pm.

To be continued

FENNY STRATFORD TOWN HALL

By 1880, Fenny Stratford's commercial prosperity had encouraged the building of a Town Hall, adjacent to the Swan Inn.

However, shortly afterwards the Fenny Stratford Town Hall Company Ltd. went into voluntary liquidation and the building was then purchased by Barclays Bank, who employed some of the ground floor offices as accommodation, for their Fenny Stratford Branch Bank.

For the local population, outdoor entertainments could seasonally be provided by such events as the Bletchley Feast, where for a small fee the antics of 'a troupe of Soudanese Yelent Zulu Fire Kings' might be observed, not to mention 'the largest lady in the world' and an American midget.

Yet for indoor entertainments the Town Hall provided an ideal venue although perhaps in deference to the present political correctness, 'entertainment' might not be the best term applied to the various political meetings held in the hall, as it also held the early gatherings of the Salvation Army.

The latter held their meetings at the Town Hall until the construction of a

Fenny Stratford old town hall.

purpose built barracks in Church Street, at the opening of which General Booth graciously pronounced that Fenny 'was a nice place'.

He also hoped that 'my coming here will cause some poor backslider to come here', and judging by some of the rowdies who turned up in later congregations, his wish was joyously fulfilled.

For the more established religion, in aid of funds for a peal of bells to be hung in Saint Martin's Church, as a commemoration for Queen Victoria's Jubilee, in Fenny Stratford Town Hall the Walford family gave an entertainment of handbell ringing, an art in which they displayed considerable skill.

By their efforts a most useful sum was produced and eventually the new peal was opened on October 12th at the Harvest Thanksgiving service.

In fact the Walfords became popular performers at the hall and at Christmas, 1887, they excelled themselves, travelling especially back from the West of England.

Not only did Miss Eva Walford perform 'Star of Bethlehem', amongst other renditions but her sister bashed out 'I know that my redeemer liveth' on no less than her 'Aquadigipsycharmonica', a collection of wine glasses, partly filled with water.

The whole family then gave of their best in an amusing little piece entitled 'The Gay Jolly Blacksmith', accompanied by a string band and an anvil. Matters were then brought to a close by the performance, for the very first time in Fenny Stratford, of the family's original Psychological Seance -'Mysteria'.

In later years it was proposed that the Town Hall could be used to accommodate the offices of the Bletchley Urban District Council but at the local enquiry the Local Government Inspector deemed the premises unsuitable.

In 1903 a purpose-built centre was constructed in Bletchley Road, instead.

As a bathroom and kitchen centre, today the building fulfils a need far removed from its earlier use but entertainments of a certain kind are still available to the local population by the provision, in a nearly premises, of an 'adult shop', whatever one of those may be!

FENNY STRATFORD'S FIGHTER PILOTS WWI

Good grief. In the wake of the Channel 5 documentaries it seems we now have 'celebrity' truck drivers.

Is there no end to this celebrity hype. Whatever next - celebrity biscuit dunkers.

But that's not to decry truckers although in the realm of unsung heroes I'm sure there are persons far more deserving of public adulation, not least those risking their lives on the front line in Afghanistan, or the dedicated army of those toiling all hours under the sun for a pittance in the NHS.

It could be said that the cult of celebrity began with the advent of the silver screen and apart from the film stars during World War One those in the celebrity limelight were not infrequently the air aces.

The story of Fenny Stratford and one such Knight of the Air, Edward 'Mick' Mannock, has been told in a previous article but Fenny Stratford also has an association with another local distinguished airman of that time, Francis Tattam.

Born at an address in Simpson Road, when aged about 14 Francis worked his passage to Canada, where apart from several jobs in Saskatchewan he also helped to build the Kansas City railway station.

He later joined the Mounties but shortly after the outbreak of war enlisted in the Army and served in the Canadian Engineers in France.

In 1916 he then gained his wings as a pilot in the R.F.C. and one Saturday in July 1918 he greatly entertained the residents of Fenny Stratford with a display of flying stunts. Indeed his performance would merit a communication to his parents 'expressing the Council's high appreciation and admiration of the splendid exhibition of flying given to the inhabitants of the District on the 16th July 1918.'

Having received his commission, in October 1918 Francis would be sent with the B.E.F. to the Murman Coast, Russia, but in early April 1919 his parents received a telegram to say that he had been posted missing since March 31st.

Then in April 1920 they received a letter from the War Office stating that he had arrived from Russia in Terijoki, on the frontier of Russia and Finland.

Arrangements for his repatriation were to be made as soon as possible and in a cable he told his parents that he was safe and well.

It later transpired that whilst on a wireless station he had been captured by the Bolsheviks, only a few days after having distinguished himself on active service. For this the French Government awarded him the Croix de Guerre which had been sent to his parents by his commanding officer at Archangel, accompanied by the following details in French:

'A very good pilot; did not hesitate to take observations at Bolchoe-Ozerki from 20th to 30th March with a machine which he had never piloted previously, and he bombarded the enemy with success, submitting himself to a violent bombardment. He returned with his machine riddled with bullets on 23rd March, 1919.'

In 1920 Francis broke his arms and legs in an air crash and returning to Bletchley he married in 1922 and began employment at the Tompkins Moss garage in the High Street.

Then at the age of 51 he joined the R.A.F. as an officer during the Second World War, after which he resumed his former employment and later became a temporary agent for the Prudential.

Continuing the family tradition his son would become a Master Pilot in the R.A.F. whilst as for Francis he died aged 71 at Renny Lodge, Newport Pagnell, in 1966.

But back to celebrity truckers. In the folly of youth, of a Friday evening a favoured stopping off point before hopefully seeking a night of debauchery in the Northampton night spots was the M1 service station at Newport Pagnell. Here we would often see celebrities of the day and on one occasion we noticed Matt Monro who, despite our unsolicited approach, quite happily signed autographs.

In his earlier days he had been a long distance lorry driver and I found him to have quite the most down to earth and unassuming charm. A confident yet not arrogant pride in his abilities - in fact just what you'd expect from a real celebrity trucker.

FIRST WORLD WAR LETTERS

Having been frequently featured in the national and local media, (and indeed being the subject of a recent article in Local Pages), the ceremony of the Fenny 'Poppers' is now well known.

By those who are unaware of their significance, it is often assumed that there must be some connection with Armistice Day, since both fall on November 11th.

Although this is incorrect, it was during the First World War that the 'Poppers' began to achieve a more widespread renown, beginning with the establishment in early 1915 of Staple Hall as the Southern Division of the Royal Engineers Signal Section.

From all corners of the British Empire, troops were sent for training and, billeted in the town, they soon began to contribute significantly to the local economy - primarily the shops and pubs.

Due to this new source of wealth, it was perhaps inevitable that the potential for a 'souvenir' trade would soon be seen, and thus at the end of 1915 a 'Popper' was despatched to the factory of Messrs. Goss, the well-known manufacturer of armorial china, to be reproduced in quantity to the exact scale.

With the person commemorated by the Fenny Poppers having begun his career as a soldier, what better souvenir could there be for those thousands of troops who would be variously stationed in the town?

In fact, apart from the vicar, it would be officers of the Royal Engineers who on at least one occasion fired the Poppers, in a field close to the Staple Hall depot.

During the Second World War the ceremony would cease due to the regulations regarding noise. However, many things pioneered during the First World War would be resurrected during the Second World War, from the entertainments staged at the Temperance Hall and Spurgeon Memorial Baptist Hall to the Blackout, which recalled the Lighting Order. No lights in the town had to be visible during Zeppelin alerts, and this truly brought home to many civilians the new danger that they now faced.

As for the frontline troops, they would endure a conflict on a scale and of a savagery that had no precedent, and perhaps the horrors are best described in the letters sent home by the soldiers serving in the trenches.

One graphic example is from Rifleman Fred Thurlow, the son of Mr. and Mrs. Harry Thurlow, of Napier Street.

Writing to his sister, Mrs. B. Kemp, of Bletchley, he tells how Corporal Sam Tompkins (who before enlisting was employed as a baker for many years by Mr. Richardson, of Bletchley Road) was wounded.

Along with four other young men from Fenny Stratford, they had enlisted in the Rifle Brigade in September 1914.

"I am getting on all right, and all the other boys are well, with the exception of Sammy. He went out on night patrol with our platoon officer, Mr. Torry.

"I was outside the trenches lying under our barbed wire, listening for the Germans, when he came out with Mr. Torry. He told me what the password would be when they came back and then they went on; and that is the last we have seen of him.

"A patrol is supposed to be out for about two hours, but three hours passed before we heard anything. Then a Gurkha came down the line and said what had happened.

"It seems that this Gurkha was out with a patrol of his men lying on the edge of a 'Jack Johnson' hole, watching a party of about 10 Germans moving about, when all at once they heard the Germans say: 'Hands up!'

Then they could see Mr. Torry, with Sammy about five yards behind him. Torry was putting his hands up, and as he was doing so he turned round to Tompkins and said: 'Run for it,' and then bolted in the opposite direction to Sammy.

"As they bolted the Germans fired at them and threw a bomb. Mr. Torry, who it so happened, was running towards the Gurkhas, was hit three or four times and fell down into the hole where the Gurkhas were. Tompkins seemed to disappear altogether. The Gurkha said he appeared to be going towards the German trenches, mistaking them for our own. Of course, it was very dark at the time and everything was hard to see.

"The Gurkhas brought Mr. Torry into our trenches, but he died the next day from his wounds. I asked for permission to go out and look for Sammy, as he might have been badly wounded and unable to get in. The Major allowed me to go the following night (Sunday). Sammy had gone out on the Saturday night.

"Another fellow and I set out. We crawled all over the ground from where the Gurkhas saw them, back to where they started from, but we could not find him nor his rifle."

The next day Rifleman Thurlow continued the letter.

"Sammy crawled in the Gurkha trenches half a mile away, as I was writing yesterday. He was captured by the Germans, but managed to get away and hide again in a shell hole. He explained how it was he was out so long. As he was running away when the Germans first saw him, he lost his direction and did not know which were ours or the German lines.

"He was light-headed when he came in and did not know how long he had been out till we told him. He had not had anything to eat or drink all the time (three days). How he came to be away so long was that he could not remember anything about Sunday night, so I conclude he must have been knocked out by the bomb the Germans threw at him.

"On Monday night he made for what he thought were our trenches, but they were the Germans'! They fired at him and shot him in the hand, but he managed to get away and stopped in a hole all day.

"On Tuesday night he made his way to the opposite lot of trenches and lay in a ditch waiting for somebody to look over. At length a Gurkha did so. Sammy yelled at him and the Gurkha officer told him to come in. This was about half a mile down the line from where he started on the Sunday night. So he had Gurkhas on one side of him and Germans on the other, and could not understand the lingo of either. He is in hospital now, and he needs it, too. While I am writing, a terrible bombardment is still going on. We have absolutely smashed the German trenches to bits."

GORDON DOWNS BUSHELL - BATTLE OF BRITAIN FIGHTER PILOT

An orphan, Joseph Downs Bushell had been apprenticed to the grocery trade in Reading, and, travelling about his duties in a pony and trap, was later employed for ten years with a wholesale and retail grocers in Buckingham. In 1912 he then moved to Bletchley, and taking over a retail shop at 39, High Street from a Mr. White, during the following year he employed his nephew, Len Bushell, in the business, as also George Guess. In 1915 Joseph married Margery, and in 1924 realising the potential for trade in Bletchley he bought a shop from Tom Brace, and went into partnership with an employee, Fred Thurlow, as Bushell and Thurlow. Yet this was also a year which would bring tragedy, for on Sunday, August 10th his 30 year old wife was found dead at her home. That morning Mr. Bushell and his two children, Gordon and his sister, had gone for a walk, and although when they returned at about 1pm he could not get into the house, Mr. Bushell was unconcerned, since he thought that his wife must be upstairs. Remaining in the garden, he later sent Gordon back to the house, but with no sounds from within, nor a smell of cooking, Mr. Bushell climbed through a window to investigate. He then discovered the body of his wife in the copper house, with her head submerged in the copper of water, and now he was left to bring up the children alone. After an education at Mrs. Fry's private school (now the 'Small Shop') in Church Street, Gordon attended the Bletchley Road Schools and then Magdalen College School, Brackley, where he became top boy. Intending to take up tea-broking, towards this ambition in January 1937 he was presented with his certificate in the Guild Hall, but having in November 1938 joined the Volunteer Reserve of the R.A.F., he was called up at the outbreak of war and posted to 213 Squadron, flying Hurricanes. On June 18th 1940 the squadron flew to the small civilian grass airfield at Exeter, and would remain in the thick of the action throughout the Battle of Britain. In fact as a veteran of aerial combat, on November 25th 1940 Gordon, as a Sergeant Pilot, was mentioned in a despatch 'for gallant and distinguished service as a fighter pilot during the Battle of Britain,' and this regarded an incident which occurred at 22,000 feet south of the Isle of Wight, when his squadron engaged over 100 enemy aircraft. Despite baling out, the Squadron Leader was attacked by three Messerschmitts, but warding off the enemy aircraft Gordon destroyed one and, by radioing the coastguard, enabled the downed pilot to be rescued. As part of 13 Group, no. 213 Squadron was 'rested' to Leconfield, Yorkshire, on December 1st 1940, but at the age of 24 on December 31st 1940 Gordon was killed when his Hurricane, no. P3267, crashed at Risby Park, in Suffolk, during a snow storm. On the very same day he was to have been interviewed by the Station Commander regarding a commission. With full military honours his body was conveyed from his home station on a gun carriage, and after the cremation the ashes were brought for burial to Bletchley, where, having formerly been a member of the choir, it was appropriate that a service was held at St. Martin's Church on Wednesday, January 8th. As for Joseph Downs Bushell, as a respected trader he continued in business in Bletchley for many years, and died at the age of 74 in 1957. Today in Fenny Stratford Cemetery may be seen his grave and that of Gordon, whose sacrifice is recalled by the wording 'JUST ONE, TO WHOM SO MANY OWE SO MUCH'. As for the scum who have desecrated the grave, by pushing over and damaging the cross, one can only wish that this low life had been the victims of Nazi oppression.

H.M.S. MEON: BLETCHLEY, RAISES MONEY FOR A SHIP CREWED BY CANADIAN SAILORS

As the conflict dragged on, during World War Two it became increasingly essential to raise the finance to continue the struggle. One means was the national introduction of annual 'Weeks', to raise money for a specific theme, and following 'War Weapons Week' in 1941 - it would be the turn of 'Warship Week' in 1942. The objective was for the townspeople to raise £120,000 as the amount needed to buy a Corvette, and as a result of these efforts Bletchley would adopt HMS Meon, a Rivers class Corvette which would see action in the D Day operations.

HMS Meon.

By March 1942 Britain's spending on the war had reached £9,050 million, more than the entire expenditure for the Great War, and as a means to raise extra funds plans were made to stage the Bletchley Warship Week from 21 - 28th March.

A representative committee had made the preliminary arrangements, and these were then reported to the secretaries of the various sub-committees.

The intention was to raise £120,000 as the cost of a Corvette, and the need for such escort vessels was imperative, since a recent convoy to Malta had lost four fifths of its number.

At 2.30pm the 'Week' commenced on the Saturday with a Grand Parade of Services and Civil Defence Units which, having assembled on the Studio car park, was then led by a contingent of the WRNS via Lennox Road, Eaton Avenue, Manor Road, Aylesbury Street, Church Street and Victoria Road to the Council Offices, where the salute was taken.

The procession included an RAF band, two contingents of WAAF's, units of the regular Army, 456 Squadron ATC, elements of the Home Guard, members of the Women's Land Army, St Martin's Church Scouts and Guides, Buckinghamshire police and Special Constabulary, Civil Defence units and local men and equipment of the NFS.

Yet also adding to the stirring spectacle was a lifeboat full of WRNS personnel, a large model submarine, (made at an RAF station!), and a model 'warship', HMS Bletchley, which, with the assistance of police sergeant Boucher and Mr. L Verrel, a member of the National Fire Service, had been built over a lorry with the help of the Council's Surveyor, Mr. A. Bates, and his staff.

Following the salute the parade then passed through the main gates of the Bletchley Road schools to Leon Recreation Ground, and here the opening ceremony was performed by Admiral Sir Lionel Halsey, 'GCMG etc'.

In fact he seemed well qualified for the task, having until his retirement in 1922 enjoyed a long and distinguished naval career.

Indeed, apart from commanding 'HMS New Zealand' during her Empire cruise in 1913, his duties had also seen action both at Heligoland Bight in 1914, and Dogger Bank in 1915, service in 'HMS Iron Duke' at Jutland, and for two years the command of the Royal Australian Navy.

On Monday evening Commander O. Callaghan, RN, then announced that so far £18,365 had been raised, and to this amount further sums would then be added by not only the loud speaker encouragement being broadcast from HMS Bletchley, which toured the local streets urging people to contribute, but also by the various money raising events being held during the 'Week'.

With kick offs at 3pm on the LBC ground at Newton Road, these included football played against an RAF XI team on Saturday 21st March and Saturday

28th March and both of these were followed by an dance in the LBC canteen.

Then at 7.30pm on Tuesday 24th March a whist drive was held at the Yeomanry Hall.

Prizes were awarded of Savings Certificates and stamps, and on the 26th March at 7.30pm Lorna Webster compered her concert in School Hall.

Artists included Belle Chrystall, 'stage, screen and radio star', and Ernest Elliot's 'Living Marionettes', whilst for the Police Dance on Friday 27th March the music was provided by Reg Millman and his Paramount Players. On Saturday, 28th March the Bletchley Warship Week then closed with a Grand Finale Concert at 7.30pm.

This was presented by the Bletchley Park Drama Group in the Senior School Hall, although also vying for public attention was a meeting held in the Co-op Hall by Ben Bradley - 'the noted communist authority on Colonial affairs' - who, as a member of the Communist Party of Great Britain, Bletchley Branch, spoke on the subject of 'India and the Colonial Question'.

By the end of the month £73,073 had been collected, and to this new total the Warship Week indicator would be raised by a former member of the 1st Fenny Stratford Rover Crew, Ashley Shouler, who was now home on leave from the Royal Navy.

In early April the final figure would reach £78,716, (of which Mrs. Hankins, for the Bletchley Road Savings Group, had collected £1,000, the Bletchley Road Schools invested £500, BUDC collected £505, the selling centres £12,629 and Bletchley Park, £5,701), and in recognition of the achievement Mr. F. Bates, the Chairman of the Council, received a congratulatory telegram from Sir Kingsley Wood, Chancellor of the Exchequer.

As a result of Warship Week Bletchley had adopted the yet to be launched HMS Meon, a River Class corvette named after a Hampshire river, and in fact the town's naval enthusiasm might have been further encouraged by the release during the year of the film 'In Which We Serve', which starred Noel Coward, who had also written the script.

Charting the career of the destroyer 'HMS Torrin', this was the first full length feature film by David Lean, and included amongst a cast of several embryo movie stars was Richard Attenborough, who would become acquainted with Bletchley on acquiring his first motoring penalty at Fenny Stratford crossroads!

The theme of the film was perhaps influenced by the naval exploits of Louis Mountbatten, (who from 18th April was appointed to command Allied operations in South East Asia), and as an interesting association with Bletchley, a member of his staff would be a Wren officer, Miss Philippa Cary, who was the great granddaughter of the late Sir Herbert Leon of Bletchley Park. However, despite the financial success of the Week there was disappointment later in the year, when it was revealed that the public response towards providing money to buy a plaque, and create a comforts fund for the crew of HMS Meon, had been less than forthcoming.

In fact it would be announced at a meeting of the Council that of the £40 needed only one small subscription had been received. Yet at least a model of the vessel had been made by police constable Boucher, and this would now be offered for display in the Council Chamber.

Fortunately matters were more optimistic the following year, for having been ordered from the firm of Inglis, 'HMS Meon' was launched on August 4th, and it was therefore appropriate that with Lord Keyes, the Admiral of the Fleet, receiving the town's plaque from Mr. Collins, Chairman of the local National Savings Committee, the exchange of plaques between Bletchley's adopted ship and the town took place on the evening of the first Monday in August. For some while the ship would be transferred to the Royal Canadian Navy, and having 'worked up' at Tobermory she joined the 9th Canadian Escort Group at Londonderry, prior to taking part in the defence of Atlantic convoys. Then in May as one of the six frigates of the 9th Escort Group she was assigned for duties in support of the Normandy landings, and was subsequently deployed in the Bay of Biscay to deter U boat attacks on the invasion fleet.

In the wake of the Normandy landings she then undertook anti submarine duties in the Channel, but on July 20th would be damaged by a near miss when attacked with glider bombs.

After repairs she then rejoined her group and helped in the defence of Atlantic convoys in the Western Approaches but, with the vessel still being crewed by Canadians, in early 1945 in a letter to the Council the Commanding Officer said that although the officers and crew felt honoured to be adopted by Bletchley, the town might wish to consider adopting another ship.

However, the matter would soon be resolved, for on 23rd April with the anti submarine equipment now removed the vessel would be decommissioned and revert to Royal Navy control, being converted by the end of the year to the role of a Landing Ship Headquarters.

In 1946 HMS Meon then joined the reserve fleet at Harwich, whilst as for the plaque which had been funded by the Bletchley donations, with the vessel now out of commission this would be recovered in 1947 from Chatham by the Clerk of the Council, to be hung in the Council chamber. HMS Meon remained at Harwich until 1952 but would again see active service in the Suez campaign of 1956, and with the Amphibious Warfare Squadron in the Persian Gulf, before being eventually paid off in 1965.

She then arrived at Blyth for breaking up in May 1966, to be scrapped on the 14th.

HEALTH HAZARDS 1886

In July, 1886, the local vicar reported that the sanitary accommodation at the National schools was 'simply abominable' and elsewhere in the town conditions were little better.

In fact at Bletchley one learned doctor repeatedly complained of the stench, from sewage discharged into the stream passing the front of his house and he was not best impressed when, possibly as a consequence, he fell victim to typhoid.

Some of the locals hardly helped matters, for one had been using the parish sanitary cart to convey water for his own purposes! Defending his action, he said that his was because the cart had been standing on his premises for so long, with no rent paid, that he thought he was entitled to use it.

Common sense on the part of the authorities also seemed lacking, when they rejected an offer by Rowland Brothers to allow a drain to be laid across their properly, on Bletchley Road, to a brook, for the better drainage of the neighbourhood. Even the surveyor said it would have been the best scheme!

Disease became rife in the town and of three cases of diphtheria in Oxford Street, one tragically proved fatal. Thereafter it was decreed that the closets of certain cottages in the street were to be immediately reconstructed.

Soon afterwards the parochial sanitary committee then decided that the oval sewer along Bletchley Road should be opened and a new one laid in its place, a distance of some 510 feet.

The work, to be completed in four weeks, or else the contractor would be fined 10 shillings for each additional day, proved unique, for this was the first time cemented joins were to be used.

Yet only one tender was received and with little choice this was accepted, at £6910s.

Measures were also now in hand to improve the local water supply and a trial well, sunk on the property of Sir Philip Duncombe, proved promising. A copious yield of water prompted the waterworks committee to investigate the possibility of supplying water to the parish from the Brickhill Hills, to be supplied by gravity feed.

The sewage problem however, had not received such a beneficial view and one irate parishioner was moved to write: "I think the members of the Fenny Stratford sanitary committee must have gone abroad and taken the sanitary Inspector, the contractor for removing the night soil, and the night soil men with them."

It had been a month since the closets had been emptied and the stench was awful! For the main sewage at Fenny, the brook in Mrs. Hammonds field was relied upon to carry away the effluent, not only from Fenny but also from Bletchley and with the smell again being dreadful an added hazard was children playing nearby.

Mrs. Hammond had threatened to take action against the sanitary authority if this went on but the only solution the Board could think of was to clean out the ditch.

In the longer term the provision of a sewage works was being considered but having been left to a sub committee, urgency seemed lacking. Meanwhile typhoid continued to plague the town and three cases were reported in Aylesbury Street, three in Victoria Road and one each in Park Street and Oxford Street.

Something had to be done and the committee decided to lay a sewer of two feet diameter from the outfall ditch, complete with the necessary junctions and manholes with an advert for tenders to be placed in the local papers.

Not that the process went smoothly for due to a printers error the date appeared as the 13th, not the 3rd, incurring another two weeks delay. Still disease was prevalent -11 more cases of typhoid were reported - two fatal - and among the worst affected areas was Woodbine Terrace, where eight cases were reported.

Matters were not helped by there being a broken spoke on the water cart and immediate repairs were ordered. Yet some progress was being made and the surveyor reported that the clearing out of the Water Eaton brook had been done, with the holes filled up at an additional cost of £812s 12s 2½d.

On the down side he also reported that a water sample, taken from a well at The Three Tuns Inn, which supplied the whole of Woodbine Terrace, was largely contaminated with sewage.

As for the tenders for the Bletchley Road sewer, the lowest cost was from Mr. H. Welsh, of Fenny Stratford at £119 10s and this was duly accepted. A further delay occurred when it was realised the pipes hadn't been ordered!

The story of an eventual water supply for the town belongs to another article but due to the shortage of manpower, during the First World War, the quality again began to suffer and a man from the Royal Engineers depot at Staple Hall had to be appointed as engineer.

At the end of the war, remedial measures were then put in hand and tenders for the supply of an eight inch water main between Fenny and Little Brickhill were invited.

The Stanton Iron Co. would only supply 1,000 yards of pipe and so the remainder was ordered from the Stavely Iron Co, at £14 4s per ton.

The inadequacy of the existing six inch main meant a depleted supply only was available to Far Bletchley and until the new main could be laid, as a temporary measure the auxiliary pumping station at Bletchley Railway Junction was to be used, for an hour a day.

This would reduce the supply to Duncombe Street and the residents were duly warned. Yet by December the new main had been laid and tested and the problems, for the moment, had been resolved.

HERO DOCTOR AND THE DARDANELLES - DR. GURNEY WHITE BUXTON

Gurney White Buxton qualified in his profession in 1891, and in 1893 settled down to a doctor's practice in Fenny Stratford, making his home at Ivy Dene, in the High Street. Prior to the outbreak of the First World War he held a commission in the 2nd South Midland Brigade, Mounted Ambulance, Territorial Royal Army Medical Corps, and thus when war was declared he was required, as a Captain, to join his unit. At first he and his corps would remain in England, but his medical practice, which he could no longer attend, was removed to Bracknell House. When sent on active service, Captain Buxton would be stationed on the shores of the Gallipoli Peninsula, from where he would subsequently write of his experience;

"We are now living in holes in the ground and sleep on the hard ground in dirt, and there is dirt all around, and we are all dirty. Water is very scarce and only just sufficient for our bottles. We are not comfortable and sleep in our clothes and boots, the nights being cold. We are, it is needless to say, in the Dardanelles, and really seeing active service. We see numbers of wounded soldiers and shells and bullets falling everywhere. ..."

However, he was soon in declining health, and although his was the opinion that the illness could be shaken off, the medical authorities thought otherwise. They transferred him to a hospital ship, and aboard this vessel he tragically died from dysentery in January 1915, being buried at sea near Malta. Before the war, for many years Dr. Buxton had been a sidesman at St. Martin's Church, where, near to where he used to sit, may now be seen a memorial tablet in bronze, mounted on an oak base.

HELLO, OPERATOR? - TELEPHONE EXCHANGE FENNY STRATFORD

There are three of us in this relationship; me, the teenage daughter, and the teenage daughter's mobile phone. Or so it seems, when frequently summoned for taxi or mobile money 'lending' services. Of course on entering the vehicle 'texting' takes immediate precedence, with the only nod to one's existence being an incredulous glance, in response to such pleasantries as "How's school?"

Yes, I really don't know how my generation ever managed without mobile phones. The phones that we had were certainly not mobile, with the public versions being enshrined in elaborate temples of cast iron and glass, and the domestic versions, after a deferential approach to the Post Office, and the tingling anticipation of a six month wait, being a thing of eternal reverence. Around which like Pavlov's dogs the whole family would expectantly salivate, when summoned by its ring.

Bletchley had first made the acquaintance of this new fangled speaking device in the late 19th century, when in July 1888 permission was granted for the United Telephone Co. Ltd. to erect 'posts and wires' in the parish. As for the use of the device, it proved a handy means for a local chess club to compete in games with a Dunstable club, by telephoning the moves.

Then around 1902 the Post Office installed a public telephone service to Bletchley and Fenny Stratford, but with only those of sufficient means and status having the need for such an instrument, the famous jockey Mornington Cannon became the fourth of the 20 subscribers in 1906, when a telephone was installed at his home of Brooklands.

The first telephone exchange in the town was in the Aylesbury Street post office, in the home of Mrs. Fortescue, and one of the first two telephone operators would be Ethel Grant from London, who in 1909 married Alfred Staniford. Along Bletchley Road the telephone wires were carried aloft on wooden poles, but in early 1919 heavy snowfalls brought down all but about two of these. Therefore, it was decided to lay an underground cable on the south side of Bletchley Road, and work began in 1920. Not that there seemed much demand, for by the opinion of one local councillor most residents 'could not now, or ever' need a phone, and it was deemed sufficient for a public call box to be installed at the post office.

Following the Second World War, with the beginnings of the migration from London the need arose for a new exchange. The original idea in 1952 had been to site the exchange on top of the Post Office in Bletchley Road, but since the council had gone to a lot of trouble securing a site at the corner of Church Street and Victoria Road, their will prevailed.

With the continuing arrival of the London 'overspill' the town was rapidly expanding, and in 1958 the area telephone manager would be asked to consider placing telephone boxes on the Rivers and Castles estates. In fact by 1961 there was an annual demand in the town for 180 telephones, expanding the present customer base of 986, and in 1964 the question arose of a suitable site in Bletchley for a telephone engineering centre, as required by the Postmaster General. However, the council had agreed to lease a site in Tavistock Street, which was no longer required by Henry Sykes Ltd., and thus the telephone manager of the Bedford area asked the council to make houses available for the staff being brought in from outside. From September 29th 1967 about 2,500 telephone subscribers in Bletchley would be able to use STD, and in the 1970s the telephone exchange was massively expanded into its present form.

High Street, Fenny Stratford.

HISTORY OF THE FENNY POPPERS

With the second Fenny Poppers Festival due to be held in August, it seems a new local tradition is being set. Local historian John Taylor investigates the older tradition of the Fenny Poppers, after which it is named.

"The whole of the work being happily finished", on May 26th 1730 the Lord

Bishop of Lincoln, Richard Reynolds, came to Fenny Stratford to consecrate the new church of St. Martin's. This had been founded by Browne Willis, the lord of the manor, and the dedication honoured the memory of his grandfather, Thomas Willis, who had died on St. Martin's Day in 1675.

Thomas, in the wake of the self-imposed financial worries of the second Duke of Buckingham, had purchased the estates of Water Eaton with Bletchley and Fenny Stratford in 1674. By also acquiring that of West Bletchley, he would reunite the local manors.

A student of Oxford University, Thomas had fought for the King in the defence of that city during the Civil War, and becoming medically qualified as 'MB' in 1646, this would be the year in which the first of his books was published, at The Hague. Perhaps amongst the more perceptive of his works was to be 'Two Discourses Concerning the Soul of Brutes which is that of the Vital and Sensitive of Man', one of the subjects of which was 'melancholy', to which the male was particularly susceptible, one cause being falling in love.

At the Restoration, when - following the austerities of the Puritan age - Charles II came to the throne, Thomas was made Professor of Natural Philosophy at Oxford University, and in London during 1664 he published - with many of the excellent illustrations having been drawn by Christopher Wren - a major work which, even in recent years, has been acclaimed as 'the most exact account of the time. It is the basis of our modern knowledge of the subject and the anastomosis between the left and right internal and external carotid arteries at the base of the brain is known as the Circle of Willis to this day.'

In Oxford, Thomas had been involved with the meetings that led to the formation of the Royal Society, but in 1666 he went to London, where he set up in practice in St. Martins Lane. It would be on St. Martin's Day, (November 11th), that he died from pneumonia in 1675, leaving two daughters and a namesake son, by whom much of the enclosed lands at Fenny Stratford would be leased to the inhabitants.

Apart from the dedication of the church, in order to further perpetuate the memory of his grandfather, Browne Willis, on July 4th 1730, settled a rent charge of £1 on Dr. Martin Benson, the Rector of Bletchley, and also on the Churchwarden of Fenny Stratford, and the Overseer of the Poor of Fenny Stratford. This would be annually raised out of a close of land in Bletchley called Parsons Piece, and the three Trustees were tasked to pay the curate of Fenny Stratford to preach a sermon on St. Martin's Day. Then on 11th February 1736 the curacy was endowed with a small farm at Bletchley, (which included Parsons Piece), and by this arrangement an income of £18 a year was now provided.

However, in January 1740, Browne Willis acquired a thatched house and grounds 'fronting the common street of Fenny Stratford', and for this he paid £33 to Mary Gibbs and her eldest son.

Thomas Gibbs, had originally acquired possession of the property from her brother, Matthew Cherry, on July 20th 1716, but the premises later became an alehouse known as The Crispin.

At the time of his purchase, the premises were in such a poor condition that, in order to render them habitable, Browne Willis had the front wall rebuilt, (duly recording this expenditure on the deed of conveyance), and as the means to both fund a sermon on St. Martin's Day, 'and to buy small divinity tracts to give to poor persons yearly', he then gave the property to the town.

With the dwelling being bounded on the north by the premises of Benjamin Pomfret, on the south by Richard Stapp and on the west by John Page, at a rent of 3d per annum, the house was at that time occupied by Mary Lovell, a widow, but by 1839 the property - which as 25 and 27 Aylesbury Street would be known as St. Martin's Cottages - had been divided into two dwellings, let at 1s a week to Richard Baseley and Conyers Burton.

The case of the latter was perhaps not without a certain irony, since he may well have been the same person who, before the building of a small church in 1805, had allowed those inhabitants inclined towards the Baptist faith to use his bouse as meeting place.

By the later 19th century, the two cottages were producing a revenue of between £8 and £10, and from this sum payment was made for a dinner, with the vicar paid £1 1s for preaching a sermon. Other sums were spent on the mundane matters of tax, rates, upkeep and insurance, but for a ceremony to commemorate Thomas Willis the sums of 2s for bell ringing, 6s on gunpowder, and 2s for firing the 'poppers' were also expended. The poppers were cast-iron vessels in which gunpowder was packed and then ignited, although it seems somewhat obscure as to whether the instigation had been by Browne Willis, since no specific mention occurs until the 1830s.

In the later 19th century, the churchwardens received a proposal from the Charity Commissioners 'for the appropriating of the charities of the town, and more especially the St. Martin's or Browne Willis charity for educational purposes', but since only one churchwarden recommended acceptance, the general opinion was it 'is not desirable in as much as the said charities have been carried out strictly according to the will of the donors'.

The intention of the charity, therefore, remained intact, although this could not be said of the fabric of the cottages, which had become so dilapidated that on May 12th 1914 the council, under the 1909 Housing Act, placed a closing order on the premises, 'as being dangerous and unfit for habitation'. Indeed, by November the situation had become so severe that they gave notice to consider demolition, and on Tuesday January 12th of the following year the order was duly sealed, at 8pm.

In consequence, the property would be acquired by a local building firm and, with the site having been cleared, the area was purchased by the firm of Manyweathers. As wheelwrights, following the outbreak of World War I, they would produce many gun carriages for the army, and it was also due to the war and the consequent national financial situation that £60 from the sale of the site was invested in Canadian Bonds. During World War I, in the search for dollars, the Government took over the Canadian Bonds and, with these eventually being replaced with other securities, in 1950 £2 5s 8d was being raised in interest.

As for the poppers, for many years the gunpowder was supplied by Pacey's, the ironmongers in Aylesbury Street, but in 1867, when fired in a field called Bull Close, at the back of Aylesbury Street, one of the poppers exploded, and a fragment partially demolished the roof of the Bull and Butcher. As a result, one of the remaining poppers was then sent as a pattern to Barwell and Co. at the Eagle Foundry, Northampton, with a new set duly forged and bored out.

By tradition, the poppers are fired on 11th November, as per the original intent, but on occasion they have also been fired on other dates. These included the Coronation of King George V, when Dr. Charles John Deyns, the chairman of the newly created council, was afforded the honour of firing the 21 'gun' salute.

In 1905 the then vicar of St. Martin's decided that the poppers were unsafe. He had them replaced by two small cannons but the loudness of the cannons caused several local inhabitants to complain. The following year, the poppers made a triumphant return!

As for the cannons, they were eventually purchased by the Surveyor to the Council, Major Chadwick, and for many years would adorn either side of the front door of his house. Then at the sale of the late Mrs. Chadwick's effects they were purchased in March 1951 for £2 by Captain Hubert Faulkner, who placed them in the garden of his home at Staple Hall Lodge.

During World War II, Captain Faulkner had been much involved in constructing extra buildings for the code breakers at Bletchley Park, and due to the outbreak of war because of the regulations regarding noise in wartime the ceremony of firing the poppers ceased in 1939. Nevertheless, the St. Martin's dinner still went ahead at the Vicarage, attended by the wardens and secretary of the Parochial Church Council.

After an absence of seven years, following the end of the war the poppers made a welcome return, with the first being exploded at exactly midday by the vicar, the Reverend Wheeler before a crowd of 'youthful and excited' sightseers. A 6ft-long red-hot poker, rushed out by Mr. Frank Duffield from a furnace at the rear of the church, was used for the firing, but after the first explosion Mr. Pacey had to add additional powder to the following five, before they could be ignited. A London film cameraman and photographer were present to record the ceremony, and after repeat firings at 2pm and 4pm about 70 people attended the associated cold spread, prepared by the ladies of the church.

From then on, the ceremony once again became well-established, but as an effect of the blasts in 1949 a piece of the glass face of the church clock was blown out - rather unfortunate since in front of the tower was a board recording the amount so far collected towards the church restoration!

Not surprisingly, the next ceremony was transferred to the Watling Street entrance of Manor Fields, but this location attracted so little public interest that the event was moved to Leon recreation ground. Here much greater attention was aroused, and in 1953 the poppers were recorded by the BBC for their feature, England in November, scheduled for transmission at 10.15pm on November 25th.

HOME GUARD - PLAYING A VITAL ROLE IN RELEASING TROOPS FOR THE FRONT LINE

As telephone traffic increased so did the number of wires required and cables began to be laid underground.

But being smaller they required the telephone signal being boosted and amplifying 'repeater stations' were built along the telephone trunk routes, typically 45 miles apart.

The repeater station at Fenny Stratford was completed in 1924 with main national phone cables passing through the building.

When WW2 broke out the need to protect such premises - especially given the lines laid to Bletchley Park and other sensitive installations - was considered and provision made, north and south, to tap into the trunk line should it be damaged by bombs.

This was justified when four bombs fell near the suitably named Dropshort Farm.

When the Home Guard was formed in 1940 the Post Office authorities realised the essential need to maintain telephone and communication facilities.

Because of their specialised knowledge PO employees were restricted to joining Post Office Home Guard units with safeguarding PO property a priority.

At Bletchley this saw a platoon attached to B Company Home Guard with the HQ at Bedford forming part of the 6th Cambridgeshire (34th Post Office) Battalion.

The Post Office platoon came under the Bletchley Garrison Commander and they received the same training as other Home Guard units.

A Mr. Herring and Mr. Bedford allowed the use of their land for a rifle range and assault course. For those assigned to guarding the repeater station there was Sten gun practice.

In the middle of 1940 the King's Liverpool Regiment was stationed at

Bletchley Park and eight men under a Corporal were sent to the repeater station on eight hour shifts.

An Austin 'Tilly' brought meals and the men had a small gas cooker and ring but local children would also fetch them fish and chips from Thurlows (now Napoli's) as well as beer from The Bridge Inn! In return the soldiers let them play with their caps and equipment.

Private Sid Lucas, a talented artist, would sketch away the hours including the portrait of a GPO Home Guard sergeant.

During the war there was a lot of activity on the canal and children would be given welcome (given sweet rationing) chunks of glucose as workmen unloaded barges for the Valentin, Ord and Nagle refinery.

Soldiers also found a ready, if unofficial, supply of coal for the guardroom stove from the barges although getting it required nightime raids using a makeshift raft - which eventually sank.

In 1942 the Suffolk Regiment took over guard duties and they were later replaced by Royal Military Police 'bluecaps' who had a blue badge with VP for Vital Points.

They were more officious than their predecessors.

As for Sid Lucas he later served with anti-aircraft units and a Mobile Field Bakery until discharged in 1944 when he went back to being a butcher.

He died aged 78 in Birkenhead in 1993.

The Home Guard was formed on May 14th 1940 as the Germans were pushing into Belgium and France. 150,000 were expected to answer the call for volunteers. At its peak 1.8m men were serving.

Home Guard soldiers were officially aged between 17 and 65.

They were too young or old to serve in the regular forces or were in 'reserved occupations'. More than 1,600 members were killed on duty.

HOUSING & HIGHWAYS 1926

As an example of the information now to be gleaned from the computerised Bletchley News archive database, being completed at Bletchley Library, this article concentrates not so much on a particular theme but a particular year - the first half of 1926.

So, by courtesy of the database, let's travel back in time 75 years and find out what was happening in the town - and what the inhabitants were getting up to.

The Christmas festivities were over but for those still needing a religious fix, there were several brands on offer. Except for the Church Army which - since their headquarters at St. Martin's Hall had been taken over, by assorted worthies from St. Martins Church - no longer had a local branch.

At the opposite end of town the faithful at old Bletchley were being rewarded by the prospect of a central heating installation in the church but the Methodists had to resort to a bazaar for the renovation of their Aylesbury Street premises.

Apart from the spiritual accommodation of the locals, for housing developments there were bursts of activity all over the place.

Plans to convert two houses into shops in Bletchley Road were approved for Mr. E. Weatherhead while anyone wishing to purchase a home in Bletchley district was invited to inspect 'homes in course of erection by us on the Staple hall Estate', advertised by Garner and Son of Denmark Street.

A detached property would cost between £550 and £950! Of those town properties already built and established, Mr. Frank Duffield paid £460 for No 25 George Street while for those in need of council housing, at a meeting of the Bletchley Urban District Council, it was recommended to accept a tender entered by four Bletchley builders.

A total of 68 houses were proposed - 36 in Western Road and 32 at Old Bletchley with the work to be completed within 12 months.

For private buyers, C. Martins, builders, of Wolverton advertised three 'very attractive ideal labour saving homes' in Windsor Street while on the Brooklands Building Estate, frontages to Brooklands Road and Westfield Road were available at 2s 6d a yard.

More unusually two years previous, at the sale of the Bracknell House Estate, the executors of William Rowland purchased land on one side of Denmark Street, then in use as allotments and gardens.

Now that the yearly tenancies were up, they made preparations to build a memorial almshouse on the site. With all this residential growth came a need to expand and improve the recreational and highways infrastructure.

For pedestrians the footpath from Stag Bridge to Denbigh Road underwent an improvement and for motorists the county council decided to enlarge the canal bridge from 20ft to 40ft.

In a commendable community spirit, for the local school the AA had promised to supply two roadside danger signs but when these arrived the county highways committee refused to allow their use, stating only those authorised by the Ministry of Transport were suitable.

Elsewhere a new road was proposed to link Buckingham and Newton Longville roads and in Western Road the condition of the road surface was causing concern, due to the heavy traffic.

IT WAS FENNY BY GASLIGHT- HISTORY OF THE OLD GASWORKS

Aylesbury Street, Fenny Stratford, with the street gas lamps still in place - electricity, supplied from Northampton, did not arrive until 1930.

Replacing much of the local heritage, during the past few years Fenny Stratford has seen many new developments. In fact one of the latest is presently taking shape on the site of the old gasworks, and perhaps now is therefore an opportune time to take a brief glance at this age of Fenny's industrial past.

'Fenny Stratford is likely soon to reap the advantages consequent upon having the shops and streets lighted with gas.'

So read a report in the Aylesbury News in 1857, and in accordance Gregory Odell Clarke and Robert Holdom, who between them had various business interests in Fenny Stratford, founded the Fenny Stratford Gas Light and Coke Co., which first lit the town by gas on December 31st, 1857.

As for their customers, from Monday April 1st 1889 the price of gas would be reduced to 4s 7d per 1,000 feet, with a discount for cash, and, as an added benefit, if they were not more than 20 yards from the existing mains new customers could have their gas laid on free, 'subject to the approval of the Directors.'

The advent of the canal, and later the railways, had allowed the bulk import of coal and with this proving an obvious advantage to the local gasworks an enlargement of the premises took place in 1891, with tenders invited for a gasholder tank, 51ft. 6in. in diameter.

With Alfred Taylor to attend to those in the town, towards the end of September, 1895, for those at the Bletchley end of the parish Mr. H Lee was appointed to carry out repairs to the street lamps. As for the cost of the gas they consumed, this would now be a matter for consideration by a committee, who were tasked to obtain a larger discount from the gas company.

Then in other concerns the gas company was asked to lay a main in St Martin's Street for a lamp to be erected at a position determined by the Lighting Inspectors. Tenders for the work were duly invited, and that of £2 12s 6d from Alfred Taylor was successful. Yet regarding the negotiations about the price of gas the cost was deemed to be too great, and in 1897 Mr. Lisling, of Messrs. Laurence Scott and Co., of Norwich, was approached to provide details of lighting the town by electricity.

However, in view of this if the Council undertook the lighting etc. of the lamps the gas company then offered to supply gas at 3s 7d per 1,000 feet, and with this agreed it was decided not to proceed with the electricity scheme.

In late 1899 the Council then asked the Company if they wanted to sell the gasworks. The Chairman, in a letter of October 1st duly replied that if the shareholders agreed he would sell for £9,750, but in the event a vote went against the proposal for sale.

At the turn of the 19th century the Company was producing 5.2 million cubic feet of gas, and with 228 customers connected to the mains, (13 of whom had gas cookers), 58 were using the new penny in the slot meter. In 1910, on a location that allowed the easy offloading of coal a new gasworks was then constructed fronting the canal, and by 1913 there were 700 customers, of whom 415 had slot meters.

Originally from Heme Bay, where for several years he served on the staff of the local gas company, Jasper Cook later become assistant engineer at the Bedford Gas Light Co., and then, at a time when gas was priced at nearly 7s per 1,000 cubic feet, he was appointed in 1920 as general manager, engineer and secretary at the Fenny Stratford Gas Light and Coke Co. With his office being that part of the house on the canal side, he lived at 'Ivydene' in the High Street, whilst as for the consumers the company would now install a supply of gas, free of charge, and also provide a prepay meter, three lights and a cooking stove. Usually taking pennies, the coin meters were in fact set to deliver slightly less than the value of the coins, such that when the money was metered and collected a welcome cash surplus could be handed back to the customer!

Calling every three months, the collector would be accompanied by a youth and with his job being to push the 'copper truck' - a strong box on a tyre wheeled chassis - he was left in charge whilst the collector emptied the meters.

In 1924 discussions again took place to supply Bletchley with electricity, but even so during the year the gas lamps along Bletchley Road (now Queensway), were fitted with automatic clockwork lighters. In fact the continuing use of gas was good news for Mr. Fowler, who in 1928 arrived as foreman at the gasworks.

He brought with him much relevant experience, for during the previous 12 years he had been foreman of the gasworks at Seaford, Surrey, and was then for a while employed at Whittlebury. During 1936 Mr. Frank Palmer was then appointed as the gas works foreman, and from a house midway along Bletchley Road he moved with his family in 1937 to a house at the gas works site adjacent to that of Jasper Cook, who was now the Company manager.

With the outbreak of World War Two it was obviously realised that the gas holders would make an inviting target for enemy aircraft, and at the gas works a refuge in the basement of the Retort House - protected with sandbags and steel shutters - was provided to accommodate ten men, who were equipped with gas suits and trained in anti gas measures.

In fact the measures were taken none too soon, for towards the end of October 1940, four high explosive bombs fell in the near vicinity, although fortunately without causing any damage.

At 83, Bletchley Road, as a sign of the times an air raid shelter was also being constructed at the rear of the gas showrooms, and in June 1940, with the shortage of manpower regular work at the gasworks was open to a gas works stoker, aged over 30 who, by working seven shifts, at £4 3s 9d per week, could thereby no doubt help produce the 'good, hard clinker', which was now being offered for sale at the works at '6s cash per ton.'

Throughout the war the manager of the gas works was Mr. Jasper Cook, and he also played an important role in presiding at local public committees during the savings week campaigns.

In aid of the RAF Benevolent Fund, after the end of the war at the gas showrooms at £1 each Victory Bells, cast from the metal of German aircraft shot down over Britain, were offered for sale by 'Mr. Therm', who in early 1946 became rather more expensive when the Directors of the British Gas Light Co. Ltd. announced that from the reading of the meters for the June quarter, the price of a therm would be increased by 2d to 15d.

Nevertheless, business remained sufficiently brisk to employ more stokers, stoker-labourers and general labourers and later during the year a works maintenance fitter would also be required, 'able to do acetylene welding and forge work.'

During the early summer of 1946 'The Manor', at Little Brickhill, became the home of 105 German POWs and although most of the men were sent to work at the Marston Valley brickworks at Ridgmont, a few were directed to the gas works at Fenny Stratford.

By the later year the restrictions on POWs visiting private homes were then lifted, and in fact Francis Palmer, foreman of the gas works, would take several of the POW's into his home for meals, even serving Christmas dinner for a number of them!

In January 1947 he and others then expressed a desire that Bletchley should 'bestir itself to stretch out the hand of friendship; to provide for the spiritual and social welfare of our ex-enemies who had been away from home for so long, and whose lives were in danger of being ruined through the monotony of having only these same 104 companions all day and all night, every day for weeks....and months....and years.'

They duly consulted Ernest Staniford, a deacon of the Spurgeon Baptist Church, and on going to the gas works he was introduced to Heinrich Dueval, 'interpreter to the Gas division', Gerd Nolte and Georg Krieger, all German POW's employed at the facility. So began a local friendship society through which many local families would take POWs into their homes, as an 'Experiment in Friendship.'

With the war now in the past it was indeed a time for reconciliation, and in mid July, 1947 in the window of the Gas Company showroom toys made by the POWs at the Little Brickhill camp were put on display.

Having been priced by a local tradesman, they would then be sold at the Community Centre on Thursday and Friday, July 24th and 25th, with the proceeds applied to the entertainments being arranged for the Belgian, and other children, who were presently visiting Bletchley.

In 1949 came the nationalisation of gasworks, and although electricity had been introduced to the town in the 1920s, even in 1950 gas was still the preferred form of lighting for the tenants of the council house at 82, Newton Road. In fact this was the only such property in the town to still rely on a gas supply, although until 1953 gas would be supplied for lighting at Bletchley station.

An unfortunate incident occurred in 1952, when gas containing too much sulphur was allowed to pass on to the town.

Compounding the matter this lapse had been detected by the gas 'Referee', and in November the following year the Ministry would bring a prosecution against the Gas Board at Bletchley Magistrates Court. Pleading guilty, the Board was fined £5, with £5 costs.

Also during 1952, in February Gerald Palmer, the son of Frank Palmer, was entrusted with installing and maintaining the private trunk line at the Royal Lodge, Nyeri, Kenya, and in fact during the later part of World War Two he had worked at Bletchley Park in the Post Office Telephones Department, and then for a few years at the Repeater Station.

Indeed, perhaps with hindsight he was wise not to pursue a career at the gas works for in 1956 the Fenny Stratford gasworks closed, and on the site in November, 1963, work began for Pergamon Press on a new printing and bookbinding complex.

This was known as the Buckingham Press, but the premises came up for sale in

February, 1966, following an announcement by the chairman, Robert Maxwell MP, that it had not been possible to recruit the skilled staff that were necessary.

For some years after the closure of the gasworks the two spiral guided gasholders on the main site remained but one, with a capacity for 140,000 cubic feet, was dismantled in 1971, and the other, of 200,000 cubic feet, in 1974/75.

LOCAL WRITERS BRING HISTORY TO BOOK.

In recent months, with the sad passing away of Ted Legge and then Ted Enever, Bletchley has lost two of its most respected resident authors.

However, their wealth of local knowledge has fortunately been preserved within their various writings and publications and perhaps now is an opportune time to glance back at some of the other people who have locally wielded the pen.

As epitomised by the impressive monument in St Mary's Church, after the Norman Conquest the de Grey family came to hold considerable influence and power throughout the district and it was at their manorial home of Water Hall at Water Eaton that Arthur, the 14th Baron de Grey de Wilton, was born and raised.

However, in 1563 he transferred the family seat from Water Hall to Whaddon, and following his appointment by Queen Elizabeth as Lord Lieutenant of Ireland, he gained the capable service of Edmund Spenser as his secretary.

In fact, it was whilst staying as a guest at Whaddon Hall before departing with his master for Ireland that Spenser, according to tradition, is said to have composed part of his monumental life's work The Faerie Queene, beneath 'a most venerable oak' on the south side of the garden.

The tree has long since disappeared although an ancient volume of The Faerie Queene was more lately to be seen in the library of Ascott House, near Wing.

Moving on through the years, in 1753 the Reverend William Cole came to live in Bletchley, pursuant to his appointment as rector of St Mary's Church, but it is for his diary dealing with some of the years that he spent in the town that he is best remembered.

In fact, it might perhaps be equated to a modern-day soap opera (for it would certainly make good content for one) since it deals not only with himself and his clerical life but also the local characters - their quarrels, gossip and everyday activities.

In 1767 the Rev. Cole left Bletchley for Waterbeach in Cambridgeshire but, regarding his time in Bletchley, The Bletchley Diary of The Rev. William Cole 1765 - 1767 was published in 1931.

As for some of the characters mentioned, under the date Sunday, March 9th 1766, is found: "Mr. Armstead, the mad and drunken Apothecary of Fenny

Stratford, about three or four days ago salivated Joe Holdom for a bad leg and yesterday morn borrowed his horse to go to some other apothecary for drugs, as he has none of his own, and has not been here since: so the patient left in a miserable way and not knowing how to proceed, sent his son this afternoon to Leighton to one Mr. Pike to come to him."

(Spelt as Armitstead, the burial of the wife of the 'mad' apothecary is recorded on October 30th 1782, although there is no mention in the registers of her husband).

Deserving of an entire article is the story of Water Eaton's very own 'mystic', Thomas Lake Harris. Suffice to say that, after his birth in 1823 at Water Eaton Mill, his parents took him at an early age to America where he eventually became minister of a chapel in New York.

He died in 1906, and is still remembered for the 'stirring' poetry that he wrote 'looking forward to an era of love and liberty and peace when there shall be visible signs of brotherhood in Christ among all Christian men'.

Not that there seemed much point in looking during the early years of the 20th century when prevailing imperial tensions would soon erupt in the outbreak of the First World War.

Despite the competition of motor vehicles, this was still an age when the horse remained an important means of travel and the Army swiftly descended to commandeer many from the local district.

These even included the 'hunters' of Lord Dalmeny, at The Grange. If a local expert should be required, then J. Albert Frost was on hand at The Homestead, Bletchley Road. Indeed at the beginning of 1915 he published his book The Shire Horse In Peace War. which for 2s, was available from the publishers Vinton and Co, 8 Breams Buildings, Chancery Lane, London, or from any local bookstall. Or it could perhaps be had by personally visiting Mr. Frost, who was also able to offer Rhode Island Red eggs for sale at 2s 6d per sitting.

As for the future role of the horse, as Mr. Frost wrote: "The motor-mad mechanic may think that his chance has come, but generals who have to lead an army over water-logged plains, or snow covered mountains, will demand horses, hitherto - and henceforth - indispensable for mounting soldiers on, rushing their guns quickly into position, or drawing their food supplies and munitions of war after them."

For those who had witnessed the horrific carnage of the First World it would no doubt seem ridiculous that a repeat performance could be staged 20 years later but so it was destined to be.

When the Second World War broke out, a well-known Canadian artist and illustrator, Herbert Sellen, was on a visit to his daughter, Mrs. Phyllis Fryer, at 59, Eaton Avenue. Being unable to return to Canada, he instead stayed at her home,

The cover of a children's book by the Canadian artist, Herbert Sellen. He was stranded in Bletchley at the outbreak of war in 1939 while visiting his daughter.

where he died in 1962, aged 86.

During the war he ran several art classes in Bletchley as well as providing artwork for the local newspapers but his reputation achieved a far wider renown, and the illustrations for *The Story Of Little Greedy* - a salutary tale for the younger generation - are just one example of his artistic talents.

Also to achieve a far wider renown, albeit for reasons of less merit, was Robert Maxwell.

On the site of the old gasworks during the early 1960s work began in a new printing and bookbinding premises for his Pergamon Press, to be known as the Buckingham Press. But with the buildings having remained unused they came up for sale in February 1966.

The reason, according to the chairman, Robert Maxwell MP, was that it had not proved possible to recruit the staff with the necessary skill.

Nowadays, with the incredible developments in technology it is perfectly possible, via 'print on demand', for anyone to produce any number of their own books to a high quality at an affordable cost and thus anyone can now have the means to preserve their life story for posterity.

An inspiration is undoubtedly Harry Hill, who was featured in the last issue of Local Pages. Conversely, such technology - if at present at the embryo stage - is also capable of 'resurrecting' books which have long been out of print.

In fact, one that must surely qualify is that written by Captain Knight, the grandson of a former rector of Bow Brickhill, who long before the 'Great Escape' broke out of a German prisoner-of-war camp during the First World War and made a 'home run' to England, there to be received by the King at a private interview.

Sadly, as a result of the cruelty and privations that he suffered in Germany, he died from illness on October 30th 1919, at 82, Eaton Square.

However copies of Brother Bosche, the story of his adventure, are still to be found and - as with many deserving titles - may soon be accessed by this new technology which will therefore quite literally have the potential to bring the past to life.

Extracts from Brother Bosch. Gazetted to the 3rd Devons in 1914, after much service in the trenches in France Gerald Knight joined the Royal Flying Corps as an observer. He then obtained his pilot's certificate but was brought down in the autumn of 1916 while bombing over the German lines. Taken prisoner, his third attempt to escape proved successful and on landing in England he was received by the King at a private interview.

LOOKING BACK - QUEENSWAY, BLETCHLEY

What, exactly, would any self respecting looter hope to find in Queensway, Bletchley.

Even more puzzling, how is the supposed cause of 'social deprivation' remedied by causing even more of the same.

Oh well, riots are nothing new, and surprisingly this was not the first time that Bletchley Road (now Queensway) had witnessed civil disturbance.

Around 1902 Paul Klameth had taken over some nurseries in Bletchley Road, but being of foreign birth his name, although he was a naturalised British citizen, was removed from the list of voters following the outbreak of World War One.

His original nationality also lead to unwelcome attentions from a small local minority, and this soon became manifest in a spate of window smashing at his premises. Consequently, on the night of Saturday, May 15th 1915 Inspector Callaway, police sergeant Snelling, and four special constables, mounted a surveillance operation, and shortly after 11 p.m. they saw a number of men and youths arrive.

Two were immediately arrested upon entering the grounds but the rest managed to run away, and in the morning it was found that more panes of glass had been broken.

In due course, on Thursday, May 20th 1915 the two persons arrested - a carter and a labourer, both of Fenny Stratford - were brought to court, and although they pleaded guilty they said they had not been intent on any unlawful purpose.

As for the facts of the matter, in court it was said that on coming from Fenny Stratford they had passed the house and nurseries but then returned, and after climbing over the fence looked in at the dining room window of the house, which stood amongst the glass and hothouses.

They then went round to the back, but were found near the door by police sergeant Snelling and a special constable.

On being asked what they were doing the pair replied that they were "only having a look," but nevertheless they were arrested, and, with the assistance of Inspector Callaway, brought to the police station to be locked up over night. Both were under the influence of drink, and were released the following morning on bail.

At their court appearance they were fined 5s costs, with each bound over for the sum of £5, to keep the peace for 12 months.

Not surprisingly the following month the nursery was sold to Mr. G. Littlewood, a nurseryman, seedsman and florist, and in late July 1915 it was announced that Mrs. Paul Klameth, who had been operating the nursery, was leaving the district, and would therefore resign as honorary secretary of the Bletchley Branch Committee of the N.S.P.C.C.

As for the two miscreants, and their somewhat lenient treatment, when arrested one had said "My mates are not having fair play at the front, so I thought I would try and get it for them."

In fact he would have even more of a chance from March 1916, for with the introduction of military conscription his future would lie in the trenches, where the opposing German infantry would no doubt soon teach him the real meaning of a 'robust response.'

A FAMILY AT WAR - LORD & LADY DALMENY AT THE GRANGE, BLETCHLEY

Forget your Eastenders, or your Coronation Streets, to become really enthralled in a 'soap' just take a seat at the Local Studies Centre, Milton Keynes Central Library, where all human life and drama can be found. Not the staff of course, with their calm and professional expertise, but the reels of microfilmed local newspaper archives, which, accessibly stored in filing cabinets, may be readily viewed on the microfiche readers. In fact in this enlightened age, when libraries are 'service providers,' and the punters are 'clients,' as a further enlightenment coffee (at a price!) is available from a vending machine. All making for a very pleasant environment, in which to spend an hour or two following the weekly paper trail of some developing news story from yesteryear. So it was in this way that the intriguing drama of Lord and Lady Dalmeny's marital relations began to unfold, and since the full story is told in a forthcoming book on Bletchley during the First World War, this article deals with the details in brief. In January 1914 The Grange was sold to Lord Dalmeny, who in 1909 had married Dorothy Grosvenor. Yet the family had only been in residence for a week when the First World War broke out, and Lord Dalmeny obtained a staff appointment with General Allenby in France. Meanwhile Lady Dalmeny remained at The Grange, but already their marriage had begun to founder, and on his first leave Lord Dalmeny discovered that when informed of his return his wife left the town, an occurrence she repeated in February 1915. Then in August 1915 came news that Lord Dalmeny had been wounded, but this seemed of little concern to his wife, since the frequency of her letters had not only lessened, but their tone had become colder. Thus in October 1915, when he obtained leave to see her in Paris he asked why she had this attitude, to which she replied she had ceased to care for him, and it was a pity they ever married. In fact she declared she would never live with him again, but nevertheless she continued to reside at The Grange with her children. After further acrimonies, Lord Dalmeny consulted his solicitor, and arrangements were made for the care of the children, since he would be away on military service in Egypt. Lady Dalmeny then took a house in her own name, without consulting him, and in further independence when he came home, due to his father being seriously ill, his request for her and the children to meet him needed an order to be obtained from the Court of Chancery. Having moved from The Grange, by April 1918 Lady Dalmeny had taken up voluntary war work on a farm in Northants., whilst as for Lord Dalmeny, he was performing distinguished service in Palestine. Eventually, after a brief meeting with his wife Lord Dalmeny began divorce proceedings, and at the hearing in December 1919 it was stated that the couple had not lived together since August 1914, and that whenever her husband returned, Lady Dalmeny would deliberately be away. Thus with all the facts presented there could be only one outcome, and a divorce was granted. In fact in true 'soap' fashion the saga would continue, and so, for real life drama, instead of slumping in front of the telly, watching the 'Vic' burn down, try sitting in front of a library microfiche reader, a veritable 'time machine,' where you can voyage through the past by just turning a knob.

MAISON BELGE

War and Peace - The Early Fortunes of No. 44, Church Street

Under the Defence of the Realm Act, (DORA), during World War One, many buildings in Fenny Stratford, including the Town Hall, were reserved for the use of the military.

Associated with this, No. 44, Church Street became a home for Belgian refugees, cared for by residents of the town - and the house therefore became known as the 'Maison Belge'.

It remained under military authority until April 1919, when offered for sale by the trustees of the late Samuel Bragg, who had given the plot of land next door to the Salvation Army, as a site for their barracks.

Hedley Clarke, the local fire agent, purchased the house for £220 and being an astute sort of chap, he then agreed to sell it for £350 to the local branch of the National Federation of Discharged and Demobilised Soldiers and Sailors, forerunner of the British Legion.

They intended to use the premises as a social centre but the deal fell through and it was purchased instead by the Roman Catholics, as a chapel.

In 1905 they had bought a piece of land, at the corner of Victoria Road and Denmark Street, as a plot for a chapel but this was never built and Mass was instead celebrated for many years at Hey Tor, in Bletchley Road the home of Mr. J.W. Watson.

During the war Mass then came to be celebrated at five or six different places in the town, including an army hut at the military camp but now witt their purchase of 44, Church Street, the Roman Catholics at last had a permanent centre of worship, capable of seating 80.

The Rev. Walker, rector of the church at Wolverton, performed the opening ceremony.

MEDIA STARS

For those of us bedraggled parents, clutching our cameras on a rainswept Platform 5, awaiting the belated arrival of Hogwart's Express, any thoughts of Harry Potter seemed more sympathetic with those of Lord Voldemort.

Yet, as perhaps the only sure means to prevent the offspring bunking off school, the chore proved well worth the eventuality and as the magical moment approached, so were conjured up those glorious memories of a bygone, steamy age.

Also aroused were those passing thoughts of some other celebs to have one time or another graced the town and Goldie the Wonder Dog, Fred Spoons and his amazing one man travelling band and Fab 1 immediately spring to mind.

However, before the multimedia merits of our present age, entertainment came in a variety of guises to Fenny, certainly travelling artistes, not least Mr. Eos Dyffryns and his International Choir.

Thank goodness also for those frequent performers at the Town Hall, the multi-talented Walfords and of course special thanks to Mr. S Walford and his quite unforgettable Coesysgwlell-Caerddgar-Peircant (a musical contraption made of broomsticks).

With the arrival of the cinema, Fenny would soon have its very own Picture Palace.

By courtesy of Mr. Stafford's mobile projector people could also have the very latest blockbuster screened personally on to their living room wall and who, of female persuasion, could possibly resist a private viewing of Bletchley's very own homespun talent, that swashbuckling Hollywood swoon merchant, Robert Douglas. Born at No 5, Albert Street as Robert Douglas Finlayson, the son of a railwayman on November 9th 1909, his first major Hollywood film came in 1948 and he later starred in the 1952 remake of The Prisoner of Zenda before progressing to an episode of Colombo.

Also in the realms of celluloid celebrities, the younger generation was not forgotten and somewhere in the Pathe archives lurks footage of Bletchley schoolchildren engaged in puppet making, or something similar.

No doubt a present day remake would feature something more contemporary - perhaps carjacking.

Apart from the visual arts, local radio celebrities have also found a voice, including that one time occupant of Yew Tree Cottage, Mrs. Aldridge, better known to her radio listeners as Catherine Campbell of the BBC Repertory Company.

Regular listeners to Riders of the Range were also in for a treat when their cowboy hero stayed at the Swan Hotel, during his journey on horseback along the Watling Street from London.

Talking of horses, that reminds me of the recent box office bonanza, The Horse Whisperer, but forget Robert Redford - way ahead of the times, Fenny had decades before been privileged to entertain no less than Prof. H. Sample, Horse Educator.

A good job too, for some horses seemed in serious need of an education. Out for a bicycle ride with his friend, a gentleman was casually pedalling towards Little Brickhill when taking exception a grazing horse leapt straight into the air and flattened him.

Well out of order and flying horses were just one example of those in need of 'the Sample System of Horse Management' now being demonstrated in a marquee on Blunt's Field, adjoining Denbigh Road, where people were invited to take along their troublesome beasts.

No doubt the idly curious were attracted, judging by the accompanying invite to the marquee to make the personal acquaintance of the professor's famed collection of 'educated fillies'!

Sunday Citizen April 21, 2002

OUR TOWERING ACHIEVEMENT - MELLISH COURT, BLETCHLEY

Mellish Court, dominating the skyline for over 40 years. It was opened on December 8th 1966, with the first resident being Mrs. Doris Gent.

Even at a time in the conflict when the outcome was far from certain, during World War Two Bletchley Urban District Council was making plans for the post war expansion of the town!

This would be primarily to accommodate the overspill population from London, and the numbers of wartime refugees, and personnel for Bletchley Park, that were pouring into Bletchley gave an early indication of the problems that might be expected, and the expansion that would be needed to the existing facilities.

As the war drew to a close, as a possible housing solution Bletchley councillors travelled to London to view a display of the new prefabricated type of accommodation, which was now being made available.

However, since the national shortage of fixtures and fittings would affect 'prefabs' just as much as permanent housing, in an innovative move they instead opted for a quota of traditional houses that, by using a steel structure, saved not only on cost, but also on the time necessary for their construction.

In fact as an additional benefit, due to the shortage of timber the amount that was allocated to each house could be used for other purposes, apart from the actual structure of the building, and the occupants of the steel framed houses could therefore be 'one up' on their neighbours by having smart wooden floors, instead of the utilitarian concrete!

Due to the housing shortage, at the end of the war many families in the town had little choice but to rent rooms but desperate for their own 'space' some were now squatting in the huts of disused local army camps - albeit with the tacit approval of the authorities.

Then in the years after the war new housing estates began to provide adequate accommodation for both locals and the new arrivals to the town, and in a solution typical of the 1960s a tower block of flats was even constructed, which still dominates the local skyline today.

The foundation stone of the 18 storey block of one and two bedroom flats, to accommodate 136 families, was laid in January 1966, by Robert Mellish, MP, the then Parliamentary Secretary of the Ministry of Housing and Local Government.

Designed by Mr. F. Henson of Stone, Toms and Partners Construction, the building, appropriately named Mellish Court, would be constructed at a cost of £465,000 by Bernard Sunley and Sons, on the Sunley-Allbetong system of industrialised building and, hailed as a method that saved time and labour, this system had been devised in Sweden.

Indeed, before the contract was placed Bletchley councillors had travelled to Sweden to view various examples.

On Thursday, December 8th 1966 with a golden key, Mr. Mellish then opened Mellish Court, and the first tenant would be Mrs. Doris Gent, a 55-year-old widow, who had lived for most of her life in London.

However, the concept of tower blocks was tarnished on May 16th 1968 when part of the Ronan Point tower block in London collapsed, following a gas explosion.

MRS. MOSER & THE REPORT CENTRE

Herbie, the newly acquired rescue dog, took me for a walk around Fenny Stratford the other evening and after playing dominant male with the local cats (from a safe distance) and investigating choice sniffs on the lamp posts, we chanced upon the old Council Offices.

The newly displayed *To Let* sign caused me to muse what next would fate decree for this iconic premises.

While as for its bygone days, with the artistic brush of imagination and a palette filled with a little knowledge, the mind's eye pictures a pastiche of perhaps romanticised reminiscence, which from times of peace and war evoke a kaleidoscope of emotions.

On the plaque is the name of the council's surveyor, John Chadwick, who designed the building and poignantly he also designed the war memorial at Old Bletchley, upon which appears the name of his only son, Douglas, who died of wounds sustained in the Battle of Fromelles in World War One.

Then in World War Two there would be further sadness when the brother of a member of the Council Office staff was killed in action in Burma.

He was Glyn Hankins and his sister, Olive, would name her son Glyn.

During World War One the council had insured the offices for £2,000 against air attack which became a much greater threat following the outbreak of World War Two, when the Council Offices accommodated the Report Centre.

Here air raid reports would be received and as a full time member of staff Olive, having worked the first shift voluntarily, helped to maintain a telephone watch for an average of 12 hours a day, seven days a week.

In fact in company with Mr. W. Bradbury she carried out not only all the clerical and administration work of the A.R.P. Dept. but others as well.

Born in Bletchley, the only daughter of Mr. and Mrs. W. Hankins, of 46, Windsor Street, Olive had attended The Cedars School, at Leighton Buzzard, and then worked in Bedford and later in the offices of J.L. Shirley Ltd., in Bletchley Road. In 1937 she married Carl Moser, who after leaving Banbury County School had joined the Banbury Advertiser before moving in 1933 to the Observer at Leighton Buzzard.

In 1934 he became the local reporter for the North Bucks Times but following the outbreak of war joined the Army in 1940 as a 2nd Lieutenant in the 135th Field Regiment. After the Fall of Singapore in 1942 he was reported missing and it was burdened with this uncertainty that Olive carried on with her duties.

Then, dated June 20th 1943, she received a postcard stating that Carl was a prisoner of the Japanese and thus with some measure of comfort during March 1944 as secretary of the Bletchley Aid to China Fund she attended a reception at the Mansion House, London, given by the Lord Mayor and Lady Mayoress. As throughout the country, on the morning of Wednesday, May 2nd 1945 the Civil Defence personnel ceased their duties and of the original members it would be Olive who worked the last shift at the Report Centre and sounded the last siren. Yet the war with Japan would continue until the dropping of the atom bombs. In the aftermath she then received a card from Carl. This was sent from Bangkok on September 2nd 1945 and on Saturday, October 13th he arrived at Liverpool aboard the Empire Pride, saying only of his experience that it had been 'jolly rough.'

He now returned to his journalistic profession and in late 1945 was offered the position of the Bletchley District Gazette. When this was bought in 1951 by Home Counties Newspapers he became the editor of the North Bucks Times and in 1972 he joined the Milton Keynes Development Corporation as press officer.

Carl died in 1993 and Olive in 2003 and their grave is in St. Mary's churchyard.

Just one tale of sadness and joy from the wartime annals of the old Council Offices. In fact just one tale from the continuing annals of human conflict.

But then I was jolted back to the present when Herbie noticed the local cats regrouping and in the ensuing commotion my musings abruptly ended, with the certainty that humans are not the only species unable to co-exist on this planet.

Milton Keynes Citizen, July 26, 2012

OLD BLETCHLEY WAR MEMORIAL

For those who had fought in the First World War, in view of the unprecedented horrors and carnage it was earnestly hoped that this would be the 'war to end wars'. While many realised that this was no doubt a little optimistic, they might be justified in thinking that their children would be spared such an experience.

Therefore, the amputation endured by Corporal Joseph Cheney, Oxon & Bucks Light Infantry, when wounded in 1917 was to prove tragically ironic. He had only just rejoined his regiment after being wounded for the first time when his right leg was blown off above the knee, confining him to the 28th General Hospital, Salonika and a series of operations.

It is therefore incredible that, at the age of 21, Frank Cheney, a former member of the 1st Bletchley Company Boys' Brigade and the Boys' Brigade Old Boys Football Club, had to have his left leg amputated, after being wounded at Dunkirk on May 21st 1940.

With the advent of the internet, details of the First World War soldiers commemorated on local war memorials are now readily available.

According to the Roll of Honour website, information concerning the fallen of the Second World War is, however, not yet available - except of course to readers of the Bletchley & Fenny Stratford Local Pages!

OLD BLETCHLEY WAR MEMORIAL

Edward Ayres, son of Mr. F. Ayres, 41, Saffron Street. Killed in action aboard the destroyer Trollope, 1944.

Sergeant Frederick Brown, RAF. Reported missing on flying operations, June 1942.

Private John Catterall, Beds and Herts Regiment. Husband of Mrs. Catterall, The Shop, Water Eaton. Died at sea while a POW en-route to Japan, September 21st 1942.

William Calver, information unknown.

Private Harry Douglas Davis, 5th Suffolks. Youngest son of Mr. A E. Davis, 114, Buckingham Road. Died as a Japanese POW in Siam (now Thailand), August 18th 1943.

Driver George Joseph Essen, RASC. Second son of Mr. and Mrs. C. F. Essen, 21, Duncombe Street. Killed in an ammunition explosion in western Germany, April 28th 1945.

Sapper Charles Arthur Essen, Royal Engineers. Eldest son of Mr. and Mrs. C. F. Essen, 21, Duncombe Street. Killed in the evacuation of France three weeks after Dunkirk, when the Lancastria was sunk, June 17th 1940.
Sergeant Pilot Glyn Hankins, RAF. Third son of Mr. and Mrs. W. H. Hankins, 46, Windsor Street. Killed while dropping air supplies to forward troops in Burma. December 23rd 1943.
Able Seaman John Jones, husband of Nora Jones, son of William and Emily Jones. Killed while serving on HMS Samphire. January 20th 1943.
Lance Corporal Albert Ernest Knight. 5th Beds and Herts Regiment. Youngest son of Mr. and Mrs. B. F. Knight 70, Newton Road. Killed during an air raid on Osaka while a Japanese prisoner, June 5th 1945.
Sergeant Pilot Leonard May, RAFVR. Only son of Mrs. A. E. Stokes, 23, Tattenhoe Lane. Killed whilst on special flying duties, July 8th 1941
Sergeant Edgar Mynard, Royal Bucks Yeomanry. Husband of Mrs. E. G. Mynard, 44, Newton Road. Killed during the evacuation from Dunkirk, May 28th to June 5th 1940.
Corporal Alec Peacock, Military Police, formerly of the Royal Bucks Yeomanry. Son of Mrs. E. Clare, East View, 18, Newton Road. Killed when his motorcycle collided with a car between Nottingham and Mansfield while on despatch duties, March 31st 1941.
Flying Officer David Foster Sinfield RAF. Only child of Mr. and Mrs. W. P. Sinfield, 53, Buckingham Road. Killed on duties with a pathfinder squadron in a night attack over Germany. February 20/21st 1945.
Flying Officer Leslie Smith, RAF. Husband of Mrs. N. Smith. 'Killala', Stoke Road, eldest son of Mrs. J. F. Smith, Water Eaton Mill. Shot down over England while giving night-flying instructions, September 7th 1943.
Brigadier John Percival Whiteley MP, formerly Commanding Officer Royal Bucks Yeomanry. Husband of Mrs. A. Whiteley, The Grange, Buckingham Road. Killed in a plane crash off Gibraltar, July 4th 1943
Pilot Officer Donald Baker, RAF. Youngest son of Mr. and Mrs. F. Baker, Ivy Cottage, Church Green Road, and fomerly of Newton Longville. Killed on a bombing raid over Germany, December 16/17th 1943.
James Tompkins, Died in India, 1947.

BLETCHLEY ROAD (QUEENSWAY) MEMORIAL
Sergeant Vincent Barber, The Intelligence Corps. Only child of Mrs. M. D. Barber, 4, Lennox Road. Killed on active service during an air raid on Southampton, July 8th 1941.
Private Leslie Barden. 1st Loyals. Husband of Mrs. L Barden of

Brickhill, and third son of Mr. and Mrs. P. H. Barden, 21, Church Street. Killed in action at Anzio, Italy, February 8th 1944.
Fusilier Frank Breedon, The Royal Fusiliers. Son of Mrs. F. Breedon, 37, Eaton Avenue. Killed in action in North Africa, May 9th 1943.
Gunner Ronald Bowler, 148 Field Regiment, Royal Artillery. Youngest son of Mr. and Mrs. C. W. Bowler, 3, Manor Road. Died as a prisoner of the Japanese, April 16th 1944.
Alfred Burgess. 9, Brooklands Road. Killed in an explosion near Rome, 1944.
Private William Gladstone Chambers, The Queens. Only son of Mr. and Mrs. W. G. Chambers, 10, Tavistock Street. Killed in action at El Alamein, north Africa, October 24th 1942.
Gunner Geoffrey Lionel Chew. 148, Field Regiment Royal Artillery. Youngest son of Mrs. E Chew. 21, Aylesbury Street. Killed when the ship taking him from Siam to Japan as a POW was torpedoed, September 12, 1944.
AC2 Albert Clements, son of Albert and May Clements. Killed on October 25th 1942.
Private Frederick Eastaff, 1st Suffolk Regimant.Youngest son of Mr. and Mrs. F Eastaff. 32, Albert Street. Killed when the ship taking him from Siam to Japan as a POW was torpedoed, September 12th 1944.
Private Herbert Richard Goodwin, The Warwickshire Regiment. Only son of Mrs. W. Goodwin, 23, Oliver Road. Killed in the Battle of France, near Ypres, May 28th 1940.
Private Henry Grace, The Cambridgeshire Regiment. Husband of Mrs. H. Grace, 13 Eaton Avenue. Died in Siam while a prisoner of the Japanese, October 11th 1943.
Private Walter Colin Harris, Beds and Herts Regiment. Husband of Mrs. Harris, 26, Brooklands Road. Died in Siam while a prisoner of the Japanese, September 1st 1943.
A Catterall, information unknown.
AC2 Joseph Reginald Haynes, RAF. Husband of Mrs. Haynes, 29, Tavistock Street. Died through illness in Uxbridge RAF Hospital, November 22nd 1943.
Private John William Thomas Levick, 10th Hussars. Husband of Mrs. J. W. T. Levick, Bow Brickhill. Eldest son of Mr. and Mrs. W. J. Levick, 48 Duncombe Street. Killed in action, June 16th 1942.
Private Alec Lingard, The Queens. Husband of Mrs. Lingard, Drayton Parslow. Son of Mr. F. Lingard, 52, Westfield Road. Killed on active service in the Middle East, September 4th 1942.
Private George Lovell. only son of Mr. and Mrs. L Lovell, 60, Victoria Road. Shot by a sniper while clearing a small German village, while

other Germans were coming out under a white flag, April 20th 1945.
Signaller Peter Eric Meadows, Royal Navy. Only son of Mr. A. T. Meadows, 67, Eaton Avenue. Killed in action aboard a minesweeper, May 20th 1940.
Frank Nursaw, third son of Mrs. K. Nursaw, 61, Duncombe Street. Killed on the Western Front, May 8th 1940.
Signaller John Eric Payne, Worcestershire Regiment. Nephew of Mrs. T. R. Bazeley, 34, Windsor Street. Killed in action in the Middle East, June 14th 1942.
Sergeant Pilot Harold Ernest Perry, RAF. Second son of Mr. and Mrs. A Perry, 4, Bedford Street. Killed in a crash following a bombing raid, May 7th 1942.
Private Kenneth Harold Walter Perry, The Loyal Regiment. Husband of Mrs. Perry, 6, Western Road. Killed in action on the Anzio beach head, February 15th 1944.
Driver Jack Shepherd, Tank Corps. Second son of Mr. and Mrs. E. Shepherd, 12, High Street. Killed in action during the Battle of Caen, August 14th 1944.
Marine Frederick Southwell, Royal Marines. Son of Mr. and Mrs. Southwell, 48, High Street. Died from illness at Ramsgate Hospital, February 1944.
Marine Charles William Tomkins. Royal Marines. Husband of Mrs. P. M. Tomkins, 57, Windsor Street. Killed during the fighting in Crete, May 31st 1941.
ADDITIONAL
Flying Officer J. E. Watts, Eldest son of Mr. and Mrs. J. Watts, 49, Eaton Avenue. Killed in action, September 6th 1943.
Sergeant Pilot Gordon Downs Bushell, RAFVR Only son of Mr. and Mrs. J. D. Bushell, High Street. Killed while returning from an air patrol, December 31st 1940.
Flying Officer James Edward Hanks, RAF. Eldest son of Mr. and Mrs. A E. Hanks, 1, Simpson Road. Shot down over Holland following an attack on Dusseldorf, April 23rd 1944.
Sergeant William Edwin Meredith, Grenadier Guards. Eldest son of Mr. and Mrs. W. E. Meredith, Hollybank, High Street. Killed while in command of a tank on the France-Belgium border. September 3rd 1944.
Private Leonard Wilfred Pettier The Loyal Regiment. Youngest son of Mr. and Mrs. W. Pettier, Walnut's Cottage, Simpson. Killed on active service in North Africa, August 16th 1943.
Sidney Fleming, The Beds and Herts Regiment. Formerly of 21, Church Street. Killed in an air raid on Formosa where he was being held as a prisoner by the Japanese, February 7th 1945.

Private Frederick Arthur Tofield Oxon and Bucks Light Infantry. Youngest son of Mr. and Mrs. E A Tofield, 6, Council Houses, Simpson Killed in an accident while home on leave, February 11th 1943.
John Whitfield, RAMC. Formerly of 19, Lennox Road. Killed by enemy action on Mersyside, November 1940.
Lieutenant Jacques Donald Alphouse Buisson, RAOC, of Cheshire. Died January 1945 at the age of 32 in a motor accident between Bletchley and Little Brickhill on Watling Street. Stationed at Bletchley, he had been living at 18, Vicarage Road and the commanding officer of the unit, Major Saxon, was among the four other occupants of the vehicle who were injured.

OPENING THE TEMPERANCE HALL

In 1889 three plots of land in George Street, Bletchley, became available, and opportunely, on behalf of the Good Templars two of these, 'on reasonable terms', were purchased from Mr. Willis of Leighton Buzzard by Mr. Kirby.

After a period of two years, as the time allowed for payment, plans for a Good Templars Hall were projected by the leaders of the movement and eventually those furnished by Mr. J.J. Stone, an architect from Leighton Buzzard, were approved.

With the building work entrusted to Mr. T.W. Clarke of Fenny Stratford, when complete the hall could seat around 200 people, having cost about £370 to construct.

Supplied by Cheshire and Co., a set of six Harp lamps, complete with opal shades, adorned the roof of pitch pine.

For the opening ceremony, in 1892, the hall was decorated with evergreens, flowers and flags and with Mrs. Heley presiding, also on the platform were Mrs. Flowers, Miss Laws and Miss Leon.

'Temperance workers toil away', sang the choir, followed by Mr. Kirby's solo rendition of the anthem 'Seek Ye the Lord'.

At the conclusion of these celebrations Mrs. Flower, in her speech, declaring the hall open, proclaimed that 'Every village should have its temperance hall and coffee tavern'.

Mrs. Heley, in her address, declared that all Christians should be abstainers and then at 4.30pm a well patronised tea was held at the Salvation Army barracks.

In the evening, prominent members of the order, resplendent in their regalia, attended a public meeting held in the new hall, which was preceded by singing and prayer.

As the secretary of the organisation, Mr. W. Sutherland, giving details of the movement, said that with a Red Indian as their chief, he was proud to serve under him.

A hymn and the benefaction then brought events to a close.

THE ROADS TO FAME: ORIGIN OF BLETCHLEY ROAD NAMES.

Many people or families who have held prominence in the local past are today immortalised in the names of various streets in the town. Examples include Duncombe Street, Durrans Court, Rowlands Close, Bristow Close and - recalling the more recent industrial developments - Bilton Road, which is named after the well-known property developer Percy Bilton.

(In fact there is still a local connection, for his grandson has recently spent £10 million renovating Tyringham Hall.) In this article, local historian John Taylor looks at the figures commemorated in Whiteley Crescent, Stuart Close and Sherwood Drive.

Whiteley Crescent

In July 1943 Bletchley received the tragic news that, whilst returning home on leave from the Middle East, Brigadier General John Whiteley, of The Grange, Bletchley, had been killed in a plane crash.

A native of South Africa, John was born at Mafeking, where his father, Frank Whiteley CMG JP, had been the mayor during the famous siege. Following an education at Shrewsbury School and the Royal Military Academy, Woolwich, he served in the Royal Artillery from 1916, and then in the Life Guards from 1926.

On retiring as a captain, two years later he became much involved in the civic and social life of North Buckinghamshire, and, as chairman of the association, he was to play a prominent role in the formation of the Conservative Club, of which he became the president. He was also responsible for many local educational improvements, and throughout much of the time that he lived in the town would represent Bletchley on the county council in Aylesbury.

During the Depression, for the benefit of those who were locally unemployed, he instigated several improvement schemes in the town, including those which enhanced St. Martin's churchyard and St. Mary's Church. Despite having retired from the army, he nevertheless maintained links with the TA becoming not only CO of the 393rd Battery, but also being responsible for the construction of the Yeomanry Hall.

As for other activities, with a clear majority he was elected MP for the local division in 1937, but at the outbreak of war he resumed military service and would accompany his men of the Bletchley Territorials to Dunkirk, and eventually to India.

In December 1942 he was promoted to Brigadier but, after 15 months of continuous military service, he planned to spend a month carrying out political work in his constituency. It was during the journey home that he was killed when the Liberator aircraft, which had been converted to an RAF transport, crashed one Sunday evening, just after take off from Gibraltar.

The crash also claimed the lives of General Sikorski, the Polish premier and Colonel Victor Cazalet MP and, not surprisingly, the cause soon became the subject of various conspiracy theories. In fact, as late as December 1968 a two-night televised debate chaired by David Frost would take place regarding the subject.

Brigadier Whiteley was buried in Gibraltar with full military honours, in the cemetery close under the north face of the Rock. On the day that his memorial service took place at St. Mary's, Westminster, a service was also held at St. Mary's Church in Bletchley, where flags were flown at half-mast at the Council Offices, the schools and the Conservative Club.

His two sons, the eldest of whom was 15, and his wife, Amy, a daughter of Mr. H. Tetley of Alderbrook, Surrey, continued to live at The Grange throughout the war, but eventually moved to Mixbury Hall, Brackley.

In 1947 The Grange was purchased by Mr. Norman Green and, with space available for other sports, the grounds accommodated an excellent hard tennis court, a squash court, rose garden, and also a swimming pool which, if they brought their bathing costumes, those attending the Grand Garden Fete (held to raise monies for the Victory Clock Fund) could use on Saturday June 7th. In fact, Mr. Green - who was noted for his business acumen - hoped to open a lido at the premises before the end of the year!

At the end of February 1967, The Grange, with the stables, and the adjoining land in Buckingham Road, was auctioned as one lot in London for £31,000. With outline planning permission having been granted for the development of 34 houses, purchase was made by the Greaves Organisation of Birmingham. In fact, this would be the first considerable auction of land in Bletchley since the announcement of the proposed new town.

Sherwood Drive

On October 1 1932, Mr. Reginald Leuty Sherwood became the Clerk of Bletchley Urban District Council. He thereby succeeded Mr. F. Capper who, succeeding Mr. W. Charter Wilson, had been appointed to the position in 1928, having formerly been the clerk, accountant and rating officer to Audenshaw, Lancashire.

As for Mr. Sherwood, from 1910 until 1919 he had been master's chief clerk at Firvale Poor Law Institution, in Sheffield, and from 1919 until 1923 he served on the Ministry of Health district audit staff, firstly in Durham and then in Doncaster.

He next became clerk of Brigg Urban District Council in Lincolnshire and, having applied for a similar position at Bletchley, he was asked at the interview what he thought of the town. "Not much," he replied - but nevertheless secured the job!

He and his wife would make their home at 'Netherleigh', Buckingham Road, until moving to Eastbourne on Mr. Sherwood's retirement in 1960.

Stuart Close

At the corner of Victoria Road and Denmark Street, on the site now occupied by the Londis supermarket, once stood the Bletchley Iron and Tinplate Works, founded by Charles Stuart.

In the late 1880s Charles was joined in the business by his son Herbert Akroyd Stuart who, having witnessed the effects of oil spilt onto hot metal, during this period had the idea of harnessing such energy in a 'heavy oil engine'.

On October 4 1890 a patent was taken out for 'Rotary motors, to be worked by the heat obtained by the combustion of oil', and consequently a number of engines were built. In fact, by the end of the century several more patents for 'Motors and Rotary Engines' had been granted, but it was the German engineer Dr. Diesel who eventually claimed the credit for the invention.

Perhaps disillusioned, Herbert, who had sold his patent to the Hornsby Company, moved in around 1910 to Perth, Western Australia, where he died in 1927.

However, in 1964 a wall plaque to his memory and achievement was placed at the corner of Denmark Street, by the Bletchley Co-op and the Bletchley Archaeological and Historical Society.

PAINTING BLETCHLEY PARK

For those blessed with a modicum of intelligence, it's perhaps pretty obvious that the fast track to the riches of life is to plan a career early in their existence, preferably to those positions which provide the maximum remuneration for the minimum ability - possibly local government, or politics. As for the rest of us, either through idleness, indifference, or just being thick, our lot is to journey along the bumpy cart lane of life, which is why having in the late 1960s drifted into the local Labour Exchange (as Job Centres were then known) I shortly afterwards drifted out again, having been directed to employment with the firm which had just been favoured to paint the buildings at Bletchley Park. Apparently little skill was needed (and indeed none was offered) and on arrival I was teamed up with Harry, whose frequent expansions on the evils of Capitalism would seem to predict the strike ridden days of the decade to come. Despite the loss of a middle finger - allegedly the result of a dive bomber attack, during his wartime service aboard a motor torpedo boat in the Mediterranean - Harry wielded a nifty paint brush, and was therefore hardly best pleased when the officious site clerk passed a derogatory comment regarding some minor blemish or other. Yet no doubt because he assigned an equal contempt to all figures of authority, Harry was commendably restrained in his response, although the eloquence of his wording in dismissing the incident remains with me to this day, and in fact "What's he think this place is - Lady Docker's ******* boudoir," more or less sealed my own opinion of Bletchley Park. That is until 1974, when the incredible achievements of the wartime codebreakers became finally known. Thus, if only in a small way, it would be pleasing to think that the application of all those tins of gloss and emulsion helped, if only a little, to preserve the place for posterity. Nowadays the story of Bletchley Park is well known, although less so is that of Whaddon Hall, upon which was centred the secret communications operation which handled the radio traffic for the codebreakers. In fact on Church Hill, Whaddon, may still be seen the concrete foundations of two huts, wherein operators received the information from Bletchley Park for transmission to military commanders overseas. However, to minimise any signals interference between the transmitting and receiving aerials the intelligence, although 'keyed in' at Church Hill, was transmitted from Tattenhoe Bare, where the buildings still remain. As for the village hall of Whaddon, this became the cookhouse for some of the secret operations personnel, and in the field at the rear still lie the bases of the huts in which they were billeted.

PREPARATIONS FOR WAR

By 1939 it seemed that The War to End All Wars needed renaming as The War to End All But One Wars since a rematch seemed increasingly likely.

Indeed, Bletchley took the situation very seriously and at the newly built schools clinic in Bletchley Road, plans were already in hand to have the premises converted into a first aid post, where A.R.P. casualties could be treated, should the need arise.

With London a primary target, the accommodation of refugees became a probability and in Bletchley 60 lady enumerators were appointed for the task, in a scheme supervised by Mr. R. Sherwood (after whom Sherwood Drive is named). When complete, the census revealed that with the number of habitable homes being 10,174, 1,601 'unaccompanied children' could be housed.

Air raid sirens were fixed at the council offices and Vaughans and Cowley and Wilson garages. But since, in certain winds, it was difficult for them to be heard at Water Eaton, an additional siren was placed at Flettons brickworks.

From the air Bletchley station would present a most inviting target and with this in mind, near the goods yard large well drained trenches were dug, lined with seats.

The subway under the station could also be opened but - in blackout conditions - 'it was unpleasant to bump into women and other people' and police permission was sought to install a screened light.

Several local firms took measures to protect employees and at Beacon Brushes large concrete bins, formerly used to hold gravel, were converted into shelters.

Concrete shelters were also erected at the W. O. Peakes factory while Premier Press preferred to convert a strong room for the purpose, complete with brick built walls to break up air concussion.

On the military scene, now at full strength the Bletchley detachment of the Royal Bucks Yeomanry were training on howitzers with other personnel on signallers duties.

Should the town be attacked, then apart from A.R.P. wardens, fire-fighters and medical personnel, provision was made for squads of specially trained council workers to deal with emergencies at the waterworks.

On June 9th hundreds of people watched a dramatic display, given by services at Bletchley Park. This included a gun and trailer, wireless cars, fire engines and ambulances.

The procession - a quarter of a mile long - then made it's way to the Report Centre, at the council offices where, upon arrival, in a simulated air attack three bombers from the aerodrome at Cranfield swept over. With explosions set off in the school grounds, 'casualties' and 'gas victims' were immediately attended to while in a second 'raid' the fire brigade swiftly dealt with a 'blaze' at the council offices.

The demonstration confirmed that, as far as possible, the town would be able to cope with the aftermath of an enemy attack but as events would prove, it was not direct enemy action that had any great impact on the town but more the arrival of evacuees and they will be the subject of a following article.

Sunday Citizen May 26, 2002

PRISONERS OF THE JAPANESE: THE FATE OF THREE WHO WENT TO WAR AGAINST THE JAPANESE IN WW2...

Many Bletchley men were amongst the thousands of Allied troops taken prisoner by the Japanese at the Fall of Singapore, in 1942.

Some would survive their captivity, many would not, and this is the story of those who, having been forced to help build the 'Railway of Death', were crowded aboard Japanese ships to be taken as slave labour to Japan.

In March, 1944, after the building of the Thailand to Burma railway a group of British and Australian POWs were duly crammed into the forward hold of the Japanese vessel 'Kachidoki Maru', and 1,318, including all the Australians, in the

'Rakuyo Maru', this being the vessel aboard which three men from Bletchley - Douglas Cresswell, Frederick Eastaff and Geoffrey Chew - would be herded.

Gunner Douglas Cresswell of 72, Victoria Road, had enlisted in 1939 from a previous employment at the brickyard and Gunner Geoffrey Chew of 21, Aylesbury Street, had joined the Royal Artillery.

In fact his first job on leaving the Bletchley Road schools had been at the local Sketchley branch whilst as for Frederick Eastaff, his parents lived at 32, Albert Street and he had been a driver in the 5th Battalion, Suffolk Regiment.

Aboard the ship each POW was handed a block of raw rubber, about two feet by two feet by one foot, and although this was to be ostensibly used as a 'life preserver' the real motive was probably to cram more rubber into the cargo.

On the morning of 6th September the two ships, with no markings to indicate that POWs were aboard, manoeuvred into a box formation with other ships to sail for Japan, but unbeknown to the Japanese a message had been intercepted regarding the voyage, and on the night of 9/10 September the decoded information was transmitted to the American submarines Growler, Pampanito and Sealion II. Thus it would be whilst crossing the South China Sea that the convoy was attacked, yet nevertheless, for Douglas Cresswell 'It was a wonderful feeling knowing our Allies were out there.'

Launched by the Sealion, one of a second salvo of three steam torpedoes missed the ship but one hit in the bow, and another amidships in the engine room.

Yet despite settling 10 or 12 feet into the water the vessel was kept afloat by the cargo of rubber, and although the Japanese survivors tried to prevent the POWs from clambering into the lifeboats, this often provided an opportunity for some of the prisoners to settle old scores.

After the torpedoing of his vessel Douglas Cresswell had scrambled on to a raft, and this was then lashed to three others to endure the coming uncertainty.

As for the 'Kachidoki Maru', of the three torpedoes fired by the Pampanito two struck home, sinking the ship.

About 600 POWs from the two stricken vessels would be picked up by Japanese ships,but not for another four days did the Americans realise that many of the remaining survivors were British and Australian.

A rescue mission was swiftly launched and - asking the Sealion to help - on 15th September the Pampanito began to pick up the exhausted POWs.

Fainting in the arms of his rescuers Douglas Cresswell was the first man to be hauled aboard, and after as many men as possible had been rescued the Pampanito and the Sealion then rendezvoused on the afternoon of 18th September with the destroyer 'Case', which transferred medical supplies, a doctor and a pharmacist to each submarine.

On 20th September the two vessels reached Tanapag Harbour, Saipan, and small landing craft then ferried the survivors to the beach and thence to the US Army's 148th General Hospital.

Wearing US Army uniforms on 1st October the British group then embarked on the Liberty ship 'Cape Douglas' for Pearl Harbour, and from there were taken to San Francisco.

From here they travelled across America to New York and duly boarded the 'Queen Mary' for the Atlantic crossing to England.

During their time in America the former POWs had enjoyed almost a celebrity status, and it therefore seemed quite appropriate that two of the other passengers would be the movie actors Mickey Rooney and Bobby Breen.

The ship duly docked at Greenock, and the POWs then underwent a week of military debriefing at a secluded country estate, Vache, at Haversham, Buckinghamshire, before returning to their homes.

Yet tragically Frederick Eastaff and Geoffrey Chew would not be amongst their number.

They had not survived the sinking, and are today commemorated on the war memorial at Kranki, Singapore.

Douglas Cresswell was the only Bletchley survivor of the sinking which claimed the lives of his long-time friends Frederick Eastaff and Geoffrey Chew.

A PLACE WITH REAL HISTORY: BLETCHLEY'S QUEENSWAY METHODIST CHURCH

2009 was the centenary of Queensway Methodist Church, which before renaming Bletchley Road as Queensway, on July 1st 1966, was known as Bletchley Road Methodist Church.

During 1813, with a small burial ground attached, the construction began of a Wesleyan Methodist Chapel in the High Street. It cost £688 13s 4d.

Despite a complete refurbishment of the Chapel and new seating in 1882, an alternative site for a chapel was considered and land in Bletchley Road was purchased in 1907. The Methodist Trustees decided to build a church to seat 350. With tenders examined the lowest, of £1,851 10s was accepted, and 250 circulars were sent out to solicit subscriptions.

On July 10th, 1909, the stone laying ceremony took place and in November 1909 the door was opened by Mr. J. Turney, using a silver key inscribed with his name and the date.

Interestingly, in 1966, when she came to Woburn Sands from London, the key was discovered amongst his effects by his daughter, Miss E. Turney, to be subsequently kept in the church safe.

The old chapel was sold in 1912 to Barber's Picture Palaces.

It became a favoured venue for entertainments not least during World War One, when the town hosted a large presence of troops.

One of the Royal Engineers stationed at Staple Hall would be Captain R. E Priestley, who having been on the Shackleton Antarctic and Scott Antarctic Expeditions gave a lecture there on his exploits.

In 1919 a recreation room, 'The Hut', was erected at the back of Bletchley Road Methodist Church providing much-needed accommodation for the Sunday School and social functions.

But with the outbreak of World War Two, following the arrival of hundreds of evacuees in the town it became the Rest Centre, or 'Bletchley Refugee Reception Centre.'

On land acquired from the Trustees was erected an ARP equipment store and (as detailed in a previous article) a British Restaurant.

By the beginning of April 1941 plans were advanced to remove the 'Rest Room' - provided for the benefit of evacuees - from St. Martin's Hall Reading Room to the newly built 'Evacuations Centre,' situated next to the Bletchley Road Methodist Church. In May a proposal that refugees using this Rest Room and social centre should be provided with tea free of charge was heavily defeated and it was agreed that tea at the Rest Room would be 1d a cup or ½ p a cup on 'milkless days.'

At The Hut bunks were to be fitted and children's clothes were still required, and would be distributed during July and August.

For the benefit of evacuees, in January 1942 the Rest Room was still open from 2pm to 6pm, with the emergency feeding and rest centres for Bletchley having been established as The Hut and the Temperance Hall.

With the launch of the German V weapons campaign the need for refugee accommodation again became necessary and responding to the emergency were the WVS who, under Mrs. Taylor, were now running the Methodist Centre in Bletchley Road as additional accommodation to the Temperance Hall.

Henry Fuller would have personal experience of a V2 rocket attack. A former steward of the Bletchley Road Methodist Church, he left the town in 1931 to become the caretaker at Whitfield Memorial Church, London.

Unfortunately he was in the building when it was hit by a V2. He survived and returned to Bletchley in 1949.

Someone with a long standing connection with Bletchley Road Methodist Church was James King, who died in 1945 aged 82.

Born at Simpson, he became a member of the old High Street Wesleyan church and would be involved with the building of the Bletchley Road Methodist Church. Employed for many years at Wilkinson's, (later Cutler) Stores, he drove a horse and cart until the age of 60 when he learnt to drive a van!

During 1946, the trustees of the Bletchley Road Methodist Church benefitted by £50 as the price the Council agreed for a plot of land at the rear of the premises, but the following month it was announced that the church was to lose the services of the Reverend Holdsworth as Minister.

Aged 24, Edward Wilson, an ex-RAF man (in fact having been released from the service the previous week) would then fill the position, having first become a local preacher at the age of 17.

The influx of evacuees during the war had been a precursor to the expansion of the town's population, and by 1951 there were 1,591 children attending the five schools in the town. Due to this, the Bletchley Road Junior School was therefore using not only their own premises but also the upstairs and downstairs of the Spurgeon Baptist Sunday school, as well as St. Martin's Hall and the Bletchley Road Methodist hut.

However, in time new housing estates and the corresponding facilities would be built, whilst for the Bletchley Road Methodist Church a long standing ambition would be fulfilled when, on the adjoining land, work began to build a Sunday School hall.

One Saturday afternoon in July 1960 four foundation stones were laid, and with the work undertaken by the firm of Tranfields, at a cost of £5,500 the new centre was opened on December 2nd 1961.

Initially only church activities were allowed on the premises, but at The Hut church activities came to an abrupt close when, due to suspected arson, it was burnt down in mid 1971.

The site has now become part of a car park, but the Church and the adjoining hall continue to flourish, and provide a much needed service for the local community.

RELIGION IN 1887

The year 1887 found Fenny Stratford townsfolk going about their daily business in a God fearing and well ordered community, excepting a few interesting hiccups.

Among unusual goings on was the local trader who sold up and 'did a runner', having been over familiar with his lady assistant.

Otherwise the population seemed industrious and church going - even marriage - was viewed much as commitment, rather than transient as it is for some today. In religious affairs, for the local non-conformists it was a time of much hope and building for the future and towards reducing the debt on their chapel the Primitive Methodists had given a public tea in their chapel on Christmas Day 1886 with the whole event raising 'a good sum.' This possibly also provided financial assistance towards the chapel enlargement which opened in October.

Also in a fund raising mood were the Baptists, who also held a public tea. Followed by a sale of 'useful and fancy articles' this event again enjoyed a good attendance, concluding with a magic lantern show, held in the evening by Mr. Daniels.

Elsewhere in the town the Salvation Army were pursuing grandiose plans. A meeting of the Fenny Stratford Parochial Authority gave final acceptance to the building of the Salvation Army barracks, in Church Street.Tartly remarking upon the decision Mr. Baisley commented that the sooner they got out of the town hall and into the barracks the better!

These also were the sentiments of one 'Mr. Angry' from the town who indignantly declared that while going along Aylesbury Street, one Sunday evening, he had encountered a group of youths, bawling the latest Salvation Army offering at the top of their voices, having learnt this particular ditty at that evening's Salvation Army service.

The rendition left him decidedly unimpressed. He likened it to a row to which 'one is accustomed to hearing in the tap room of a public house'!

Hopefully more acceptable was The Christian Union, for 'Here young gentlemen and ladies receive such training as shall fit them for the stern duties of active life.'

For those of whom these 'stern duties' had proved too great a burden, however, perhaps Underwoods Charity, founded in 1793, offered a measure of relief.

The Baptists were certainly on a financial 'roll', which now enabled them to pursue their ambitions of constructing a new chapel. Indeed, as the Reverend C.H Spurgeon himself observed: "They have enjoyed considerable prosperity and need a fit building to meet in."

Apart from attending their own particular needs, in the wider community the varied religious entities were also preparing to play their role within the realms of education. In the Wesleyan schoolroom a sizeable meeting of the town's non-conformists met, to select the candidates and arrange affairs in connection with the forthcoming School Board. Yet, as has been touched upon in a previous article, that is another story!

Sunday Citizen March 17, 2002

ROBERT MAXWELL

Cor, cheers gal. That's some awesome wheeze, bunking off from the day job for a jolly in the jungle.

And all to enlighten us plebs about the importance of politics: Our adulation knows no bounds, especially since the viewers didn't seem to give a stuff.

This is supposedly not for financial gain, since the taxpayer funded salary is to be donated to charity. So don't fret poppet, of course you didn't need to ask our permission. We understand.

We may presume the 40 grand fee was just for expenses. Indeed praise be on high, for by this noble sacrifice our eyes are now wide open and, yessir, it's a loadsamoney Parliamentary/showbiz career for me.

In fact pursuing this stunt, regarding the former profession it should now be OK for nurses to skive off for a spell of high profile lap dancing at Stringfellows.

Not of course for the sizeable wedge to be earned – far in excess of the pittance on the wards – but purely to heighten public awareness of the NHS.

Good grief, it now seems that we have to treat MPs as the fools they seem to take us for.

On the subject of fooling, who could forget another one time local MP, Robert Maxwell, who by raiding the pension fund of his employees consigned many to a retirement of penury.

Born in the Czech Republic in 1923, Jan Ludvik Hoch, as was his original name, was the son of Jewish parents.

But while many of his family would perish in the Holocaust, in 1940 he escaped to Britain and served in the British army, being awarded the Military Cross for bravery. After the war he settled in Britain and now as 'Robert Maxwell' was naturalized in 1946.

Acquiring a small publishing firm he expanded its fortunes and in 1951 changed the name to Pergamon Press.

Then some years later at Bletchley, on the site of the old gasworks, work began for the company on a new printing and bookbinding complex.

This would be known as the Buckingham Press, but in 1966 the premises came up for sale, after Maxwell announced it had not been possible to recruit skilled staff.

Somewhat ironic, for in the same decade he had bought Bletchley Printers, the staff of which on being moved into a factory in Tavistock Street would later all be made redundant.

Apart from business, Maxwell also had Parliamentary ambitions and standing for Labour was locally elected in 1964.

In fact it seems he had the endorsement of the party's leader, for when Bletchley railwaymen had a brief conversation with Harold Wilson, whose train had stopped at the station, they were told that Bob Maxwell was 'a very good man.'

Indeed Maxwell involved himself in many local matters and in 1970 was guest of honour at a social evening at Little Brickhill, held for members and friends from the reformed Brickhills' Labour Party.

About 40 people attended and Maxwell accepted a bouquet of flowers on behalf of his wife, who was indisposed.

However, he was defeated by the Conservatives that year and concentrating on business in 1980 took over the British Printing Corporation, turning it into the Maxwell Communications Corporation.

In 1984 he then bought Mirror Group Newspapers. Yet he still retained local interests and in 1985 purchased the old Cigarette Components building in Bletchley, where the company of Oyex Stationery would store all the back issues of the Daily Mirror.

Due to mounting financial difficulties he floated Mirror Group Newspapers in 1991, the same year that he sold Pergamon Press, and in November he sensationally went missing from his yacht at sea.

The body was duly retrieved but the death remained a mystery, as did his alleged role as an agent of Israeli Intelligence, Mossad, a conundrum compounded by the great honour with which he was buried in Israel.

But back to more recent times and the antics of the jungle queen. Did I really read that by her own admission much of her blog is pure fiction? Well, say no more. If true, that's all we need to know about politicians.

Milton Keynes Citizen, December 6, 2012

ROMANTIC ENCOUNTERS

'The wild bird woos his mate with long and melliferous song; and woman feels it her right to expect homage before marriage.' So philosophised one contributor to the early newspapers but in today's throwaway society it sadly seems that even marriage has almost became a disposable commodity.

In a previous age, when through either social conditions, circumstance or religious belief, marriage was considered a lifetime commitment, one might optimistically have expected the pillars of local society to set an example beyond reproach - but sadly no!

An eighteenth century Fenny Stratford doctor expected rather more than domestic servitude from his maid and the birth of the resulting child was quietly - but hurriedly - hushed up.

Then, in the following century, as the sole manager of a local school, 'in a glaring infringement of the Education Act', the Reverend promptly sacked the schoolmaster, when he learned that the schoolmaster's wife was

expecting her second child! - This was even despite Her Majesty's Inspector having declared himself completely satisfied with the running of the school and that at the resulting enquiry the Chairman pronounced the dismissal illegal.

Not surprisingly the matter was taken further.

Illicit liaisons

As for illicit liaisons, these could provoke social outrage and when it was discovered that a girl in a local village was 'carrying on' with a married man from a neighbouring village, the locals grabbed pots, pans and whatever else came to hand and drummed her out, never to return.

As always, in times of national distress, when the prospects of a continued mortality become ever less certain, romantic encounters become heightened and with a large military contingent stationed in the town, during the First World War many couples were hauled before the beak for 'laying in the mowing grass'.

Ten shillings was the usual fine but some young ladies acquired a more permanent legacy and the 1918 report of the North Bucks Association for Preventative and Rescue Work stated that 69 girls had been admitted to the shelter in the High Street where four babies - perhaps as less obvious casualties of war - had already been baptised.

As for one of the more prominent military personalities from that period, John French had married Eleanora, one of the 'Eight Belles' Selby Lowndes daughters and they made their early home at Bracknell House, ironically now the Register office.

In later years the marriage unfortunately faltered but the grave of Eleanora, who survived her husband by 16 years, may be seen in Bletchley churchyard.

SCHOOL EVACUEES

Anyone afflicting themselves with a modern day teaching career must surely soon realise the attractions of compulsory birth control, especially since accepted wisdom now seems to decree that little more than a pat on the head and the promise of an extra sweetie is sufficient to stop the little blighters from running amok.

In an historical context, from the moral high ground, much the same approach was applied by the world community when Hitler began getting out of his pram, and several million dead, weapons of mass destruction and a world changed forever, are the legacy for which we may be eternally grateful.

World War II became the first total war in which civilians had no choice but to become involved. For children the realities were cruelly harsh, causing many to become uprooted from their homes and families and dumped into alien culture.

However, when the rhetoric stopped and the shooting began "there was a general expression of relief that the tension had ended, even though the decision might mean hardships and sorrow" and initially it did seem more like the start of an adventure holiday for the first batch of evacuee children who arrived, one Friday morning, at Bletchley station.

Dutifully gathered on Platform Seven, a welcoming party to include Mr. Cook, the Billeting Officer, members of the police, clergy and teachers, endured an extended wait - caused by the disruptions of entraining and detraining at London before the train finally arrived at 2.45pm.

Local children had gathered to watch but were soon moved onto the station approach as the first 800 "refugees" alighted in one "happy throng, clutching haversacks, cases or parcels of clothing in one hand and steadying their gas mask cases with the other".

Formed into a line, they were then walked over the bridge to the station entrance and led to the Duncombe Street market entrance by the teachers.

Mr. E. Jones and his helpers then took charge of the rationing and, apart from the obvious lure of a l/4lb slab of chocolate, the children were also intrigued by a postcard of Bletchley with the printed greeting: "Bletchley has welcomed your child." On the reverse, a space allowed them to post back their address details.

Having received the rations, the children were then assembled into groups. Eventually, under the charge of a marshall and helpers, the children were taken to the various areas and, at the road junctions, handed over in small sets to the relevant officer, who then saw them to their final destination.

As for the host families, they received 10s 6d for one child, 8s 6d for more than one and 21s for an adult. For their "keep" vouchers issued by the Evacuation Officer could be exchanged at Bletchley Road or Aylesbury Street post offices.

Now in use as a centre for the evacuation organisation, schools for the meanwhile remained closed for education and, as for their potential new charges. all from Islington, the first batch comprised 407 children and 47 adults from Ecclestone School, 300 children and 31 adults from St. Pauls School, seven children and two adults from Beresford School and five children and two adults from Arundel House School.

On the next day, from Highgate and North Paddington, 700 more evacuees arrived, many mothers with small children, for distribution to the Winslow Rural Area. The evening brought a further 500 by bus and 800 by train.

In an organised manner, Bletchley had now received its involuntary young population, but how would they settle in and how would the communities integrate? Well, the future held both laughter and tears, but, of course, that is a story for another article.

SHOULDER OF MUTTON AT OLD BLETCHLEY & RECTORY COTTAGES

At Old Bletchley, the Shoulder of Mutton was for many years a picturesque feature of the original community, and stood near the village stocks.

In fact James Cook, who died in 1914, could recall that within these he, as a constable, had frequently during his younger years imprisoned various wrongdoers, as an embarrassing punishment for their misdeeds.

Then owned by the Ampthill Brewery Co, in 1921 the pub was taken over by Mr. and Mrs. Bowden.

Born in Torquay, Mr. Bowden had later become a native of Wiltshire, and it would be whilst employed as a butler that he first met the girl destined to become his wife, when she was also working in domestic service.

Shortly after their marriage in 1907 the couple moved to Bletchley, and for 10 years were engaged in the service of Sir Herbert Leon, of Bletchley Park. In 1927 Greens Brewery then purchased the Shoulder of Mutton, and in 1942 the extended premises unexpectedly became the setting for one of the most important events of World War Two when, following an inspirational visit by Winston Churchill, some of the staff at Bletchley Park felt that, in place of the exisiting regime, a 'Bletchley council' could run the organisation better.

In consequence, four of the key cryptanalysts met at the pub and, having decided that a petition outlining their grievances should be sent directly to Churchill, wrote a letter on October 21st 1941.

In this they voiced their concerns, not only at the lack of clerical staff, and the delays that this inevitably caused, but also the impending call up of skilled male staff, engaged both in the British Tabulating Co. and in the huts at Bletchley

Park.

Indeed, such a combined loss of talent would be irreplaceable, and by one of the signatories the letter was duly taken by train to Downing Street. The day after its receipt Churchill then issued his famous instructions to 'Make sure they have all they want on extreme priority and report to me that this had been done', although when news of this unauthorised action reached the intelligence hierarchy they were, of little surprise, far from pleased. Nevertheless all the desired requirements were swiftly met.

During World War Two, Mr. Bowden's son served with the Army in Burma, and on his return he would be best man for the wedding, on December 15th 1945, of his only sister, Nora. The marriage took place at St. Mary's Church, and following a reception for 60 guests, held at the Yeomanry Hall, the bride and her husband, John Davies, of Birmingham, left for a honeymoon at Gosport. After the war, for many years a Mr. and Mrs. Harvey ran a weekend cockles and whelks stall outside the pub, and this understandably proved to be very popular with the newly arriving Londoners!

In fact being a Londoner himself Mr. Harvey, as a member of the heavy rescue service of the Civil Defence, had endured several narrow escapes during the Blitz, and it was perhaps with some relief that in 1942, Mrs. Harvey had come to Bletchley, since for eight months the couple had been living in a London shelter, to escape the bombs.

In the post war years, with the increasing potential for house building Messrs Tranfield, a local building firm, had by 1950 acquired 38 acres of freehold land at Old Bletchley which, as part of Manor Farm, had since 1928 been farmed by Mr. Mattinson.

He also ran a butcher's business, and prior to moving to Manor Farm had previously farmed Cow Farm at Water Eaton, having moved there on his marriage to Mabel Garrat, a member of the family from Caldecote Farm, Bow Brickhill.

On the proposed 'Manor Farm estate' the council planned to build 450 houses, although since Bletchley already had a Manor estate the theme for the road names became 'castles', as chosen in November 1952.

Thus came into being the Castles estate, and in keeping with the new development, Flowers Brewery, the contemporary owners of the Shoulder of Muton, were offered a site in 1961 opposite their existing premises, on which to build a new pub. The need had arisen due to a proposed road widening scheme, and would no doubt prove popular with both the landlord and his customers, since the existing pub had no bar, with beer sold through a basement doorway.

Destined for demolition, in March 1962 the old thatched Shoulder of Mutton duly closed, and on the following day an inn of the same name (now the Three Trees) opened across the road. Mostly it comprised the greatly rebuilt Manor Farm, yet despite the benefit of central heating the premises still retained the old fireplaces, to avoid the 'glass and brass modernistic effect.' However, as a concession to the modern age the provision was made of an automatic tape recorder, which played low volume background music.

The new pub also included a children's room which, by featuring a one way partition, enabled the staff to exercise an ongoing supervision.

Rectory Cottages

Apart from St. Mary's Church, Rectory Cottages has claim to perhaps be the oldest building in Bletchley.

The hammer-beam roof of the 'hall' dates from around 1425, and, from being too ornate for a humble dwelling, may possibly have once been a part of Water Hall.

This was a manor house that stood in the riverside meadows at Water Eaton, but in 1562 Arthur Grey de Wilton, on succeeding to the manors of Bletchley and Whaddon, caused the manor house at Water Hall to be demolished, with the materials used to enlarge his preferred manorial home of Whaddon Hall.

Perhaps deemed as surplus to requirements, the hammer beam roof was employed at Rectory Cottages, a first definite mention of which occurs in 1619.

During the early years of the 19th century a school was held on the premises by a Miss Sears, of a long established local family, but in 1838 this became united to the National Society. Then in the wake of a National School being built in the early 20th century the premises became the home of Alice and William Clarke.

Married in 1892, in 1900 they were appointed as the caretakers at St. Mary's Church, and in fact in appreciation of this service would be presented in 1928 with a comer cupboard, made of oak from the belfry.

In fact the couple would live at Rectory Cottages for over 30 years, and following the death in 1936 of her husband, Alice in 1938 went to live with her brother, William, at Noke Cottage, Church Green Road.

Aged 76, she died on Wednesday, June 11th 1947.

After World War Two the premises fell into an unfortunate decline until, with an estimate of £10,000 being given as the sum necessary for restoration, the Bletchley Rectory Cottages Museum Trust Fund was set up in 1960.

With £7,000 being eventually raised, in 1964 the Bletchley Archaeological and Historical Society then began a determined effort to save the building, and in consequence an architect from the Society for the Preservation of Ancient Buildings declared the structure to be fairly sound.

A scheme was accordingly prepared to convert the barn into a small lecture hall, with the rest of the cottages to accommodate an office, two exhibition rooms downstairs, and a caretaker's flat upstairs.

In July 1965 a grant of £500 was then made by the Ministry of Public Buildings and Works, and with an appeal launched for £5,000, necessary to preserve the hammer beam roof, the council announced that they would also grant £500, as long as Bucks County Council and the Ministry of Works paid a similar sum.

However, matters were hardly helped by repeated vandalism and, allegedly started by school children, the effects of a small fire, which occurred one Saturday morning in the roof.

Yet thankfully no damage was caused, and this proved especially fortunate since the building had now been afforded the status of Grade Two.

Following further efforts for restoration, not least by Milton Keynes Development Corporation, Rectory Cottages was restored to a habitable condition, and is today in regular community use.

SPREADING THE NEWS: WEATHERHEADS

OK. I've checked the bank balance, but it seems there's absolutely no way I can afford a Super Injunction. So before it hits Twitter, yes, it is true, in the junior school I did have a crush on the form mistress. But it was only adulation from afar, and the infatuation soon paled when I discovered Biggles books.

Of course, nowadays through 'social networking' any indiscretion has the potential to become public knowledge, and the embryonic nature of the medium has ensured that farce and confusion surrounds those trying to police the content. However, in times gone by 'mass communication' was very different, and in the days of medieval serfdom very unnecessary, since social circumstance, and the state of the primitive tracks, meant that the next village might just as well have been a foreign country.

In many communities the focus for local gossip would be the village well, that at North Marston being of particular interest, and in later years came the introduction of town criers, whose job was to impart news of local or national importance to the often illiterate inhabitants.

In the 19th century, one of the most notable was the one legged, poetical, Sam Ashton of Stony Stratford, while in villages official proclamations would often be posted on the church door. However, regarding the 'Enclosure' of the common acres at Stewkley, such discontent was caused in 1803 that only when Sally Sear hid the document under her skirts, and so thwarted a defiant vigil of the church, was the official notice able to be posted on the door, as required by law.

From as early as the 18th century local newspapers would provide a popular mass media, but two soldiers just back from the South African war put their own news in print on their own 'message board' at the Three Tuns, in Fenny Stratford, which, found many years later during renovations, read 'This matchboard was fixed by Pte. Coleman and Pte. Bowes in the year 1900, just back home from the Transvaal War, Gordon Highlanders was wounded in the thigh.' (sic) In the 20th century, with the advent of national radio came the potential for 'personal messaging,' and in November 1941 in a BBC Anniversary radio broadcast Mr. & Mrs. Harrington, of Bedford Street, Bletchley, were surprised to hear themselves being congratulated on their golden wedding. As for Rhoda Maddox, of High Street, Fenny Stratford, she was also rather surprised, when 'Trees' was played especially for her by Sandy Macpherson. The request had been made by her husband, who during World War Two was training to be an air mechanic in Canada. In a pre Facebook age, children could create distant friendships through 'pen pals,' and in 1945 a letter was received by Miss Audrey Hughes, of Cottingham Grove, Bletchley, from Sonya Muchina, a Russian girl who lived about 25 miles from Moscow. Audrey was also corresponding with a girl in the US, and a girl in France, and it had been via the 'Anglo Soviet Youth Friendship' that she had been put in touch with Sonya, who began her letter, 'Dear friend Audrey, how good it is to know that this short letter is to fall into the hands of one of our Allies'.

For the technically minded, assuming they passed the exams they could become 'radio amateurs,' and via their sets 'socially network' even across the oceans. In fact in a competition held by the Radio Society of Great Britain, in 1947 Philip Tandy of North Street, Bletchley, an employee of Weatherheads, had been recognised as the second best radio 'ham' in the country, for having via his home made radio set communicated with 86 other 'hams' Nowadays any non entity has the ability to spout their two pennyworth worldwide. But discretion is to be definitely advised, as some local glamour queens of the teaching profession recently discovered, regarding their rather interesting antics at a hen night!

SPURGEON MEMORIAL BAPTIST CHURCH - BLETCHLEY

Currently dominating the skyline of Fenny Stratford is a tall tower crane above what was the old Spurgeon Memorial Baptist Church in Aylesbury Street, writes Local Pages' resident history man John Taylor (the site will soon become a McCarthy & Stone retirement complex) John has been delving into the church archives.

Built in 1892 for £3,050 it survived until 1976. In recent years the land became a car showroom (finally a Toyota dealership?).

The Church, as with many important communal and civic buildings in the town, played a vital role in WW2.

With the outbreak of war many children came to Bletchley from Islington in London and school accommodation was stretched to the limit.

On October 30th 1939 they began using the Spurgeon Memorial Baptist Chapel Sunday School.

Apart from accommodating a school by late 1940 the church also found room for 'Sunday at 7.30' concerts to entertain troops in the town. With 21 attending the initial gathering community singing proved a much appreciated feature among the several entertainments.

They became very popular and on Sunday, May 11th 1941, a request programme marked the close of the winter season. Promoted by Reg Snelling and Robert Storey 29 concerts had been given by that time, averaging an attendance of between 50 and 60 soldiers. They recommenced on October 12th.

By now a nursery school had opened in the Baptist school hall providing care for infants under five who had been evacuated from bombed cities.

As part of the children's routine emphasis was placed on 'clean habits, an afternoon sleep, body building and mentally exercising games' and with two upstairs rooms converted to make the nursery school, the main room contained beds and toys with the smaller room fitted out so that each child had their own place for a toothbrush, comb and towels.

A little picture, each one different, identified each child's place and the same picture was by each clothes peg.

Teachers painted the children's chairs bright pink and green and the left over paint was used on the walls.

In 1942 the popular troop concerts continued and for the 30th of the season drew a record audience of 150.

The ladies who under Mrs. S. Whitlock managed the catering, were all cheered.

The Spurgeon Memorial Baptist Church - demolished in 1976.

In November 1942 a former member of the church and the Boys Brigade, Cpl Reginald Keen, Royal Engineers, wrote recalling a day in the Mediterranean.

"Returning to Egypt from Crete we were under attack for 12 hours and after we sustained three direct hits I saw men who I thought were hard cases praying.

"If people rag you it is all bluff. Call it and they will respect you all the more!"

In March the church received a letter from Private Fred Marsden who wrote on behalf of 'all the boys who used to be in Bletchley' and many of whom attended the 7.30 concerts.

"What would we give to be sitting in the Baptist Schoolroom when the cakes and buns and all those things we now miss very much came round."

One of his comrades still had the caricatures he sketched during the performances.

By June 13th 1945 and the end of the war in Europe the people of the Baptist Church bid farewell to Miss B. Eden the headmistress of the Ecclesbourne Road Infants School.

ST. MARTIN'S HALL

As implied by the name, *St.* Martin's Hall has associations with Saint Martin's, the parish church of Fenny Stratford, founded in 1724 by the then lord of the manor Browne Willis.

The dedication commemorates his grandfather Thomas, a noted physician who died on November11 Saint Martin's Day, in the parish of Saint Martin's-in-the- Fields, London.

Known as the St. Martin's Soldiers Institute, during the First World War a 'hut' was employed for the use of the many soldiers, billeted around the immediate district, and after the war the local Co-op applied to buy this as a temporary branch shop to be erected on a site that they owned in Victoria Road.

Then in May 1919, came the decision to build a permanent social centre and hall on a site in Vicarage Paddock. Fifteen voted for the name Saint Martin's Hall and 12 for Saint Martin's House and during August plans were duly submitted to the council for building the proposed 'Saint Martin's Hall and Social Centre' at the lower end of the paddock, on a site adjoining the Council Schools.

Real progress was being made by April 1920 and although it had not been possible to secure the large entertainment hut put up for sale at the Royal Engineers depot, Staple Hall, a larger hut 'at a smaller price' was obtained from Rugely, Staffordhire.

For the while this would then suffice as a temporary measure, until funds,

St. Martin's Hall, now demolished.

now amounting to £929, allowed for the construction of a permanent building.

Entertainments were held for the raising of funds and on one occasion even featured an imitation jazz band! By July a small hut had been erected as the caretaker's quarters and the larger hut, the hall, now lying in sections, would also be shortly assembled.

Indeed, by November the 'Church Army Social Centre' at last neared completion and included the provision of a reading room and a billiard club with full size tables.

Captain Sturdy, of the local Church Army, had responsibility both for the building and of those who used it and he moved into the caretaker's quarters with his family.

The first event to be held in the new 'Saint Martin's Hall and Social Centre' was a New Year's parochial gathering and as for the final financial costs, these had totalled £3,488 which left an overdraft of £1,457. Such was the popularity of the hall that the premises had already been in use for nearly two months, before the Bishop of Buckingham performed the official opening ceremony, on the last Saturday of April, 1921.

Additional to the main buildings, accommodated by a separate entrance, the premises also included a brick built room, which served as the Fenny Stratford Parish Room, or Church Council Chamber. Previous to this, parish gatherings had to be held in either the parish room of the Vicarage or the Saint Martin's Mission Room, in Bletchley Road. Today, much extended and modernised, Saint Martin's Hall still remains, fulfilling an important role in the community activities.

Sunday Citizen September 3, 2000

STARS IN OUR EYES

Strange as it might seem, Bletchley has been home on occasion to several stars from the realms of cinema, stage and literature. In an age when it appears that 'celebrity' status is achieved with very little effort and even less talent, local historian John Taylor recalls some of those who have helped to put Bletchley on the cultural map!

In times when education and learning were the preserve of the few, clergymen were among an articulate elite. As regards Bletchley, one of the rectors would invent the first form of shorthand to be introduced into America, while another, the Rev. William Cole, would record his local observations of 18th century life in a diary which, fascinating to read, contains sufficient characters to form the basis of a modern day 'soap'.

In later years came the invention of photography and eventually cinematography, and in 1909 at No 5 Albert Street would be born Bletchley's very own Hollywood star, Robert Douglas Finlayson.

Coincidentally, the year of his birth would also be the year in which Bletchley acquired its first cinema. For when the Wesleyan Methodists moved to new premises in Bletchley Road, the old building in the High Street was purchased for use as a cinema by Mr. Barber.

Having been successively known as the King George Cinema and the Picture Palace, it then became the County Cinema in 1932, as part of the Odeon circuit.

As for Robert Douglas, (this being his screen name), after studying at RADA he made his first film in 1931, but it was in 1938 that he appeared in the epic that was perhaps intended to make him a star.

The Challenge featured him as the Victorian mountaineer Edmund Whymper, but as an Anglo-German production the timing of the release was perhaps hardly opportune!

Nevertheless, the film would be shown at the County Cinema in 1939.

During World War II, Robert served in the Fleet Air Arm, whilst playing the role of an airman in The Way to the Stars was the well-known actor Michael Redgrave.

In the film he starred as Flight Lieutenant David Archdale, and he was in fact the cousin of John Palmer Redgrave, the brother of Mrs. L Kent of 22,

Buckingham Road.

John had chosen a military career, and as the youngest of four soldier sons he would rise from the ranks to be granted a commission of full Lieutenant in the Royal Corps of Signals.

At the age of 60, during December 1940 the death occurred of Charles Thrupp who, being a renowned woodcut artist and illustrator, had carried out much work to beautify St. Mary's Church, including work on the Lady Chapel ceiling.

For several years he had lived at Walnut Tree Cottages, in Old Bletchley, but it would be at 59, Eaton Avenue that another well-known illustrator had now come to live.

He was the famous Canadian artist and illustrator, Herbert Sellen who, whilst on a visit to his daughter Mrs. Phyllis Fryer found that, because of the outbreak of war, he was unable to return to his Canadian home.

Instead he would stay at his daughter's home, and he soon became a familiar sight riding around the town on his racing cycle.

During the war he ran several art classes in Bletchley, as well as providing artwork for the local newspapers. But his reputation had achieved a much wider renown, and the illustrations for *The Story of Little Greedy* - a salutary tale for the younger generation are just one example of his artistic talents.[1]

After the war he continued to live at his daughter's address, and there he died, aged 86, in 1962.

Becoming an art teacher at Bletchley Grammar School, also possessed of an artistic talent, was his granddaughter, Kathleen, who at the age of 15 inadvertently became a film artist during a trip with a friend to Maidenhead.

At Beaconsfield they had stopped to watch the shooting of an outdoor scene for a Just William film and, asking if they could take part, they were then given the job of extras, standing at a garden gate and pointing at William as he sprinted past, carrying a bunch of flowers with his dog!

Perhaps it was because John Clark, the 13-year-old actor who played William in the BBC series, had opened the Bletchley Company Boys' Brigade fete the previous year that they were given the role!

During the war the Bletchley Park Drama Group, the 'Parkites', had staged many acclaimed productions in the town, these having been arranged by Major Douglas Jones - whose chief qualification appears to have been a singing engagement at the end of Weston Super Mare pier in the summer of 1938!

A couple of years after the war Bletchley Park then played host to another artistic talent when Constance Cummings, 'star of radio, stage and screen', opened the Bucks Divisional Labour Party Fete. As for other film stars, after the war an officer stationed at the Bletchley RAF camp was granted special leave of

1 See picture of cover on page 88

absence to portray his real life POW experience in the film The 'Wooden Horse.' He subsequently attended the well-received premiere in London.

Another Bletchley serviceman to be immortalised on film was Mr. S. Prat of Water Eaton. Disabled during the war, he was now a resident at the Star and Garter Home in Richmond, and there he had been selected for an appearance in the movie The Lady With a Lamp, featuring Anna Neagle as Florence Nightingale.

In fact, in the film he and his co-stars would play the role of wounded Crimean War soldiers.

As for the younger generation, 43 pupils from the Bletchley Road Primary School were destined for their 15 minutes of fame when, in the school hall on Wednesday, February 6th 1946 they were filmed by Pathe Gazette giving a demonstration of puppet-making.

The premises had been especially transformed into a film set, complete with lights and a camera, and, although the film would last for only 15 minutes, the cameraman stayed for four hours!

With Mr. Brann as the producer (assisted by the educational adviser to Pathe Pictures, Miss Wilson), Pathe Gazette had first developed an interest in the subject following a successful demonstration of the craft in London, and, with a shortened version of the footage, (Pathe Pictorial No. 77) being screened in those cities on Sunday, March 2nd, audiences in Manchester and Birmingham would be the first to be shown the completed production.

In fact, on the day after the original filming, on Thursday, February 7th International Photos Ltd, an American company, had taken more than 100 stills at the school, and with these intended for distribution to magazines and journals in Britain and the US, the pupils would then once again become the focus for media attention.

By now television transmissions had been resumed, and provided the medium for Mrs. Bloggs to achieve national renown when she appeared on What's My Line. She was employed as a Bletchley signalwoman, and her occupation was correctly guessed by the panel!

Another TV star would be an employee of the Cowley and Wilson garage who, on an inventors' programme, demonstrated his revolutionary 'kitchen pot stirrer'.

Despite the advent of television, radio programmes still remained popular and, for a while, Bletchley would accommodate a well-known wireless celebrity Catherine Campbell, as she was known to her fans.

A member of the BBC Repertory Company, she was in fact Mrs. Aldridge, who lived in Church Walk at Yew Tree Cottage.

Coincidentally, at one time this would also be the home of Dr. Ronald Connor, the brother of the film and television star, Kenneth Connor.

As for Bletchley's original film star, Robert Douglas, he continued his film career after the war, including a role in the 1952 remake of The Prisoner of Zenda.

However, by the end of the decade he had become more involved in television directing, being associated with such programmes as Lost in Space and The Fugitive, but nevertheless he still made an occasional on screen appearance. Indeed, only a few weeks ago it was pleasing to see him cast as a ship's doctor, in a repeat episode of Colombo, which also starred Robert Vaughan.

The Studio Cinema.

SUICIDE AT STAPLE HALL DEPOT

Personally, the dates and Kings and Queens approach to history bores me rigid.

For unfettered by encyclopaedic formalities the past should be a dimension through which to voyage, dreamlike in the waking hours, a land of strangeness where the figures one meets are not figments of the imagination but persons who have gone before. From the records of the past, one can often empathise with their emotions and especially with those inflamed by the affaires de coeur in wartime. Such was the scenario in the First World War when thousands of troops made the acquaintance of the Royal Engineer Depots at Staple Hall, in Fenny Stratford, and Newport Pagnell.

Often lonely, and facing a shortened life expectancy, passions would sometimes run high with the opposite sex and not infrequently with the lady of the house in which they were billeted. With the husband away at the war temptations could soon prevail although, as with Corporal John Jackson, the ending would sometimes be tragic.

It was in a field on Galley Lane Farm, Great Brickhill, that his body was found with a bullet hole in the left breast and with this reported to the police it was discovered the man was a South African stationed with the Royal Engineers at Staple Hall.

At an inquest at the Police Court, Lieutenant George Weston, the Adjutant at Staple Hall, identified the man as having belonged to B Company, Royal Engineers. Married with four or five children he had been popular with comrades and being in charge of the mess hut had proved to be a very good NCO. Having previously been in the Army he held several campaign medals and at the outbreak of war re-enlisted in August 1914 at Bury.

He transferred to the Royal Engineers and served in France until invalided home. He then served in Salonika but was again invalided and went to the Newport Pagnell Depot and then Staple Hall Depot.

Giving evidence Sapper Albert Ernest Ansel, of the South African Royal Engineers, said that while walking near Galley Lane Farm he saw a dead soldier lying close to the hedge. A pistol lay near by and he at once returned to Staple Hall Depot and reported the matter.

James Hill, a corporal in the Royal Engineers Regimental Police, said he had seen the man in the camp, who when asked how he liked the job replied "Not so bad." Inspector Callaway said he went to the scene and found letters to the man's family and one to a Mrs. Emily Mapley, 32, of Newport Pagnell.

The content of the letters suggested an intent to take his own life. Mrs. Mapley, the woman mentioned in the letters, said her husband was serving abroad and she had met Corporal Jackson when he was sweeping the road outside her house. They spoke and she agreed he could be billeted with her.

However, one night although she struggled and fainted he took advantage of her, but knowing he was married with children she decided not to say anything. In fact when 'her condition' became evident she went with him to Bedford intending to see a doctor but they did not go through with the plan.

On a second journey she took out a gun licence in a false name at Bedford Post Office and purchased a revolver from a shop in the town. The couple then cycled back to Newport Pagnell and when Jackson test fired the pistol she knew he intended to commit suicide.

Nevertheless he had seemed cheerful when she last saw him but having often talked about committing suicide he said he would shoot her first and then himself. The inquest recorded a verdict of 'Suicide whilst in a perfectly sound state of mind.'

SUPERINTENDENT ERNEST CALLAWAY

As public servants, it is really about time some political plebs knew their place. got off their bikes and stopped being abusive to police officers.

One police officer it would not have paid to be abusive to was Edward Callaway who rose from the ranks to the position of Superintendent and, having marshalled the facts, stood no nonsense from any strata of the great unwashed, least of all those possessed of a pompous self importance.

Of a military family at Chalvey, near Slough, Edward was born on December 31st 1876 and although in 1938 he retired from a distinguished police career, he would fulfil many important roles in wartime Bletchley.

During his youth he had worked in a newspaper office but he then joined the Slough Company of the Bucks Volunteers and at the age of 18 enlisted in the Scots Guard for three years.

He joined the Bucks Constabulary in 1898 and in May was sent as a constable to Newport Pagnell, being later transferred to Whitchurch.

At St. Gabriel's Church, Pimlico, in June 1899 he married Elizabeth, the matron at the Chesham police station, and at the outbreak of the Boer War he rejoined the Scots Guards. In fact the diary that he kept of his exploits makes fascinating reading.

Afterwards he returned to a police career and was posted to Bletchley on his promotion to sergeant in 1904. Then followed various postings elsewhere, during which he was promoted to Inspector in 1913.

After 10 months at Brill he returned to Bletchley and here he would duly remain, enforcing with vigour the various rules and restrictions which prevailed during the First World War.

In fact he would bring the town a certain renown by being the first police officer in the country to raise a case under the Air Navigation Regulations.

In 1922 he was promoted to Superintendent and, serving on several police committees, was soon elected to the Police Council at the Home Office.

In fact for two years he became the chairman of the Superintendents' Conference and took part as the police representative in the funeral procession of King George V.

In 1936 he received the MBE from Edward VIII at Buckingham Palace and with the rank of Superintendent he retired at Bletchley in May 1938.

Yet he would not be idle, for in 1939 he was elected to Bletchley Council, remaining a member throughout the war, as well as fulfilling several other roles to include those of Sectional Organiser of the Local Defence Volunteers (forerunner of the Home Guard), Chairman of the British Legion, and positions with the Bletchley Food Control Committee.

Then in the wake of a letter of June 25th 1942 from Sir Arthur Willert, Regional Information Officer, he was proposed as a Deputy Information Officer, since the Ministry of Information had now prepared a scheme to establish 'Emergency Information Officers'.

However, it would not be until a meeting of the council on August 11th that his appointment was formally approved, shortly after which in November 1942 he was made chairman of a committee to arrange entertainment for Bletchley war workers.

At Burton on Trent, in November 1943 the wedding took place of Sister Lily Wallis and Edward's youngest son.

He was serving aboard HMS Maidstone while as for Edward's other sons, one was a corporal in the Military Police, another was a member of the Buckinghamshire Constabulary, another was a corporal in the RAF in Rhodesia and the eldest was employed in the Control Office at Bletchley station, having joined the railway in 1913.

Tragically, he died of pneumonia at Northampton Hospital aged 41 in 1945.

In 1944, after an illness of 13 years, Edward Callaway's wife died, but in November 1945 at the Register Office he married Edith Sexton of the Bull Hotel, Fenny Stratford, the licence for which she had held since the death of her husband some seven years before.

Mr. Callaway would then sell his house at 'Belmont', 143, Bletchley Road, by auction for £2,000 to Hedley Clarke and would subsequently live at the hotel until his death in 1950.

Milton Keynes Citizen, October 4, 2012

SYCAMORE FARM

A listed 18th century building, Sycamore farmhouse, Water Eaton, is today linked to the local activities centre of the Sycamore Club.

However, until the building of the Lakes Estate it had been a working dairy farm to where Mr. W.J. Makeham, a native of Fenny Stratford, whose parents farmed at Home Farm, brought his bride, Edith, in 1892.

She was a native of Kytes Hardwick, and their first son, Eric, was baptised in Bletchley on April 12th 1894. Their other children would be Kathleen, Betty and a son, Clarence, who following the outbreak of World War One joined the Beds Yeomanry.

As for Eric, as a farm labourer he had emigrated to Australia and having enlisted at Rockhampton, Queensland, would serve in the Australian Machine Gun Corps.

Meanwhile, at Sycamore Farm in early December 1915 his father had the need for a good all round farm labourer.

The position offered a tied cottage and then in July 1916 a good cowman was required, who could also expect a cottage and good wages.

After the war the Water Eaton peace celebrations took place in July 1919 and in the short time available the elaborate preparations had been made by the Committee of management. This included Mr., Mrs. and Miss Makeham but there was a sadder occasion in June 1921, when a tablet bearing the names of men from Water Eaton who had served in the war was unveiled in the Weslyan Chapel.

Five of this number had been killed or died of wounds and with the lesson, from Revelations, read by Mrs. Parker and Mrs. W.J. Makeham, the rector of Bletchley in addressing the throng said that in Australia one of the soldiers, Eric Makeham, had recently died from war wounds, being buried at Cloncurry Cemetery, Queensland.

Sycamore Farmhouse.

In his memory a wreath was attached to the tablet 'from all at home, and Aunt Gerty' while as a further tribute his parents presented a solid brass vase to the chapel. During 1929 the acres of Home Farm succumbed to brickwork development but across the road Mr. Makeham continued farming, which after his death in 1932 would be carried on by his widow.

Allowing the village fetes to be held in her orchard, she also took an active interest in the community but in later life had to retire from all her involvements due to ill health. In 1939 she died at the age of 72 and during January 1940 her executors instructed the sale by private treaty of the freehold Sycamore Farm and also a cottage, paddock and semi-detached house.

However. it would be by auction on Thursday, April 25th 1940 at the Park Hotel that the sale took place, to include 'Blue Cottage', the paddock, and no. 65, Water Eaton Road.

By August 1940 Mr. A. Cook, who had been recently registered as a cow keeper, was farming at Sycamore Farm where soon he could offer one hundred tons of swedes for sale.

Later, having begun married life at Eaton Leys Farm, William Gurney moved to Sycamore Farm where in February 1944 to assist in the farm work, and also on a milk round, he had the need for two youths or members of the Women's Land Army (In fact of the latter a local girl, Lorna Logan, would work on the farm for over three years, until her marriage.)

On Whit Monday, 1944, in aid of the Bletchley NFU Agricultural Red Cross Fund many local riders competed in a gymkhana at the farm by permission of Mr. Gurney, whose tender in March 1944 had been accepted to supply the British Restaurant with TB tested milk, at 3s per gallon less 10 per cent.

Having served as a sergeant in the Royal Bucks Yeomanry in Burma, where he would be mentioned in despatches, his son Cyril returned home from the war on Friday, November 15th 1945, and in consequence his father held a celebration at the farm for his safe deliverance and for the delivery of a full harvest.

Around 1961 William moved from Sycamore Farm to a bungalow in Drayton Road and now Cecil with his family took over, duly moving, after many years, from Mill Farm.

However with the coming of the New City he would move elsewhere but that, and the beginnings of the Lakes Estate, is a tale for another day

Milton Keynes Citizen, September 6, 2012

TALE OF THREE CHURCHES.... BLETCHLEY

In our multicultural age, Bletchley now accommodates several religious faiths, but in this issue local historian John Taylor investigates the story of three of the more established churches, both past and present.

St. Margaret's Mission Church

At the instigation of the Reverend Alfred Barrow, vicar of St. Martin's Church from 1883 to 1891, Saint Martin's Mission Room, as it was then known, was built by Henry Walsh of Fenny Stratford, with the iron cross on the building having formerly graced Woolstone church.

Originally in the possession of the Holdom family, the land for the site had been sold by Rowland Bros., and, with the railway company donating £45, the costs of the building amounted to £458 5s 8d. This included £88 2s 9d for the land, £28 for the wooden block floor, £7 10s for glazing with 'cathedral glass', £5 for the bellcote and £3 3s for the new bell, which was first rung by George Campbell at the opening of the premises by the Bishop of Oxford, on 1st March 1886.

St. Margaret's Mission Church.

George would long be associated with St. Martin's Church. Whilst on Army service in India in 1893, he was one day incredulous to see a church notice proclaiming that the Reverend Barry, formerly of Fenny Stratford, would be present on Sunday. However, before he could renew this acquaintance George was posted to the North West Frontier!

The addition of a chancel was made in 1888, and St. Margaret's Mission Church became licensed in 1890, the year in which a porch was built. With a wooden hut built to connect with the main building, in 1907, further land was then acquired.

During 1945, because of the increasing dilapidation, discussions took place about replacing the building. However, it would not be until Low Sunday, April 29th 1962, that the centre finally closed for worship, with the site being auctioned at the Conservative Club at the end of May.

For £31,000, purchase was made by the estate agents Marcus Leaver and Co of London - 'almost certainly for a supermarket-type shop, with flats and accommodation above'.

Yet despite the demolition of the church, the name would still be recalled by St. Margaret's Court. This was built on the site of the old vicarage in Fenny Stratford, and in 1965 offered two-bedroom maisonettes with central heating on a 99-year lease, available from £3,810 plus £10pa ground rent.

As for the proceeds from the sale of the site, a third of the amount was expended on providing St. Martin's Church with a new vestry and sacristy, which were blessed by the Bishop of Buckingham on the first weekend of October in 1965.

The Methodist Church, Queensway.

The Methodist Church, Queensway

The complete refurbishment of the Methodist chapel in the High Street (Watling Street) had taken place in 1882 at a cost of £155, but nevertheless the Methodist trustees set up a committee for a new building in 1908, with the land in Bletchley Road having been purchased the previous year from a Mr. Lee and the trustees of the Duncombe Estate.

Eventually it was decided to build a church at a cost not exceeding £1,800. With plans prepared by Mr. E. Harper, an architect from Birmingham, the lowest of the 13 tenders received, of £1,851 10s, was accepted.

The following year, 250 circulars were sent out to solicit subscriptions, and on July 10th 1909, the stone-laying ceremony took place to a musical accompaniment by the Luton Town Band. Also included was singing by the Wolverton and Woburn Sands choirs, and this was again a feature at the official opening by the Reverend William Perkins in November 1909, with Mr. Turney using a silver key inscribed with his name and the date.

Interestingly, in 1966 the key was discovered among his effects by his daughter, Miss E. Turney, when she came to Woburn Sands from London, and was subsequently kept in the church safe.

From 1934, a wooden hut in the grounds was used by the Methodist Girl Guides. The large vestry room of the church, being set aside as a social amenity, would see use in the early months of the World War II to cope with the influx of evacuees into the town. For the most part the evacuees were afforded a genuine welcome by the townspeople but, when the hut began use as the 'Bletchley Refugee Reception Centre', the notices proclaiming this purpose were mysteriously ripped down.

After the war, in 1955 the wooden hut was destroyed by fire, and one Saturday afternoon in July 1961 four foundation stones were laid for the new Sunday school hall, built alongside the Methodist chapel by Tranfields, at a cost of £5,500.

44, Church Street, formerly the Catholic Church

During World War I, the building had provided accommodation for Belgian refugees, and for a while afterwards found a military use until, in April 1919, it

The former Roman Catholic Church at 44, Church Street.

was offered for sale by the trustees of the late Samuel Bragg, who had given the adjoining plot as a site for the Salvation Army barracks.

Hedley Clarke, the local fire agent, purchased the property for £220 and, being possessed of a noted business acumen, duly agreed to sell the house for £350 to the local branch of the National Federation of Discharged and Demobilised soldiers and Sailors - the forerunner of the British Legion.

They intended to use the building as a social centre but, when the deal fell through, the Roman Catholics purchased the house, which was subsequently opened for religious use on Trinity Sunday 1920, by the Reverend Walker, rector of the church at Wolverton.

In the earlier century, the Catholics had held their services at Hey Tor, 115, Bletchley Road, the home of Mr. J.W. (Bibby) Watson, who eventually retired to Worthing, but a site in Victoria Road had been acquired in 1905 for a permanent facility. Since this was never built, and having celebrated Mass in five or six different locations in the town, (including an Army hut at the Staple Hall military camp), the local Catholics then decided to purchase the Church Street property.

A room on the first floor was solemnised for marriages in 1941 and until his move to Cromer in 1946, the Reverend Father Tomlinson would be the priest in charge. With the building only able to accommodate a congregation of 90, in the years after the war a decision was taken to provide an alternative venue - especially since otherwise three services had to be conducted to cater for the average Sunday attendance of 300!

Thus, to the design of Mr. J. Comper, FRIBA, work was scheduled to begin on a new centre in April 1955, at the corner of Manor Road and Sycamore Avenue. But during the initial stages, work was delayed by an intervention from on high, when a blackbird decided to nest on top of the electrical switchboard!

Under the direction of the aptly named Father Carey, the five chicks were allowed to hatch, and during the interim the workmen put up a notice reading: 'Supply when they fly'!

TELEPHONE EXCHANGES

Apparently it's now possible to buy an 'app,' some sort of cyber gizmo to 'download' on to a phone.

Although quite how to install one on my 1940's Bakelite model, complete with dial, braided cord and – I kid you not – nifty little pull out tray, is not entirely clear. But if it was possible, one I'd part with some pennies for would have the ability to decipher 'teen speak,' especially as regards teenage daughters.

A pre-requisite would be to obviously filter out the word 'like,' after which the much reduced content could then be played at a civilized speed with, of course, a pause facility, such that unintelligible abbreviations such as 'LOL' and 'OMG' could be looked up.

Stone the crows, how the world has changed since I was a lad, when mobile phones consisted of two empty treacle tins and a taut length of string. Regarding Fenny Stratford, it had been in July 1888 that permission was granted for the United Telephone Co. Ltd. to erect 'posts and wires' in the parish and in many photographs of the early 1900s often to be seen along the main highways is a line of wooden telephone poles, this overhead arrangement being used to limit the signal loss between the very large distances spanned. The town's first telephone exchange was installed on December 18th 1905, in the Aylesbury Street post office and occupied one side of the double fronted house which served as the premises.

The Early Telephone Exchange.

Initially there were 30 subscribers and they were given a 24-hour service due to a bell being fitted into the bedroom of the post mistress, Mrs. Rose Symington. She had succeeded her father, John Riddeford, and her husband had a drapery and men's outfitters shop in Aylesbury Street. (This would later be occupied by Mr. Cook, a greengrocer, but the building has long been demolished, with the site now a part of Durrans Court.) Together with Miss Ethel Grant, from London, Mrs. Symington and her daughter Juliet (later Mrs. W Elmer of Northampton) were the first 'Hello girls' in the town and in the year following the installation of the exchange Herbert 'Morny' Cannon, a famous jockey, had a telephone installed at his home, 'Brooklands,' being the fourth of the 20 subscribers that year.

In 1909 Ethel married Alfred Staniford (who for 52 years would work in the office of Rowland Bros, a local timber merchants) and with her daughter Alice she began a newsagents and stationers at 61, Aylesbury Street.

This continued until 1929 while four years later in March a new telephone exchange in Aylesbury Street came into operation.

The 185 subscribers were transferred automatically and with extra staff engaged provision was made for a caretaker's flat in the upper half of the building, which in 1900 had accommodated the International Stores, later becoming premises for a Mr. Croxford, of Leighton Buzzard and then, during the First World War a Soldiers' Institute. By 1949 the staff comprised one supervisor, nine female operators and three male operators for night duty, with the number of subscribers being 449. However, by October 1955, this had increased to over 800, who were allocated new four figure numbers to replace the old two and three figure ones. This was in preparation for a switch in February 1956 to a new automatic exchange in Victoria Road – work on which had commenced in July 1954 – and when complete it would be possible to dial direct not only to subscribers in Bletchley but also to those on nine other automatic exchanges, all within 15 miles.

Then in further progress from September 29th 1967, about 2,500 telephone subscribers in Bletchley would be able to use STD while in 1973 to cater for the town's expansion a vast extension of the exchange began. All a far cry from the early days, when one council official disdainfully remarked that most ordinary residents could not 'now or ever' have the need for a phone. To which of course the requisite teen speak would nowadays be, 'Yea, whatever.'

Milton Keynes Citizen, December 13, 2012

TEMPERANCE HALL IN WW2

During World War II, many established buildings in the town would be put to uses that had never been originally intended.

The Temperance Hall, in George Street, was no exception, and would variously accommodate a school, a community centre and a temporary refuge for evacuees fleeing the German flying bomb and rocket attacks on London.

At the instigation of the Buckinghamshire County Education Committee, in February 1939 a letter proposing to transfer the County Lending Library from the Temperance Hall to the Bletchley Road Schools had been sent to the county council. The work would now be taken over by a voluntary committee, and the position of part-time paid librarian was, in consequence, abolished. Following this rearrangement, from October 21st books would be issued from the Bletchley Road Junior School on Saturday afternoons from 2pm until 4.30pm.

With the arrival of evacuees in the town, those boys belonging to the 45th

London Company Boys' Brigade, of Salters Hall Baptist Church, Islington, had now been formed into a separate group under the enthusiastic command of their captain, Charles Ricketts, and their meetings were held in the Temperance Hall.

Having been in use as an evacuation centre, on January 10th 1940 the Bletchley Road Schools then reopened. Mr. E. C. Cook, the Senior School headmaster, had received information at the end of the previous year that under the headmistress, Miss K. Stearns, who had accompanied the pupils from London, the Ecclesbourne Road Senior Girls' School would now be accommodated in the Temperance Hall.

Yet apart from this educational role, as with the Methodist Hut in 1942 the premises were also designated as an emergency feeding and rest centre for Bletchley and, if necessary, would be opened on a four-hour basis from 7am until 11pm, staffed by a rota of volunteers.

As for the educational use, on Tuesday December 15th 1942 the London Senior Schools, both at Bletchley Park and the Temperance Hall, combined their breaking-up party, and 83 scholars accordingly joined in a carol-singing concert. Amongst those present were the headmaster, Mr. Taylor, and the headmistress, Miss K. Stearns but, with the Temperance Hall school scheduled for closure from the end of the current term, during the new year she would resume her work in London.

Thus in February 1943, at a Tuesday meeting at the Council Offices, the opening of a social club at the premises was agreed by representatives from Bletchley firms and organisations, with the objective being primarily to provide general entertainment for workers. The Ministry of Labour were prepared to release the centre for this purpose, and one room would be especially set aside for rest purposes.

Miss Bezzant, welfare officer for the Ministry of Information, said that, having seen the achievements in other districts, she fully realised the similar need for Bletchley and, with a full-time warden to be appointed to organise the activities, for the benefit of shift-workers the facility would be open all day and every day. Mr. H. Jones was subsequently appointed as secretary of the committee which, at the opening of the centre, would then be replaced by a council and their elected committee.

Thus, on Saturday August 28th 1943 the 'Bletchley Community Centre' was officially opened at 3.30pm by W. Blakiston, regional controller, Ministry of Labour & National Service, and in the evening a concert by the Jollities Concert Party took place at 7pm. This was followed by a dance at 9pm, with admission for the concert priced at 1s, and the dance at 1s 6d.

With Mr. F. Bates as chairman and Mr. H. Jones as honorary secretary, as previously agreed the management of the centre now came under a local committee, and in fact the idea had aroused the interest of many firms locally, whose workers paid a subscription of 4d a week, or 2d if under 18. The membership was expected to eventually total around 800, and attractions would include two billiards tables, table tennis, darts, draughts etc. It was also hoped to start an amateur dramatic society and debating clubs, and concerts and dances would be an additional feature, with light refreshments and baths available on the premises.

The Temperance Hall.

On Wednesday May 17th the following year at 7.30pm, the re-election of the committee took place at the AGM and, reporting that he found it easier to get people to dance than listen to lectures, Mr. Mort announced that the membership now numbered 170 - although people were not allowed to come to the centre to play games seven nights a week, nor was the centre to become 'a playground for older people'!

Public dancing on Tuesday nights drew a welcome attendance of about 40, but a talk and discussion held on Wednesdays only attracted around '12 interested and 12 disinterested persons'. As for the Thursday music appreciation class, this was a fiasco, in contrast to the whist drive on Fridays which proved a huge success!

Saturday concerts and social evenings also proved popular but on Sundays the centre opened only in the evening, due to a drop in the afternoon attendance. Mondays also drew an unusually low attendance, and it seemed that the faults of the centre lay with the lack of co-operation and communal spirit. Therefore, an all-out effort would be needed to get the Entertainment & Social and Sports & Education Committees working efficiently, and he proposed to enrol all members aged under 18 as associate members, and not as full members as was presently the case.

Mr. Mort also proposed setting aside two nights a week for young people, allowing them the run of the premises, but since several of the 18-year-olds had been behaving like children of nine and 10, this caused understandable problems.

Yet the problems would soon become irrelevant for, with the launch of the German's V1 flying bomb campaign, the premises were closed as a community centre, and from Sunday July 2nd were made available as an evacuation centre for displaced persons. On being offered a similar position in Aylesbury, Mr. Mort would shortly resign, and with a local advisory committee the centre was now administered from Aylesbury by the Public Assistance Committee.

Based at 45, Bletchley Road, Muriel Manlove became the centre organiser for the Bletchley Urban District, and she was therefore tasked with supplying helpers to the staff, who would be under the direction of the full-time supervisor, Mrs. Breeze. Also responding to the emergency were the WVS who, under the charge of Mrs. Taylor were now running the Methodist Centre in Bletchley Road as additional accommodation. With a consequent shortage of assistants, an appeal was duly launched to persuade Bletchley housewives to become volunteers and interested persons were asked to apply to Mrs. Warren at 20, Cambridge Street or Mrs. Fennell at 14, Oxford Street.

As for the entertainment of the refugees, one Sunday towards the end of July a small party of artists came to the centre to entertain the London evacuees and, although there was a piano on the premises, it was alleged that permission to use the instrument had been refused. Instead, from Stoke Hammond a piano had to be borrowed from the RAF, 'who came flying to the rescue'. Despite the report of a number of 'desperate cases', the use of the telephone had also supposedly been disallowed.

Hardly overjoyed by these allegations, Mr. Mort, who was still fulfilling the role as warden at the community centre, was unsurprisingly swift to respond, exclaiming: "What is all this baa-ing of sheep and bleating of lambs?"

He explained that, as the property of the community centre, the telephone was subject to Post Office regulations and, although a delay in reaching an agreement regarding its use had resulted in some 'interference' (in fact for 36 hours), even then the interests of the evacuees were safeguarded, since incoming calls could be taken. As for outgoing calls, there was a public telephone box about 100 yards away. Regarding the piano, this was the property of the Ministry of Labour and, despite Mr. Mort and the committee being held responsible, "no one, at any time, has applied for its use for concerts either to me or anyone else", and in fact if anyone could disprove this, "I'll buy him a piano."

He sympathised with the plight of the evacuees, having during the previous week experienced the effects of a VI, but his comments concerning the complaints of the artists could have been hardly more disparaging: "It is easy to provide one hour's cheap entertainment per week and be absolutely impervious to the fact that for the other six days and 23 hours evacuees are herded like cattle with inadequate supplies of gas and water."

Nevertheless, conditions at the centre were clean and efficient and, with the men's quarters situated in the old games hut (as well as the hospital bay and medical depot), by mid-August, from a one-day peak of 51, now 19 'happy' evacuees were being accommodated, with Mrs. Hayward in charge.

However, during October the Rest Centre authorities then unexpectedly released the 'Bletchley Centre', and it was now scheduled to reopen with 'a social' on Saturday, November 4th. Thus, with the unforeseen need for a replacement, during the day four candidates for the position of warden were accordingly interviewed by the Bletchley Community Centre Committee, and by the end of November Mr. E Halsey, of Chingford, would be appointed. In fact, he seemed an appropriate choice for, having arrived from an East End educational settlement, he and his wife had already been wardens in a rest centre, as well as being involved in the Citizens' Advice Bureau. On Saturday, January 13th 1945, Mr. Halsey acted as MC at a social and dance at the centre, with admission being free. Mr. Papworth's band provided the music.

Following the end of the war, the community centre would accommodate a new use, and not without a certain irony. For with rationing still in force, in 1946 it became a centre where people could bring 'points' foodstuffs for Germany. In fact, tins of powdered milk, eggs, beans, etc had already been received by the warden, Miss Challenger, and gifts could be left any morning or evening, as well as on Wednesday and Thursday afternoons. With the collection being taken over by an official body, a good response was anticipated, and this proved to be the case. Each weighing 15lb, the first gift parcels to Germany were despatched on Wednesday, December 18th via the Save Europe Now Fund.

THE AMERICAN DREAM - TALES OF BLETCHLEY'S GI BRIDES

Given the continuing austerity of a Britain ravaged by war, it was perhaps not surprising that many young British women found not only the charms and affluence of the American servicemen enticing, but also the prospect of beginning a new life in a country which, to many, must have seemed like stepping into a Hollywood film set.

In fact, perhaps tempted by this vision, several Bletchley girls would find romance, and, for better or worse, gladly embrace their chance to become a part of the 'American Dream'.

As part of the 33rd India Corps, commanded by Lieutenant General Sir Montague Stopford, on their journey to Rangoon between April 3rd and May 27th the Royal Bucks Yeomanry, in which many Bletchley men served, had covered some 1,127 miles, and liberated 50,000 square miles of territory from the Japanese.

With the war finally at an end, preparations were made to bring the men home, but during the journey they were entertained at Bombay with a showing of the film Objective Burma, in which it seemed that Errol Flynn, assisted by a few American paratroopers, had been solely responsible for the task that the British and Indian troops had just accomplished. Not surprisingly, in view of their recent experiences and this gross distortion, the real heroes became so incensed that they tore down the screen.

While serving overseas, several Bletchley men had kept romance alive by regular correspondence with their girlfriends, and among them was Sergeant Lewis Waller, the eldest son of Mr. and Mrs. Waller, of Railway Terrace. Indeed, it had been while on active service in Burma that the bride's brother, Leslie Litchfield, had promised to act as best man, and thus in due course, Eileen Litchfield, of Bedford, and Lewis were married.

With Lewis now employed at the London Road garage, Loughton, the couple settled down to married life, but for other girls their vision of domestic bliss lay further afield - and not least through having made the acquaintance of many American servicemen, who often frequented the local dances. In fact that several Bletchley girls had succumbed to American charms was perhaps not surprising for, according to one source "The Yanks were the most joyful thing that ever happened to British womanhood."

Indeed, as one aircraft factory worker recalled: "A British soldier would take a girl for a drink, bore her to death talking about cars or sport, etc. Then if he saw any of his mates, he abandoned the girl except to buy her a drink now and then until it was time to go home. "With a GI it was very different. He would buy me a drink and entertain me as if I was the only person in the room. I know that when my back was turned he would probably make a date with another girl, but this didn't really seem to matter."

Fortunately, this had not been a problem for Celia Saunders, the daughter of Major and Mrs. J. Saunders, of 135, Bletchley Road, for on Wednesday, April 18th 1945, at the Catholic Church she married Staff Sergeant Howard Buis, of Greencastle, Indiana. He had been stationed with an American bomber squadron.

The reception for 80 guests was held at the home of the bride and amongst those attending were Brigadier and Mrs. Gambier Parry. The presents included a canteen of cutlery from the officers and staff of Special Communications Unit 1 and afterwards the couple left for a honeymoon at Ilfracombe.

By late January 1946, for the several wives now waiting to join their husbands in America, the arrangements for free travel had been made "down to the last safety pin", and among those about to sail was the now pregnant Celia, who would subsequently join her husband in Indiana, where he was employed as a bank teller.

Already in America was the former Miss Burbury, of Bletchley Road. She was now Mrs. E. Slusser, the wife of Major Robert Slusser of the US army, and had flown to America with her daughter, Virginia, as a private passenger with Pan American airways in November 1945.

As for those now travelling to join their husbands, "We sure had a boom welcome," would be the comment of Mrs. Joan Glace, the only child of Mr. and Mrs. Harding, of Cottingham Grove, who arrived in New York with her eight-month-old son, Alan, on February 10th 1946. Ironically, her voyage had been aboard the Queen Mary, the same vessel which during the war had brought her husband to Britain!

Having been stationed with the 8th USAAF at Cheddington, he had returned to America by air in August 1945, but now in the company of his parents, two sisters and a brother, he would welcome his wife and son to their new life.

The ensemble duly drove to Philadelphia, where, due to a housing shortage, Mrs. Glace would live with the family for a while and, under the auspices of the Red Cross, she would give a broadcast of her experiences on a Philadelphia radio station.

Another Bletchley girl now crossing to America was Mrs. June Watkins, formerly June Howe, of Brooklands Road, who would be travelling with her seven-month-old son, Russell, to Scranton, Pennsylvania, where her husband, Alf, was a mechanic.

As for Mrs. Nick Garza, formerly Nancy Sears, of 'Ernbay', Osborne Street, she would be setting up home in San Antonio, Texas, where her husband Nick, who had been stationed in England with the USAAF, was a YMCA PT instructor. The couple had been married on Friday, March 30th 1945, at the church of St Thomas Aquinas, in Church Street, but unfortunately the bride's father, Captain Sears, could not attend the wedding since he was serving with the Pacific force.

During the war, a contingent of Americans had been working at Bletchley Park and billeted at The Manor, Little Brickhill, they would often cycle en masse to the County Cinema, parking their bikes outside.

As this caused an inconvenient obstruction however, Peggy Sears, the girlfriend of one of the personnel, arranged an alternative location in the garden of the family home across the road, although this quite perplexed her grandmother, to whom the American English spoken by the riders seemed almost a foreign language!

It had been while awaiting her mother at Bletchley railway station that Peggy, the daughter of Mr. and Mrs. W. Sear, of the High Street, had met her future husband, Eugene Griffiths, and in due course they were married. On Wednesday, March 13th 1946, in the company of her mother, father and brother, Peggy travelled to Waterloo, to be taken by a special train to Tidworth, prior to sailing to America. Now discharged from the Army, her husband was already back in the United States, and had been busy setting up their home in South Carolina.

On Monday, November 6th 1945, at St Mary's Church, Frances Mattinson, ATS, had married Sergeant Harry Huebner, of the American Medical Corps. She was the only daughter of Mr. and Mrs. Mattinson of Manor Farm, Old Bletchley, and the groom was the only son of Mr. and Mrs. Henry Huebner of Maplewood, New Jersey. The bride's only brother, who was currently undergoing aircrew training with the RAF in South Africa, sent a telegram of congratulations and, following a reception at Manor Farm attended by several US personnel, the couple left for a honeymoon in Scotland. Then in early 1946 the destination for herself and her baby son, William, would be Maplewood, New Jersey, where her husband was now employed by Chase National Bank, New York.

Yet in 1947 Mrs. Huebner returned with her small son, Bill, to visit her parents at Manor Farm, where she was welcomed on Monday, December 15th. It had perhaps been to provide more playing room for their grandson that Mr. and Mrs. Mattinson had decided to sell a 6ft l0in by 4ft billiard table, "in good condition", complete with cues, marker and balls! Their daughter, and Billy, would then return by air to their New Jersey home the following February.

In time another Bletchley bride would also be paying a return visit. From her home at 325 Hudson Street, West Columbia, South Carolina, Peggy Griffiths came back to England to visit her ailing father. Despite all the labour saving devices of America, she found she still preferred England, saying: "All I do now is stand and look at Brickhill Woods and the wonderful view."

Also of the same opinion was one of her three children, Debbie. She did not want to go back, but sadly the situation would be resolved when, following her husband's death in a tragic accident, Peggy returned to Britain for good.

While Bletchley brides had been leaving for America, one bride was destined to make a new life in England - although, because members of the Forces serving in Germany had initially to abide by a 'no fraternising' order which forbade any familiarity with German civilians, the relationship had at first been a little distant.

Yet this could not quell the romance which developed between Albert Wesley, a private in the Essex Regiment, and Melanie Stechert. She was the only daughter of Herr and Frau A. Stechert, of Berlin, and it had been outside a Berlin cinema that Albert, the only son of Mr. and Mrs. S. Wesley of 102, Western Road, had made the family's acquaintance. An ongoing friendship developed and, following Albert's 'demob', Melanie was allowed to travel to Bletchley where, on Saturday, September 6th 1947, the couple were married at St Martin's Church.

THE BAPTIST CHAPEL

Fenny Stratford the origins of a Baptist congregation really dates from the autumn of 1797, when a small number of 'brethren' met in the house of Conyers Burton.

During 1801 a church was formed and by 1803 services were being held at the home of Mr. Linnell, Woughton.

Despite Mr. Linnell's house being registered for worship, the members decided to build their own church at Fenny and bricked and slated, this was constructed between May and October 1805, at a cost of £100.

Opened on October 13th the first sermon was peached by the Rev. William Bull, from Newport Pagnell.

By 1807 18 names were recorded on the church roll and Mr. Smith became the first pastor on March 28th. He served the ministry well but only briefly, before being called into the foreign mission field.

Easter Monday 1891, witnessed a Public Tea and Entertainment being held at the 'ruinous' Baptist chapel, in aid of funds for the new organ and with the finance duly acquired, a few weeks later the newly arrived American organ then gave its first majestic performance, played by Mr. T. G. Kirby at the Sunday Service.

The Baptist church then decided to invite tenders for the building of not only a new chapel but also a new school, on the site of their existing chapel.

The plans made inclusion for the existing vaults - which would otherwise

Spurgeon Memorial Baptist Church remained, for nearly a century, among the most impressive of Fenny Stratford's architectural features.

be overlaid by the new building - to be opened with the bodies re-interred, in a separate vault, to be constructed outside the building.

Tenders for the chapel and Sunday School were invited and at the old chapel the closing services were conducted in March, by the Rev. H. S. Smith.

That month the demolition began and services were temporarily transferred to the Town Hall.

Mr. Fathers of Bedford was selected as builder and Mr. Sloan, of Leighton Buzzard, the architect, obedient to 'the improved style of Christian Architecture'.

Excluding Mr. Sloan's fee the costs totalled £3,050 with the completed building able to accommodate 520 people.

By Thursday, April 28th the building stood 'joist high' for the laying of the foundation stone.

The crowds were entertained by the Fenny Stratford Town Band.

Under the foundation stone was placed a tin box including a Bible, a copy of a document relating to the history of the church, a copy of Rippon's hymns and a programme of the days proceedings.

So began the beginnings of the Spurgeon Memorial Baptist Church which for nearly a century remained amongst the most impressive of Fenny's architectural features.

The site, however, is today used for car sales, a reflection of modern worship upon which it is perhaps best not to dwell!

Sunday Citizen February 10, 2002

THE GIGGLES, A WWI CONCERT PARTY

An affliction of the modern age is that seemingly the talent less are being increasingly thrust upon us in the guise of 'celebrities.'

Indeed, despite having allegedly penned hardly a word of 'her' tomes there's supposedly some woman - and I kid you not - who's acclaimed as a 'best selling' author.

Apparently the initial fame was based on a couple of rather prominent attributes, on which subject we're now being pestered by some little chap who keeps popping up to try and optimistically rekindle a singing career.

That's when not advising lesser mortals on how to achieve some ambition or other - presumably not a singing career.

But continuing this month's theme of the First World War, in those days before radio and television it was usual to be able to play an instrument, or to sing without the need for electronic enhancement, and to lift the nation's morale such talent was regularly showcased in local concerts.

In fact at Fenny Stratford many of these would feature the Wallsgrove Orchestra, founded by John Wallsgrove, who, as an accomplished flautist, had played in the orchestra of the Fenny Stratford Musical Society.

For his daily employment John was in business as a fully qualified pharmaceutical chemist with his uncle, Mr. H. Hands, in Aylesbury Street, but in the evenings he and his orchestra would regularly play to raise local morale.

However, in March 1916 his own morale had to be sadly raised, following a letter from an officer of the 6th Battalion Oxon & Bucks Light Infantry; "Dear Mr. Wallsgrove. I am sorry to have to tell you that your son was killed last night. He was on sentry duty and was hit through the head by a machine gun bullet..."

Yet throughout the country such news was a daily occurrence, and in the local district a welcome diversion would be provided by 'The Giggles' concert party which, as 'a military combination of vocalists and musicians,' was drawn from the wealth of amateur talent to be found amongst the contingent of Royal Engineers at Staple Hall Depot, Fenny Stratford.

Indeed, being in great demand they regularly brought mirth and merriment to many a local village and town, and at Newport Pagnell one Wednesday evening in February 1918 the Electric Theatre was crowded for their amusing entertainment.

The artistes included 'Cherub' (Lieutenant E.V. Appleton), 'Horace', a 'piano and card manipulator,' and 'Whizzbang,' alias Corporal Atkinson, 'the not so famous baritone.'

The major portion of the programme was given in the guise of a pierrot troupe, consisting of concerted numbers, duets, humorous songs, stories and jokes, and for the rendition of his song 'Kissing,' Corporal Walmsley received a vociferous encore.

All the acts were enthusiastically received, and the entertainment concluded with the sketch 'Plum and Apple,' or 'Does the Chewing Gum lose its Flavour on the Bedpost Overnight.'

Depicting life behind the lines the plot dealt with the adventures of the three well known characters from the sketchbook of Captain Bairnsfather, and for the trench scene there were clever stage effects for machine gun fire and shell bursts.

During the concert Lieutenant A. Carpenter received special applause as 'the world renowned tenor,' but not to be forgotten was Lieutenant Woods, who, as 'Blossom,' 'exuded a mixture of angelic sweetness and girlish grace.'

Much like those babes of more recent years the Bangles, who, may the gods be praised, are rumoured to be re-forming for some forthcoming events. Now there in every sense is some real talent, for whom - well at least in the hearts of some ageing males - a flame shall eternally burn!

THE RED HOUSE - FENNY STRATFORD

At Fenny Stratford, a familiar sight along Watling Street is the lofty prominence of the Red House, which, with the present three-storey building dating from 1817, would from 1797 serve for many years as a doctor's house and surgery.

Today the premises are in the private ownership of the Gregory family, and it is due to their care and attention that the house has received an ongoing restoration.

The height of the building is emphasised by the lowered course of the road, and this reminds one of the days before the advent of the Ml motorway, when Watling Street continued to be a major artery of the nation's transport system.

In fact, it was due to Thomas Telford that, during the 19th century, local improvements to the road were made, including the demolition in 1828 of two old cottages at the corner of St. Martin's churchyard, with half of the land being used to widen the road. It was by his advice that the level of the road was later lowered, which accounts for the Red House now standing at a raised elevation.

A Scotsman, Telford had initially been a stonemason but, having moved to London in 1782, by 1787 he began his career as a builder of bridges, canals and roads, eventually becoming known as 'the Colossus of Roads'.

With the introduction of the stagecoach, the need for adequate major roads had become paramount. The usual method of road repair in the 17th century had been just to fill the potholes and ruts with stones or gravel, using hand rammers to firmly compact the material.

But clearly this was no longer adequate, since by 1705 the 14 mile length of Watling Street between Hockliffe and Stony Stratford was in such a bad condition that ruts three feet deep were commonplace, and "the ordinary Provision made

The Red House.

by the Laws and Statutes of this Realm now in force are not sufficient for the effectual repairing and amending the Road... neither are the Inhabitants of the several parishes and townships, through which the road leads, of ability to amend the same."

A partial solution to the national problem would be introduced the following year by the Parliamentary creation of the first Turnpike Trust, by which tolls were charged for the traffic using the roads. This revenue was then expended on road repairs, although the roads that were infrequently used could only generate small amounts of money.

Then in 1739, due to the considerable amount of traffic, an Act of Parliament "for amending the Highway between Hockliffe and Stony Stratford" was passed, "by reason of many heavy Carriages passing through the same, is become so very ruinous and bad that horsemen, coaches, waggons and other carriages, cannot pass, especially in the winter season without danger".

Eighty-five trustees were duly nominated, and they were empowered to appoint surveyors and "Collectors of the Tolls of the Turnpikes", which would be erected along the roads. As for the tolls, these included "For every coach, Berlin, landau, chariot, or calash drawn by six horses, 1/6d; if by four horses 1/-; if by two horses 6d." Free passage was granted for the conveyance of the material for the road repairs, and also "on the days whereon there should be an election of a Knight of the Shire, or of a Burgess or Burgess to serve in Parliament for the Counties of Bedford or Buckingham".

Free passage was also granted for other purposes, including the conveyance of "dung, mould, soil, or compost", to be used as manure on gardens and lands.

The penalty for transferring a toll gate ticket was 10s, both for giver and receiver, and with half of the fine being given to the 'informer', the other half went towards road repair.

The tolls would take effect from March 25th 1740, for a period of 21 years, and around 1766 the keeper for the toll gate at Fenny Stratford was Joseph Ray. The condition of the road greatly improved, not least when the trustees appointed Thomas Telford as their adviser.

Even until recent times the Red House was often the home of medical practitioners, and, following the sale of the premises in 1976 by Dr. Francis Carter, this association is continued today with the naming of the Red House surgery, in Queensway.

Lynch Conway Gent.

Daniel Atkins, in his will of September 13th 1793, stated that after his death his property - consisting of a cottage in Fenny Stratford known as the White Hart, (formerly the Rose and Crown), which was formerly two tenements, and another cottage known as the Cock, (first mentioned in 1753), as well as four acres of close adjoining the Cock - should, pending their sale, be held in trust by Thomas Brett and Robert Atkins.

Daniel died soon afterwards and, in accordance with the terms of his will, the property was auctioned at the Swan in December 1800. The purchaser, who had already been the tenant, was Lynch Conway, a surgeon, with the description in the particulars of sale reading that it is "pleasantly situated by the site of the turnpike road from London to Chester".

For some 30 years, the building had been used as a pub, "for which purpose its situation is particularly desirable or for any other business which requires room. It is within a very short distance of the Grand Junction Canal many miles of which is now in full trade and the greatest part of the remainder is expected to be finished in the course of the next summer."

As for Dr. Gent, he was an officer of a Friendly Society registered in the town in 1795, which met either at the Kings Head or the church and, as the surgeon and apothecary, he received a payment from each member for his service. As suggested by the name, the Navigation Inn, now renamed the Bridge, had been built to cater for the needs of the canal diggers, and it would be here that Dr. Gent set up an association for the prosecution of robbers, following the theft of his horse.

In fact, horse stealing had once been prevalent in the town, and at the site of since demolished cottages in the middle of Aylesbury Street the complete skeleton of a horse was unearthed. It was assumed that, having stolen the horse, the thieves, considering its sale too much of a risk, slaughtered the animal and buried the carcass under the floor of their living room.

In 1817 the present Red House was built by Charles Warren who, at the age of 19, was also the architect, and it was also at this period that Dr. Gent had the three adjoining tenements, (formerly the Cock Inn), demolished, with the site converted into gardens.

As for other matters, by a covenant he instructed that no wife of his should be entitled to dower from the property, although in October 1817 William Wilson of Adderbury, trustee of the marriage settlement of Lynch Conway Gent to Mary Gardener, was, as trustee, assigned £500 due to Mary on a note of land from John Bellow of Adderbury.

Thomas Camps

Lynch Conway Gent died on January 31st 1847, being buried at St. Martin's Church. The previous year, his will of September 25th had devised his property to his trustees, George Maydon of Winslow, maltster and butcher, and John Sleath Gent of Stony Stratford, a surgeon.

Charles Ridgway, a draper of Leighton Buzzard, then purchased the property as agent for Thomas Camps, surgeon, of Fenny Stratford, for £650 with the interest to include a 'messuage and garden' and close, (part of which had been sold to the railway).

Thomas Camps had previously worked at Great Berkhampstead and during his medical career would contribute to many learned publications. He made his will in April 1855 and, after his death in September 1856, a trust for the sale of his property was set up in October 1856.

At auction, 'Lot 4' was purchased for £500 by Thomas Lucas, and on September 29th 1859 a conveyance was made of 'a messuage in the High Street in Fenny Stratford late in the occupation of Thomas Camps and now of William Lucy; and also the paddock ground'.

Doctor Frederick Deyns

Born at North Walsham, he lived and practised at the Red House, where his second son Charles John Deyns, was born. He then took over the Red House practice from his father around 1890.

Doctor Lieutenant Colonel Charles John Deyns

A staunch Freemason, he joined the St. Martin's Lodge in 1905 and, being a councillor for 25 years, would be the chairman of the council in 1909, 1910 and 1911.

He also became captain of the town cricket club and, apart from his general practice, would also be a medical officer with the Bucks Volunteer Rifle Corps.

Indeed, although officially too old during World War I, he felt it his duty to be with his men, and not only took part in the Gallipoli campaign, but also served in Alexandria. For his military service he would be awarded the prestigious Territorial Decoration.

Known also as Lieutenant Colonel Deyns, among his appointments was that as head of the school board, and as a Justice of the Peace. He was also chairman of the Fenny Stratford Gas Company until it was taken over by the British Gas Light Co.

Having moved to The Gables, in Bletchley Road, he retired from medical practice in 1927 and subsequently lived at his home in Tattenhoe Lane until his death, after failing health, aged 87, in January 1950.

Doctor Edgar Nicholson

After training at Middlesex Hospital, in 1896 Dr. Edgar Nicholson MRCS LRCP, a Yorkshireman from Whitby, came to work in the High Street practice of Dr. Charles Deyns, by whom he was subsequently offered a partnership.

A frank and outspoken man, Dr. Nicholson was greatly respected in Bletchley and when Dr. Deyns later moved to The Gables, in Bletchley Road, he maintained the practice at the Red House until his retirement in 1929. He died in Northampton, on January 7th 1945 at the age of 80.

With the estate amounting to £47,595 12s 5d, he left an annuity of £25 and the use of the house and furniture to his housekeeper, Margaret Robinson. He also left an annuity to his sister Louise, with the rest of his estate to be disposed of equally in trust to Geoffrey Hudson and Christopher Fulton.

Ernest Marchant

A veteran of World War I, in 1924 Ernest Marchant acquired 'the relics' of a solicitor's practice, and for a while set up in one room of the Red House. He cycled every day from his home in Woburn Sands and had to use the lavatories at the nearby railway station!

One of the four children of James and Lucy Marchant, he was born in north London on May 12th 1887. Educated at Christ's Hospital, Ernest was admitted to the Court Rolls in July 1913 and then gained employment in London.

Enlisting at the outbreak of World War I, he married Elsie Cotching, "a rare, golden-haired beauty", and served with the 18th Royal Fusiliers - the Public Schools Fusiliers - becoming an instructor in musketry.

However, in the aftermath of the Somme, seeing a friend return wounded for the second time from France, he immediately asked for a posting to the front. This granted, at the age of 29 he was commissioned as a lieutenant in the 17th Middlesex, and at the ill-conceived assault on Beaumont Hamel he was one of the few who on November 13th survived the long struggle through the mud to penetrate the German lines.

A grenade put an end to his war and he was taken prisoner. After two unsuccessful attempts at escape, he remained a POW after the Armistice. With no prospect of early release, in December he and two prisoners crawled under the wire and reached Denmark in an open fishing boat, having nearly died of exposure during the voyage.

In his solicitors practice he would eventually be joined by his two sons Andrew and James, and the business developed into the successful firm of Ernest Marchant and Sons. Ernest died in 1967 at the age of 80.

Doctor William Edgar Carter

On the retirement of Dr. Nicholson, in 1929 the practice was taken over by Dr. William Edgar Carter, who came to Bletchley with his wife from Soham, Cambridgeshire. On November 12th 1931 the Red House was conveyed to them by local property developer Hubert Faulkner for £500. Also at the Red House would live their nurse, dispenser and secretary Barbara Curtoise, who had travelled with them.

Since 1803 successive members of the Carter family had qualified with the Royal College of Surgeons, the first being Richard Carter. He became the ship's surgeon of the sloop Ranger at the battles of the Nile and Trafalgar, and eventually settled in Leeds where, after qualifying in 1843, his son, Joseph Barton Carter, practised until 1893. He died in 1897 but his son, Francis Richard Carter, would also practice in Leeds for over 30 years.

After his death in 1907 the tradition would be continued by his son, Dr. William Edgar Carter, who was a GP near Cambridge for 14 years. For transport, he first owned a single-cylinder car, but because of the non-electric lighting system which was unsuitable for night driving, had to cycle miles in the Fens when attending night calls.

In 1939, Doctor Carter became the deputy coroner for North Bucks and in other capacities was the rector's warden of the parish of Simpson, of which village he was offered the vice-presidency of the cricket club in April 1950. He retired in 1952 at the age of 65.

Doctor Francis George Temperly Carter

On the retirement of Dr. William Edgar Carter, his son Francis was appointed by the National Health Service authority to take over the practice at the Red House, which his parents conveyed to him in March 1952 for £4,000.

Educated at Aldenham School and Barts, Francis qualified in 1950. His sister Wendy had married a doctor, and in November 1951 a daughter, Nicola Jane Royle, was bom to the couple at the Red House.

On March 31st 1976 the Red House was conveyed by Francis to Milton Keynes Development Corporation, for £40,000.

Barbara Edith Curtoise

Barbara was born in Lincolnshire, the eldest daughter of Mr. and Mrs. Arthur Curtoise, of Branston. Having been granted the Lady Ampthill Scholarship, she became a VAD during World War I, and in 1919 trained as a midwife at Rotunda Hospital in Dublin.

On coming to the Red House, in 1931 she and Dr. Carter opened the Red House nursing home. In fact, Nurse Curtoise would be the actual owner of the town's first private maternity clinic, at the back of the premises which soon needed a temporary building to be erected as an extra ward.

During World War II Mrs. Carter, a well-known local nurse, would become greatly involved in dealing with the many cases. With the last baby to be born at the Red House maternity clinic being Michael Bell, the son of Dr. Bell of Aspley Guise, the facility closed in 1956 on the retirement of Nurse Curtoise. She had been much assisted by Mrs. Rose Smith, who lived opposite, at 26, High Street.

Barbara Curtoise died in 1967, "vesting assent of Red House Bungalow" by the terms of her will to Dr. Francis Carter.

Doctor Cyril Baker

With the increase in the local population, the need for medical facilities increased and Dr. Cyril Baker, the only son of Mr. and Mrs. Frank Baker of London, began his practice at the Red House. In 1957 or 1958 he married Sybil Edwards, a district nurse and midwife, of Tring, and they would shortly depart for a practice in Barnes.

The Red House today

Having lain unoccupied for years, in 1981 the Red House (excepting a small plot of the surrounding land) was purchased from Milton Keynes Development Corporation by the noted sculptor Ernest Bottomley.

From Stoke Hammond, he moved with his wife into an almost derelict house "in desperate need of restoration". Additional buildings were added to the property, including a large studio space to the rear, and a pitched elevation to the 1950s built flat-roofed extension.

Living in the premises with their two children, the current owners are a local businessman, Jon Gregory, and his wife, Emma. As the daughter of Ernest Bottomley, Emma purchased equity in the house in 1989, and has since continued the work necessary to maintain this impressive property

THE TETLEY TEA STORY

Oh, dearie, dearie me. It seems so sad when an icon of children's literature feels the need to break with the creation of magical innocence, of an appeal to young and old, and become debased by a venture into the supposed 'adult' realms of expletives and sexual depravity.

Which is precisely why I've decided to pull the plug on 'Half a Dozen Hues of Slightly Off White,' my milder counterpart to '50 Shades of Grey.'

Instead, with retirement thankfully looming, I've decided to capitalise on over 40 years in the workplace by encapsulating this experience in the potential block buster, 'All Based on Bovine Manure. The Secrets of Success in British Management' (of course in the actual title Bovine Manure is replaced by a single word of equivalent meaning, but this would hardly be suitable for a family newspaper).

As for the content, this will range from that ubiquitous essential, 'meetings' – where only the most verbose and those well versed in theatrical body language survive – to those manoeuvrings necessary to preserve an empire, by obviating the career threatening need to deal directly with some toxic department.

Yeay, it's always a joy to behold the wailing and gnashing of teeth when such baggage is suddenly dumped on an unsuspecting subordinate. As also is the dumper's expression of sheer relief, at having secured damage limitation through the welcome installation of an insulating fall guy, while still preserving the imperial boundaries. Of course by pleading, histrionics or sheer skulduggery the more savvy of underlings then swiftly replicate the process, leading to a scenario where in the more incompetent of companies the number of chiefs almost equates to the number of Indians.

But all this is for the future, and so back to scribbling about the local past and the story of one British company that was everyone's cup of tea, Tetley. The firm had originated in Huddersfield in the 1830s, when from the back of a pack horse two brothers began peddling tea and salt across the Yorkshire moors. They then opened in London in 1856 in Commercial Road and later moved to Aldgate, but during early WW2 their warehouse and head office were bombed out.

New offices were then opened in London but the manufacturing side was moved to a safer refuge in the former premises of the Sterilised Milk Co. in Osborne Street, Bletchley. Originally this had been the Bletchley Sanitary Laundry, whose custom had come to greatly benefit during WW1 from the Royal Engineer's Depot at Staple Hall.

Hopefully the factory was now removed from the perils of bombing but as a reminder of the possibilities it would feature as a target in a Civil Defence exercise.

During the 19th century the company had opened an agency in America and there teabags were first introduced. Then between the wars the teabag trade developed, but it was not until 1953 that Tetley first introduced this innovation to the UK retail trade.

Two years later their introduction of coffee bags to the British Catering Trade proved successful and the demand for their products eventually caused a staged move to a new factory in Denbigh Road in December 1957.

The firm of Vavasseurs Food Products then took over the Osborne Street premises. By 1968 demand had overtaken the capacity of Tetley's factory and a new facility began operation in Stockton on Tees in 1969.

As for Bletchley, with 450 people employed, further expansion was planned and the factory was now producing 40 million teabags a week, 80 per cent of the business, for sale in 63 different countries.

With an office still retained in London the head office remained in Bletchley and in 1972, as part of a £23 million package, the company was taken over by Lyons.

However, in the year of a massive coffee theft from the premises the factory closed in early 1977.

Four hundred people were thereby put out of work, with the reason cited being a drop in demand for teabags and the impending cost to replace obsolete equipment.

Milton Keynes Citizen, October 18, 2012

THE WAYWARD SERVANT GIRL AND MYSTERY OF THE MISSING PURSE

On Tuesday, May 26th 1914 at 10, High Street, the Fenny Stratford Branch of the Diocesan Society for the Refuge and Reformation of Girls opened, and 'for preventative and rescue work amongst girls' was run in connection with the North Bucks Association of the Oxford Diocesan Council.

In charge of the home was Miss Frances Cother, the lady superintendent, and she gave a talk to promote her work at the Wing Parish Room on the upbringing of children. Due to the mired state of the roads only about 40 participants turned up.

Nevertheless, Miss Cother remained committed to her work, not least the case of a 26 year old housemaid who, at the Bucks Assizes at Aylesbury in January 1917 pleaded guilty to the charge of having concealed the birth of a child at Bletchley on October 7th 1916. The infant's body was discovered while she was in the employ of a local household.

Said to have an excellent character for honesty, integrity and morality, the girl had been in service for most of her life and fully intended to tell her mother about her condition as soon as she knew.

However, finding her mother was grief stricken at the death of one of her brothers killed in the war, she felt unable to bring any fresh misery and so remained silent.

Following the discovery of the infant's body, hidden in a drawer, pending her trial the girl was placed on bail in the home and during this three months Miss Cother noted she performed her housework duties very satisfactorily and would be taken back into the home if required.

Indeed, partly because of this opinion the judge took a lenient view at the trial and having lectured the girl about the need to provide for the birth of a child allowed her to go, on her own recognisance, to come up for judgement if called upon to do so. No doubt this was a verdict that greatly pleased Miss Cother although her views were less favourable regarding another girl, described as a cigarette packer, in her charge, who was brought to the Special Sessions on June 8th 1917.

Aged 16, she was taken into the home on May 19th but on May 29th was alleged to have stolen a leather purse from Miss Cother containing 6s 2d, a medallion and pawn ticket.

The girl had been put to work cleaning the steps and then the passage, but on reaching the room where Miss Cother was having breakfast, she asked if she could dust the front room first.

Permission was duly given, but a while later having heard no movement in the room Miss Cother became suspicious, and upon investigation found that not only was the girl missing, but also her hat.

Also missing was Miss Cother's purse, which had been left in a bag on the table in another front room, where the girl had no reason to go.

At 4.30pm Miss Cother reported the loss to the police and, in the company of Inspector Callaway, later in the day went to Bletchley station to identify the girl, who had been detained by one of the railway officials.

On being asked by Miss Cother for the whereabouts of the purse, the girl admitted the theft saying that 'I was looking at it at Woughton' - but said that she had now lost it.

However she still had the medallion, which she produced from her pocket.

It had first been on May 7th that the girl attracted the attention of the police when a police sergeant found her wandering at the railway station at Wendover.

Feeling compassion he took her to his house to be attended to by his wife while he made enquiries but this hospitality was then abused when some ten days later the girl stole some clothes and a purse containing 17s 6d and left the house in the middle of the night.

She was soon caught near Great Missenden and having been charged before the Aylesbury magistrates was convicted and bound over in the sum of £5 being then taken to the home in Fenny Stratford.

Despite refusing to provide any details about herself the complete history of the girl was nevertheless revealed when her photo was sent to the Enquiry Department, London, for on consulting their records they were able to forward all the necessary information.

In fact it appeared that she had been more 'sinned against than sinning,' but even so would remain in custody to appear at the next Quarter Sessions for Bucks at Aylesbury, on June 25th.

As warden, Miss Cother's dedication was recognised in June 1917, when the annual meeting of the North Bucks Association of the Oxford Diocesan Council for Preventative and Rescue Work expressed their deep gratitude for the work she had done for the past three years.

The home was full during the past 12 months with girls staying a night or two to a couple of months or more.

In many cases it proved the beginning of a new life for them but perhaps not the 16-year-old servant girl accused of stealing from Miss Cother.

At the Bucks Quarter Sessions on Monday, July 2nd, 1917, she pleaded guilty and was sent to a Borstal for three years.

Also accused of stealing was another 16-year-old servant charged with the theft of money, jewellery and clothing from the Rev. Field, of Milton Keynes Village.

Mrs. Field said she employed the girl as 'cook general,' but gave her a month's notice on July 23rd. On August 21st she asked the girl to complete some work but on refusing was told to pack her bag and go.

This she also refused, and Mrs. Field sent for Miss Cother.

The girl was asked what the matter was but no reply seemed forthcoming.

When opening the girl's box several stolen items were found.

Following the arrival of a police constable other items were discovered in her handbag and at the ensuing proceedings the prisoner pleaded guilty but said nothing further.

It was decided she should be sent for trial and dealt with under the Borstal system.

Towards the end of the year it seemed that Miss Cother was to leave the home, for the Oxford Diocesan Magazine reported: "We cannot speak too highly of the way in which she has carried out her difficult duties."

"She has been a real power of good amongst the girls and by her patience and sympathy has gained their entire confidence."

Miss Cother had a change of heart for she was back at the home to have her patience further tried by a case in June, 1918.

This concerned a 21-year-old woman in the RAF who in early May attempted to strangle herself at Halton.

Some four years earlier she threatened suicide having given birth to a child but after being in the RAF for a few months her conduct had been good. Having no idea what to do with her the case was sent to the Bucks Assizes.

Her friends were unable to influence her behaviour.

In fact since leaving school she was a constant source of trouble to her respectable parents from Surrey who did not attend the trial saying they had done all they could for her.

Miss Cother, under whose charge the woman was accommodated, refused to take her for longer considering the prisoner was not sorry and might commit a similar act.

It appeared the girl had been reprimanded in camp and was afraid 'certain things' might be made known to her parents.

The judge sentenced her to three months in prison.

In Aylesbury, on Thursday, June 20th, 1918, Miss Cother presented an account of the work which had been performed at the home.

The chairman said the premises had been run for £250 a year which proved excellent value and during 1918, 69 girls were admitted with 14 sent to service, three to other refuges, 16 to 'long Homes,' 17 returned to relatives, three to the infirmary, and one to prison. Fifteen girls spent their holiday at the home!

Additionally, seven babies were admitted with their mothers with four baptised while at the shelter.

Nevertheless, by May 1919, Miss Cother left the parish and the Fenny Stratford Home disappeared into the mists of time.

Judging by the state of some of the young ladies seen spilling out of the local hostelries at chucking out time, perhaps now is the moment to seriously consider a swift reintroduction of such a facility!

THOMAS LAKE HARRIS & THE REVEREND ERNEST SILL: WHAT DOES HAPPEN TO US WHEN WE DIE?

A while ago, 'The Way We Were' featured Dr. Richard Sandy, the Great Linford rector who talked to angels, and another mystic of local note was Thomas Lake Harris, who was born in 1823 at Water Eaton Mill.

At an early age he moved with his parents to America, and there he became the minister of a chapel in New York. Having earned a certain reputation as a mystic he died in 1906, and amongst his legacies left the vision of "looking forward to an era of love and liberty and peace, when there shall be visible signs of brotherhood in Christ among all Christian men."

However, perhaps he meant in the very distant future, for within nine years of his death there would be the most horrific war in human history. In fact a war in which there would be further mysteries, from the 'Angel of Mons' to the tale told by a local soldier, who, in a letter to his parents in July 1915, wrote; "There is a big chateau near us which the Germans shell every day, and yet there is one picture they have failed to touch - it is a picture of the Virgin Mary.

The rest of the place is in ruins, and yet they cannot seem to touch that picture. It is very funny, but it is the same in many cases." Perhaps the Reverend Ernest Sill, the vicar of Little Linford, could provide enlightenment, for in January 1915 at Newport Pagnell he gave a lecture on 'What happens at death,' and 'Our condition after death' - 'There will be music and solos between part 1 and 2.' Included would be the experience of those who had returned after death, and perhaps he recounted the story told to him by his friend Dr. Ingram; "A Mother whom he knew well lost her son in an air battle. He fell 13,000 feet. On hearing the news she was broken hearted. Suddenly she saw her son and felt his arms around her, his lips on hers, and in a voice of indescribable tenderness he said: "No Mummy. I am not allowed to come back to you on earth again," and vanished.

The Reverend Sill was as equally mysterious in earthly matters, for during the war he had occasion to discuss 'important matters of national interest' with the Prime Minister's secretary at 10, Downing Street. The prediction that the First World War was a war to end all wars sadly proved a little premature, and following the outbreak of the rematch, in 1940 a gentleman from Newport Pagnell caused a minor stir by unearthing what seemed to be a relevant 300 year old prophecy, written in Latin by the 'Monk Johannes.'

Extracts included; 'Near the year Two Thousand the Anti Christ will appear. His army will surpass in numbers anything before imagined; there will be Christians among his hordes and many defenders of the lamb. … On the whole of the Christian world there will not be space that will not be red, and the heavens, the earth, the water, and even the air will be red for the blood will flow in the sphere of the four elements at the same time. … The Anti-Christ will be recognisable by several masks.

He will chiefly massacre priests, monks, women and children and old people. He will show no mercy, he will pass along holding a torch, like the barbarians, but invoking the name of Christ. … The white Eagle, which will come from the north, will surprise the black Eagle and the other Eagle will completely invade the land of the Anti-Christ from one end to the other. …

Then an era of peace and prosperity will commence for all the universe, each nation being governed according to its wish and living in justice.' Oh well, not a bad try, but perhaps his crystal ball got a bit frosted over with the onset of the Cold War. As for the present troubles, it's interesting that the recent Wikileak disclosures allude to an atomic device being ready for activation 'somewhere in Europe.'

For in the 1970s a mystic of international repute 'foretold' that regarding trouble in the 'Middle East' such an incident would occur in the French capital. Blimey, let's just hope that the accuracy of fortune telling hasn't now arrived at the nuclear option.

WARTIME ATTRACTIONS

In an age where musical 'icons' seem now to consist chiefly of semi-adequate karaoke singers, riding on the skill of session musicians, it certainly is refreshing to note that for the boosting of wartime morale, Bletchley audiences often had the benefit of real entertainment - the Studio cinema being the usual venue.

London 'artistes' and radio broadcast bands were all featured, as of course a screening of Albert Street's very own home-grown Hollywood heart-throb, Robert Douglas, who put his career on hold to assume flying duties in the Fleet Air Arm.

Elsewhere, to divert local minds from the imminence of war, Fenny Stratford Cricket Club staged a Friday whist drive at the Temperance Hall, in George Street, whilst for those feeling a little more frisky, Eddie Friday and his band, from Leighton Buzzard, were on hand to provide musical entertainment at the Coronation Hall, Water Eaton, for a Grand Dance.

Casting their aspirations further afield were the members of the Bletchley Silver Band - now having reached full strength - who began rehearsals to compete in the Leicester Band Festival, scheduled for March 4th. Of a more local entertainment, in April children from the various Sunday and day schools in the town united to present 'Children Through the Ages', a pageant held in aid of the Waifs and Strays Society and for grown-ups, during May members of the Water Eaton WI could indulge an enjoyable Wednesday afternoon learning to make 'attractive yet economical dishes', as demonstrated by the untarnished Miss Rust, of the National Milk Publicity Council.

Men, thankfully, had the welcome refuge of the Workingmen's Club which could boost seasonal funds by hiring out two marquees for summer fetes. Perhaps in fact they were suitable for the British Legion Fete, held on Whit Monday in Bletchley Park, where attractions included a darts tournament, talent competition and pony rides.

A couple of weeks later came an addition of thrills with another 'Grand Fete', this time held in the orchard of Sycamore Farm at Water Eaton which, as an adornment to anyone's back garden, offered the opportunity to win a pig. Girls from the Bletchley schools gave a demonstration of dancing and for those wishing for more of the same, along came a Folk Dance Festival at Bletchley Park, on June 24, the same date as the local Conservative fete. However, here much consternation was caused when 100 buns were nicked until, eventually, several young boys were arrested as the culprits.

Meanwhile, off on their summer jaunt to Clacton were the members, patrons and friends of the Studio cinema, enjoying an occasion that would prove to be their last excursion before the storm clouds of international conflict broke.

Storm clouds were also a nuisance for the Bletchley Baptists, whose Summer

Carnival, promising a Terrific programme of attractions', had to be held indoors after a severe downpour waterlogged their Denmark Street sports ground.

The war would be an immediate, if temporary, halt to the local entertainments in the town but perhaps as compensation, the antics of those hauled before the police court for contravening wartime regulations could often provide a measure of light relief.

Not least the comments of one irate lady from Manor Road who, on being told that her blackout precautions were inadequate, replied in no uncertain terms that the policeman had probably broken down all the fences to get there and it was a pity he hadn't fallen into the stinging nettles.

Not surprisingly her consequent fine reflected her outspoken insolence!

Sunday Citizen July 7, 2002

WARTIME BOMBS: DARK DAYS WHEN THE BOMBS FELL ON BLETCHLEY PARK

Nowadays, it is perhaps with almost a certain glibness that Bletchley Park is mentioned to have been the best kept secret of World War Two.

Yet at least three occasions had the potential to either compromise the security, or disrupt the vital work, and it seems to have been that only pure luck prevented such a catastrophe. Local historian John Taylor deciphers the details...

During World War Two, the confidence of the Germans in their Enigma coding system would cost them dear, especially since they had early knowledge that the Government Code and Cipher School, 'GC and CS' was located at Bletchley.

In fact this had been revealed following the 'Venlo incident', which, some two months after the outbreak of war, had occurred when, in the company of a Dutch Army intelligence officer, two British agents, Major Richard Stevens, and Captain Sigismund Payne Best, had driven from The Hague to an afternoon rendezvous at the Cafe Backus.

On the border between the neutral Netherlands and Germany, this was situated a short distance from a customs post near Venlo, and although the agents had been advised not to go, they disregarded the warning and kept their intention to meet a German general who, it was alleged, was plotting a coup against Hitler.

However, as the agents approached the cafe despite being greeted by their German contact with an amicable wave they did not know that he was really a Major in the SS and, as they drew near, a car suddenly pulled in front of their vehicle, with troops firing machine guns from the running boards.

The Dutch officer was mortally wounded, whilst as for the British agents they were hurriedly bundled into the car and driven at speed into Germany.

Through subsequent interrogations - during which they were apparently never tortured - the two agents revealed a wealth of information regarding the British intelligence service, and in fact in a subsequent German intelligence summary prepared for Operation Sealion - the proposed invasion of Britain - the mention was made that regarding the British code breakers 'Stevens says most of the staff have moved to Bletchley.' Yet in confirmation that the Germans paid little heed to the revelations no mass bombing was ever launched, and thankfully the only bombs that Bletchley did endure caused no substantial damage to the Bletchley Park huts.

Indeed it was just as well that Bletchley would be spared from such attention, since many of the local brick kilns were used as a storage facility for vast quantities of ammunition!

With the outbreak of war it was realised that railways would become a prime target for enemy attack, and at night only dim blue bulbs were therefore provided for lighting the interior of carriages, in which yellow notices had been placed instructing passengers to 'Lie down on the floor in the event of an Air Raid.'

In 1940 it then became the official procedure that 'Where a bomb weighing 250kg or more has fallen within a distance of 100 yards from a railway (including an Underground Railway) the full restrictions should be enforced until the bomb has been disposed of. This proviso is necessary in view of the risk of detonation due to vibration', and in fact Bletchley station became a probable target on October 3rd 1940 when having machined gunned a train and caused two casualties - one by splintered glass, and one by a bullet - a German aircraft dropped four high explosive bombs.

However, they missed the station and landed in the vicinity of Bletchley Park, one falling near Hut 4, then in use for processing naval intelligence, and another demolishing an already derelict greenhouse.

Given the importance of Bletchley Park, after this incident anti aircraft guns were not surprisingly sited for a while between Shenley Road and the railway, and in further measures the buildings of the Park were subsequently strengthened.

Indeed, the competence of the builders would be dramatically proved in recent years when wrecked machinery, brought in to demolish some of the constructions, was itself wrecked whilst attempting the task!

Apart from the mansion, and the huts in the grounds, the code breakers at Bletchley Park also made use of nearby 'Elmers', (now the site of the Elmers Park housing development), which as with several houses in the vicinity would be damaged by enemy bombs.

The imposing residence had originally been the home of the Selby Lowndes family, and of the children of Richard Selby Lowndes, (whose tomb may be seen near the porch of St. Mary's Church), a son, Reginald William, was born at Bletchley Cottage in January 1853. Unfortunately he did not survive infancy, but of the eight daughters - who became known as the eight belles, (from which the nearby pub - previously known the Old Bells - took its name) - Eleanora became the second wife of Sir John French, 1st Earl of Ypres.

Elmers then came up for sale in June 1920 by the direction of Mrs. Richard Selby Lowndes, who was leaving the district, and the substantial accommodation, which included 13 bedrooms, four reception rooms and 'a park like meadow' of seven acres, was then bought for use as a school by Professor Alfred Holloway. He had previously run a school in Bletchley Road, and the premises, built in 1891, would become a centre for the Conservative Club, founded in 1930.

After the outbreak of war, during its use by the code breakers Elmers, including a classroom, would be damaged by high explosive bombs on 20th November, 1940 and with these also causing damage to several houses in Church Green Road, this seemed somewhat ironic, since it was at 'Lindthorpe' that Arthur Bates, the ARP Officer and District Sub Controller, lived.

The bombs brought down telephone wires and an electric standard, (which fell, blocking the road), and as a further cause for alarm bombs were variously dropped near the town on other occasions.

Damaging ten yards of hedging, these included a high explosive bomb at Borough Farm, Newton Longville, on 8th September 1940, whilst in early October four high explosive bombs fell on open fields, with incendiary bombs dropped later in the month at Galley Lane Farm, and a field next to the Pulman Cafe. Then on 15th November, 1940, two high explosive bombs fell a mile south east of Bletchley, but fortunately they only caused slight damage.

Two years before the outbreak of war, with a prudent foresight the insurance companies had stopped cover for war damage, and in consequence in 1940 the War Damages Commission was set up, intending to recoup the cost of the payments by an Inland Revenue scheme.

This would provide financial compensation to those people who had suffered damage to their land and/or buildings through enemy action, and the local authority was directed to categorise the extent of such damage into four sub headings: a) Total destruction b) Damage so severe that demolition was necessary c) Severely damaged but capable of repair i) still usable ii) evacuated or to be evacuated d) Slightly damaged (excluding broken windows only).

Four copies of the report were then to be made, one to be kept, one for the District Valuer of the area, one for the Ministry of Health, and one for the Regional Office of the Ministry of Health.

Taking charge at the scene of any 'major occurrence' would be Incident Officers, supplied by the police, and having fully assessed the situation they would therefore be able to provide guidance to the arriving emergency services.

An Incident Officer's post would be marked by a blue and white check flag and two blue lamps, set one above the other, and - if needed - that for Bletchley would be established on the car park outside the Council Offices.

Should an incident severely disrupt communications, then the ARP service would use the organised system of the police, whereby urgent messages could be delivered by car to the Regional Headquarters at Reading and with two routes always being available, contingency plans were in place should alternatives be needed.

WARTIME ENTERTAINMENT

For the boosting of morale and generally taking their minds off the trauma of war, Bletchley residents had the often benefit of various entertainments in the town, held at such venues as the Social Centre, nowadays more locally known as St. Martin's Hall.

As for the dance music, hotfoot from Leighton Buzzard, Fred Groom and his band were regularly engaged. For the more ambitious productions, artists might be sought of a national renown, Mantovani and Jack Payne and his orchestra, of BBC fame, to name but two.

As for troops in the town, apart from a few amorous adventures they also had special entertainments staged on Sunday evenings in the school hall of the Baptist Church and here a varied home-grown talent could exercise their contributions, to include Mr. W. Webster, delighting the squaddies with his Cockney sketches, and Peggy Sharpe, recounting a formidable selection of Lancashire monologues.

One well-meaning young lady, in aid of funds for those Bletchley men now held as POWs, even arranged for local soldiers to explore their own uncharted talent although it perhaps may be a little cruel to intimate that possibly some of these renditions might well have heightened the captives' appreciation of their present predicament.

Spicing things up, fresh from her recent cavortings in cabarets of the West End, at the Conservative Club Miss Dell presided over a very successful fancy dress dance while, as members of the National Academy of Dancing, Mr. and Mrs. Kirby - winners of several bronze and silver medals - staged a dance at the same venue, as part of their efforts to raise money for a Bletchley Dancing Academy.

By now, the organisation of local dances had largely polarised into a friendly rivalry between a gentleman who lived at 31, Osborne Street and a gentleman who lived at 10, Albert Street - except, that is, for one memorable occasion when toes, metaphorically speaking, were severely trodden on.

One of the parties had unwittingly booked a hall on the same night that the other had arranged a dance and, in the best traditions of human psyche, he was not best pleased.

In fact he marched straight round to the upstart's home intending to have rather sharp words, but unfortunately got rather carried away and smacked him in the eye.

Glasses askew, blood streaming from his nose, the object of his annoyance then retaliated with some vigorous face slapping, at which his assailant selected a choice piece of nearby fencing and whacked him over the head.

Unsubdued, the householder then ran inside, grabbed his wife's broomstick and proceeded to flail his antagonist until the broom handle broke.

In terms of entertainment value, no doubt these antics were well on a par with their more usual pursuits, but now saner forces had to prevail and one of the battling barmpots was hauled off for a spot of attitude correction at the local nick-and a consequent fine - while as passably a badge of courage, the other proudly sported a stitched eyebrow.

Oh yes, that to soothe the savage breast in these troubled times, Bletchley could indeed rest safely assured that for the organisation of dances and music, matters were surely in the most capable of hands!

Sunday Citizen August 25, 2002

WARTIME ESCAPEES: GREAT ESCAPE WAS FULL-TIME

In a previous article mention was made of Captain Gerald Knight RAF who during the First World War escaped from an enemy prison camp and made it back to England.

He was the son of a former Rector of Bow Brickhill church and it was somewhat ironic that during the same period - not many miles from Bow Brickhill - was a camp for German prisoners of war.

Indeed several made bids for freedom with one being recaptured emerging from a wood at Battlesden and another in Hockliffe.

As for British POWs another to have experienced incarceration in a German camp was Ernest Marchant who in 1924 set up a solicitor's in Bletchley's Red House.

He would cycle from his home at Woburn Sands, having secured an arrangement to use the toilet facilities at Fenny Stratford station.

Ernest was born in North London on May 12th 1887. Enlisting in the army at the outbreak of the First World War he married Elsie Cotching 'a rare golden-haired beauty' and after military training with the Public Schools Battalion served with the 18th Royal Fusiliers - the Public School Fusiliers.

He became a musketry instructor but after the Somme and seeing a friend returning wounded - for the second time - he asked for a posting to the front.

Aged 26 he was commissioned as a Lieutenant in the 17th Middlesex and at the assault on Beaumont Hamel on November 13th was one of the few to penetrate the German lines.

A grenade put an end to his war and on being taken prisoner he was escorted to the German rear.

As a POW Ernest kept himself occupied by writing, producing and performing in camp shows - and making two attempts to escape.

Even after the Armistice in 1918 he was still a prisoner and with no prospect of early release he and two others got under the wire and reached Denmark in an open fishing boat, almost dying of exposure.

Ernest would eventually be joined in the firm by his two sons and he died aged 80 in 1967.

These days, as made famous by several films, more well-known are stories of prison camps during the Second World War and with British bombers over enemy territory it was inevitable many allied airmen would come to sample their dubious hospitality.

In the later stages of the war one was Jack Bromfield, of Albert Street, Bletchley.

Among the crew of a Halifax III bomber of 158 Squadron he was shot down on January 5th 1945 during a raid to Hanover.

Despite injuring his ankle on landing Jack remained on the run but on January 13th was captured and sent to a prison camp.

The bomber was shot down by night fighter ace Heinz Rokker (who with 65 kills was awarded the Knights Cross with Oak Leaves).

Incredibly, the former adversaries were reunited when Jack, who still lives in Bletchley, stayed with Herr Rokker in Germany.

Another Bletchley airman prisoner was Thomas Cloran whose Lancaster was hit by flak over France in 1944.

Preparing to bail out he saw a young engineer holding back. Realising he had no parachute Tom held on to him and they jumped together.

Sadly the engineer lost his grip and fell helplessly to earth.

On landing Tom made his way to a farmhouse where two old ladies agreed to hide him but his injuries and burns were so severe they had no choice but to surrender him to the Germans.

After treatment Tom wrote to his wife: "Out of hospital, much better, don't worry. Food is good thanks to Red Cross, kiss the children - be home soon."

Many months of captivity followed and he would be interned in a camp in Poland for 12 months until the long trek made by all the POWs held in eastern Europe before the Russian advance.

At the end of the war Tom returned to his home in Staple Hall Road and took up his former employment.

As for the two old ladies - they were shunned by villagers who thought they had betrayed the airman.

Hearing this, Tom returned to Poigny le Feret near Paris to set the record straight. One of the ladies had died but the other, Mdme Langdale, was still being ostracised until Tom revealed the real reason for their action.

He began a grocery store and delicatessen in Bletchley Road, later becoming a supermarket manager in Reading.

Perhaps the most harrowing experience was that of Lance Corporal Stan Corby of Oxford Street, ordered to be shot by Himmler. He was captured during the Italian campaign spending 18 months in Stalag 4c in Czechoslovakia.

Following his fourth escape attempt the execution order was imposed but listening to a secret wireless set he and other inmates knew the war was almost over and with little to lose they hid a revolver and shot their way out of the camp.

They were rescued by the Americans and flown home.

After seven weeks leave Stan returned to army life.

In concluding there is one story that neatly links the experiences of a British POW during the First World War with the liberties won by those who sacrificed their own freedom or life during both wars.

In April 1947 at St. Mary's Church, Bletchley, Muriel Ellingham married William Mason, the son of Mr. and Mrs. J. Mason of Edgware.

The couple were invited to spend their honeymoon with a family in Belgium after a chance meeting during the First World War by Muriel's father who, as a liberated POW, was making his way through Liege with a friend, when a family offered him hospitality. The friendship continued through the years and when the Belgians heard his only daughter was to be married they extended their invitation to the newly weds.

WARTIME IN THE BARN

Nationally, 1942 began as a very bleak year, writes local historian John Taylor. Even Bletchley Park would have little success, for with the Germans shortly to change the Enigma key for U boats, these transmissions would become virtually secure, leading to almost unsustainable shipping losses in the Atlantic.

Perhaps it was therefore not surprising that a day of continuous prayer was held in St. Martin's Church on January 1st in response to an appeal by the Archbishop of Canterbury.

Elsewhere in the town, various organisations were doing their best to maintain morale and the Rest Room Committee reported that the room - actually a brick building next to the Methodist Hut in Bletchley Road - was open for evacuees between 2pm and 6pm.

In other entertainments, a dance at the Senior School Hall featured the Melody Makers Dance Band from Woburn Sands, and the Spurgeon Baptist Church hosted a Youth Week.

For youth activities of a more permanent nature, good progress was being made with the new Service of Youth sports ground in Albert Street, where with the fencing complete, work now began to renovate the pavilion.

Eventually facilities would be available for football, hockey and netball with the ATC, Boys' Brigade and Boy Scouts having the alternate use on Saturdays during the season.

Former members retain fond memories of the club, including the lady whose reminiscence of The Barn is now recalled.

Sixty years ago, in the summer of 1942, the Bletchley Co-operative Society offered the youth of the town the use of the sports pavilion and sports ground at the top of Park Street and Albert Street.

The pavilion was in a very poor state and the understanding was that the young people would clean it and paint the windows with black paint (curtains were not possible) for the black out. They were given some rations in order to have cheese rolls, etc, and cups of tea.

Marjorie Wells (later Leonard, now sadly passed away) was a terrific artist and she would design the decorations for the various theme evenings, for example Halloween, etc.

Somebody also provided a small wind-up gramophone with a supply of records - in the main Victor Sylvester.

Mr. Horlock, the manager of Flettons Brickworks, was in charge and he was very kind, unobtrusive and the young people really responded to him.

All in all there used to be 30 to 40 people who used the facility, but of course some of the lads were called up during the war. The club was open several evenings a week, but Saturday evenings were something special with dances being held.

Unfortunately after the war people grew up, started to go their own way, and the spirit of the club died.

However, fond memories are still recalled of the good times spent there - so much so that one former member would be interested in arranging a reunion for any 'old members'.

Sunday Citizen December 1, 2002

WARTIME LIFE

We start our column this week by reading that in 1943 a local minister has suddenly upped sticks and done a runner for reasons totally unspecified while a village vicar has been hurriedly put out to grass for instructing the choirboys in rather more than singing practice!

Still, on a more positive note the Freeman Memorial Church raised £10 for the National Children's Home by carol singing and a concert while in St. Martin's Hall a short service had been held for the Army Cadet Force and other town youth organisations. Meanwhile at a social evening in the Salvation Army hall it was a joyous occasion when 45 scouts and guides waved goodbye to fellow scout Albert Blackwell, off to take his place at the Front.

For those on leave, Mr. Papworth's band provided community singing entertainment and the Billeting Officer, Mr. Jones, also boosted morale by arranging a selection of film shows.

Yet despite the uncertainty of the times, as always romance could blossom and at the wedding of two of the town's more prominent religious workers the Methodist Scouts formed a guard of honour.

The bride, a lay preacher, had been teaching at a local school while, as a native of Liverpool the groom, the Rev. Arthur Yates, had not long arrived in the town.

They probably would not have approved of the antics of a group of American airmen, who managed to persuade a young lady to participate in some rather unorthodox night manoeuvres.

Elsewhere the Bletchley Fur Fanciers Society was a recently formed offshoot from the previous Bletchley and District Fur and Feather Domestic Club.

Gardeners were not forgotten and at their gardeners Brains Trust the first groundbreaking question was 'Are parsnips worth growing?'

This sorted those a few peas short of a pod from those who knew their onions, and it was finally decided that parnsips would be an excellent standby if the brussel sprouts failed.

Perhaps it was opportune that at 73, Bletchley Road, Weatherheads were putting their 49ft by 12ft greenhouse, complete with heating installation, up for sale - a snip for anyone with £35 to spare.

Now back from her honeymoon in Richmond, as Captain of the 2nd Bletchley Methodist Guide Company Mrs. Yates was holding a party in the Bletchley Road church and to enliven proceedings all the scouts came along as well.

Meanwhile, at St. Martin's Church the Rev. Wheeler announced to a hushed annual meeting of the Church Council that the Rev. Snell would be leaving the town to seek 'wider experience' - in Willenhall - and his place would eventually be taken by the Rev. Sutters, from Oxford.

Bletchley United Christian Council, fearing it would lead to a commercialisation of the Sabbath, were up in arms about a recent council decision to sanction the opening of local studios on Sundays.

The manager of the Studio Cinema was hardly in a Christian frame of mind when someone pinched his cinema screen!

Further violating the Ten Commandments, the husband of a local pub landlady was then discovered to be having an affair with a woman in Victoria Road and a decree nisi resulted.

However, at least for the local Baptists perhaps happier times were prophesised by the welcome arrival of the Rev. Walter Richardson, fulfilling a position left vacant, for some 18 months, by the mysterious disappearance of the previous incumbent.

With all this scandal around it could drive a person to drink and small wonder that the bar takings of the Bletchley Workingmen's Club were £2,000 up on the previous year.

So we close our brief glimpse at religious affairs in Bletchley, played out with the joyful news that the last instalment had just been paid on the Freeman Memorial's new piano.

Sunday Citizen October 13th 2002

WARTIME MISDEMEANOURS

This week we take a look at how times have changed in punishment for criminal activities by turning the clock back 60 years to World War Two.

We start with the tale of three Bletchley boys who received six strokes of the birch when all they'd done was smash their way into a railway hut and pinch a few inconsequential items, (not to mention a yellow flag, binoculars and cooking utensils).

Although this was not the first time they had been in trouble, with a shameful disregard of their personal dignity at their appearance at the Juvenile Court, they were told they were a disgrace to their parents and the town.

Meanwhile, other culprits were also proving a nuisance by stealing pieces off a Messerschmitt Me 109, displayed in the grounds of the Bletchley Road Senior School.

However, perhaps this was understandable in view of being charged 3d to sit in the cockpit.

In other misdoings, by contravening the blackout regulations, a fine of 7s 6d was imposed on Mr. Judge for cycling without a light at 11.15pm.

Asked to explain himself, he brightly countered that he couldn't keep his oil lamp alight in the wind - hardly surprising since he didn't have any matches.

Also contravening the regulations, a resident of Park Street was more than a mite miffed when fined £1, with 5s costs, for 'displaying a light from a chimney'.

The pots had caught fire.

In an excuse worthy of our present railway authorities, he suggested that perhaps 'the sweep's rods could not have been long enough'!

Evacuees sometimes proved an unwitting problem, as a woman at Brooklands Farm discovered to her cost. Attending to the blackout, she was suddenly distracted by thoughts of a steak and kidney pudding, that was on the boil for her evacuees supper.

Rushing to move the saucepan, she completely forgot about the blackout and promptly earned herself a £1 fine, when she switched on the light.

Of more pleasing matters, the caring side of youth paid a welcome visit when the Methodist Youth Circle discussed 'drink problems in wartime', whilst at the annual distribution, prizes were presented to members of the Baptist Church Sunday School.

Helping to steer the young on the straight, and narrow, it was decided to form a Bletchley youth organisation, for those not involved with the existing movement.

Six boys had been hauled before the Juvenile Court for taking sandbags from houses and piling them up in the road and their defence was not greatly helped by the fact that during the blackout the local Pc had crashed into the heap, chainwheel over crossbar.

Even some local traders were up to no good, including a local licensee who swapped one bar for a complete set of bars when he was caught trading meat on the black market.

At least in name, another character then proved worthy of his produce when caught flogging dodgy duck eggs at above the maximum price. He'd palmed them off to an unsuspecting lady on condition that she didn't bring them back, which she didn't, for on finding every single one to be bad she went straight to the Bletchley Food Office instead.

During his consequent interview, the trader admitted he had bought 45 duck eggs for 9s but couldn't remember who he'd bought them from. Perhaps the fine of £2 with £1 6s costs helped jog his memory.

Another shopkeeper also came a cropper when he tried to sell a jar of sweet pickles at above the regulation price. Just his luck, the cus¬tomer turned out to be an assistant from the Chief Inspector's Office!

As for Mr. Kemp of Bengal Farm, fortune had certainly gone walkies the day he let his cows go walkies through a gap in a rotten fence. Off they trundled to Mr. Speed's house, at 146, Buckingham Road, where in contented fashion they promptly 'ate everything in the garden'.

Before Mr. Speed and Mr. Kemp could lock horns, however, a fine of £5 sorted out the matter.

Cows in the garden were one thing but tanks down the back lanes were quite another, unfortunately with tragic results. On army manoeuvres, just off the Buckingham Road, a lieutenant was directing one of his tanks into a gateway when there was an almighty crash.

Coming round the bend, a motorcyclist had smashed headlong into the parked traffic and was thrown under the tracks of the tank. One of the army personnel died from the consequent injuries.

Sunday Citizen January 26, 2003

WARTIME SCOUTING IN BLETCHLEY

It seems that the Scouts may be re-introducing Bob a Job Week. With the garden chalet in need of a couple of coats of weatherproofing, there could be no better way to expend 5 pence. But on the downside I suppose I'll have to supply the preservative. Bob a Job Week used to be a regular feature of the Scouting year, usually mundane tasks, but during World War Two there was nothing mundane about the tasks they performed in the defence of the nation, not least at Bletchley. In fact with the imminence of war the local Scoutmaster had organised messengers for immediate service, and so it was just as well that the Bletchley Scouts would, in view of the worsening situation, stay within their district instead of going to camp at Salcombe, Devon. As throughout the country schoolchildren were being evacuated from London to safer places, and at Bletchley in early December 1939 the Bletchley Girl Guides provided a room on Sundays in St. Martin's Hall, sometimes known as the Social Centre, for mothers visiting their evacuated children. As for one mother she could feel especially proud of her son Maurice. An 11 year old evacuee from Islington, he was now living at Water Eaton, and having saved his five year old companion from drowning, whilst fishing in the canal, received the Gilt Cross for Gallantry from the Boy Scouts' Association. The end of January 1940 witnessed a meeting to organise a Group Committee for the newly formed 1st Fenny Stratford (St. Martin's) Scout Troop, which a while later held a camp at Great Brickhill in camouflaged tents. As for other measures, by early 1940 many Rover Scouts (an advanced form of Scouting, 'enabling young men to obtain the benefit of Scout training') were providing much useful service as Wardens, First Aid Workers and Messengers. Yet there was also entertainment to lighten the tension, and in aid of the Scout funds a 'tanner hop' took place at St. Martin's Hall on Friday, January 26th 1940. This had been organised by the Bletchley Fire Brigade Social Club, and there was a certain irony when a call was received to attend a fire at the Observer Corps post! With the need to accommodate more evacuees in the town, in September 1940 temporary sleeping quarters were prepared at the Bletchley Road Schools, and with Mr.. Sherwood, the Clerk of the Council, having managed to obtain 600 empty palliasses, members of the Boy Scouts and Boys' Brigade swiftly filled these with straw, assisted by the Guides. Later in the year another good deed was recognised when Thomas Allen, of 10, Saffron Street, a Patrol Leader in the 1st Fenny Stratford (St. Martin's) Boy Scouts, was awarded the Parchment of the Royal Humane Society. This was for having in August saved nine year old Cyril Ellis, of 31, Saffron Street, from drowning, when he got into difficulties whilst bathing in the Mill Pond at Water Eaton. Concluding 1940, with the Guides and Brownies as their guests on Saturday, December 30th the 1st Fenny Stratford (St. Martin's) Boy Scouts Troop held their first annual party in St. Martin's Hall, at which Private Douglas Cliffe, 'an old Scout,' entertained the audience with various impressions. The members of the Troop then made their own impression in September 1941 when, by working in squads of four, they began assembling the recently arrived Morrison indoor air raid shelters in the town. In fact despite weighing more than 7 cwt., and with over 200 parts, three Scouts would construct one table in the record time of 25 minutes. With the blackout now in force there could be no outdoor campfires, but on November 12th, 1941 as a substitute the members of the Troop held a 'Radio Campfire' in St. Martin's Vicarage Room, with each patrol giving a number of skits on popular radio features. Today, in our soft society in some quarters there has been a perception that Scouting is perhaps not 'cool.' However, in time of peace or war their standards have always been of the highest. With the Chief Scout being an S.A.S. veteran, who's going to argue.

WEATHERHEADS: HISTORY OF A FAMILY FIRM

Around 1900, Fanny Isobella Alderman, from Swanbourne, married Edward Weatherhead and, having lived in Kent and Wendover, prior to World War One the couple moved to Bletchley.

Here, Mr. Weatherhead became a gardener at Elmers, a school that was situated near St. Mary's Church. Then, as one of the earliest commercial developments in that part of the town, in the mid-1920s he converted two houses, nos 71 and 73 Bletchley Road (now Queensway), and began in business as a florist, fruiterer, and seedsman.

At no 71 a confectionery and cooked meats shop was started two years later and, after employment in the greenhouses at Bletchley Park, Mrs. Weatherhead's niece, Miss Elsie Alderman, began work in the new family business.

Tragically, in 1929 Edward was knocked down by a car and killed at Water Eaton crossroads but his widow continued the business and, on October 17th 1931, replaced the greengrocery business at no 73, (now 103, Queensway) with a music and radio shop. This would be successfully run by her younger son Herbert (Bert) and her daughter Gertrude (Trudy).

In addition to Bert and Trudy there were three other offspring: Edward Cecil, (popularly known as Cecil), Leslie and Elsie. Leslie had a senior position with the

Post Office and Elsie married George Morgan. (Their son, Paul, would become senior organist at Exeter Cathedral).

Becoming 'a reasonably able' carpenter, during his early teens, Bert had helped Fred Higgs, his close friend and cabinetmaker, in Fred's workshop at 19, Regent Street (no 17a has now been built on the site of the garden), and in 1931 he asked Fred to help him run the radio and music business.

The friends duly started working together, and with Bert having obtained the Murphy dealership in 1931 (at the age of 16!) for the radios Bert had made from kits, Fred made the cabinets.

As for the confectionery and cooked meat shop, in July 1940 Mrs. Isabella Weatherhead retired from running the business and, thanking customers for their loyalty, announced that her eldest son, Edward Cecil, would now continue the shop. Married to Madge Thurlow in 1928, Cecil had begun his working life at the Co-op Bakery but later joined the LMS Railway, where he stayed for seven years. For a year he then ran a poultry farm in Stoke Road before purchasing a grocery store at the corner shop, 79, Victoria Road.

His mother died at her home at 1, Leon Avenue in 1941 aged 66. Although the funeral took place in March 1941, the month also witnessed a less sombre event when her youngest son, Herbert, married Gladys Hurst of 35, Leon Avenue. Gladys was the daughter of Albert Hurst, who had been the manager at Randalls engineering works in Bletchley Road until it closed in 1926. At the age of 45, he then not only designed his own home - on his former allotment - but also began a general engineering works in Denmark Street, which in fact continued until recent years.

Following the outbreak of World War Two, with military requirements now obviously paramount, by 1942 Weatherheads Radio business was engaged in fitting radio apparatus into American tanks, and on joining the RAF Bert Weatherhead was involved at Potsgrove on wireless work for the Secret Service.

Fred Higgs also joined the RAF and, although he was initially involved in servicing the radio equipment fitted to American Liberator bombers, he was later also posted to secret broadcast duties at the radio station at Gawcott, near Buckingham. The story of this secret wireless section is told in the book *Bletchley Park's Secret Sisters.*

As for Cecil, by the direction of himself and the personal representatives of his late mother, the freehold smallholding known as The Poultry Farm, on the outskirts of Water Eaton, came up for auction at the Park Hotel on Wednesday February 25th 1942. Comprising 28 acres, which were currently let at £61 pa, it would be purchased for £1,075 by Mr. Valentin, of Stoke House.

Also on an agricultural theme, in early 1943 a greenhouse was offered for sale - 49ft x 12ft complete with heating installation - at Weatherheads, 73, Bletchley Road and, although the nearest offer to £5 would secure, the purchaser had to arrange the dismantling and removal. Then at the same premises in September half a ton of rockery stone came up for sale, or perhaps the proceeds helped Mr. Weatherhead to buy Tudor House in Western Road the following month for the sum of £340.

With the continuing call-up, Ron Pearson, and John Oliffe, two former employees of Weatherheads, were now serving in the RAF and around the beginning of 1944 they had an amazing coincidence when they met in a Glasgow street. Not only did they discover that they were taking the same course, but also that they had been assigned billets at the same house, an old warehouse!

John, of 9, Leon Avenue, would later be attached to Radio SEAC which, as well as producing the Forces Radio Times from studios in Colombo, Ceylon, also broadcast programmes to the British Forces in the Far East. In fact, during 1946 thoughts of home were kindled for Signalman Ken Buckingham, serving abroad at Ahmednagar, by a programme for which John held responsibility. As one of a series of programmed entitled Sunday in the Park, this was a selection of brass band music which had been played one Sunday afternoon by a band in Central Gardens, Bletchley.

Long since demolished, Central Gardens was a pleasant local amenity, the site of which is now partly covered by Princes Way, opposite the Leisure Centre.

At the end of May 1945, Mr. William Johns took over the grocery business from Cecil Weatherhead at 79, Victoria Road, which had now been established for nine years. Persons who had been registered with Cecil were automatically transferred for their rationed goods to the new proprietor, who would continue trading at the premises until his death in 1950.

Cecil died one Thursday in early December 1945 at the age of 39, leaving a widow and two young boys, Terry and David. After his father's death, the latter would for many years carry on the grocery business at 71, Bletchley Road, with his mother and Sam Whitlock.

Claiming that they could provide a service "in the shortest possible time", with the end of the war Weatherheads Radio shop could now direct their priorities to the retailing and repair business. In September 1945, they purchased a small supply of domestic appliances, which not only included a small number of bowl fires at 26s 3d including Purchase Tax, but also some of the first post-war Murphy radios.

Although televisions were not available, the firm realised the potential for their popularity and, duly declaring that the technology had made great strides, stated that 'after the war a set will probably come within the means of many householders. Then of course they will turn to Weatherheads, pioneers of Television in Bletchley.'

Weatherheads held the first public demonstration of television in the town in 1946 at St. Martin's Hall, where Fred and Bert erected a 40ft pole to pick up the relatively poor-quality signals from the Alexandra Palace transmitter. With only one channel, and within limited transmission times, initially these demonstrations were in black and white on a 9-inch screen. But to prepare for the anticipated demand, in addition to their shop at 73, Bletchley Road, from Monday May 27th 1946 they would also trade from premises at 33, Aylesbury Street. Here, to coincide with the re-opening of television programmes, television sets were demonstrated on Friday June 7th. On the following day at the Assembly Rooms of the Conservative Club, the company held further viewings which, watched by an audience of around 600 people, featured the Victory Celebrations in London.

Apart from televisions the firm also dealt in many other electrical goods and in February 1947 they were appointed as agents for Hoover vacuum cleaners: 'Supplies are limited but demonstrations will be given and orders taken for early delivery.'

Nevertheless, televisions remained the predominant novelty and, in the company of around 50 other people in May 1947 a young David Higgs (the son of Fred Higgs) remembers sitting cross-legged on the floor in Weatherheads showroom from midday to 5pm., watching the first-ever television transmission of the Cup Final, between Burnley and Charlton. (Charlton were the winners, with the winning and only goal scored by Duffy).

In 1950, David then joined the firm, which at this period was still providing a service charging the lead acid cells (accumulators) needed to power radios, since many homes did not have mains electricity. The firm operated a van service to collect and deliver accumulators for customers in the surrounding villages. A high standard of technical knowledge was of course a prerequisite for the engineers of the company, as proved by Philip Tandy of 7, North Street who, during a competition held in 1947 by the Radio Society of Great Britain, had been recognised as the second best radio 'ham' in the country. Having held his licence since 1933, from one Saturday night to 9am the next morning, via his home-made radio set, he had managed to communicate with 86 other 'hams' - a feat that the winner could beat by only 12 contacts.

That same year, on Saturday May 31st, the wedding took place of Pam Tricker, the only daughter of Major and Mrs. Tricker, of Maida Hill, London, and Neville Bedford, the youngest son of Mr. and Mrs. J. Bedford of 1, Model Cottages, Newton Longville. The couple had met during the war when Major Tricker was stationed at Bletchley Park, and both had been employees at Weatherheads.

In fact, on Saturday, November 9th of the previous year, Trudy Weatherhead had married Edgar Bedford, of Newton Longville, who having been an army staff sergeant during the war was now employed as chief motor mechanic by the Bletchley Co-op. Among the wedding gifts had been a Pyrex dish in a silver stand, given by the staff of the Weatherheads shop, while in recognition of Trudy's musical talents a congratulatory telegram was sent from Stanly Riley and

Margaret Rees, the BBC singers who had often sung to her accompaniment in the Baptish church.

An accomplished organist, in 1947 Trudy sat for the examinations for Associate membership of the Royal College of Organists and after her assessment at Kensington she would be awarded an ARCO degree. As the resident organist at the Spurgeon Memorial Baptish church in Aylesbury Street, Bletchley (now the site for a new development of retirement homes), she had written many songs for the church including Bedford, so named because the BBC Singers, who lived in Bedford, had once especially come to the church to perform a concert. In fact, after the war the tune, now renamed Bletchley, would be accepted as a hymn in the new Baptish Church Hymnal, published in 1962. As for her other works, a well known firm of music publishers accepted compositions submitted in 1946 and 1950 for inclusion in Sacred Children's Songs.

Due to the increasing competition from supermarkets, at 71, Bletchley Road the established retail grocery business of Weatherheads was finally closed in July 1961. The premises were then incorporated into no 73, and, after a major refurbishment, formed an additional and more spacious display and retail area for the radio and television shop.

Weatherheads Television continued to expand throughout the 1960s and the 1970s and eventually became a group of 15 branches in the Bucks, Beds and Herts area.

Sadly, Bert Weatherhead died in 1971 after unsuccessful heart surgery, and, due to pressure from supermarkets and national companies, the business closed in December 2001.

It had finally become too expensive to provide the personal service for which the firm was deservedly renowned.

WINTERS OF YESTERYEAR

The recent wintry conditions have come as rather a shock to many people, with transport disrupted, schools closed, and many working days lost to industry.

So goodness knows how the country managed when harsh winters were the norm, rather than the exception.

My own memory stretches back to struggling into school for weeks on end in 1963, when any attempt not to do so was met with suitable admonishment. There could certainly be no excuse for temerity in 1939/1940, for with the country fighting for its very survival a few feet of snow was the least of the worries. At 30, Windsor Street, Bletchley, one of those then resident in the town was Herbert Bennett, the chief rose grower for Ramsbotham's Nursery, and throughout the war he kept a diary which included many local events.

By the kind permission of his grandson, David Higgs, and his cousins, I have recently been privileged to access these pages, and the following quotes reveal just how severe the weather was.

Regarding December 29th 1939 the entry includes; "Saturday morning opened with the roads and pavements like glass. A proper silver thaw and there were several minor accidents to people slipping up."

As for January 1st; "--- severe frost and the roads like ice, making travelling very treacherous."

Then for January 22nd 1940; "The first thing I must mention is the weather. It has been bitterly cold with 24-30 degrees of frost all the time. It started snowing yesterday afternoon and has been snowing all day today." As for a week later; "The weather has been the worst in living memory."

After the war severe winters remained a seasonal feature, and no doubt that of 1947 is remembered as the most notorious. Yet despite a blizzard, a small and distinguished company braved the elements at Bletchley on Monday, January 6th 1947 for the opening of Tompkins and Moss new showrooms - opposite their garage premises at Fenny Stratford - and in fact the weather had been very icy for several weeks, as indicated by the thermometer outside the Council Offices, which on Tuesday, January 28th recorded 23 degrees of frost.

Not surprisingly the conditions made driving extremely hazardous, and road users on the Watling Street had been inconvenienced on the afternoon of Thursday, January 23rd when, of a combined weight of about 80 tons, a fully laden tractor and trailer encountered difficulties on the icy surface near the Repeater Station. As the driver tried to pull up he collided with a lorry passing the other way, and by blocking the road broadside on caused a 12 mile tailback.

Nevertheless, despite the weather volunteer 'taxi' drivers were needed to ferry disabled guests to the Old Peoples Party at the Community Centre, in George Street, where on Saturday, February 1st the festivities were greatly enjoyed between 4.30p.m. and 8p.m.

The wintry conditions had even caused large ice floes to form on the canal, and a canal ice breaker had to be used to clear a passage, not least because several ice bound barges were laden with prefabricated parts for local house building. Then on the first Tuesday and Wednesday in March heavy snowfalls caused the biggest hold up of transport in living memory, and, with many villages isolated in North Bucks, a farmer's wife drove a tractor from Swanbourne all the way to Bletchley, to fetch the shopping for herself and the villagers. As equally enterprising was a Wavendon man, who wearing an Alpine outfit reached Bletchley on skis. As for Winslow, there was a huge cheer at the market place when the Co-op bread van got through.

Thus when people nowadays complain about the inconvenience of a few days' of ice and snow, don't be surprised if amongst a certain generation this meets with an icy smile, and a somewhat chilly response.

WW2 CASUALTIES

A stalwart breed prevailed in 1940 with qualities much needed to deal with the increasingly harsh realities of war, especially when news arrived of the death of a loved one, a relative or a friend.

Such an occasion was the tragic loss of Peter Meadows, the first Bletchley man to be killed in action. The minesweeper, aboard which he served as a signaller, received a direct hit.

A second fatality was that of Frank Nurshaw of 61, Duncombe Street, who at the age of 34, was killed on the Western Front.

Before the war he had served for several years as a soldier but then left to work on the railways until the declaration of hostilities, when he found himself called up as a reservist.

News as equally distressing could be brought when soldiers were posted as missing, for until official notification arrived, it could only be hoped that they were prisoners of war.

In fact Private George Shackleton, a Bletchley lad from Brooklands Road, had been initially reported as missing but was later confirmed as a POW.

However, the fate of Corporal Jack Wise, aged 21, still remained unknown, he being the only son of the late Mr. Warren Wise, who had once practised as a dentist in Bletchley Road.

Another uncertainty concerned Sapper Frank Cheney, a member of the Royal Engineers, but on a happier note, advancing through the ranks Second Lieutenant Ellingham gained promotion to Captain. His had so far been quite an eventful war, for having been evacuated from Boulogne he later returned to France, only to be evacuated once again, from Cherbourg.

Amongst those now enjoying the hospitalities of a German prison camp, Private Robinson of the Oxon and Bucks Light Infantry was held in Stalag XXA 3A whilst Sgt Souster RA languished as an inmate at Stalag XXIB.

Meanwhile, back in Bletchley, at last some good news arrived when Mrs. Plumb, of Brooklands Road, learned that her husband, although in hospital, remained otherwise well.

Mrs. Adney, of Osborne Street, also received a card from her husband, saying he was 'comfortable' in Stalag V111B, along with another Bletchley soldier, Henry Mason.

Less fortunate, however, were the wife and young son of John Whitfield, formerly the manager of Wyman's bookstall, for confirmation came through that he had been lost on active service.

Official notification was also received regarding the fate of Engineer Commander Chappell.

For many years he had worked in the offices of Rowland Bros before then going to the L&NW loco sheds as a fitter.

During World War One he served as an engineering officer on merchant transports and at the outbreak of World War Two was engaged as chief engineer on the SS Matakana, before volunteering for the Navy.

As the war dragged on, so the casualties inevitably increased, including another member of the Oxon and Bucks Territorials, Charles Essen.

Called to the colours at the outbreak of war, he later transferred to the Royal Engineers but was killed just a few weeks later.

His burial took place at Bouin cemetery but for those whose remains were brought back to Bletchley, an especial area of the churchyard was set aside.

However, as we shall see, with several years of conflict still ahead, even this could soon prove insufficient.

Sunday Citizen August 11, 2002

BOW BRICKHILL

ALL SAINTS CHURCH, BOW BRICKHILL

All Saints Church, Bow Brickhill, has achieved national renown from having been the setting for the painting 'A Village Choir,' by the famous artist Thomas Webster. This - which portrayed real village characters - was exhibited at the Royal Academy in 1847, being bequeathed in 1857 to the Victoria and Albert Museum by John Sheepshanks, for whom it had been painted. Situated 535 feet above sea level, All Saints Church is first recorded in 1185, and, with the nave and chancel dating from the 12th century, saw the addition of the tower in the 15th century, plus the north and south aisles. Becoming the alleged haunt of poachers, during the late 17th century the church fell into disrepair, but was restored by the lord of the manor, Browne Willis, in 1756/7.

As such a lofty vantage, during the Napoleonic war the tower was used as a telegraph station, and during World War One the prominence served as a look out post during Zeppelin alerts, with those on duty knowing that the danger had passed when the lights came back on at Bletchley station. During World War Two the tower proved an ideal vantage for the Royal Observer Corps, and when shortly after the war the church bells couldn't be rung the rector, of an enterprising nature, employed an electronic amplifier from Weatherheads, in Bletchley, to broadcast a recording of church bells! Presently the tower (from which on a clear day six counties are said to be visible) is in need of urgent restoration, and in consequence the villagers have formed the All Saints Tower Restoration Appeal.

Apart from having once been a reputed haunt for poachers, another disturbing tale is told from around the turn of the 19th century, when a man trying to open a grave on the south side of the church was disturbed by a watcher, who had been lying in wait in the church porch. The grave robber immediately opened fire, but was killed by the return fire. An addition of land, conveyed on February 17th 1904, enabled an eastwards extension of the churchyard, wherein lies buried Antliff Edward Burton, the son of a village schoolmaster. Antliff had been a popular member of the Aylesbury Street Primitive Methodist Chapel, in Fenny Stratford, and in appreciation of his services, both as organist and choirmaster, on Tuesday, February 13th 1917 he was presented with a handsome wristlet radium watch, on the occasion of having been called to the colours to join the Cyclist Section of the Queen's Own Oxfordshire Hussars, at Ipswich. Yet all too soon he would be the subject of another farewell, for, aged 18 years and 8 months, he died on March 29th 1917 from spotted fever, in the military hospital at Ipswich. Before joining up he had been a student teacher at Bow Brickhill Council Schools, and had recently passed the Oxford Local Examination.

Also buried in the churchyard is Charles Lake, an engineer and author of many books on railway matters. In fact in 1919 during a railway strike he blacklegged the strikers and drove a train from Bletchley to Euston. During his later years he lived at Bow Brickhill, and died in 1942. All Saints Church is one of the features in an interesting booklet recently issued by the Bow Brickhill History Society, and of other places of interest Plough House is mentioned, sitated at the beginning of the incline to the church. As a pub, this continued selling ale until the 1960s, and was the scene of a gruesome suicide in 1924, when the landlord cut his throat with a razor. Now the only pub in the village is the Wheatsheaf, a fairly modern building that replaced the 17th century thatched original, and for any persons interested in Bow Brickhill, from here copies of the booklet may still be available.

BOW BRICKHILL WAR MEMORIAL

Oh joy. Yes, in the wonderful world of work it's that time again - 'Appraisals'!

How times have changed. We never had those when I was a lad, but then we had 'Personnel Departments,' run by 'Personnel Managers.'

Of which, as I recall, one old dear in a previous life had been an MI6 operative, whilst the distinguished gent at Marconi Avionics had flown Lancasters during the war.

But now we have 'H.R.' Departments. Staffed mainly it seems by 25 to 35 something fillies, a decorative species for whom the sales team of Hello magazine must no doubt be truly thankful. It seems these denizens of the latter day all communicate in some strange tongue, whereby the 'bleedin obvious' is often expressed in terms of pretentious strangulation.

But enough of the present, and so to past times of national crisis, when regarding recruitment there was little time for frills or fancy. The outbreak of the First World War had caused few to think that this would be anything but short lived, but after Mons this notion was dispelled, and so came the need for 'Kitchener's Army.'

Yet as the conflict stagnated into trench warfare it became apparent that even this patriotic surge was insufficient, and so to provide potential replacements the Derby Scheme was introduced, whereby men could register their willingness to serve, and thus be called upon when needed.

However, not all were willing to serve, which then lead to conflict with the authorities when conscription was introduced. So on Friday, January 12th 1917, Lieutenant J. McFarlane, from the Bletchley Recruiting Office, represented the military at the Fenny Stratford Police Court when a young man of Bow Brickhill, claiming to be a conscientious objector, was charged with being an absentee from the Forces.

To this he pleaded not guilty, stating that he had a conscientious objection to all forms of military service. In evidence police constable Hedges said that the previous evening he had seen the man at his father's house at Bow Brickhill, and

told him he had orders for his arrest. The man said "All right," and was then taken to the police station. In court, Lieutenant McFarlane said that on December 16th an 'action' had been issued to the prisoner to report and join up. However, he had failed to comply, and when the chairman of the Tribunal asked if the man had been rejected by the military medical authorities, Lieutenant McFarlane said that he had been classed B1 Reserve, and, because this was a category in which men were not immediately required, had been told to go home until called.

Inspector Callaway, of the police, said that the man had been fined 40s last April for a similar charge, and that the money had been paid. On that occasion the prisoner was taken to Oxford, where after demanding a medical re-examination he was offered some papers, which he refused to accept.

The man confirmed that he had received the notice to join up, but had paid no attention to that, nor a letter from the Bletchley Recruiting Officer. In further evidence, Lieutenant McFarlane said the man had appealed to both the Local Military Service Tribunal and the Area Tribunal, but the verdict of each was that he was not a bona fide conscientious objector.

Saying that he would rather face the death sentence than do any military service, the prisoner was fined 40s and handed over to a waiting military escort, which took him the same day to Oxford.

Yet he didn't remain there for long, for the following morning he left by train and was driven from Bletchley to Bow Brickhill.

However, following a telephone message 'a man in blue' was waiting, and he was taken back to the police station. As for the sequel, in May 1917 at a meeting of the Newport Pagnell Board of Guardians it would be reported that a young man -'from a village near to Fenny Stratford' - who had been taken into the army against his will, had been admitted as a patient to the county asylum. As one member commented, "The Army have done him to death and sent him to the Asylum. It is a scandalous shame."

Payment would duly be sought from the War Office for the man's maintenance.

BROUGHTON

BROUGHTON: ST. LAWRENCE CHURCH, WALL PAINTINGS

At Broughton, consisting of a chancel, nave, south porch and embattled west tower, the church of St. Lawrence dates mainly from the late 13th and early 14th centuries, and from this period on the walls of the nave may be seen several magnificent 'morality paintings.' Having been covered over at an earlier date, they were discovered by the rector in 1849, and are amongst the finest to be seen in our region. As an age of general illiteracy, in medieval times the intent was to portray religious scenes to the congregation, and more especially the consequence of straying from the Biblical teachings. Thus it is no coincidence that on entering the church by the south door the first depiction to be seen - directly opposite, above the north doorway - is that of the Last Judgement. On the south wall is portrayed St. George on horseback, slaying the dragon, and also on the south wall are to be seen two figures, one of whom is holding a T shaped cross (known as the Tau Cross.) In fact this is held by St. Helena, the mother of the Emperor Constantine, who reputedly discovered the true cross. Beside her is probably St. Eloi, the patron saint of blacksmiths, since the tools of his trade are depicted below the painting. As for the north wall, here may be seen a 'Pieta,' ie. a representation of the mutilated body of Christ in his mother's arms.

Apart from the paintings, also of note in the church are two ancient chained books, resting on shelves either side of the chancel arch, and one, by Bishop John Jewel, is an 'Apologie,' or defence, of the Church of England. Regarding the nation's religion, between 1549 and 1662 the English Acts of Uniformity were passed, but with this provoking reaction from the 'Dissenters,' - those not accepting the established church - the Bishop's book, printed at Fleet Street, London, and dated 1567, is an early defence of the accepted practices of the Church at that time. In the then rector's handwriting, on the opening pages of the other book is recorded that its purchase was made in 1632 for the church and parish, the volume being by Erasmus and entitled a 'Paraphrase of the New Testament.' Erasmus, who occupied the Lady Margaret chair of Divinity and the chair of Greek at Cambridge in the early 16th century, attempted to introduce a more rational Christian doctrine, and in fact his tutor was William Grocyn, who, as a past rector of Newton Longville, is commemorated in the village church

by a brass on the north wall as the 'First Teacher of Greek in the University of Oxford.' In this day and age, the murals of Broughton church may be viewed on the appropriate web site, but for anyone wishing to see them as they were intended, please note that the key to the church door has to be inserted into the lock upside down!

CALVERTON

LADY GRACE BENNETT - BUTCHERED BY THE BUTCHER

Grace Norwood, the daughter of Gilbert Norwood. of London, became the wife (nine years his junior) of Simon Bennett, who through family descent had acquired the manors of Beachampton and Calverton.

He died at the age of 60, being buried at Beachampton on August 26th 1682, and thereafter Lady Bennett would live alone at the Calverton manor house.

However, she was widely disliked for her 'mean and covetous' ways, and being 'a terror to the village' she would have anyone found gathering firewood on her land severely beaten.

To ensure that her orders were being obeyed, she one day dressed in peasant's clothes and went about the fields to gather sticks, whereupon, in a commendable response, a keeper swiftly pounced. Feigning ignorance of his victim's identity, he then proceeded to administer a sound and thorough thrashing.

Lady Bennett would often neglect to pay her poor rates, and as a result was frequently hauled before the Justices at the Quarter Sessions.

She also proved rather reticent in paying her dues for highways maintenance, and, in further misdemeanours, in 1689 she was fined for having made a forced entry upon the lands and tenements of three of her Calverton neighbours.

Her skills in estate management also seemed amiss, and it was said that she kept all the arable land 'in her owne hands laid downe and untilled so that the parish is almost depopulated and the fields looke like a wildernesse little being moved and that which was generally so late and kept so long till it was spoyled.'

Many people believed that Lady Bennett kept a large fortune in the manor house, and this tempted a local butcher by the name of Barnes, or Bates (who had a shop in Stony Stratford, where the post office would later stand) to break in and relieve her of such worldly burdens.

However, she suddenly stumbled across him in the servants' quarters, and there she was brutally murdered for her interference. In fact the servants' hall remains little altered from that time, and has lately been used as a storeroom.

After the murder, the butcher escaped over the orchard wall into Gib Lane, but he could not evade an eventual justice and, in a room above the Cross Keys inn of Stony Stratford, he was convicted and sentenced to hang from the gibbet in Gib Lane.

With the execution complete, his body was left to swing in irons and rot.

On the outside of the orchard wall a stone may be seen - some three feet above the ground - on which are two crudely carved gibbets, flanked by the inscribed date '1693'.

It was said that this marks the position where the butcher escaped over the wall, but more probably it marks the site of the actual gibbet, since Lady Bennett was murdered on September 19th 1694, and the Beachampton registers record her burial on the 27th.

Whatever the explanation, there is little doubt regarding the fate of the butcher, for in an eye witness account Celia Fiennes, a lady famed for her 17th century travels throughout England on a donkey, would write '...and by the rich Mrs. Bennett's House remarkable for her coveteousness which was the cause of her death, her treasures tempted a Butcher to cut her throate, who hangs in chains just against her house.'

Perhaps of little surprise, both the murderer and his uncharitable victim are still said to walk their ghostly ways, and for many years in the servants' hall could be seen a red stained stone that defied all attempts to clean it.

However, when the stone was eventually taken up a natural red vein was found to run right through it!

CHICHELEY

GWEN FARRAR

Born on July 14th 1899, Gwen Farrar was one of the six daughters of George Farrar and his wife, Ella.

George had prospered in gold mining activities in South Africa, and during the Boer War would be mentioned in despatches and awarded the D.S.O. Then in 1902 he was knighted, and after the Boer War he became leader of the opposition in the first Transvaal Parliament. In 1911 he was created Baronet Farrar, for his role in the creation of the Union of South Africa, whilst in other activities, at a farm that he owned outside Johannesburg many prize winning cattle were bred.

Having rented Chicheley Hall, it would be here that he would stay whenever he was in England, and he and his family were in residence when the First World War broke out.

Intending to serve in France and Belgium, Sir George was instead sent to South Africa, but in 1915 he died in a tragic rail accident. Afterwards, Lady Farrar and her daughters continued to live at Chicheley Hall, and in January

1917 it was announced that, with honours, at the recent examinations of the London Royal Academy of Music, Miss Gwendoline Farrar had qualified in violoncello playing, and was entitled to use the letters L.R.A.M.

Indeed, she was billed as such when performing at two concerts at the Electric Theatre, Newport Pagnell, which included Gervase Elwes, a world renowned tenor. During the closing stages of the war, with Miss Norah Blaney, a singer and pianist, Gwen performed at concerts and entertainments for the troops in France and Belgium, and the pair continued their partnership after the war, appearing at leading theatres all over the country, including London.

In fact she soon became celebrated as a world class entertainer and a brilliant cellist, who delighted 'in making weird noises with her voice much to the discomfort of her partner,' Norah. In 1926 they went to New York to perform, and having begun a short professional partnership with Billy Mayerl, a popular pianist, it was due to her organisation that in March 1928, on the evenings of Monday 12th and Tuesday 13th an excellent variety entertainment took place in the Electric Theatre, Newport Pagnell. Here she sang syncopated songs, imitated animals and poultry in the farmyard, and then played the cello.

In fact despite her excellent musicianship her act always had a comical element, and for the theatrical effect she would sometimes go off the stage dragging her cello behind her, or slung over her shoulder! A few years after the war her mother, Lady Farrar, died at Chicheley Hall, from internal injuries sustained whilst moving furniture, in preparation for a children's party, and although some of Gwen's sisters would continue to live at the mansion, she, having been left a considerable financial sum by her father, divided her time between her 17th century country home in Northants, and 217, King's Road, Chelsea, which she maintained as a base for her musical career.

Renowned as a popular entertainer, she died after a short illness on Christmas Day 1944.

As for other musical talent from Chicheley, in the 1920s Lawrence Easson, the son of the local vicar, enjoyed radio fame when his song 'I wish I could go where the birdies go' was broadcast on 2L0 and 5XX. "It is a delightful composition and was greatly enjoyed by hundreds of listeners in this neighbourhood. The words and music of the song revealed Mr. Lawrence Easson as a composer of great promise and with an ability to suit the tastes of the music loving public. The song has not yet been published and printed." Oh, how we'd wish the same for that more recent birdie classic, 'Chirpy, Chirpy, Cheep, Cheep.'.....

CRANFIELD

GUY GIBSON

Oh dear. It seems that one of the nation's favourite 'luvvies' is trying to be ever so trendy, and tinge history with the airbrush of political correctness. Yes, in the remake of the film 'The Dambusters' apparently Guy Gibson's dog will now be named 'Digger,' and no doubt by the same token the Third Reich will be portrayed as a bunch of social reformers, who were just a little bit misunderstood. Yet it's hardly a surprise that throughout the war one of the main reasons that the BBC was avidly, if clandestinely, listened to by the oppressed peoples was that, in contrast to the enemy propaganda, the content could be trusted as factually accurate. Therefore it should be pretty obvious that those who seek to sanitise the past play straight into the hands of totalitarian regimes, by giving credence to ad hoc re-writes of the nasty bits. It's only by understanding the mistakes of the past that there can ever be hope for the future. The real story of the Dambusters is now well known, but perhaps less well known are the following two local connections. Of those who took part in the raid, one would be the grandson of the Reverend James Chadwick Maltby, the rector of Aspley Guise from 1880 until 1915, whilst as for Guy Gibson, he would spend three months as Chief Flying Instructor at Cranfield aerodrome. When the war finally arrived Cranfield was reformed as a Group Pool under No. 6 Group, providing replacement aircraft and personnel for the Advanced Air Striking Force in France, and in December 1939 hard runways of concrete were laid - in fact the first in Bedfordshire. With this work complete in April 1940 No. 14 Service Flying Training School arrived from Kinloss, and Cranfield was next transferred to No. 23 Group, Flying Training Command. It was then decided that the unit should concentrate on twin engine training using Airspeed Oxfords, and as the fighting intensified Cranfield came under attack from the Luftwaffe, and even until recent years several pillboxes and air raid shelters could still be seen. On consecutive nights in August 1940, 52 bombs plus incendiaries were dropped on the neighbourhood, but the decoy service units, dispersed in the surrounding fields, ensured that the bombs were widely scattered. Nevertheless Astwood church suffered damage, and a German parachute mine caused damage to several shops and houses in the High Street of Cranfield. In fact probably from the same raid another mine, complete with parachute, was discovered three weeks later hanging from a tree in Hulcote Wood. The bomb was detonated the following day by bomb disposal experts.

Throughout that year and into the next the German attacks continued, although the damage was fortunately limited to the creation of a few craters on the landing ground. In August 1941, No. 51 Operational Training Unit arrived at Cranfield for the instruction of night fighter crews, and the aerodrome now became part of No. 81 Group, Fighter Command. As recuperation from operational flying, during which he had not only destroyed enemy aircraft but also gained the DFC on December 29th 1941 Guy Gibson was posted to 51 OTU, and of the appointment he wrote in block capitals in his log book; 'WITH THE NEW YEAR I AM POSTED AS CFI TO 51 OTU CRANFIELD. THIS BEING HELD AS A REST FROM OPERATIONS!!!.' Yet with his duties being to organise the flying aspects of the courses, and monitor the progress of the trainee crews, he would do very little instructional flying, and soon began to yearn for operational service. In consequence he wrote to Air Marshall Arthur Harris, Commander in Chief of Bomber Command, and having attended an interview on March 12th 1942, two days later he was appointed as commander - at the age of 23 - of 106 bomber squadron, Coningsby. Subsequently he would become involved with 617 Squadron, and of course the rest is history. Let's keep it an accurate history, shall we, and not one 'dogged ' by political correctness.

CUBLINGTON

CUBLINGTON AIRPORT RESISTANCE CAMPAIGN

One of the joys (!) of living in Milton Keynes is that whilst all the amenities of pseudo city life are on the doorstep - big brand name shopping centres, sporting facilities, entertainment venues etc. - by virtue of the grid roads a ten minute drive can pierce these urban bounds, and transport one back to that green and once pleasant land of rural England; a land of country pubs, cosy thatched cottages, and quaint village tearooms. Perhaps even now within the farthest depths may lie communities as yet unknown to civilised man, and where the rustics still practise such timeless pursuits as wurzel chomping, or fondling ferrets; where yokels throng the muddy tracks to gawp in awe at the passage of a flying machine. On which subject, not so long ago there was a real threat that flying machines would sweep away much of the local farming acres, for Cublington was scheduled to become the site of London's third airport. However, by a long and hard fought battle the residents of the area saw off the authorities, and the intriguing tale is told in the DVD 'Over our Dead Bodies.' (www.stewkleyfilms.org). So thanks to their yeoman tenacity Cublington remains an unspoilt village in an unspoilt setting, and in a field to the west may be still be seen the 'Beacon,' an ancient artificial mound surrounded by earthworks. This indicates the location of the early community, although for reasons not entirely apparent the village, probably during the 15th century, was moved eastwards, to the present situation. Following the Norman Conquest, in the Domesday survey Cublington is recorded as 'Coblincote', and being in the possession of 'Gozelin the Breton' the manor comprised ten 'hides,' with a hide approximating to 120 acres of mainly arable land. Of the nine ploughs that are mentioned four farmed the 'demesne,' this being the land owned by the lord, whilst the other five cultivated the remainder of the estate, which was held from the lord by his subjects. According to the Domesday Book these comprised eight 'villeins', eight 'bordars', and five 'serfs', which made a total (not including the lord of the manor, his family and their servants) of some 21 households. 'Villeins' each normally maintained a virgate, which, comprising an area of around 30 acres, would lie in a scatter of various strips of an acre or less across the manor, thereby balancing the good situations with those less favourable. A 'bordar' cultivated around 10 acres, also held in scattered holdings, whilst the menial 'serf' had no land, and as a simple labourer endured a status little better than a slave. In fact even the oxen, which pulled the ploughs, seemed more fortunate, since they had the benefit of water meadows set aside to provide them with hay. At the time of the survey the manor was valued at £6, but other values are also given, and these can indicate whether a manor had suffered from rough treatment at the time of the invasion. Thus because the value at the time of King Edward the Confessor (before the Norman Conquest) is the same as that at the time of the survey, the manor of 'Coblincote' seems to have been left untouched. A priority for the invaders was to build a fortification from where to oversee the vanquished locals, and the 'Beacon' was a stronghold of the 'mount and bailey' type, constructed in quick and easy fashion by digging out an enclosing ditch for a moat, piling the earth into a central mound, and placing a strengthened refuge on top. Probably the fortification was built by the de Chesney family, from whom the ownership later passed by marriage to the Lucy family, who subsequently retained possession for several generations. As for today, the Beacon reminds of a time when the land suffered the ravage of foreign invaders. But locally there now stands another monument, and one that reminds of more recent times, when the locals successfully repelled an airborne invasion by their own countrymen.

DRAYTON PARSLOW

THE DRAYTON PARSLOW BELL FOUNDRY

At Drayton Parslow once flourished the most famous bell foundry in the land, founded by Richard Chandler. He was the son of Anthony Chandler, who came from Soulbury to work as the village blacksmith, and the earliest known bells date from 1636. When Richard died the business passed to his teenage son, Anthony, and so not until 1650 does it seem that the next bell was cast, that of the treble in Simpson church. That the enterprise continued to prosper is evidenced by at least one entry in the church registers; 'Henry, son of Richard Chandler, bell founder, and Mary, his wife, baptised April ye 28, 1702.' Yet mentions are also to be found in the records of the Quarter Sessions, with George, Richard and Thomas Chandler summoned in 1686 for 'riot and assault' on Richard Chandler senior. They were each fined £1, and perhaps regular ding dongs seemed an apt way of life for a bell founding family! The Chandler foundry continued until the later sons of the family felt disinclined to continue the interest, and, as master founder, it was taken over in 1726 by Edward Hall, who, by his marriage in 1741 to Mary, the daughter of Richard Chandler, returned a family connection to the foundry. Yet as the transport systems of the country began to improve, so the Drayton Parslow foundry faced increased competition, and the decline is evidenced by an entry in the burial register penned by the contemporary rector, Dr. John Lord; 'Edward Hall poor old Bellfounder, Feb 9 1755.' Possibly Edward's son, William, tried to continue the business, but the smithy would be acquired from his son by John Baldwin who, as 'a bedridden village worthy,' recalled in later life how, whilst digging for clay, not only had pieces of bell metal been recovered, but also castings, moulds and a quantity of sand. However, no material evidence now remains, although the past fame of the foundry is echoed by the naming of Bell Close, which overlies the old bell founding site.

EMBERTON

Bell Close at Drayton Parslow, so named after the foundry.

EMBERTON MEMORIAL

As throughout the country, amongst the local towns and villages the war memorials are a ubiquitous and poignant feature, and, as befits a conflict of such horrific proportions, the names relating to World War One are not infrequently the most numerous. That being an age long before the mass media of radio and television, the letters sent home by the soldiers were readily published in the local press, and modern day readers may be interested to know that all the letters published in the contemporary newspapers have now been collated (alphabetically by town/village) for non profit publication in book form. (In fact those regarding Newport Pagnell were recently uploaded onto the website of the town's local history society.)

Apart from the 'village green memorials,' there are also many monuments to be seen in the local churches, and none is perhaps more startling than the alabaster angel at Emberton, which commemorates the seventeen local men who fell in World War One. This was given by the Sams family, and of their number the Reverend Frederick Hulton Sams is separately commemorated, for he was killed on July 31st 1915 on the wastes of the Hooge battlefield, 'whilst crawling from cover to fetch water for his wounded men.' Prior to the war he had spent five years as a 'Bush Brother' in Queensland, and the story of 'the Fighting Parson,' or 'Mr.. Fred,' as he was affectionately known, will be the subject of a future article. On the wall behind the alabaster angel may be seen a brass plaque to another angel of Emberton, Nurse Nellie Decima Brown, the daughter of

The alabaster angel memorial at Emberton church.

the village blacksmith, who, 'after three years of suffering following four years of active service in the Great War,' died on July 2nd 1921, from a lung disease contracted during her nursing devotions. All the men from the village who served during World War One are commemorated on the village clock tower, and on the subject of 'angels' the mention of F.C. Stanton D.C.M. is somewhat significant, for after courageous service in the trenches - indeed being regarded as the smartest man with the bayonet in the 6th Oxon and Bucks Light Infantry, and decorated not only with the Distinguished Conduct Medal but also the Croix de Guerre - he was gazetted in 1917 to a second lieutenancy in the Royal Flying Corps. In fact as a pilot he would also excel, and, as will be seen in the forthcoming publication, his consequent aerial adventures could have well been a chapter for a Biggles book.

COUNTERING THE ESPIONAGE - SIR VERNON KELL

In an almost a semi-state occasion, at Emberton church in March 1942 the funeral took place of Sir Vernon Kell, who, by his almost singular efforts, was responsible for the creation of the counter espionage and intelligence organisation of Britain. In 1909, the year when many nocturnal sightings were made of a mysterious airship in British skies, concerns regarding German intelligence had lead to the creation of the Secret Service bureau, and although this initially comprised a military section and a naval section, within a year these had been replaced by a home department for counter espionage, the forerunner of MI5, and a foreign department for espionage, the forerunner of MI6. Widely travelled in Europe, and competent in five languages, Vernon Kell, a 36 year old army captain, became the first head of the military section, and - having been experienced since 1902 in German intelligence analysis at the War Office - he began his operation with just one clerk and the assistance of Special Branch, Scotland Yard. They were now investigating suspicious Germans in Britain, and in consequence Kell began the compilation of a secret register, listing those aliens believed to be of hostile intent. Then by chance he overheard a conversation on a train, and this enabled a German spy ring to be kept under surveillance for a number of years before the outbreak of World War One. Thus when on the evening of August 3rd 1914 he received secret notice of the intent to declare war, instructions were immediately issued for the arrest of the 22 paid German spies, and all except one, who had returned to Germany, were duly netted. In fact (although this was not realised at the time) the entire German spy network in Britain was thereby neutralised. As for Kell's staff, they had numbered just three officers, one barrister and seven clerks. In August 1914 the counter espionage department became formally reconstituted as sub section MO5g of the War Office, and in view of the hostilities the staff was increased to nine officers, three civilian assistants, four female clerks and three policemen. Yet by 1919 his empire comprised 844 employees, and now the main priority for MI5, which had been created in 1916, would be the threat of Communist Russia, for in 1920 the British Communist party was established. In the ensuing battle of wits Vernon Kell was to play a significant role, and although in 1923 he officially retired, in reality he remained as the head of MI5 for many years to come, which seemed just as well since 25,250 persons were now registered as being a threat to the national interest. With MI5 having taken over the Scotland Yard intelligence, the period for the best progress against the Soviet codes would be the 1920s, although, apart from a lack of resources, matters were not helped when the Prime Minister read out decrypted information in Parliament. Immediately the Russians changed their codes, and not before the wartime alliance would they again be broken, following which Churchill ordered a ban on such espionage against the Soviets! At the outbreak of World War Two, MI5 moved to a well known London prison, but with a degree of acrimony Churchill asked Kell to vacate his position, and thus at the age of 67 he finally retired. Understandably embittered, he moved with his wife and two servants to Emberton, where, becoming a special constable, he lived an active existence amongst the local community at 'Stonepits,' a house alongside West Lane. Nowadays the Communist threat has been consigned to the past, although with Russian bombers regularly probing British air space, and 'femme fatales' popping up in Parliament, might there still be a cause for concern. In fact whatever next, the infiltration of the local press? Surely not, although - come to think of it - the name of my editor does seem just a little bit suspect!

EMBERTON: FRED STANTON, WWI HERO

In the workplace, no doubt we've all come across a few; 'The Apprentice' types who purport to be the dynamic young dudes of British commerce, seemingly based on a 'life experience' of binge drinking in Benidorm, and educational qualifications about as much use as a degree in collecting Pokemon cards. At least so it appears in peacetime, but in time of war ordinary individuals, when thrust into extraordinary situations, often find leadership qualities they would not have otherwise discovered, and by which they gain positions of real worth, and earn the accolade of true respect. From the First World War, one of the most remarkable stories concerns Fred Stanton, the only child of Mr. and Mrs. Charles Stanton, of Emberton post office, who, having been a well known footballer in the district, joined Kitchener's Army at the age of 18½, and in September 1914 was amongst those sent to Oxford for a medical. He soon proved to have the makings of a fine soldier, but in March 1915 had to be sent home suffering from a dangerous illness. Yet he soon recovered, and in September 1915 whilst serving in Flanders with the 6th Oxon and Bucks Light Infantry was promoted to lance corporal on the battlefield. Then in October 1916, again on the battlefield he was promoted to sergeant, and with his leadership qualities having been recognised he was sent to England to study for a commission. At a large troop parade at Reading, there it would be on his 21st birthday that he was presented with the Distinguished Conduct Medal, for having rallied his section under heavy fire and not only capturing an enemy trench but, with his comrades, taking nearly 200 Germans prisoner. Then for carrying a French officer to safety under fire he would also win the Croix de Guerre, which was presented on Tuesday afternoon, November 27th 1917 at a large parade of troops at Kingsthorpe Hollow, Northampton. Having passed his exams with distinction, as a Second Lieutenant he was now a pilot in the Royal Flying Corps, and during this service would even be recommended for the V.C. In fact this seems of little surprise, judging by the following extract from a letter that he sent to his parents; "I went over the lines on Saturday with another officer looking for trouble as usual. We had penetrated over the enemy's territory some distance when we met five to seven Hun planes. We had a good scrap, but weren't quite sure of the damage we did. I set about one hard and fast, and when I had put a good burst of shot into him, he did a sharp turn and dived as hard as ever he could into the clouds."

After the war, for awhile he continued his flying career, but eventually left the service, with the right to retain the title of Lieutenant. He then took a smallholding at Emberton, and on February 7th 1928 at St. Matthew's Church, Ashford, Middlesex, married Miss Dorothy May Olive. After a honeymoon tour of the south coast they returned to Emberton to take up residence at Clay's Farm, whilst as for Fred's parents, who had lived for over 50 years in the village, at their home of Four Views, Petsoe End, in 1952 they celebrated their 57th wedding anniversary. (Their bungalow, built in the same field, replaced the Swiss Cottage that Mr. Stanton had bought at an Ideal Homes Exhibition.) His wife having

Emberton post office.

been a cook at the Rectory, Mr. Stanton had worked for the Reverend G.F. Sams for 25 years, as firstly a groom and then chauffeur, during which in early 1915 he volunteered to be a driver to the Red Cross. He later spent 26 years as the village postman, until illness caused him to retire around 1948. Nevertheless, despite being aged nearly 80 he still maintained a large garden. Replete in her old straw hat, for 30 years Mrs. Stanton would be the sub postmistress, and in the photo the initial 'K' stands for Kate, she having been Miss Kate Dunkley, until her marriage to Charles on June 3rd 1895 at Litchborough, Northants., his native village.

GAYHURST

GAYHURST HOUSE

In the unlikely event that anyone actually reads these pieces, I've been a little concerned of late that, having been couched in the educational system of the 1960s, perhaps the style of writing, especially as regards punctuation and grammar, may seem a little alien to modern youth. Also, for all I know history may have even been dropped as a required subject, to be replaced by some topic more appropriate to the modern culture - perhaps binge drinking, or football studies. So regarding these concerns I've decided - just for this topical piece - to use a wording and style which might hopefully connect with today's school population, with of course an accompanying sub text for the older readers. So having listened to the word on the street, here goes. Yo, dudes; (hello, everybody.) I'm like (frequent interjection, inserted into most sentences) gonna (going to) tell you about Sir Everard Digby, some ream (good looking) burly (virile young man) who hung out (lived) at a massif crib (large mansion, actually Gayhurst House) at Gayhurst. He ain't like no townie (he lived in the country) and was well sharkle (awesome) with the sword and well into rappin (an accomplished musician). Also right peng (very attractive) to the ladies, and well choice in the nut huggers (especially in tight fitting hose.) Then one day in October 1605, instead of cooching (chilling out) at the pad (Gayhurst House) he meets one of his bred'rin (friends), Robert Catesby, at Harrowden, near Wellingborough, and this blad (bloke) tells him that cos (because) some dudes bin (have been) dissin (disrespecting) their religion, he and the crew (his gang) are well vexed (rather upset). So they lay it down that this grief ain't gonna happen no more (they're not going to put up with this persecution any longer), and they're bustin (very keen) to blow up the Houses of Parliament. Now Sir Everard is well up for this (he's keen on the idea) and making sure they ain't caking (lying) or frontin (being fake) he joins these skanks (good friends) in the Plot and gives them 1,500 golds (£1,500) to buy gunpowder. He's then like appointed Commander of the 'Warwickshire Rising,' so that when the deed is happened (when the Houses of Parliament are blown up) this will like rally as a hunting party and seize the King's sprog (daughter) at Combe Abbey. But bad times; (what a calamity). The Plot is discovered and the breds (conspirators) have to uppit it and bounce the endz (hurriedly flee the neighbourhood.) But Sir Everard is gripped (arrested) at Holbeach, Staffordshire, and with the Stabz (in this context, the authorities) going pure mental (not very happy with him), penned (put in prison) and brought for trial at Westminster Hall. When sentenced, with a bow he then gives it large to the bench (he addresses their lordships) and says "If I could hear any of your Lordships say you forgive me, I should go more cheerfully to the gallows." Whoa, sympathy card, for these nobs (persons in authority) say; "God forgive you, and we do." Coolbins; (that's a result.) But his fate is right gantin;' (horrible). He's dragged on a hurdle to St. Paul's courtyard, and hung, drawn and quartered. Yo, what a dark off; (what a bad experience.) But Sir Everard is well blench (strong) and when the executioner plucks out his heart, and proclaims 'Here is the heart of a traitor,' the dude with his final breath says 'Thou lyest.' Massif respect; (a deep appreciation for his dignity). His remains are then bigged up on Tower Hill (put on ostentatious display), and of all the conspirators he alone confessed and accepted all blame. Double massif respect; (as before, but increased by 100%). And so breds, if this account has proved intelligible to both young and old alike, then it would seem that like when it comes to 'teen speak' like, then what is there not to like, like.

GREAT HORWOOD

GREAT HORWOOD: FIRE, PESTS & PESTILENCE

After the Norman Conquest, the manor was granted to Walter Giffard, as a reward for his military assistance, but he then gave it to the priory of Newton Longville, with which it passed in 1441 to New College, Oxford.

As for the parish church, this dates from the late 13th century, and of the subsequent rectors one would become Archbishop of Canterbury. Several memorials commemorate the Barker family, who for many years were resident at the early 17th century Manor House, but during the later century they were probably succeeded by John Harris, who had previously rented Calverton Manor Farm.

As for the less privileged inhabitants, in 1693 a woman had her parish relief reduced from 5s to 2s 6d when her husband, who was supposed to be a soldier, was discovered to be living in London, 'and gets a sufficient livelihood by his trade.' As for the lady's response, this was to use 'insolent language towards the officers of the said parish,' whereupon the court ordered that she should 'keep herself and her children at hard work and behave herself.' Some hope, for in 1701 she was committed to the bridewell at Newport Pagnell for a month, since inhabitants had cause of suspicion that she 'may in her passions commit some rash and violent act.'

As for her husband, in January 1706 he was handed over to the Regiment of Foot commanded by Sir Richard Temple. In fact with the advent of the Napoleonic menace an urgent need for men would arise, and in consequence in 1798 a list of males aged 15 to 60 was compiled, 'capable of acting in a military capacity.' However, at Great Horwood it seems that an allowance would have to be made for John Cox, for he had 'rheumatism.'

As for another menace, in less than two hours on Monday, May 28th 1781 a great fire destroyed 16 farmhouses, four malt houses and 40 cottages, whereupon the 'poor sufferers (whose loss upon the most moderate computation when all Insurances are deducted amounts to the Sum of Seven Thousand Four Hundred and Forty-four Pounds) are reduced to the utmost distress'. Thus the subsequent reconstruction accounts for the several Georgian brick cottages in the village, whilst the Crown dates from about 1795, built by John Harris. On the subject of ale, when the Reverend John Adey came to the village, around 1823, he encountered such drunkenness that he began to preach on the Green.

Then a farmer, Mr. Hogg, presented a brick barn in Wooden Lane, and this duly became an independent chapel. In fact there would be such a marked improvement in local behaviour that chapels of other denominations would also be established.

As for the parish church, in June 1874 this reopened after a restoration, during which consecrated earth was used to fill in the pond on the Green. Indeed, this was a blessing long overdue, for, with farm animals turned out on to the Green twice a day, dead beasts floating on the surface had been a common sight.

Yet this didn't deter the village baker from washing his oven mop in the water, until eventually the pollution became so bad that the pond was pronounced detrimental to health.

However, the wells were little better, for with the farmers throwing stable manure into the streets the gutters flowed with black water, and pigs wallowed in the fetid mud. Indeed, in 1858 a virulent form of typhoid broke out, and with Great Horwood becoming known as the 'Fever Village' many locals died.

But nevertheless perhaps a few still retain a local presence, at least to judge by the recent Citizen 'ghost hunt' at the Swan Inn.

GREAT HORWOOD: GHOST HUNT, SWAN INN

As recently reported, lead by the bolder representatives of the Citizen a ghost hunt lately took place at the Swan, Great Horwood, to be rewarded by flying bottles, emotional outbursts and blurred visions. Humm, sounds like a typical night down my local. But so to the Swan. On May 28th 1781, during the space of two hours a great fire destroyed much of Great Horwood - including 16 farmhouses, 4 malt houses and 40 cottages - and practically all of the village had to be rebuilt. In consequence the Crown, constructed by John Harris, dates from around 1795, and no doubt the Swan is of a similar vintage. Indeed many of the landlords were members of local families, with Henry Harrup pulling the pints in 1847. Including a plumber and glazier, several of his family were engaged in village trades, as were those of George Viccars, who by 1864 had taken over the pub. However, although there were still Viccars in the village, John Tolson was the landlord by 1877, to be succeeded by Daniel Canvin by 1889. Arthur James held sway at the beginning of the 20th century, Francis Middleton was in residence in 1907, to be followed by William Sampson by 1915, and Alfred Marks by 1924. Within four years the position was occupied by Frank Jacocks, and perhaps he is remembered by some of the present residents, since he was still the landlord at the beginning of World War Two. During their investigation it seems that the Citizen's ghost busters definitely witnessed some strange goings on, but nevertheless the present landlady seems sufficiently unfazed to continue happily serving her retail spirits amidst her resident spirits. Of little surprise, ghostly happenings have been reported elsewhere, and at Milton Keynes village at the 17th century Swan a 'grey ghost' supposedly haunts the rooms. As for Fenny Stratford, a ghostly presence was allegedly apparent at Dropshort Farm, on the Watling Street. This had been a coaching inn, but when the arrival of the railways decimated the trade the landlord hanged himself. Woughton on the Green also has a tale to tell, for even in recent years the ghost of Dick Turpin has supposedly been seen along Bury Lane, astride a dark horse and clad in a cloak, fancy waistcoat, black thigh high boots, and tricorn hat. As the story goes, prior to carrying out a daring robbery he called at the blacksmith's shop, at the village pub, and paid the man a handsome fee to reverse the horseshoes of his mount. Thereby his pursuers were supposedly foxed when they tried to give chase, but whatever the truth it makes a good yarn. As for the Citizen investigation, an unreserved admiration must be afforded to the female reporting staff who, with note pad and night vision camera to hand, boldly ventured where others have feared to tread. But then this seems of little surprise, for - as my gender has long been aware - the realms that transcend understanding are not only the province of ghosts.

GREAT LINFORD

GREAT LINFORD: BRANCH CANAL

As early as 1793 the Grand Junction Canal Company had considered the idea of a branch canal from Great Linford to Newport Pagnell, but the plans did not begin to take a serious form until 1813, when a meeting was convened at

Newport Pagnell to discuss the project. However, by now the Canal Company seemed less than keen, for apart from a monetary shortage they also held concerns regarding the increasing water leaks in the main canal between Fenny Stratford and Wolverton. Nevertheless the inhabitants and traders of Newport Pagnell pressed ahead, and at a public meeting, chaired by the local M.P., on August 20th 1813 they resolved to apply to Parliament for the necessary bill. A survey estimated the cost at around £12,000, and on June 17th 1814, Royal Assent for the Parliamentary Act was awarded 'for making and maintaining a navigable canal.' By December a contract had been awarded, and in January 1817 the new waterway opened, with tolls charged at 2s per ton on all goods excepting coal,

The former Wharf Inn at Great Linford.

manure and coke, which were separately levied. Leaving the Grand Junction Canal (later renamed the Grand Union Canal) by the Great Linford road bridge, the branch canal descended some fifty feet through a series of seven locks to Newport Pagnell, and at the Great Linford end featured a wide basin bordered by a busy wharf. Today the basin is still evident, and near to the old wharf lies the former Wharf Inn, which until recent years remained as a public house catering for the canal traffic.

Whilst coal initially formed the greater part of the canal cargo, stone, manure, bricks and timber were also important, and for a while the waterway enjoyed a moderate success, although an extension to Olney was considered uneconomic. Then at the end of 1845 a proposal was made to lay a railway from the London to Birmingham line at Wolverton to Newport Pagnell (to continue on a curved progress to join the Bletchley to Bedford branch line at Ridgmont) and to ease the construction Robert Stephenson suggested taking over and draining the Great Linford to Newport Pagnell branch canal, such that a part of the track could be laid on the dry bed. Raising no objections, the local Canal Company agreed to sell for the sum of £14,230, and although by February 1846 negotiations with the railway company had reduced this amount to £10,000, opposition from the main Grand Junction Canal Company ensured that the deal did not go through. Then in 1862, encouraged by the proven success of the railways a new scheme for the branch line was proposed, and, despite objections from the Grand Junction Canal Company, authority was duly obtained from Parliament to close and sell the canal to a railway company for £9,000. Their intention was to lay the track on the dry canal bed, and with the Newport Pagnell Railway Act duly passed in 1863, the branch canal came to an end. A closing down sale took place at the Great Linford wharf on September 26th 1863, and so began Great Linford's acquaintance with the railway - but that's another story.

TALKING WITH ANGELS - DR. RICHARD SANDY

Many of the estates in Milton Keynes have place names that recall an aspect of the local past, and in fact Sandy Close, at Great Linford, recalls perhaps the most mysterious of all the local parish rectors, Dr. Richard Sandy, alias 'Napier.' For the cure of the sick he would hold conversations with angels, and, according to the superstitious, he would even 'upon great occasions' converse with the Angel Gabriel, having before attending a patient retired to a closet to pray. Dr. Sandy had been instituted in 1589, and he received so much money from his work that he was able to purchase much of the village. Yet nevertheless he was renowned as a generous benefactor to the poor, and in his daily devotions he would spend at least two hours in worship, with it being said that 'his knees grew horny by much praying.' In fact it was in this posture that he died at a great age on April 1st, 1634, having foretold the date and the time of his death to the very hour. He was buried at Great Linford on April 15th, and of his surviving manuscripts a special mark denotes those which are said to be 'medical recipes,' given to him by the Angel Raphael. Nowadays there seems little to connect Great Linford with such goings on, although as I seem to recall there was, in the days long before the completion of the New City, at least one resident vision of angelic blonde loveliness, who was not infrequently to be found in the front bar of the Nag's Head. From one of the more prestigious of village addresses, sadly she moved away when the family left Great Linford, and then for spotty, post pubescent adolescents, it was only to be from afar that such heavenly beings could ever be worshipped.

HANSLOPE

HANSLOPE PARK WW2

Many, many years ago, and for reasons still not entirely apparent, my first job on leaving school was as a trainee radio technician with the Diplomatic Wireless Service.

However, despite passing all the exams it was decided that my fingers and thumbs approach to the practical side was hardly suited to the repair of sensitive electronic equipment in British embassies abroad. But from those days I've

An aerial view of Hanslope and the surrounding countryside.

always retained the greatest respect for technical persons, for unlike a host of 'arty' subjects there's no margin for waffle or 'blagging it'. A circuit either works or it doesn't, and if you calculate voltages incorrectly it might well be the last calculation that you make.

The training school was at Poundon House, in a village near Bicester, with the centre for the D.W.S. being at Hanslope Park. As with Bletchley Park, just before World War Two this had been bought by the Foreign Office for secret radio communication purposes and from June 1941 reported to Colonel Richard Gambier Parry, who had charge of the communications for the Secret Service.

As his deputy he appointed a fellow Etonian and personal friend Colonel Edward Maltby to take charge and in August 1941 the administration staff began their duties. They were soon followed by the first of the radio operators and officially Hanslope Park opened in May 1942.

At the outbreak of the war radio amateurs had been asked to scan the airwaves for transmissions being sent by enemy agents in Britain and when it became clear that there were none these 'Voluntary Interceptors' were then given the brief to monitor enemy transmissions from the Continent. Their organisation became known as the Radio Security Service and eventually moves were made to bring it within the Secret Intelligence Service.

Thus it became Special Communications Unit 3 and with several subsidiaries was centred on Hanslope Park. Essentially the role was to monitor enemy radio transmissions but other activities were also carried out, one of which would involve Alan Turing, of Bletchley Park code breaking fame. In late summer 1944 he gave up his lodgings at Shenley Brook End and transferred to Hanslope Park, where he occupied a room on the top floor of the mansion before later moving to a cottage in the kitchen garden.

His task was to develop a speech enciphering programme because the Germans now monitored 'scrambler' telephone transmissions across the Atlantic via a large antenna near Eindhoven. By the spring of 1945 Turing's 'Delilah,' as the name for the project, was complete and for a test of the system a 16 inch disc was recorded at the Milton Bryan 'black' broadcast station.

However, during the event Alan's braces burst and in remedy Harold Robin, the chief engineer of the organisation, produced some bright red cord from an American packing case. This Alan then used everyday thereafter. As for Delilah, by the end of the war the Post Office had a system of their own and dismissed Delilah as too 'crackly'.

As for the main purpose of Hanslope Park, the centre attained such competence that even Field Marshall Montgomery and General Eisenhower were shown around. After the war it became the centre for handling all Foreign Office radio communications and operated under the title the Diplomatic Wireless Service.

Today, including support to S.I.S, the centre accommodates Her Majesty's Government Communications Centre although the forest of aerials which for long were a feature are no longer required in this age of satellite communication.

Following his wartime work Gambier Parry was made Director of Communications at Hanslope Park, from where he retired in 1955. As for my own 'career,' contemporary with these times most jobs of late have seemed much akin to toothache or marriage – something at best to be endured.

Milton Keynes Citizen, July 12, 2012

THE MURDERED SQUIRE

Many tales of the local past are well known and have often been told.

However, to refresh the reminiscence of the region's heritage it is as well to retell a few. One such story is the sensational murder of Edward Watts, a popular squire of Hanslope.

Well regarded by his tenants, he had initially undertaken all the game keeping duties on his estate until, heeding the advice of his son in law, in 1910 he employed two gamekeepers instead.

One, an ex-miner, was William Farrow, who with his wife and small children moved from the Old Wrestlers Inn at Mursley to take up the occupancy of a small cottage at Tathall End, Hanslope.

A middle aged man, well built and about six feet tall, he seemed to possess a quiet disposition, until in 1911 while out shooting with the squire he was badly affected by sunstroke, having to be carried home as a result.

Thereafter, his behaviour became increasingly strange, and concerns were raised about his bouts of heavy drinking. Nevertheless, during the early part of 1912 when Edward and his wife went abroad for a holiday they entrusted him with the care of their favourite retriever.

However, through supposed neglect the animal died and Farrow was given two weeks immediate notice. Then it seems that the gamekeeper began to plan a deadly revenge.

A memorial to the murdered squire.

Since estate keepers were expressly forbidden to carry firearms on the Sabbath, he hid his gun in a roadside spinney and, when Sunday arrived set off on his deadly mission.

Along the way he briefly stopped at Manor Farm to ask for a drink of beer but, as the farmer's wife would later recall, 'his eyes were glassy, and he did not seem natural'. Farrow then made his way to the North Spinney and having retrieved his gun concealed himself in the undergrowth.

On that lovely summer day, Edward was strolling home from church when, as he approached the gates of his mansion, a gunshot suddenly rang out.

As he fell Mrs. Watts rushed to his aid but on glimpsing the assailant half hidden in the trees she dropped to the ground and shouted, 'he's firing again'. The first blast had embedded over a hundred pellets into Edward's head, while tearing his black frock coat to shreds the second shattered his back.

Hearing the shots, the coachman's wife and son hurried to the scene and meeting his father on the way the boy told him about the tragedy. Displaying great courage the father climbed the fence to search for the murderer, but the sound of a third gunshot brought the gruesome deeds to an end. With his gun beside him William Farrow lay dead in the long grass and, having been summoned by telephone, police officers arriving by car from Newport Pagnell discovered several cartridges in Farrow's pocket. His body was taken to his cottage while the lifeless form of the squire was conveyed to the mansion by a stretcher party.

In a distant corner of Hanslope churchyard, Farrow was buried after dark, his suicide having left a widow and three daughters to fend for themselves. Since Mrs. Farrow had been unaware of her husband's intent, much sympathy was extended to her and the family but this vanished when she erected a gravestone inscribed with the words, 'waiting 'till all shall be revealed'. This so enraged the locals that a police guard had to be placed at the graveside to prevent the stone from being smashed.

Edward's body was cremated at Golders Green and the ashes returned to Hanslope, to be carried into the church at the funeral by two of the estate tenants.

As for Sophie Watts, she never recovered from her husband's murder. Often she would wander alone to the scene of the tragedy and by arrangement with the county council the road was diverted from the location. The site of the killing was left to become overgrown and forgotten, but today a plaque marks the site.

HAVERSHAM

HAVERSHAM: MRS. TYSOE'S EVICTION

For those who bristle with indignation at the present abuses of the welfare system, and certain ridiculous awards of housing benefit, perhaps it's best to skip the rest of this article, since it recalls not only the injustices inflicted upon a previous generation, but also the sacrifices which paradoxically helped to create the unchecked liberalities which have allowed such a farce to exist. Born at Haversham, Frederick Tysoe had been employed before the First World War as a labourer by Mr. Souster, but as a Reservist at the outbreak of hostilities he joined up at the age of 40, and, serving with the 1st Northants Regiment, would be involved in much of the savage trench fighting at the Front. Nevertheless, regarding his cottage at Haversham ejectment proceedings were taken against his wife and three young children, and, as the respondent, Mrs. Tysoe wept bitterly at the Newport Pagnell Police Court, pitifully asking the magistrates; "Where am I to go? My husband is now in the trenches." Shamefully there was no provision for alternative accommodation, and in fact on Tuesday, February 23rd 1915 the question of the eviction of soldiers' wives was raised in the House of Commons, with the case regarding Mrs. Tysoe being specifically mentioned. Eventually it seems that Mrs. Tysoe and her young family found shelter in Chapel Yard, Great Linford, but tragically the injustice of her circumstance would be compounded later that year, when news arrived that her husband had been killed in action near Ypres on May 9th. In contrast to the plight of Mrs. Tysoe, with shades of the present day extensive assistance was afforded to those seeking sanctuary from oppression abroad, and the local district would become host to many Belgian families, fleeing from the German atrocities in their homeland. In fact one family who could well testify to the horror was that of Henri Vandenberg and his wife and four children, who, as poor labouring class refugees, arrived at Tyringham from Belgium on the evening of Monday, December 19th 1914. They had been living near Ashot, near Louvain, but when the Germans burned down their humble cottage they fled to Antwerp, and on reaching Holland came to the notice of the Belgian Refugee Committee in England. Subsequently - having ensured that the premises were in good repair - Mr. and Mrs. Konig, of Tyringham House, placed the lodges of their mansion at the disposal of the family, and there they would be provided for rent free. As for furniture, this was supplied through the kindness of Miss McFerran, of Tyringham cottage, and Mrs. Carlile, of Gayhurst House, who also did much to help the family feel at home. No one of course would begrudge such hospitality, but for those British men fighting at the Front, or at least for those who had been engaged in agriculture, it would seem that home was certainly not the place to seek charity, when their own families were in need of accommodation.

HOCKLIFFE

COLLEGE FARM, HOCKLIFFE

Four hundred grand for a flippin' party book? Good grief, I've been Pippa'd at the post.

If I'd known that sort of money was on offer I certainly wouldn't be scribbling local history, but instead be hawking my hazy memories of wild parties in the 1960s to Penguin books.

Although to quote the old saying, if you can remember such times then you weren't really there.

What does it matter if my rear end doesn't look as good in a bridesmaid's dress - it's nothing that can't be sorted by a couple of mouse clicks on a digital photo editing suite.

But enough of this modern 'celebrity' nonsense, and so to proper books and proper writers, of which locally one of the most famous was the novelist Arnold Bennett.

After some 10 years in London, in October 1900 he came to live at Trinity Hall Farm, Hockliffe, and this was to not only pursue the ambition of becoming a freelance writer, but to also provide a home for his ageing parents.

By his own account he chose the town because it was 'on a certain main-line at a certain minimum distance from London', and while at Trinity Hall Farm he, or the 'Heir of Hockliffe' as he was known to his friends, received many offers of work. In fact during this period he would write 'Teresa of the Watling Street', a novel that based the farm as a background.

However, the book proved somewhat disappointing, and even he later described it as 'the world's worst novel.'

In January 1902 Arnold's father, Enoch, died, and since his widow left shortly afterwards, to live among friends and relatives, Arnold, with little to keep him at Trinity Hall, began to spend more time away.

Increasingly he began to live in a rented flat off Red Lion Square, London, and thus when in January 1903 the lease of Trinity Hall expired he left Hockliffe, and would move to Paris.

During the First World War he would become involved in a secret propaganda department, while during World War Two his old home at Hockliffe would .also become involved in secret activities, the story of which has been recently documented in a book by a local author, Neil Rees.

By his research it seems that in great secrecy a Czechoslovak radio communications station was built in the fields of Trinity Hall Farm, to where in September 1942 the radio station of the Czechoslovak military intelligence was moved, from a bungalow called 'Funny Neuk' in Woldingham Garden Village, in Surrey.

Here, through transmitting and receiving facilities contact could be maintained not only with the Czech resistance in German occupied Bohemia-Moravia, but also agents on Czechoslovak missions, and embassies in neutral and unoccupied countries.

From their offices in Bayswater, London, the work was overseen by the Czechoslovak military intelligence services, and from the Hockliffe station the information would be passed via the on site teleprinters to the Special Operations Executive (SOE), and British Intelligence.

Under the command of Captain Gold, around 10 radio technicians operated the facility, and also accommodated was their dog, Jack, who having been a past inmate of Battersea Dog's Home was supposed to have been the guard dog, but instead became a pet.

At the station some of the radio equipment was made in a Nissen hut, which housed the workshop and power unit, while of two other huts one contained the kitchen and Captain Gold's bedroom.

After the war the huts were occupied by farm workers, but all were pulled down in the 1970s. In fact nothing now remains of the old radio station, although as a romantic remembrance some of the station personnel married local girls, and would settle in the district nearby.

LATHBURY

DAPHNE TREVOR

As yet, it seems impossible to travel back through time, and that's perhaps just as well, since, cosseted by our modern standards of comfort, hygiene, and medical care, no doubt the discovery that awaits would sadly disappoint our often rose tinted perception. Yet in the mind the past always seems present, and here we may voyage wherever we wish. When imposed upon reality, such imaginings seem to flee this dimension of dreams, and through their ethereal being awaken those scenes which are laid in the past. As when from the gates of Lathbury Church one sees Miss Daphne Trevor, approaching in the company of her father, along the pathway from Lathbury Park. For this is her wedding day, and she wears the gown that her mother had worn, and on her finger will sparkle a ring of diamond and sapphire, the gift of the groom. For he had been the best man at her brother's wedding, and could it have been then that she had first harboured those plans for her own future happiness.

The only daughter of William Trevor, and his wife Emily, Daphne lived with her brother and parents at Lathbury Park, and had been instrumental in raising a village section of the Baden Powell Scouts, which, under her supervision, became one of the finest in North Bucks, indeed winning a silver cup as the best troop in the district. Following the outbreak of the First World War, she then became a nursing sister, to be firstly attached to the VAD Hospital at Barford Hill,

Warwickshire, and then to the institution at Brooklands. But when the VAD Hospital at Tickford Abbey, Newport Pagnell, was opened, it would be there that she conscientiously continued her duties, earning respect for her kindness and devotion.

As for her brother, having volunteered for service at the outbreak of war he went to France in early 1915, and, having seen much hard fighting, was gazetted to Captain for his excellent work in the field. But he was subsequently invalided to light duties, although whenever able he would join in the local concerts to entertain convalescent soldiers. As at the Tyringham Military Hospital one evening in 1916, where, to accompaniments played by their mother, Daphne sang popular songs, and her brother performed several humorous items, as well as a whistling solo. As the friend of her brother, whom he had known since their youth, Daphne had made the acquaintance of Captain Richard Pemberton who, as an officer in the Suffolk Yeomanry, saw much active service, until severely wounded a month before the Armistice.

From their acquaintance would blossom romance, and then, in the aftermath of the war, their engagement. With Richard having secured an important position at the Treasury, at their wedding it would be a member of the Foreign Office who was the best man. With the church beautifully decorated, the service was choral, and with the reception held at Lathbury Park, a large marquee accommodated the 200 guests. Then to a rousing send off, and the ringing of the church bells, during the afternoon the couple left for a honeymoon in the South of France,

Lathbury Park and Church   Valentines Series 4688x

whilst in the evening the ladies of the village were invited to tea at Lathbury Park, and to view the beautiful wedding gifts. Daphne and Richard would make their home at Bilsdon, Ipswich, but several years later would again be acquainted with Lathbury Church, to attend the memorial service for Daphne's father. In fact despite all of the sacrifice made by their generation, soon there would be further tragedy in the form of another war. For the same cause; and which would only bring further bereavement. So let the past dwell in the province of dreams, for romantic expectance - at least in this world - is never to be how we'd wish it to seem.

LITTLE BRICKHILL

SIR PEXALL BROCAS

Oh to have been a lord of the manor in days of yore.

A rollicking role of wanton wenching, or so to judge by the 17th century antics of Sir Pexall Brocas at Little Brickhill, where no female appears to have been safe from his amorous intent.

Indeed he is said to have sired between 70 and 100 illegitimate children while as for legitimate offspring he troubled his wife to produce only one. Pexall had acquired his unusual name from a marriage between the Pexall and the Brocas families, which by a legal settlement stipulated that the name of Pexall should be kept alive, and although he inherited the manor of Little Brickhill in 1589, it would be in London that the 21 year-old preferred to spend most of his time. As for other mischief, in 1601 he was involved in the attempt of the Earl of Essex to rise against the advisers of the ageing Queen Elizabeth, but while Essex was beheaded for his actions Brocas was charged with causing a riot and publishing a forged deed of perjury. He was then saved from further punishment by the accession of James I who not only pardoned but knighted him.

And so he continued his worldly ways, until having been convicted before the High Commissioners for 'Secret and notorious adultery with divers women' on Sunday, October 24th 1613, for his promiscuous pursuits he was sentenced to stand at St Pauls Cross, London, in a white sheet emblazoned in red with the letter 'A' for adulterer, holding a stick in his hand. Many of those thus convicted actually welcomed this punishment, since it thereby advertised their dubious appeal to a more widespread audience of the more wanton of womenfolk. As for further impudence, at Little Brickhill in 1624 he refused to pay a church rate because the south side of the parish church had not been reserved for the exclusive use of himself and his servants.

Yet in later life perhaps the pleasures of the flesh began to wane for, believed to have been the last private person to do so, he employed a jester to keep him amused.

Perhaps from exhaustion Pexall died on August 13th 1630, to be buried the next day at Little Brickhill. Yet an alternative version states that his heart was buried at Little Brickhill, with the rest of his body interred at Ivingoe Aston, another village of the family influence.

Whatever the truth, a reminder of his prolific legacy is said to be found in the parish register, with the baptism entries of some of his progeny.

Also in the registers are entries marked by a small cross in the margin and these indicate a grim record of 42 people who by the verdict of the Assize 'suffered death and were buried.' In medieval times crimes of a more serious nature were tried by travelling justices, and due to the position on the important Watling Street, and because of the nearness to the county border, Little Brickhill became the first stop on the Norfolk circuit.

Until 1638 the Assize Court met in a building now known as Court House and portions of the original construction still remain. Leading off from an upstairs room a little closet is supposedly where the judge retired to powder and put on his wig and as seen from the Watling Street this room is now evident as that small and upper projection on the front of the house.

Additionally, on either side of the doors to certain of the upper rooms remain iron brackets, which once held bars to prevent the door from being opened by anyone on the inside. When a sentence had been pronounced the condemned was led away to await execution, and by tradition the gallows stood 'on the Heath, about three furlongs out of the town, on the road to Woburn.' Indeed, this corresponds to that spur of land at the junction of Sandy Lane and the Woburn road, and not surprisingly became known as 'hangman's corner.'

In 1638 Little Brickhill then ceased to be a centre for executions, and with these now carried out at Buckingham and Aylesbury so came to an end the village's judicial status.

Milton Keynes Citizen, June 28, 2012

LITTLE WOOLSTONE

LITTLE WOOLSTONE: SISTER DORA

How times change, and not least in education. During my schooldays the 'internet' consisted of a set of Encyclopaedia Britannica, stored on suitably stout shelving in the local library. Whilst as for 'text messaging,' the nearest we had was passing grubby bits of paper around the class, not infrequently to the blonde bombshell at the back who, by dint of looks, and certain other attributes, held the monopoly of being able to pick and choose from the spotty herberts vying for her attention. Yes, it would certainly be a shock for today's generation to endure the classroom of 50 years ago. Yet this would be nothing compared to the teaching methods of earlier times, for it was not without good reason that Dr. Richard

Busby, the headmaster of Westminster School, was known as 'Sir Richard Birch-Hard.' 'Addicted to flogging,' he literally left a lifelong impression upon many of his notable scholars, whilst as for his local impression, this he left in the form of the architectural excellence of Willen church (designed by Robert Hooke), which was built following his purchase of the manor. Another teacher of local renown - albeit of a more benign philosophy - was Dorothy Wyndlow Pattison, who is considered by many to have been a civilian counterpart to Florence Nightingale. As a child, Dorothy had lived in the Yorkshire village of Hauxwell, but she suffered so badly from a weak chest that she often had to stay away from school, and it would be during these absences that she indulged in 'washing and attending to people and dolls.' Seeking escape from a rather unhappy home life, Dorothy had considered joining Florence Nightingale's Sisters of Mercy, but since this was forbidden by her father, instead in 1860 she answered an advertisement for a schoolmistress at Little Woolstone, being duly chosen from the 25 applicants. Until the schoolteacher's house was complete she stayed at the rectory at Great Woolstone, and apart from her primary role as a teacher she would also nurse any pupils who fell ill. Yet eventually the strains proved too much, and she had to return to her Yorkshire home. However, when recovered instead of resuming her teaching career she joined the nursing 'Sisterhood of the Good Samaritan' at Redcar, and being known as 'Sister Dora' in 1865 undertook hospital work at Walsall, in Staffordshire. Unfortunately, due to her conscientious devotions her health began to suffer, and in 1878 she died at the age of 46, with her wish having been that 'no vain eulogy' should be made to her. But nevertheless a statue was unveiled in the market place at Walsall in October 1886, whilst at Little Woolstone a small locally made plaque was placed in the church, on the north wall of the nave. Later, this was moved during the New City restorations to the chancel, and it was also due to the New City that Pattison Lane came into being, as a further commemoration of the famous schoolmistress. As for today's education, Dorothy would no doubt be pleased that the little petals no longer have to endure corporal punishment, and of course any oik worth their salt will now be fully clued up on 'Human Rights.' And so to the surviving kin of Miss Nora Bone (real name withheld for legal reasons) I say beware. For regarding that clip round the ear I received in 1959, for knocking over the water pot during the art lesson, I shall be advising my 'no win, no fee' lawyers to seek substantial 'compo' for 'hurt feelings,' contravention of the E.U.s 'Dignity at School' policy (I'm sure there must be one), not to mention the constant 'flashbacks' and stress related illness. And besides, I reckon most of the kids' paintings looked a darn sight better, having been smudged with 2½ pints of murky tap water.

LOUGHTON

LOUGHTON: NATIONAL SCHOOL

For many years the old National School of the village stood in a state of ruin and neglect, but in 1981 it was rescued from decline and converted into a private residence. At least since 1848 a small school had been held in two upper rooms of Elm House, but, with this accommodation as hardly adequate, plans were put in hand - largely through the efforts of the local rector - to construct a proper building, and of the 17 subscribers the local squire made two contributions amounting to almost a quarter of the £400 cost. Being a Harley Street physician by profession, a resident on the Green made a significant donation of £20, and with the remainder of the expense soon amassed the school was built in 1865 on a corner of a common meadow, owned by the church. However, due to the perils of flooding, posed by a nearby stream, a banking up of the site had been necessary, and indeed before the coming of the New City flooding still remained as a periodic problem.

Amongst the expenditures for the school, the architect's bill came to £41 6s 0d, and a foot scraper, 8s 3d, and with the school initially able to accommodate about 40 children, a doubling of this capacity was enabled by the provision of a new classroom around 1894. At this period educational control lay with the Shenley and Loughton United District School Board, but when such bodies were later abolished the Council assumed control. In 1916 the Loughton school closed when the headmaster of Shenley Council School, Mr. Melton, joined the Army,

Loughton Church School.

and it was therefore to Shenley that from May 1st 1916 the Loughton children and their headmistress, Mrs. Maud Cresswell, were transferred. However, it was soon made very clear that many people would have preferred a man as the new head, and with trouble arising from the start not least would be the occasion when, instead of being in class, one of the pupils was found to be working on the land. Then in a later incident it became necessary to punish the lad, and the subsequent caning so enraged his parents that when his mother came to the school the police had to be called, such was the disturbance she made. The father also made his opinions felt, for on meeting the headmistress in the street his tirade of verbal abuse expressed the earnest hope that "We will kick you out ..." Therefore, when Mr. Melton returned from the Army many hoped that he would return to the school, but instead he moved elsewhere, and a petition was subsequently raised asking the Education Committee to appoint a man as the headmaster. On May 19th 1919 this was duly presented to the Managers, who attending a meeting on the same date with the boy's father heard him make several slanderous accusations against Mrs. Cresswell. However, following the evidence of Mrs. Cresswell and a number of other witnesses the jury returned a verdict in her favour, and, with this also being the opinion of the judge, she was awarded damages of £200.

MILTON BRYAN

MILTON BRYAN'S COMMEMORATIVE PLAQUES

Whilst perhaps not blessed with the ability to walk upon water, those of the Methodist faith in Milton Bryan were at least once able to walk across the waters, for their chapel was supported on stilts above the village pond.

By the later 19th century they had been holding their meetings in a local cottage but their ultimate aim was to have a purpose built chapel.

Yet no one would allow them a site and when one farmer who had bitterly opposed their plans died from a wasp sting many considered it to be an act of Divine retribution.

Possibly not wishing to suffer the same fate, the Duke of Bedford then granted the use of the village pond - which was then much larger than at present - but due to a stipulation that the chapel had to be erected between sunrise and sunset, and not during the day, the sections of the building were made at Dunstable and then, supposedly in the middle of the night, brought to Milton Bryan to be bolted together.

Supported above the pond on stilts, in the early days the chapel was known as the Tabernacle and for some 100 years would become an unusual centre for weekly worship. Initially an annual rent of 2s 6d was payable to the lord of the manor but in time the Duke of Bedford relinquished this 'peppercorn' amount and sold the right to the trustees.

Of little surprise, in such a moisture laden situation by the late 1970s the chapel had begun to deteriorate and the slated roof and much of the internal furnishing had to be removed.

Then damp set into the woodwork and in consequence during the early weeks

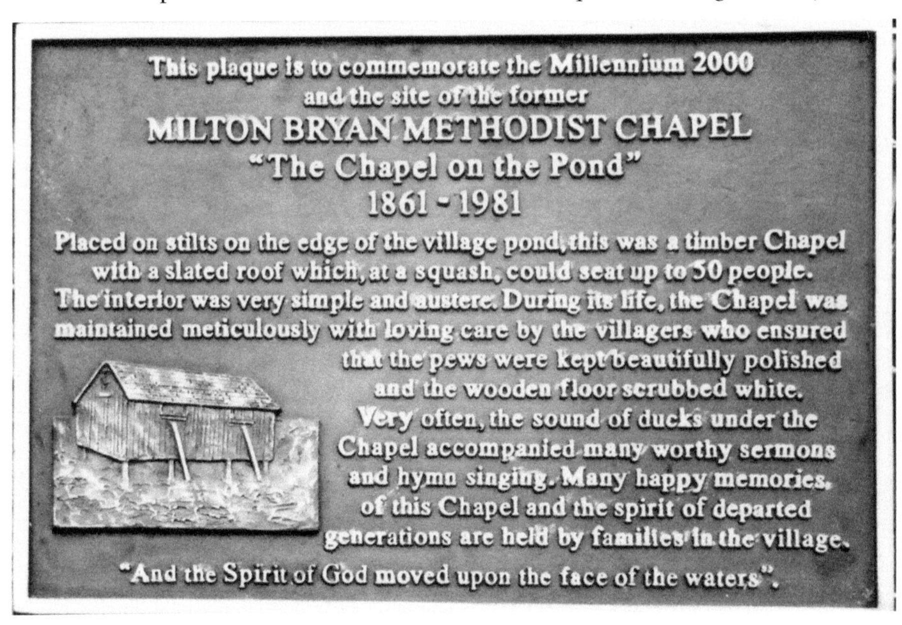

of 1981 the building was demolished.

The timbers were piled up at the side of the pond and no trace of the chapel now remains. However, a plaque to commemorate the chapel and the millennium was erected in 2000, for which year the village also saw the beginnings of another commemoration and plaque, for the 'black propaganda' World War Two radio station situated at the other end of the village.

It had been during 1942 that on a remote corner of the Woburn estate construction began of this squat, symmetrical, brick building, guarded when complete by steel fencing and armed personnel.

During the earlier years of the war information gained from German prisoners had been used by foreign teams, housed in the local area, to record 'black broadcast' programmes onto wax discs at Wavendon Towers, which were then taken by Secret Service cars to covert transmitting stations in the district.

The intention was solely to deceive, dishearten and demoralise the German audience, and convince them of a growing underground movement deep in Germany. Indeed upon this belief hinged the whole credibility of the operation and pornography to appeal to the enemy soldiery, as well as language offensive in the extreme about the British, was deliberately employed.

However, the physical size of the discs limited the length of a programme to 20 minutes each side and so in 1943 the purpose built station at Milton Bryan came into operation, with broadcasts transmitted on shortwave.

Then at Crowborough, in Sussex, an ultra powerful transmitter from America was installed and, with this being able to swamp any German radio station, a direct link was laid to Milton Bryan.

Thus here the studio announcers could mimic and take over a German station and with the German audience none the wiser all manner of false information was relayed.

Also mimicked were the ground controllers directing German fighter aircraft, sending them all over the sky on false missions.

In 2000, the research regarding this wartime story formed the basis of a website created at the Open University and when this came to the attention of Channel 4 it provided much information for their documentary on the subject.

The full story is also told in a recent book and DVD whilst as for the plaque, this was unveiled by the now Duke of Bedford on September 4th 2002, in fact possibly being the first to carry a website address!

Milton Keynes Citizen, April 5, 2012

MIDDLETON KEYNES

A TROUBLESOME MAID

The centenary of the beginning of the First World War is just a couple of years away, and it's encouraging that the Government is planning appropriate measures towards recognising the sacrifice made by an entire generation.

As for efforts to recognise the contribution from our immediate district, it may be of interest to know that a book containing letters from local men serving at the various fronts is now available, as also a book detailing the story of Bletchley during WWI.

Companion volumes detailing Newport Pagnell and Stony Stratford are in preparation, as also is one which chronicles everyday life in the local communities during that period.

In fact included in the latter is the then village of Milton Keynes, regarding which a recent article featured the early arrival of Belgian refugees.

Prominent in securing their accommodation was the rector of the village, the Reverend G. Hawkes Field, who on Whit Sunday 1915 took up the position as a chaplain to the Forces and spent several weeks among the troops in Norfolk.

He then left his name on the list and on Friday, November 26th 1915 took up duty as temporary chaplain to troops stationed at Plymouth.

Meanwhile, his wife remained at the Rectory and with this still being an era of upstairs, downstairs. in the course of domestic life she advertised the need for a household servant.

Consequently a 16 year-old girl began employment as a 'cook general' but matters did not work out, for one morning Mrs. Field went into the kitchen and told the girl to accompany her to the bedroom, where some work had not been done.

The girl refused and was then told to pack her box and leave at once.

This she refused to do, whereupon Mrs. Field said: "Very well, I will wait till you have packed."

When the girl still did not comply Mrs. Field made arrangements to fetch Miss Cother, the lady superintendent of the Preventative and Rescue Home at Fenny Stratford, from where the girl had originally been sent.

On arrival she asked what the matter was and on receiving no reply opened a cardboard box belonging to the girl, in which were discovered several articles stolen from the house.

Miss Cother then said that this was a case for the police and following the arrival of Police Constable Britnell, two purses were found in the girl's handbag.

It duly transpired that the girl had a considerable criminal record and at the subsequent hearing it was thought advisable to send her for trial at the Quarter Sessions.

Here she pleaded guilty with it being revealed that she had originally been in a situation near Leicester but was dismissed for petty thefts and sent to a Refuge Home.

She was next placed in a situation at Henley-on-Thames, from where, having opened a missionary box and stolen the contents, she was dismissed and sent to another Refuge Home.

Subsequently she was placed in service at Maidenhead but was again dismissed for bad conduct and petty thefts.

During the trial the girl wept bitterly with the verdict reached that she should be detained in Borstal Institution for two years.

As for the other end of the social spectrum, on Wednesday, May 23rd 1928 Miss Elizabeth Field, the daughter of the Reverend and Mrs. Field, was presented by her aunt, Lady Coote, at his Majesty's Court.

Continuing such social ascent she would marry the widowed husband of her mother's sister, to live in style at a local country mansion, but, as always, that's a tale for another day.

Milton Keynes Citizen, November 1, 2012

MILTON KEYNES VILLAGE: BELGIAN REFUGEES, WWI

Across the country, at the beginning of World War One Belgian refugees were given refuge in English villages, typical of which was Milton Keynes

At the beginning of the First World War, when Belgium refused to allow the German armies to cross their territory the population suffered a terrible consequence.

But it was the bravery of the Belgian army that initially stalled the enemy advance and so prevented the capture of Paris and thus the fall of France.

German reprisals against the Belgians were characteristically brutal but for those who could escape Britain provided a ready refuge, not least in appreciation for the heroic stand of 'Brave little Belgium.'All over the country, in towns and villages, accommodation was being made ready and at the village of Milton Keynes it was Mrs. Harley, of Walton Hall, the Reverend G Hawkes Field, rector of Milton Keynes, and Mrs. Field who were the prime movers in securing comfortable homes for two Belgian refugee families.

Mr. Alan Finch - affectionately regarded by the villagers as 'the squire' - provided two thatched cottages rent free near the village centre, situated in a meadow off the main street, and with furniture etc. provided, it would be one Monday night in October 1914 that the refugees arrived. Before the war they had earned their livelihood working small plots of land at Buggenhout, a village a few miles from Antwerp, and when Mrs. Harley and the others had approached the Belgian Refugee Committee they had made clear they needed people who would be of use on farms in the district. One of those duly forwarded was Frans Van Eyken, a middle aged labourer, who in Belgium had kept two cows, some pigs and poultry.

His wife Rosalie, and 18 year-old daughter, Philomena, would also help for, "They can milk the cows and do all kinds of work on the land." Until 12 months ago their son, August Van Eyken, had helped on the smallholding but more recently he had turned his attention to coal mining.

As for another son, he was in the army fighting the Germans. Fortunately the family received good warning of the enemy advance and managed to flee but sadly on the afternoon of Wednesday, October 28th 1914, Madame Van Eyken passed away from acute erysipelas. Since arriving in the village she had complained of acute pains in the head and was attended by Dr. Holmes of Woburn Sands, and Dr. Bailey of Newport Pagnell.

The other Belgian family was that of 32 year-old Madame Mathilde Rosa Segers, with her aged mother and six small children. In their urgent flight her father was lost and his whereabouts unknown and when the Germans discovered that her husband was a Belgian soldier they set light to the cottage, and destroyed all the pigs and chickens.

In fact Madame Segers had many tales of German atrocities, against men, women and children, and with no love for the species the refugee families had prominently placed the Belgian flag on the front of the cottages which, prior to the arrival of the families, had been painted by the men of the parish, with the interiors papered and the floors scrubbed and the windows cleaned by the women, who also brought food. As for those foreigners who were resident in Britain, as 'aliens' those who were not interned were subject to various restrictions and within this category was a Dutchman. He had been in the country for a while but by 1918 still seemed confused by the requirements, for he was summoned for not giving notice of his arrival at the village of Broughton and for having failed to notify his departure.

Police Constable Bunce said he had seen the man on the Newport Pagnell road at Broughton under the influence of drink and when questioned the man said he lived at Newport Pagnell but was staying at Broughton as he had come to see his wife. Thinking it unnecessary to register as a Neutral - "and a friendly one at that" - he pleaded ignorance and said he hadn't read the last instructions pasted on the back of his identity book. A fine was imposed and when the chairman told him he was careless not to read the instructions he replied, "I have read them since."

Milton Keynes Citizen, April 19, 2012

MILTON KEYNES VILLAGE: ELM TREE LEGEND

In a previous age, when it was discovered that a girl of Broughton was 'carrying on' with a married man from Milton Keynes, the retribution of the villagers was swift, for she was drummed out of the village to the sound of banging on dustbin lids. No doubt if the same criteria were applied to present standards, it would be bonanza time for every hardware shop for miles. In fact it seems that bankrolled by the welfare state, the promiscuity spawned during the 'Swinging Sixties' began the meltdown of the nation's morals, and, as I seem to remember from the 1970s, savvy females made a career choice of having a few sprogs out of wedlock, to thereby obviate having to find some mind numbing job, and instead be guaranteed state provided accommodation, and all the benefits that went with it. (As for feckless males, they couldn't believe their luck, for now there seemed to be a local network of easy lodgings offering easy liaisons, which not infrequently left the legacy of yet another mouth to feed - on benefits, of course.) But on the question of babies, illegitimate or otherwise, at the village of Milton Keynes there once stood a great elm tree next to the Swan, and by tradition it was said that should ever this tree wither and die, then no more babies would be born in the village. Then in 1974 the tree became a victim of Dutch Elm disease, and for reasons of safety the woody landmark had to be reduced to little more than a stump. Yet even this became a victim of fate, for as an immoveable object it was demolished in 1989 during a high speed police chase. However, in 1990 Milton Keynes Development Corporation presented the villagers with a new elm, and in June of that year this was planted by a 75 year old resident. Thus in a way the old legend came true, for with the end of the great elm came the end of babies being born in the village, for Milton Keynes was now no longer a village but a part of the new city - with all the social modernity which that entailed. In fact regarding the now accepted phenomena of 'partners' and 'single mums,' goodness knows what the Victorian rector of Broughton would have thought, for, whilst about his early morning walks before breakfast, his wrath was even incurred by the shabby holes in the pinafores of any girls that he encountered, who, with the shortcomings of their attire having been pointed out by the Reverend with his walking stick, were swiftly despatched back to their mothers with the words 'a stitch in time saves nine' ringing in their ears! Trying that today would probably result in a foul mouthed tirade and a charge of child abuse. Oh dear, it does seem that one can only sigh and despair at the breakdown of moral standards. But never mind, now where I did put that list of guests for next Saturday's Swingers Party.

MURSLEY

IN MEMORY OF SIR JOHN FORTESCUE

Desended from Richard Fortescue, Knight, 'Cupp-bearer to King William the Conqueror', Sir John Fortescue, (or 'Sir John Ffoscue', as he appears in writings of the time), purchased the interest of Salden, near Mursley in the later 16th century.

He also owned the manor of Drayton Parslow, but repeatedly had to complain that the keepers and rangers of Lord Arthur Grey de Wilton, lord of the neighbouring manor of Whaddon, trespassed on his land in pursuit of deer.

In fact his servants had to beat off the intruders with bows and staves and eventually the matter came before the Lords of the Privy Council.

Here, Lord Grey contended that he had a right to fetch any deer of Whaddon Chase which strayed into Salden but the decision of the Lords was that Sir John had the right to 'absolute uninterrupted possession of his Manors.'

Declaring that "there hath been a continual custom time out of mind for the keepers with hound and horn to hunt and "make in" the deer that had strayed from the Chase," Arthur got a little upset by this and a while later whilst in London he laid in wait for Sir John with a number of armed men.

On seeing their quarry coming from Chancery Lane they then "strake him so sore" that he fell off his horse, and he might have been killed through further blows had a servant not pulled his 'insensible' body into an adjoining house.

However, Sir John recovered and at the impressive mansion that he built at Salden would entertain Elizabeth I and James I, having enjoyed great favour during their successive reigns.

In fact shortly after his succession it would be here that on June 28, 1603, King James knighted 22 worthies in one session.

Built on the site of an old manor house, the mansion was constructed around a courtyard from locally made bricks at a cost of £33,000, with the principal width measuring 175 feet.

One man was solely employed to open and close the numerous windows, and during his wanderings would no doubt greatly admire the many family coats of arms, richly depicted in stain glass.

In the grounds of the mansion bowling greens for recreation were laid out although due to a wayward ball it was said that here one of the family members had been killed.

At a local windmill corn was especially ground for the house, while for the impoverished of the district broken victuals were served daily in a nearby field appropriately known as Beggars Mead.

Indeed, any poor people encountered by the Fortescues on their daily walks would be given 2s 6d. As for the opposite end of the social spectrum, when during her famous travels Celia Fiennes encountered the mansion she wrote '6 mile to Horwood, thence we pass by a lofty pile of building called Salden, a Gentleman's house.'

Sir John Fortescue died at Westminster in 1607, and although this was the initial place of his burial his body was later moved to Mursley Church, where notable monuments to the family are to be seen in the chancel.

As for Salden House, this was partly demolished in 1738 and when the remainder succumbed in 1743 the various building materials were sold for about £450 to Thomas Harris, a builder of Cublington.

Only that part of the mansion used as a passage from the kitchen and great parlours escaped demolition, to be later converted into Salden House Farm (however, as a reminder of the former glory the ornate ironwork that graces the balcony of The George, in Winslow, was supposedly once a feature of Salden

House).

At the demolition of the mansion the noted antiquarian, Browne Willis, purchased a vestige of the stain glass 'for a trifle' (30s) and into the three lights of a north window this he inserted into St. Martin's Church, which he had founded at Fenny Stratford.

There it may still be seen and especially interesting are the arms of Fortescue

impaling 'Bolein,' dated 1556, since, possibly due to his relationship with Anne Boleyn, Sir John's father, Sir Adrian Fortescue, had fallen foul of Henry VIII, and, despite his distinguished career as a soldier, was consequently attainted for treason.

Milton Keynes Citizen May 24, 2012

MURSLEY WATER TOWER

Judging by the online response, the recent venture into the language of modern youth (Gayhurst, 11-11-10) seems not to have met with universal approval (!) But as stated, and no doubt to all our relief - not least the lady from the Citizen, who kindly types these pieces - this was definitely a one off. However, it proved gratifying to know that people do like to read about local history, and, as always, I am totally in awe of anyone who has the technical savvy to be able to post comments on this new fangled Internet. And so back to traditional English, albeit with one exception, for in my schooldays it was taught that beginning a sentence with 'and,' or 'but,' was a cardinal sin. But times have changed. And so to the theme of this week's piece, the water tower at Mursley. Despite being almost as far inland from the sea as possible, in the skies around Mursley aircraft of the Fleet Air Arm were a frequent sight before World War Two, engaged on cross country exercises. However, on one occasion a Fairey Swordfish biplane tragically crashed in a local field, and the track of its last erratic movements was gouged into the ground by the under slung practice torpedo. Tragically all the crew were killed, and a few years later there would be a poignant reoccurrence when, on April 11th 1943, a Wellington bomber, from the airfield at Wing, crashed into a water tower, which had been constructed in an adjoining field. Eighty feet high, and with the foundations said to be as deep as the height, this had been built just before World War Two at a cost of £23,995, and the capacity of 500,000 gallons - supplied from the pumping station at Battlesden - provided a reservoir for a large area of North and Central Buckinghamshire.

The R.A.F. airfield at Wing had been opened on November 17th 1941, and here No. 26 Operational Training Unit was formed in January 1942, predominantly equipped with 'war weary' Wellington bombers. Inevitably accidents occurred, and on one occasion whilst on a landing approach a Wellington had to be warned off by firing a flare, when another aircraft occupied the runway. The incoming pilot immediately opened the throttles, but on climbing away one of the engines lost power, and the aircraft crashed to the ground. Only 150 yards away a workman had been operating a dredger, and rushing to the wreckage he pulled the unconscious rear gunner clear of danger. In fact the gunner was the only member of the crew to survive, and after eight months of treatment and rest he returned to duty in November. Then on April 11th 1943 he was detailed as part of a Wellington crew scheduled for early morning dual circuits and landings, but in the foggy conditions the aircraft collided with the water tower, and all the crew were killed. A resulting fire greatly blackened the exterior, but although the engines of the bomber had gouged two large holes in the tower, apart from the distortion of some large diameter pipes there was no major structural damage, and repairs were carried out within a week. In fact the wartime scars would be visible until a general renovation in 1968, when during the work the crane driver decided to climb the jib of his machine to free a twisted cable. However, it would then be him who had to be freed, by the local fire brigade! In the grounds of the water tower, on May 8th 1995 (this date being chosen to coincide with the 50th anniversary of D Day) a memorial plaque, organised by Mr. Peter Abbey, was unveiled to those who perished in the crash, and their names are recalled in the wording.

THOMAS BEECHAM: KEEP TAKING THE TABLETS

Thomas Beecham, who began life in the 1830s as an Oxfordshire shepherd boy, became wealthy and famous for his Beecham's Pills - widely advertised by such slogans as 'Beecham's Pills save doctor's bills', and 'Beecham's Pills - worth a guinea a box'.

Tradition has it he was given the formula by an old shepherd on his deathbed, who asked for them to be patented and the money used to look after his wife.

Exploiting the opportunity, Tom gave up shepherding, and began to hawk his herbal remedies around the streets of a then thriving Lancashire.

In time, he and his first wife, Jane, settled in Wigan, where their first son, Joseph, was born. With the business continuing to prosper, the family moved in 1858 to St. Helens.

After Jane's death, Tom married Mary Sawell, whom he had met on Banbury station in September 1879, and in deference to her dislike of the industrial north, plus the advice of his doctors on health grounds to seek a more agreeable climate, he decided to move south.

Having many relatives in the area, eventually he chose Mursley, and duly purchased a large acreage adjoining the churchyard where, in 1881, construction of the couple's new house began. Meanwhile they lived elsewhere in the village - although Tom would be at the site almost every day to motivate the workmen in his forceful fashion!

SIR THOMAS BEECHAM

Good grief, it just beggars the imagination.

Apparently in today's world of 'pop star poppets' one woman has been known to prance around warbling with a telephone on her head, while for reasons somewhat obscure another seems to have a thing about umbrellas, ellas, ellas.

O' would that the Royal College of Music could produce such icons of melodic magnificence. But from the farcical to the fulsome, and a look at someone acquainted with our region who was truly possessed of musical talent, Sir Thomas Beecham.

He was the grandson of his namesake of Beechams Pills fame, whose story, and association with the village of Mursley, was the subject of a previous article.

At St. Helen's, Lancashire, Thomas's father, Joseph, had courted a local girl, Josephine Burnett, and with the couple being married in 1873 it would seem that Thomas, born on April 29th 1879, had inherited his mother's musical talents. Even at the age of five he displayed an early promise but the distractions of youth would soon take precedence and not least when he made the acquaintance of Utica Welles.

She was the daughter of the staff doctor at the American Embassy and when

Thomas proposed, Utica accepted.

However, this happiness was to be marred by the lessening health of his mother who, due to her many pregnancies and her advancing years, had contracted a mild form of epilepsy.

Supposedly 'for her own safety' Joseph then made covert arrangements to have her committed to an asylum, and so one day Thomas and his elder sister, Emily, returned home to discover that their mother was missing. When Joseph refused to say where she was a dramatic scene ensued and in culmination he threw them both out.

Disinherited, they went to London to fight their father in the courts and for a while lodged at the home of the Welles family. During this period Thomas kept his mind occupied by composing operas and attending concerts but not until the whole unpleasant business was resolved would he feel free to marry Utica.

Eventually Josephine was traced to a Northampton home and with Thomas and Emily having sent solicitors to visit her, not surprisingly she began a petition for divorce.

Following a settlement of £4,500 a year she was then taken into the care of Emily and the Welles family and with the situation now resolved Thomas married Utica in July 1903. Joseph did not attend the wedding. Indeed the rift between father and son had become so great that Thomas could expect no form of paternal allowance although one day as a gift Joseph, without warning, sent a pony and trap to Mursley Hall, an accommodation that had been presented to the couple as a wedding present by Thomas's grandfather.

In 1911 this then also became home to Josephine and Dr. Welles and his family, when they all moved from London. Yet less harmonious was the relationship between Thomas and Utica, who despite her husband's infidelity had no wish to divorce him.

Apart from the gift of Mursley Hall, Thomas Beecham had also presented his grandson with an allowance of £300 a year, but even with this welcome reprieve dire financial straits would have been the result, had not a timely reconciliation occurred with his father. In fact Joseph had developed an increasing admiration for his son's musical ability, and after a rift of nearly ten years he suddenly announced "You dam' well annoyed me." "And you annoyed me too," replied Thomas, after which they shook hands and that was that.

In October 1942 Sir Thomas Beecham (as he had now become) filed a suit for divorce from Utica and subsequently married Betty Thomas in New York. In later years he would retain an interest in Mursley by visiting village fêtes and today the family is remembered by The Beechams, built on the site of Mursley Hall. As for other local musical connections, Wing has a connection with Henry Purcell while as for my own musical abilities, well modesty forbids disclosing too much. But suffice to say I'm just off to practise my air guitar, for a star billing at the forthcoming Age Concern karaoke night.

Milton Keynes Citizen, October 11, 2012

THE MILLENNIUM WINDOW AT ST. MARY THE VIRGIN, MURSLEY

For the celebration of the Millennium, a commemorative window was placed in Mursley church and with a theme of local historical aspects included was a depiction of Mursley Hall. Previous articles have covered some of the story of the Beechams family, and their association with the village, but for this week's piece some of this is retold but with extra details.

At a cost of £10,000, as his country residence Thomas Beecham, of Beecham's Pills renown, had a mansion built at Mursley in the robust and solid manner of the period. On completion he named it Mursley Hall and crowned it with a weathervane enhanced with his own initials.

His initials would also grace Beechams Row, a terrace of cottages built at the northern end of the village to house the employees who were engaged in the gardens, on the farmlands, or on the small farm which Tom had established in the grounds of the Hall.

In addition to the outdoor workers, many domestics were also employed. In fact, Tom supposedly had such a reputation for his antics with the female staff that the windowsills of Mursley Hall were allegedly built higher than usual, to screen any untoward goings-on.

Nevertheless, he appears to have been well liked as a landlord, and took a genuine interest in the activities of the village. For the celebration of Queen Victoria's Golden Jubilee in 1887 he organised a sports event for the over 50s, followed by a sumptuous tea at Mursley Hall, where each of the female winners received dress lengths, and the men stockings and handkerchiefs. Widows and the very old were given new sovereigns.

Mursley Hall was, without doubt, among the most palatial of the local mansions, and children invited into the kitchen by the cook would stand in awe of all the numbered bells and the lovely spiral staircase.

Yet missing his involvement with the business, Tom began increasingly to spend weeks in the north, and Mary soon came to resent her spells of enforced loneliness - a situation frequently compounded by the absence of regular maids, as a consequence of Tom's amorous attentions.

Mary began to seek company elsewhere, and especially the friendship of a lady schoolteacher, whom she invited to share the Hall almost at will.

Whenever Tom returned, arguments would follow.

Returning from one of his jaunts, Tom announced that his wife Mary looked unwell and, before leaving that night, gave her two pills. Falling violently ill shortly afterwards, she became convinced he had tried to poison her.

Now more than ever she sought the support of her schoolteacher friend, and whenever Tom returned the two women would sleep in the same bed, with the door of the bedroom firmly locked.

Predictably, the marriage came to a premature end and, following a separation, a settlement was made. For good reason, Mary demanded the payment in cash.

Despite having many relatives in the district, Tom felt increasingly lonely at Mursley Hall and, with drink as his primary solace, his thoughts turned again to life in the north.

In 1892 he had a house built at Southport, and with all the stock and furniture at Mursley Hall sold, Tom's acquaintance with the village carme to an end.

But this would not be the end of the Beechams' association with the village.

As a young man, his nanmesake grandson proposed to Utica Welles, daughter of Dr. Welles, the staff doctor at the American Embassy, and she accepted.

Sadly, his happiness was marred by the deteriorating health of his mother. Due to her many pregnancies and advancing years, being in her late 40s, Josephine had developed a mild form of epilepsy and supposedly for her own safety, Joseph made secret arrangements to have her committed to an asylum.

So when Thomas and his elder sister, Emily, returned one day, they discovered their mother was missing. Joseph refused to say where she was and, in a dramatic scene, threw them both out.

Now disinherited, in the early 1900s they went to London to fight their father in the courts, and during this period would lodge for a while at the home of the Welles family. Here Thomas was allowed a room of his own and kept his mind occupied by composing operas and attending concerts, for until the whole unpleasant business was resolved he could not feel free to marry Utica.

Josephine was eventually traced to a Northampton home, where Thomas and Emily sent solicitors to visit her. Unsurprisingly, she then began to petition for divorce, and the case attracted widespread publicity.

Following a settlement of £4,500 a year, Josephine was taken into the care of Emily and the Welles family and, with the situation resolved, Thomas married Utica in July 1903. Joseph did not attend the wedding.

In fact, the rift between father and son had become so wide that Thomas could expect no form of paternal allowance. So it was fortunate that his grandfather, Tom, had given the couple Mursley Hall as a wedding present - to where Joseph one day without warning, sent a pony am as a belated gift.

In 1911 Mursley Hall also became home to Josephine and Dr. Welles and his family, when they all moved to London. The relationship between Thomas and Utica was becoming less, harmonious but, despite her husband's infidelity, she had no wish to divorce him.

Apart from the gift of Mursley Hall, Thomas Beecham had also presented his grandson with an allowance of £300 a year but, even so, he would have been in dire financial straits had there not occurred a timely reconciliation with his father.

Joseph had developed an increasing admiration for his son's musical ability and, after a rift of nearly 10 years, suddenly announced: "You damn well annoyed me."

"And you annoyed me too," replied Thomas, at which they shook hands, and that was that.

After the death of Utica's parents, Josephine continued to live alone at Mursley Hall, except for her servants, although occasionally Utica would come to visit with her two sons, Adrian and Tommy.

With the outbreak of the First World War they all came for a more prolonged stay, having deemed Mursley to be safer than London, and Utica would soon become an everyday sight, taking her sons around the village in a buggy cart.

Also to be sometimes glimpsed was 'Charlie', supposedly a brother of Lady Beecham, who had to be escorted on local excursions by a keeper, 'a big burly man' to whom he was handcuffed. Children ran when they saw them coming.

Known by the locals as the Dowager Lady Beecham, in her old age Josephine became ever more reclusive, and on November 3rd 1934 she died at Mursley Hall, having not once received a visit from Joseph.

As for Sir Thomas Beecham, as he had now become, in October 1942 he filed a suit for divorce from Utica, and subsequently married Betty Thomas in New York. Through continuing neglect, Mursley Hall began to fall into ruin and, following a sale of the household goods and furniture, was eventually disposed of.

In more recent years a fire ravaged the building. The site was bought by developers and is now overlaid by the Beechams housing estate.

Two monkey puzzle trees still recall the former grounds which, according to new residents, continue to yield lumps of coal that were once stored in the old fuel bunkers.

NEW BRADWELL

NEW BRADWELL: BRANCH RAILWAY

In 1862, encouraged by the success of the railways a scheme was proposed for a branch line to initially link Wolverton and Newport Pagnell, and, as the subject for a future article, despite the objections of the Grand Junction Canal Company, Parliamentary authority was obtained to close and sell the branch canal from

Great Linford to Newport Pagnell, such that a part of the track could be laid on the dry canal bed. Hauling 17 wagon loads of navvies, a steam locomotive made the inaugural passage on September 30th 1865, and with the line opened the next year for goods, parcel and cattle traffic, passengers would be carried after September 2nd 1867. The provision of a single platform was made at the intermediate stops of Bradwell and Great Linford, and at the latter a man was employed to deliver parcels in his spare time within a radius of one mile. Plans were even made to extend the railway to Olney, but shortly after the work began in 1874 the scheme was abandoned.

As for the existing railway, often being a London and North Western side tank, the little steam engine, pulling the three or four coaches, would be affectionately known as 'Nobby Newport' (or more usually by the railwaymen as the 'Wolverton Worker'). Then in 1964 railway economies forced a closure, although at Great Linford the naming of Station Terrace still reminds of a steamy past. However, there was hopefully nothing steamy in the past of Mrs. G. Tupper of 3, Station

Terrace, for in a testament to the wonders of Doan's backache kidney pills she, in the early years of the 20th century, would pen the glowing recommendation; "It was pleurisy that left my back weak. I used to get dull, aching pains there, which made it miserable moving about. I hardly knew at times how to raise myself after stooping, owing to the pains. But I found Doan's backache kidney pills very helpful to me; they relieved my back splendidly, and I could move about in comfort afterwards. I always speak well of Doan's pills now."

Since the arrival of the New City, at New Bradwell the course of the old track has become Railway Walk, but possibly an additional remembrance remains in the shadowy form of a group of ghoulish Victorian passengers, who, on occasion, have supposedly been seen awaiting their phantom train at the site of the old station. However, with shades of the modern day railways perhaps one got fed up with waiting, for a few years after World War Two a ghostly form was sighted by a couple outside their home at 21, High Street, New Bradwell. Waiting up for their daughter, one Sunday just after midnight they were startled to see a figure in "a long white night gown" gliding towards them down Glyn Street. Then the apparition suddenly turned around and went back towards the junction of Glyn Street and Spencer Street, where - having been chased by the husband - it just disappeared on the spot. The man then confided to his wife that he had experienced a similar encounter some two weeks before, when the apparition had passed him along the back way of the High Street, to vanish in almost the same location. All very strange, and although it may all be a load of old cobblers, I for one won't be investigating, for there can be no more shocking an experience than to be suddenly grabbed by the ghoulies.

NEW BRADWELL: CHURCHES AND A VERY 'TURBULENT PRIEST'

At St. James Church, New Bradwell, in February 1951, the Lord Bishop of Oxford dedicated a new east window.

The work, by prominent artist Christopher Webb commemorated various former parishioners and priests of the parish since its foundation in 1860.

For many of those present, the most vivid recollections would be of the Reverend Allan Newman Guest, whose local antics had been almost as colourful as the glass in the new window.

But in earlier times the most famous of the clergy was the renowned poet John Mason, who served as vicar of the church at Stanton Low from 1668 until 1674.

As a small agricultural village, the community had been devastated by the 'enclosure' policy of the then lord of the manor, Sir Nicholas Vaux, who converted some 36 of the Stantonbury acres to sheep farming. As a rich and powerful man, who was a counsellor to King Henry VIII, he had the authority to have 40 people summarily evicted from their homes, and by 1563 only three households remained.

A further decline would be evident following the arrival of the railways in the 19th century, when the township that was initially termed Stantonbury, but became more popularly known as New Bradwell, began to be built nearby.

The London to Birmingham railway line had been completed in 1838, and with Wolverton chosen as the location to construct both a major station and the central engine works, the urgent need had arisen to acquire land on which to build housing for the workers.

However, at Wolverton, the landowning lords of the manor, the Radcliffe Trustees, were unwilling to continue the sale of their acres, and when suitable sites at Stony Stratford, Newport Pagnell and even further afield had been exhausted, the railway company decided to create a new township.

In 1852 they purchased not only 15 arable acres lying between the Newport Road and the canal, but also four acres of field next to Bradwell Brook and the Bradwell Road. And with Mr. Parnell engaged as the contractor, by the end of 1853 more than 100 terraced dwellings had been built, as well as the Foresters Arms public house. With the railway company now being the major landowner, the new town would eventually become known as New Bradwell.

To serve the spiritual needs of the population, the foundation stone of St. James Church was laid by the chairman of the LNWR railway company, the Marquis of Chandos, on Monday, May 24th 1858. The ensuing construction was undertaken by Mr. J. Mills, of Stratford-upon-Avon, to the designs of Mr. G. Street, of London, architect of the Strand Law Courts. The costs would total £4,430, partly paid for by subscription, plus a further £1,000 for the provision of a spire and upper tower.

On Thursday, December 6th 1860, the Bishop of Oxford, addressed the assembled railway workers in the great engine shed and then consecrated the new church.

A stone font bearing the inscription 'Presented to God and the service of the Church of St. James, Stantonbury, by the Marchioness of Chandos' was placed at the western end of the north aisle. The pulpit was a gift from the engine factory foreman and the workmen of Wolverton.

Despite the building of St. James Church, services continued to be held at St. Peter's Church.

The Reverend Allan Newman Guest, 'a strong-willed Irishman' who was born in County Kerry in 1862, became the vicar of Stantonbury cum New Bradwell in September 1908.

Then, with New Bradwell now well established as a thriving community, on July 1st 1909, St. Peter's Church was demoted to the status of a chapel. Nevertheless, a restoration took place in 1910, at which an altar and credence table dating from the time of King Stephen was found.

However, there would now also be a need to restore the faith of the congregation in their new vicar, for after an evening service in March 1909, he announced that, the 'instrument' necessary to convey the rights and privileges of St. Peter's Church at Stantonbury to the new church of St. James did not exist. Having been either lost or never made out. Therefore those couples who had been married at Saint James were technically living in sin, conferring an unfortunate status upon any children born of those unions. This naturally caused great consternation, and in 1909 a special Act of Parliament had to be passed to swiftly legalise the hundreds of marriages in question.

With the outbreak of the First World War and the consequent sense of national unity, it might be hoped that there would also have been an increased unity between the Reverend Guest and his flock. But sadly this was not to be, and on one occasion some of the congregation even pelted him with hymn books.

It was perhaps just as well that he was tall and well built and able to defend himself. Indeed, he had fostered boxing competitions in the vicarage gardens, 'and issued challenges which created a considerable amount of controversy at the time'.

However, it was a one-sided attack which led to him being fined £3 for assault at Newport Pagnell Petty Sessions, the summons having been taken out by a lady of Bridge Street, Stantonbury, for beating her 14 year-old daughter.

The girl had only just recovered from a bout of pneumonia, and while standing outside her home with some friends the vicar approached, and asked why she did not attend church.

She replied that as a member of the Primitive Methodist faith she could not attend, whereupon the vicar retorted: "There is only one church in England, and that is my church," and gave her a vigorous blow on the cheek. The mark was still visible the next morning, and when he later tried to apologise, the girl's mother slammed the door in his face. Not only was he fined, but also ordered to pay the expenses of six witnesses.

Apart from such notorious instances, the Rev. Guest also became known for championing Sunday gardening, sports and pastimes on Sundays after church service. He threw out a challenge to all comers, 10 years his junior, to swim 100 yards at Wolverton's new bathing place. Unfortunately he lost.

After the war, despite the installation of a new organ in 1930, the services at St. Peter's Church became ever more occasional, although an increasing interest in the history of the building caused a great deal of excavation to be undertaken between 1930 and 1936.

During the Second World War the vicar was in the news again when fined at Stony Stratford Police Court for an assault upon Israel Bloom, an elderly tailor, and his wife.

The couple, who were at the vicarage, alleged that the minister had struck them during an argument about an open door. His defence was that, even though five people had been killed when bombs fell locally, he had received little co-operation from the pair in keeping the door closed to prevent light from shining onto the church. It was alleged that the door must have struck Mr. Bloom when forcefully closed by the Reverend.

A keen archaeologist and historian, 'Father Guest' would remain in the parish until 1946, when, on Sunday, October 6th, news of his resignation from the vicariate of the parish of Stantonbury and New Bradwell was posted on the door of St. James Church. The living was then entrusted to the Rev. E. Steer, vicar of Stony Stratford and Rural Dean.

For the past three years the church had been empty on many Sundays, and in the aftermath of this prolonged neglect during the ensuing week a band of willing ladies began a thorough clean of the church interior. Attention was also needed for the churchyard, which had similarly suffered.

At the end of October services - now more fully attended - were recommenced, taken by Canon F. Howard, a former vicar of Aylesbury. He had recently retired from the active ministry and lived at Wavendon.

As for the Rev. Guest, he died in December 1946 at a Bedford nursing home, aged 79, and was cremated at Golders Green in London.

NEW BRADWELL: SCRAP YARDS: WHEN SCRAP METAL WAS VITAL TO THE WAR EFFORT.

Much as expected, many of the specimens involved in the current spate of metal theft seem to be the less finely honed implements in the tool box.

And not least some sub species who apparently tried to hack through a high voltage cable at an electricity sub station, with predictable results.

Oh well, thieves will always be with us. But those who steal war memorials, to melt down for a few quid, are the real sad life and hardly worthy of the freedoms for which those commemorated sacrificed their lives.

Such as during World War One, when in July 1916 an example of German 'scrap' metal was displayed in the window of Berwicks shop in Fenny Stratford.

This was in the form of a Prussian helmet which, recovered from one of the enemy trenches, had been sent home to his father by Corporal Sid Wodhams.

After the war another example of German steel was then sent to Bletchley but under more peaceful conditions.

This was a 40 foot girder, for when building the Co-op stores in Bletchley Road (now Queensway) the firm of Tranfields found that a single section girder of this length was not available in this country. Therefore they had to order one from Krupps at Essen, Germany, which was duly shipped to a north east port.

A few years after the war the youngest son of Mr. E.W. Morgan, of Duncombe Street, Bletchley, would receive the MBE for his role in recovering a large quantity of gold, and other valuable metal, aboard the White Star liner 'Laurentic,' which had been sunk by enemy action in January 1917.

But more locally, with just a horse and cart Edward Goodman began a scrap metal business in New Bradwell which after his death his widow relinquished to her sons, of a family of 12 children.

For nearly 30 years in a paddock opposite the Cuba Hotel she lived in a caravan and having been ill for awhile it was there that she was attended by her doctors, before being removed to Northampton General Hospital, where she died aged 61.

Towards the late 1930s there came an urgent need for scrap metal for re-armament and the need became even more acute following the outbreak of war.

"Very few of us can be heroines on the battlefront, but we can all have the tiny thrill of thinking as we hear the news of an epic battle in the air, perhaps it was my saucepan that made a part of that Hurricane."

So said Lady Reading in a radio broadcast when, as the head of the W.V.S., she launched a campaign to collect scrap metal.

In fact the Government had especially asked the W.V.S. to concentrate on aluminium, 'One ton of aluminium makes a Spitfire,' and in 1940 Bletchley Urban District Council launched a general appeal.

A 'salvage canvass' began and of great surprise from Water Eaton came an aluminium pipe rack labelled, 'A bit of the Germans' own metal, to hit back at them.'

It had originally been part of a Zeppelin brought down at Cuffley during World War One!

In fact the need for metal was so great that although for his 63 years' of farm work 81 year old Dick Faulkner, of Loughton, had been awarded a Long Service Certificate by the Royal Agricultural Society of England, there was no metal for the associated bronze medal.

At New Bradwell, about 1964 Fred Cox started a scrap metal business, moving to Bleak Hall Industrial Estate in May 1974.

Also at New Bradwell, at this time on the original site W. Goodman Bros. were operating a scrap yard whilst of the same family there were three other independent companies; E. Goodman Bros. in Old Bradwell Road, New Bradwell, J.G. Goodman in Old Bradwell and A. Goodman and Son in Bletchley.

A feature of the Newport Road yard was a large metal crown which had supposedly been used during the coronation of King George 6th being then brought to Luton for the coronation celebrations of Queen Elizabeth.

As for the yard in Old Bradwell Road, here for many years was an old steam engine, which many people incorrectly thought was 'Nobby Newport,' from the adjacent branch line.

As for Bletchley, the scrapyard is still to be seen, with a large sign on the old United Counties bus depot.

Milton Keynes Citizen February 23, 2012

War Effort: The Cockerel auction.

NEWPORT PAGNELL

A RED CROSS SALE, WW1

Every picture tells a story although in this age of digital manipulation if it's a truthful one is open to debate.

But with postcards and snapshots of yesteryear what you see is what you get, albeit with the misfortune of often having no clue as to the event or specific location.

Yet there's no doubt about the story regarding this scene and it's all thanks to no less than the 'V.C. Cockerel,' 'Mr. Fyson's famous bird.' This wording is just discernible on the notice on the platform and identifies the event to be a Red Cross sale held on Market Hill, Newport Pagnell, on Wednesday, April 24th 1918.

The cockerel had been purchased by Frank Fyson for 2s at Warboys Red

Cross Sale in October 1915, and being above military age, and with no sons, he determined to raise at least £1,000 for wounded soldiers.

A legend among its feathered friends, during 103 previous sales his 'V.C. Cockerel' had raised £8,212 for the Red Cross and the intention was for it to be auctioned and then handed back for re-auction.

In the photo the cockerel's cage is seen almost centre in front of the platform. As for the human element, this photo epitomises how in times of crisis the nation's population swiftly unites. On parade to the left are the Royal Engineers stationed in the town. Opposite, sporting their distinctive armbands, are the Special Constables - men not eligible for the Army but who, apart from their normal employment, have taken the place of those members of the regular police now in the Forces.

Behind them, in their distinctive floppy hats, are women of the Women's Land Army, among whom are perhaps the daughters of the Reverend Easson, from Chicheley, who by touring the town attired in their WLA Uniforms collected £14 6s 6d with a barrel organ.

Within this vicinity are the wounded soldiers from the VAD Hospital at Tickford Abbey, and some of the nurses can be seen in the upper right. Having gained the necessary qualification many girls would fulfil this role, including Daphne Trevor from Lathbury Park.

The proceeds were to be divided between the British Farmers' Red Cross Fund and the Bucks Branch of the Red Cross Society and even before the sale substantial donations had been received.

Mr. P. C. Gambell acted as the honorary auctioneer and his office staff - Miss Geary, Miss Cox, Miss Inns and Mr. Hedge - all worked hard throughout the day.

Having been invited to open the sale, the Marquis of Lincolnshire inspected the Guard of Honour of the Volunteers and Special Constables and, after a similar inspection of the WLA and wounded soldiers, took to the platform.

He recalled his boyhood memories of the district and praised the Army, Volunteers, Special Constables, WLA and nurses, saying that although for three years he had acted as Lord Chamberlain to Queen Victoria, thus attending many Drawing Rooms, he had never seen a better group of young women than the representatives of the WLA.

He then called for three cheers for the King, plus an extra cheer for the Prince of Wales. Bidding £5 he put the 'Cockerel' up for sale, after which Mr. Gambell took over and a sum of £60 6s was obtained.

In the afternoon at a meeting of the Farmers' Union he again offered the bird and this time a further £69 10s 6d was secured, plus a further £23 7s 6d in the evening.

So had it not been for a famous chicken this postcard scene would have remained a complete mystery. In fact by the end of the war the bird had been sold 12,237 times and raised £14,517.

And so if any descendants of the V.C. Cockerel get to see this article, then they'll certainly have something to crow about ....

Milton Keynes Citizen, May 31, 2012

NEWPORT PAGNELL: CIVIL WAR

During the English Civil War, the Royalists realised the strategic importance of Newport Pagnell, and at the end of summer 1643 they seized the town and "forced the inhabitants to come in and intrench it and draw the river about it the better to strengthen and fortifie it ..."

Thereupon the Earl of Essex sent a force under Major General Skippon to drive them out, and with this accomplished on Friday, October 27th they took possession, and not only continued the fortifications but also launched attacks on the Cavaliers in the proximity, including a night raid on Stony Stratford, in which 18 prisoners were taken.

Establishing his headquarters at the Saracen's Head (adjoining the Swan) in January 1644 Sir Samuel Luke became the Governor of the town, and his attention would soon turn to repairing the fortifications, for in March heavy rain caused the earthworks to give way.

In fact with Royalists stationed at Buckingham the rebuilding was imperative, as evidenced by the 3,500 or so labourers. Barracks were built in the Market Place (part of the building being used in later years for waterworks), whilst as for the townspeople, no one was allowed out after 9 p.m.

By June the garrison comprised 1,200 foot, and with one of these being John Bunyon, of Pilgrim's Progress fame, the town also gained note as the situation where Cromwell's namesake son is said to have died, from smallpox. As the sometimes haunt of the notorious Captain Pollard, by whom the rector of Tyringham was badly maimed, Whaddon Chase provided a space where Luke's falconers could exercise their feathery charge. However, it was also a useful source of timber for the town's fortification, and - by an order of the Buckinghamshire Committee at Aylesbury - on March 28th 1645 Luke was commanded to procure '100 loads of timber out of the woods of the Earl of Antrim at Whaddon, and 2,000 poles out of the College Woods there.' Apart from the Cavaliers, on occasion Luke had to deal with hostility from his own ranks, especially when Henry Andrewes failed to receive a promised promotion from Captain to Major. This was despite Luke's earnest endeavours, and when the rank was awarded to a Captain Ennis, Henry mistakenly believed that Luke had been responsible. A feud then developed between the two troops, and 'I cannot hope for any good from him or his troop, he being heightened and cherished in his discontents by his friends.' In fact by the spring of 1645 all the local Roundheads seemed demoralised, largely due to want of pay, whilst in other needs Luke wrote "in my company two that had but one payre of Britches between them soe that when one was up the other must of necessity be in his bed." However, having raised the siege of Oxford, Sir Thomas Fairfax reached Sherington on June 7th and at Newport Pagnell was shown around the fortifications by Luke. In the wake of the decisive Parliamentary victory at Naseby, Luke ordered a public thanksgiving to be held in the parish church, but on the day it became apparent that many people had been drawn to an unorthodox gathering, organised at Lathbury by two Captains of Colonel Fleetwood's Regiment. Enraged by this impertinence, Luke had the two soldiers arrested as 'stragglers' and swiftly sent them back to Sir Thomas Fairfax, Supreme Commander of the New Model Army, in the expectation that 'such Anabaptistical companions trouble us no more.' Sir Samuel Luke's local command came to an end on June 26th 1645, and he was succeeded by Captain Charles D'Oyley. However, during the autumn and winter the troops seem to have become quite lawless, and soon the garrison was reduced to 800 foot and 120 horses.

Nevertheless, in 1646 parliamentary dragoons from Newport Pagnell 'seized upon a poore Bone lace man and a shoemaker near Stony Stratford, robbed them of what they had and sent them away prisoners to Aylesbury …" Therefore it was no doubt a local relief when, in the autumn of 1646, the order came to dismantle the fortifications at Newport Pagnell, and disband the garrison.

NEWPORT PAGNELL: WORKHOUSE CONDITIONS

In these days of recession any job is welcome, although for persons of a certain age most of those available could of course be quite happily performed by Bobo the chimp and his mates on day release from the local safari park - and for far less peanuts.

But then whingeing about employment, or lack of it, is of course as much an endearing trait of the British psyche as moaning about the weather. Yet not so long ago - in the days before the Welfare State, and 'the world owes me a living' culture - there really was something to whinge about, since, as touched upon in a previous article, for the destitute the horrors of the Workhouse awaited.

And so to put things in perspective it's perhaps time to reflect upon those conditions that prevailed at the Newport Pagnell Workhouse, as told by 'one who was there.'

"Up to recently breakfast and supper at the Newport casual ward comprised 6 oz of bread and a pint of gruel.

However, if you should at any time desire to take yourself to a casual ward don't fall into the error of thinking you are off to a convalescent home.

Otherwise you will soon find that a very rude awakening awaits you in the discovery that it is a place where there is a wealth of work and a paucity of food. But let me commence my rigmarole from the beginning.

Casuals are taken in at six o'clock, and the Guardians dislike turning away any tired and hungry mortal on account of the lateness of the application and therefore admissions are sometimes made quite late.

"The first item on the programme on entering is making a record of the usual personal details - name, age, occupation, where from and to where going, and so on.

"Then comes the search of pockets for hidden treasure - lucre, tobacco, matches, and other things barred in such establishments.

"A usually by no means unwelcome bath follows, and then a newcomer gets outside his supper, after which he may adjourn to his bed and slumber away the hours of darkness in the sure and certain knowledge that on the morrow he is in for nine hours work at wood sawing, scrubbing, stone breaking, oakum picking, cleaning up, garden labour, or any general employment on hand.

"The dinner hour is from twelve to one, when work is resumed and continued till 4.30, supper being served soon after, and then follows a general turn-in for the night, so that while tarrying at the expense of the Newport ratepayers a vagrant's life is all work and bed.

"Those due for discharge are not eligible for readmission till they have "tried their luck" for work elsewhere, and if they apply again within a month they are liable to three days' detention, although with the more costly dietary under the new regulations the Guardians are by no means anxious for more detentions than necessary.

"On leaving each casual receives half-a-pound of bread and two ounces of cheese. "

Poor as is the hospitality at the Newport casual ward, those who are compelled to take advantage of it may derive some consolation from the more or less comforting reflection that hard as life is there it is harder in some similar establishments.

"For instance, in some places a wood bed and wood pillow is the order, with as much as 13cwt. of stones to break up; the men being detained on the second day till the task is completed, in addition to which the work is done under the superintendence of officers who are mere bullies, whereas at Newport one does fall in for a little more reasonable treatment at the hands of the Master and his subordinates if one makes a proper attack on the work.

"It seems hard that our Poor Law system should compel a man to be absolutely destitute before he can take advantage of the casual ward, and then when he does so afford him no chance of earning so much as a copper with the result that he comes out as hard up as he goes in ..."

Quite a simple philosophy really; if you didn't work you didn't eat. Well, I suppose death by starvation was one way of keeping the unemployment figures down.

NEWPORT PAGNELL'S FLU PANDEMIC

In fact at an estimated 25 million this would claim more lives than were lost during WWI, and it was a tragic irony that locally several soldiers who survived the carnage of the trenches would fall victim to the outbreak on their return.

The flu strain occurred in three waves, with the first, in the early summer of 1918, being comparatively mild. However, in August a more lethal strain emerged, and it would be from this that 26 year old Sergeant Instructor F. Fincher, of the King's Royal Rifles (Cadet Battalion) died on October 25th 1918.

A Territorial before the war, he had been mobilised with the County regiment, but was discharged after sustaining a serious wound to his neck in the trenches.

He then joined the King's Royal Rifles (Cadet Battalion), and it was their members who formed a firing party at his funeral, held at St. George the Martyr's Church, Wolverton.

Boosting local morale, throughout the war the talented musician, Mr. C.K. Garratt, from Newport Pagnell, had locally arranged numerous concerts and entertainments, but sadly his young wife died from the epidemic in late October.

In fact such was the severity that with many teachers being affected it had been necessary to close the Council Schools at Wolverton, whilst at the railway works, and McCorquodales printing works, some 40% of the workforce was absent.

At Stantonbury over 500 inhabitants were ill, and amongst the hundreds more at Wolverton there would be several deaths, including that of Mr. George Scrivener, a body maker at the railway works.

Aged 37 he had succumbed on October 22nd 1918, and it was because his wife and six children were also affected that he had moved to his mother's home in Victoria Street.

Twenty two year old Miss Gladys Sykes, 'a bright and attractive person,' also became a victim. Her parents lived at 1, Radcliffe Street, Wolverton, and for some while she had been employed delivering milk for the Co-op.

In Europe the disease was also raging, and at No. 9 Casualty Clearing Station, Italy, 34 year old Driver Frank Lamble, of the Royal Horse Artillery, died from pneumonia following influenza on October 30th 1918.

He had seen much severe fighting in his three years in France and one year on the Italian Front, and at 95, Church Street, Wolverton, he left a widow and a five year old son.

Also on October 30th Eddy Leonard, the only son of Mr. & Mrs. Leonard, of Bletchley, died from influenza in France. He had been a bell ringer at St. Mary's Church, and in his memory on the Sunday the bells were rung half muffled.

Also regarding Bletchley, here there were now many cases of influenza, and dated October 28th 1918 a lengthy document- signed by the Medical Officer of Health for the district, Dr. E. Nicholson, and the Clerk to the Council, by which body it had been raised - had been issued headed 'Epidemic Catarrh and Influenza,' giving advice on preventative measures.

Despite 30% of the pupils being absent the schools were still open, although bills posted in the town announced that because of the epidemic the Picture Palace had been closed.

In other manifestations a shortage of staff caused some shops to occasionally close, or only be open for reduced hours, whilst as for the Bletchley Road Sub Post Office, this had been shut for several days towards the end of October.

In fact emphasising the seriousness of the situation, 34 year old Lieutenant Newbery-Boschetti, of the Royal Naval Reserve, had died from the epidemic at Maidenhead.

For some years his family had been resident at Far Bletchley, and it was after the death of his father that they assumed the name of Newbery, being known as such until Mrs. Newbery and her children went to live elsewhere.

Through the winter of 1918/1919 came the third deadly strain of the virus, and at Hanslope the funeral took place on Saturday, November 2nd 1918 of Miss Cox, the 60 year old headmistress of the Church End Schools.

During the previous fortnight, by the end of the first week of November there had been over 20 deaths in Stantonbury, and, with these being mostly from pneumonia following influenza, no other town had suffered to such an extent.

Abroad on active service, there was tragic news regarding Lance Corporal Herbert Staniford, for having been admitted to the General Hospital, Salonika, on November 5th, 1918, he died the following day from pneumonia.

Before joining up he had been well known in Leighton Buzzard and Fenny Stratford, being a special constable and a brother of the St. Martin's Lodge of Freemasons.

The flu epidemic continued throughout the month, and Mr. and Mrs. S. Johnson, of 48, Queen Anne Street, Stantonbury, would receive official news that their youngest son, twenty eight year old Sergeant David Johnson, of the 7th Oxon and Bucks Light Infantry, had died at a military hospital in France on November 27th 1918.

After three years of strenuous service in Salonika he was on his way home on leave when he contracted the illness. Locally the disease was still widespread, as also much further distant, for on December 5th 1918 Private Victor Page, the second son of Mr. & Mrs. Victor Page, of Aylesbury Street, died of pneumonia at Salonika, to where he had been sent a few months after arriving in France 3½ years ago.

His youngest brother, Gunner B. Page, was still in France, whilst the eldest brother had lost a leg in the earlier part of the war. Within two hours of each other, Mrs. Annie Dorrill and her five year old son died on Saturday, December 7th 1918.

Mrs. Dorrill's husband, Bombardier Joseph Dorrill, had served throughout the war with the Royal Horse Artillery, and it was while on the Western Front with the victorious British troops that he heard the news.

His other children were daughters aged 7 and 2½, with the family being resident at 29a, Mill Street, Newport Pagnell. Her home being in London Road, Newport Pagnell, also on December 7th, and also from influenza, at Northampton Hospital the death occurred of Mrs. Louisa Woolhead, whose husband was serving in India as overseer of a regimental tailoring department.

As for 21 year old Private George Daniells, the second son of the late Mr. George Daniells and Mrs. Daniells of 44, Caldecote Street, Newport Pagnell, he tragically died on the eve of his anticipated return to civilian life.

Hopes had been expressed for his recovery, but he was deemed not strong enough to make the journey from No. 32 Casualty Clearing Station, where he died on January 16th 1919.

He was buried the following day in Valenciennes cemetery. Previously in the employ of Dr. C. Bailey, he had enlisted in the Oxon and Bucks Light Infantry in May 1915, but on account of his health was transferred two months later to the Ammunition Column of the R.A.S.C., with which he served on the Western Front for almost two years.

The following month on the 27th Sergeant Alfred West, M.M., of the 2nd Battalion Oxon and Bucks Light Infantry, died at the Gravesend Military Hospital from influenza. Aged 27, he was the eldest son of Mr. and Mrs. A. West, of Broughton, and being on the Special Reserve had been mobilised with his regiment. Wounded in the retreat from Mons, he subsequently witnessed much hard fighting in France and Flanders, and would receive his promotion on the battlefield. Then for having carried an officer to safety under heavy fire he was awarded the Military Medal.

After the Armistice, Sergeant West served with the British Army of Occupation, and it was whilst on his way home to begin work on the farm of Mr. Adams, at Broughton, that he contracted his illness.

Only nine months before he had married Mrs. Lake, of Priory Street, Newport Pagnell, whose first husband had been killed early in the hostilities.

From Gravesend, the body of Sergeant West was brought for interment in Newport Pagnell Cemetery on Wednesday, March 5th, and amongst those present were several soldiers who had been on active service.

Even in April the flu epidemic was still claiming victims, and on Wednesday, April 2nd 1919 Aircraftsman Harry Sear, of the R.F.C., died in the Military Hospital, Norwich, from pneumonia, following influenza.

He was the son of Mr. and Mrs. Sear, of 83, Newport Road, Stantonbury, and had been apprenticed in the finishing shop at Wolverton Works.

Aged 17 he voluntarily enlisted in September 1918, and after a while at Halton Camp, Wendover, was transferred to an aircraft station at Yarmouth.

There he contracted the illness, and his remains were brought for interment at Stantonbury. By now the Reverend Bennitt, of Bletchley, had returned to England from active service with the R.A.M.C. in Salonika, but no sooner had he arrived than he became seriously ill.

He was then sent to the Military Hospital at West Bridgford, Nottingham, from where he wrote in a letter; 'Early in November I was sent to Salonika; at about the time when the troops advanced against Bulgaria.

There was a great deal of malaria and influenza, and a strong reinforcement of R.A.M.C. was sent out. However, by the time we arrived, an improvement had taken place, and only about half our number were needed.

Personally, I was put in the Army Pay Office at the Base Depot, and have done very little R.A.M.C. work at all. However, from another point of view, my work in the Army has been of value.

I have frequently taken services, both week-days and Sundays, and it does seem to have been a good thing for me to have shared in the ordinary daily life among the men on an exact equality rather than as a Chaplain.

At any rate, I have learnt more of the general point of view of the men of all branches of the service than otherwise could have been possible.' As printed in an issue of the parish magazine he continued 'I expect to be back at home by the second Sunday in April,' and indeed having made favourable progress he was able on Sunday, April 13th to conduct the services at St. Mary's Church, where he was heartily welcomed by the parishioners.

By now the flu strain had thankfully run its course, and although there would be further outbreaks during the 1920s, these would prove far less severe.

ODELLS, IN WAR & PEACE

In these days of super stores it's increasingly difficult for small, family run shops to survive.

Yet at Stony Stratford the name of Odell still flourishes although the Odell's shop in Newport Pagnell closed in 1991 after many decades in business.

Born in 1849 into the ironmongery and agricultural implement business, John Odell was the eldest son of John Odell and after a period working in his father's establishment in the High Street, Newport Pagnell, he completed his apprenticeship in Banbury.

At his father's death in 1896 he then took over the Newport Pagnell business and built it up into one of the largest in that part of the county.

In other activities in his younger days he served in the Bucks Regiment of Volunteers and for many years would be a member of the Volunteer Fire Brigade.

He married the eldest daughter of Thomas Shakeshaft, of Ravenstone, and within an hour of the outbreak of the First World War on August 4, 1914 their eldest son, Percy, volunteered for active service saying, "I am prepared to do anything."

With many men now volunteering for Kitchener's Army the need for replacement shop staff would increase and in the following month John had the need for an active man as a porter and also an errand boy.

As for the staff who joined up, Harry Bunker was an early casualty, killed in action at Mons. In December 1914 Reginald, John's second son, volunteered for active service while the third son, Cecil, was serving in Egypt, having been in Australia when the war broke out.

In September 1915 news arrived that Reginald had been wounded for the second time in Flanders and then on December 31st 1915 he became a casualty for the third time, when a bullet smashed his rifle and caused a wound in his side.

Then in May 1916 came news that Lance Corporal Percy Odell had been

Large assortment of Lawn Tennis Balls and Rackets in stock by all the leading manufacturers : --- Ayres, Bussey's, Slazenger's, etc.

VACUUM CLEANERS,
BRUSHES,
GARDEN FORKS
& SPADES.

LAWN MOWERS

GARDEN ROLLERS,
GARDEN ARCHES,
WOOD TRELLIS.

Agent for all the Leading Agricultural Implement Makers & Horticulturists.

Engineer. J. ODELL. Ironmonger.

slightly wounded by a bursting shrapnel shell, which fractured his right thumb.

However, for Reginald he would suffer a fourth wound, to be subsequently treated in Chelsea Hospital for serious shoulder injuries.

Then came the tragic news that Corporal Percy Odell had been killed in action on the Somme and today a plaque to his memory may be seen in the parish church.

As for Reginald he would be discharged from the army and once back in Newport Pagnell would become one of the night orderlies at Tickford Abbey V.A.D. Hospital.

His sister Dorothy was nursing and following the crash at Lathbury of an aeroplane, which spun from 400 feet to crash into a large elm tree in a field, she on several occasions would sit up all night with the unconscious pilot at the home of his father in law in Newport Pagnell, to where he had been taken.

On January 13th 1920, her mother, Elizabeth Annie Odell, died and now with the help of his sons Mr. Odell carried on the business.

As for Dorothy she was a pioneer of the Girl Guide movement in the town, being captain of the Parish Church Company, and she also taught in the Sunday School, of which in 1927 she became superintendent.

Apart from involvement with his business at Newport Pagnell her father was a Freemason and also served as a Governor of Northampton Hospital, of which he was a member of the Board.

Aged 83 he died on Friday, January 9th 1932, at his home, Blair House, High Street, to be buried in the grave of his wife.

Reginald and Cecil now took over the business while on Saturday, April 16th 1932, Dorothy left Newport Pagnell to begin a training course in religious and social work at St. Andrew's House, Portsmouth Training College.

Cecil Odell died in 1970 aged 85 and Reginald in 1976 aged 93 and it would be in December 1991 that the Odell's shop at Newport Pagnell finally closed

Milton Keynes Citizen, November 8, 2012

ORSON BULL

Floundering with style, is perhaps the best way to describe my response to the Bletchley Road Junior School's 1950s technique of swimming instruction.

Which in exasperation as a last resort involved being towed by a rope through the icy cold waters of Queen's Pool (now the site of the new leisure complex.)

And on the subject of complexes, after that experience I never did master the art of progressing gracefully through the water.

So perhaps the renowned instruction of Orson Henry Bull, a respected local head teacher, should have been employed. Aged 82, Mr. Bull died in May 1937 at his home, Colville House, Newport Pagnell, and although ill for about four years he had been able to take fresh air in his bath chair until the last three weeks.

The only son of Henry Bull, a lime and cement manufacturer, he was born at Oulton Broad near Lowestoft and after training as a pupil teacher at Carlton Colville, a suburb of Lowestoft, progressed to a distinguished period of study at Culham College, Oxford.

He later took his B.A. at London University and at the age of 20 was appointed headmaster of the National School at Newport Pagnell, attracted to the town by the fine parish church and organ.

When the Riverside Schools were condemned he continued as headmaster under firstly the School Board and, when this was abolished, the Council. He was also active in the town's civic life and having gained election to the Parish Council in 1904 remained in public life until resigning for health reasons in April 1933.

As the founder of the Swimming Club it was due to him that the Bathing Place was opened as a Jubilee Memorial in 1887 and for many years he gave a three penny piece to boys from his school whenever they swam across the River Lovat.

Orson Bull.

Marrying the daughter of a local butcher, he lived with his wife and daughter, Ethel, at 49, High Street, but from a consortium that included his father in law he purchased two plots of land opposite Lovat Bank and built Colville House.

Following the outbreak of the First World War, in his capacity as chairman of the U.D.C. he organised a recruiting meeting held on the Market Hill and in November 1915 his married son, Lorenzo, enlisted. He was an assistant master at Wolverton Council School and would be called up when required.

Nevertheless, an applicant who had failed to secure military exemption reprimanded Mr. Bull in the street, alleging that none of his relatives were taking part in the war.

Thus in response at the Newport Pagnell Urban Area Tribunal on Wednesday evening, January 17th 1917, Mr. Bull, as chairman, made clear that he didn't mind slurs against himself but he would not tolerate those against his family.

Putting the record straight he said that he had one son in South Africa who had sold his business and been in the Army for some time. Lorenzo had attested at the start of the Derby Scheme and been graded B1, and ten of his nephews had joined up, three being killed.

On the afternoon of April 1st 1918 Mrs. Bull sadly died at Colville House. Born on January 26th 1858, she was aged 60 and it had been during the previous morning while getting dressed that she suddenly became unwell. Falling unconscious she failed to recover, despite every medical attention.

On August 31st 1919 Mr. Bull retired from teaching on a pension but the following month he married the headmistress of the Girls' School, Miss Catherine James. As for the children of his first marriage, his daughter would become Mrs. Potts, resident at Harrow; his second son, Edward, a chemist who had trained in Newport Pagnell, would become an executive of the Pharmaceutical Society for the Transvaal, in South Africa, whilst as a graduate Lorenzo, of 37, Cambridge Street, Wolverton, would remain as a teacher at Wolverton, where he played a major role in establishing the College of Further Education. He died in early 1965 aged 83, after an illness of a week.

As for swimming, had I been a pupil of Mr. Bull I might have mastered the art. Whilst as for being towed by a rope, now that really was a load of old bull.

Milton Keynes Citizen, August 16, 2012

RAFFAELE MAZZONE

Italy: renowned for hot cars and hotter women.

And on a cooler note also for ice cream, which was introduced to Newport Pagnell and district by Raffaele Mazzone.

A native of Italy, in 1900 he came to Bicester where during the next year he was joined by his wife and two young children. He began a fish merchant's business, but in 1908 came to Newport Pagnell to become the proprietor of a lodging house at 22, Silver Street.

From the premises he also ran a fish and chip saloon and traded as a general fish merchant. Also he introduced ice cream, selling his product from a horse drawn cart.

At ½d and 1d this he sold in small glasses but some adults were unimpressed saying, "you will freeze our children on cold days."

Nevertheless the children loved it and Mr. Mazzone further endeared himself with his broken English.

Following the outbreak of the First World War he readily became involved in charitable events although there was no charitable outcome for his contravening the lighting restrictions, for which he received a lenient fine.

As a loyal subject Mr. Mazzone was naturalised during the war and after the war his eldest son, Michael, who had seen much active service, including a while in Egypt, returned to Newport Pagnell where he went into business with his father at 7, St. John Street, which the latter had bought in 1920.

Here was built up a successful enterprise and in 1926 Michael married Miss Antonette Secondine at St. Michael's Roman Catholic Church in Birmingham, his sister Mary being a bridesmaid. Another of his sisters was Adeline, who as a talented pianist often played at local concerts and gave music lessons at her home in Silver Street.

With a passageway in between, in 1927 Mr. Mazzone acquired the premises adjoining his own in St. John Street, and thus from 22, Silver Street (of which they retained ownership), in January 1928 a move was made to St. John Street by the Mazzone family consisting of Raffaele, his wife, their sons, Michael and George, and, with her young son Anthony, Mrs. Giovanne 'Ginny' Valente.

She was one of the five daughters and sadly a widow for her husband, Stefan, whom she had married during the First World War, had died in 1920.

Sadly in the month of the family's move there was another bereavement when Raffaele's wife, Andoniella, died. George and Ginny would now live at no. 5, selling fruit etc. while Michael and his father occupied no. 7, where they sold fruit, vegetables, fresh fish and fish and chips. As for Adeline in January 1931 she married Leslie Griffin of Spring Gardens, who was in business with his father, Harry, as a painter and decorator.

Adeline was given away by Michael, and one of the guests would be Toni Arpino, a boxer who had recently fought at the Albert Hall.

Tragically in 1932 Raffaele suffered a seizure and being unable to take any further part in managing the business, on his occasional short walks he had to be accompanied by family members, of which he gained much comfort from 'Ginny,' who was a member of the Newport Pagnell Nursing Division of the St. John Ambulance Brigade and for many years would undertake nursing at Renny Lodge Hospital.

Raffaele Mazzone outside his shop.

At 5, St. John Street, aged 70, Raffaele died on June 9th 1942, and was buried in the grave of his wife.

After the war, in 1946 Ginny married Mr. Nicky Pelle and with her son, Anthony, moved to 8, Silver

Street, to begin a general stores. Unfortunately she developed a serious illness, but was making a good recovery until in late 1955 she broke her thigh in a fall.

At the beginning of December she returned to hospital for a minor operation, but died in Northampton General Hospital aged 59.

As for George Mazzone, in 1955 he bought Colville House, in Silver Street, while as for the shops in St. John Street they were scheduled for demolition for road widening at the end of November 1956.

However deliveries would be made from 5, Wolverton Road, while as for the trademark ice cream, in a contemporary competition Peter Mazzone would beat his father, Michael, to take the accolade of champion ice cream maker.

Milton Keynes Citizen, June 21, 2012

SALMONS MOTOR CARRIAGE WORKS

With this being the month in which we celebrate Armistice Day, perhaps now is an appropriate time to mention the little known First World War story of Salmons Motor Carriage Works, of Newport Pagnell, and 6,7,8, and 9 Upper St. Martin's Lane, London.

Following the declaration of war many of the employees volunteered for

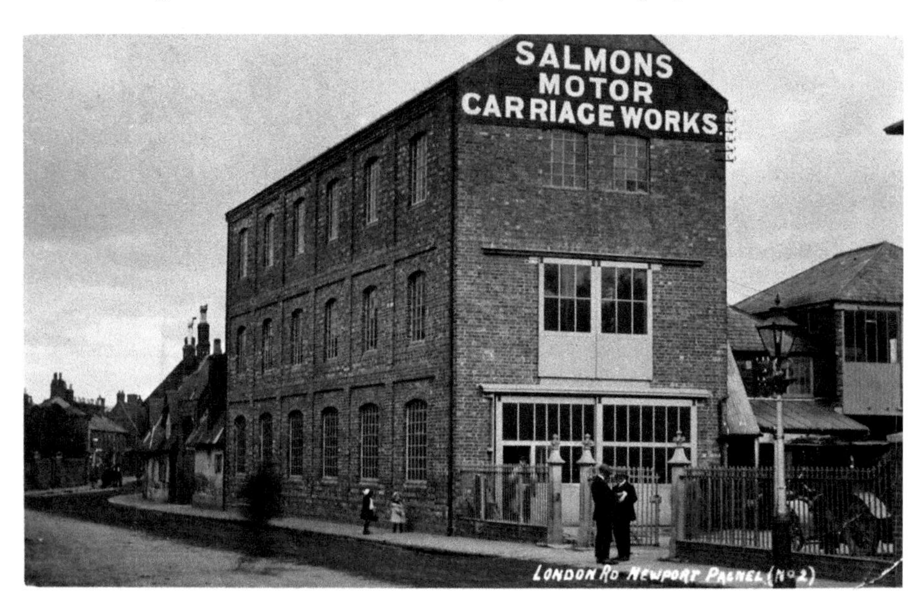

service, but for one, a German mechanic by the name of Otto Schonebrook, he was arrested and conveyed to the compound at Newbury, Berks, as a prisoner of war, this being the first occasion that a police officer had been noticed to be armed with a rifle.

At their own expense, for military use several local worthies now ordered ambulances from the firm, whose reputation was such that a feature even appeared in the Daily Telegraph. Indeed, as evidence of the importance a motor ambulance designed and supplied by Salmons, and built to the order of the London Panel Doctors Committee, headed the City of London Red Cross Detachment in the Lord Mayor's procession through London.

As the war progressed a fleet of 10 motor ambulances were built to order as a gift to Russia, but apart from the best type of ambulance on the market, incorporating the ideas of Colonel Broome Giles of Bletchley, the firm were also building a motor field kitchen, which was featured in two editions of the Daily Graphic.

In a demonstration of its capability personnel aboard one example, which joined up with the transport column of the City of London Red Cross, in front of the Guildhall, London, cooked a meal for 300 people during the route march to Hyde Park, where the food was then distributed. As for other activities, Salmons were agents for King cars, but unfortunately a consignment of 12 eight cylinder models was lost with the sinking of the S.S. Inkum, by a German submarine.

Later in the war, to the special order of the War Office the firm would complete four Rolls Royce cars fitted with landaulet bodies for the use of the General Staff in France. These were equipped with folding tables and other accessories, to enable British officers directing operations on the Western Front to transact map work etc. while on the move, and one had already been used by General Sir Douglas Haig, the Commander in Chief.

With no private work now being undertaken the firm had a War Office contract to turn out ten 3 ton lorries a week for as long as the war lasted, as well as eight ambulances a week, and in addition they were entrusted by the British War Department to build the bodies for 75 motor cars for use by the Headquarters Staff of the Russian Army, for despatch to Petrograd. Incredibly, the firm was also making toys from the left over scraps of wood, with girls, due to the shortage of manpower, being employed for this work.

THE ROYAL ENGINEERS HOSPITAL - NEWPORT PAGNELL

Hopefully not from a purely political motivation, one of our illustrious M.P.s seems to have taken a sudden interest in the rejuvenation of the High Street, Newport Pagnell, to the extent of optimistically seeking the help of a retail celebrity guru.

And so at this topical juncture it's perhaps opportune to remember the lesser known past of some of the remaining buildings, and more especially no. 36. In the early days of World War One, Miss Helen McFerran and Miss Annie M. Wood organised a Voluntary Aid Detachment, and gave the use of their home at

Tyringham Cottage, Tyringham, (which they rented from Mr. Frederick Konig, of Tyringham House) to accommodate the making of medical and other 'comforts.' Having subscribed for the supply of the necessary materials, here, at this 'War Hospital Supply Depot, Regd. No. 1531,' from November 16th 1915 ladies from the local area voluntarily worked two days a week from 10a.m. to 3.30p.m., and despite the somewhat remote location regularly attended whatever the weather.

Soon, with the war having stagnated into the stalemate of trench bound attrition, the increased volume of work caused the need to seek larger and more convenient premises, and in consequence Mr. F. W. Taylor offered his premises at 36, High Street, Newport Pagnell, rent free.

Thus on Monday, October 16th 1916 a meeting of all the subscribers and workers of the 'North Bucks War Hospital Supply Depot' adopted the necessary standing orders, passed a hearty vote of thanks to the owner, and began operations from their new premises the following month. The accommodation proved ideal, and on Tuesday and Wednesday of the first week in March 1917 an exhibition of the work carried out was held, with the ladies to be seen busy with fabric and needle in the upper rooms, and on the ground floor a host of articles displayed for distribution to various war hospitals. In fact with a need for more voluntary ladies the Committee hoped to secure 50 workers a day, and indeed since moving into the Newport Pagnell premises it had been possible to forward 25,200 articles to various hospitals.

Apart from Newport Pagnell there were associated depots at Wolverton

The premises on the High Street used as a WWI hospital.

and Addington, whilst in mid June 1917 in a room at the Old Vicarage, Old Wolverton, a workroom would be set up by the vicar's wife to make slippers.

As for the raising of funds, two excellent concerts were given at the Electric Theatre, Newport Pagnell, on Tuesday afternoon and evening May 1st 1917, and from October 1916 to December 31st 1917 the output from the Depot would include 28,680 surgical swabs, 15 pairs of pyjamas for the Newport Pagnell V.A.D. Hospital, and 40 pairs of collars for the same.

Then in November 1918 came the signing of the Armistice, and at the quarterly committee meeting on Tuesday, December 18th it was decided to close the Depot, due to the now diminished demand for hospital requirements, and pass a vote of thanks to Mr. F.W. Taylor. However, there was still some unfinished work, as also, in view of the flu epidemic, the need for pneumonia jackets, and so it was decided to work from a room in the Auxiliary Hospital, Tickford Abbey, for a few hours from 11a.m. on Tuesdays. This would open on Tuesday, January 14th 1919, but was intended to only run for a few weeks.

Then at the close of the ordinary business Mrs. Knapp rose to present a silver afternoon tea tray to Miss McFerran and Miss Wood, the original founders of the Depot, on which was engraved ;

'Presented by the Workers of the North Bucks War Hospital Supply Depot to Miss McFerran and Miss Wood in recognition of their able management and organisation, 1915 – 1919.'

There remains much more to tell regarding Newport Pagnell during the First World War, but the story of the staff cars built by Messrs. Salmons for the Russian Army, which now lie at the bottom of the sea, will have to wait for another day.

NEWTON LONGVILLE

BRICK MAKING AT NEWTON LONGVILLE

By the later 19th century an agricultural decline had set in, and for the rural village of Newton Longville only the arrival of the brick making industry would return a local prosperity. There had been local brick makers since 1847, but around 1890 it would be Thomas Read and his son, John Thornton Read (born in 1869) who were to establish a more substantial operation, employing about 12 men on a five acre site near the railway, about half a mile north of the village. They would later be joined by Richard Andrews, and so was formed Read and Andrews, 'The Bletchley Steam Brick Works.' In fact the row of houses that they built for their workers may still be seen. The firm enjoyed a local success, and around 1919 (when the works acquired the distinctive addition of two chimneys) they were joined by W.T. Lamb and Sons, builders merchants. As for the next development, it is often stated that 'The Bletchley Brick Company' came into being in 1923, but it was actually before then, and in 1921 there was even talk of a takeover by 'The Amalgamated Housing Industries Ltd,' with plans for large extensions. Now having the capability to make roof tiles, in 1925 the Newton Longville works began the manufacture of 'flettons,' produced from an underlying clay that mostly contained its own source of combustible material. Indeed the name arose from Fletton, near Peterborough, where this type of clay had first been exploited. Then in 1929 the London Brick Company and Forders purchased the works, and during the 1930s greatly extended the operations. Indeed, in 1933 new works were constructed on the opposite side of the road, and the old site then became allotments and a half acre lake. In 1936 the name of the company was shortened to the London Brick Company, whilst as for the wartime use of the works, here in 1943 the Ministry of Supply established an ordnance depot, where vast quantities of ammunition were stored in the kilns. After the war, with widespread bomb damage there came the national need for housing, and to accommodate the local employees of the flourishing brick works the Council, as elsewhere in the immediate district, built many new houses and bungalows in the village. In later years the Hanson Trust took over London Brick, and following their closure of the works there would be little to remind of the former industry, excepting the use of the clay excavations for landfill.

NEWTON LONGVILLE - THE PRIORY & MANOR HOUSE

Cottages at Newton Longville.

After the Norman Conquest, William Giffard, for his military service to William the Conqueror, was rewarded with many estates, and locally these included that of Newton. The name, as a legacy from the Saxon period, meant 'new settlement,' and Walter would, amongst other local interests, bestow the manor on the Cluniac Priory, of his foundation, of Saint Foy (Saint Faith) at Longueville, near Rouen. After his death he was succeeded by his namesake son, by whom the gift of Newton was reaffirmed, and with royal confirmation being received around 1109, it was probably soon after that the priory at Longueville built a cell in the village, thereby accounting for the second part of the name. (Interestingly, in the village church the moulding of the north west pillar of the nave is said to be very similar to that of Longueville Abbey.) In 1316 the prior of the parent order is returned as the lord of the manor, but during the 14th and 15th centuries the cell, due to the wars with France, would often be in the hands of the King. He consequently made various grants to various people at various times, until in 1414 it was finally suppressed as 'alien property,' to be given to the Warden and scholars of New College Oxford. They, apart from making alterations and additions to the church, constructed a new moated manor house on the foundations of the old priory (a part of the cloisters of which are possibly in the grounds of the nearby St. Anne's Grange) and, as a manorial privilege, near the Manor House around the late 15th century a dovecote was built. Notably, this featured a construction of closely set timbers, with brick nogging laid in between, and with 360 oak nesting boxes lining the walls the structure was topped by a pyramidal roof. In fact the dovecot was the only example of this type in the county, and although in 1923 New College, as lords of the manor, were willing to contribute a considerable amount for its restoration, the preservation fell through, since the Society for the Protection of Ancient Buildings required an extra £100 or so, to provide an income for the continued upkeep. Thus within a few years the dovecot fell into ruins, and had to be demolished. As for the Manor House, generally this was occupied by a lessee of New College, with the lease period in 1826 being 20 years. In 1918 it was the home of the head of Rowland Brothers, Mr. William Alfred Lailey Rowland, whilst as for later occupancies, at it's sale in 1985 the asking price - to include 'a master bedroom with bidet' - was £150,000. In view of the monastic past, not surprisingly the area is supposed to be haunted, and it has even been said that a presence is felt in the telephone box near the churchyard gate. However, if it's trying to communicate with an overseas call centre, it hasn't a ghost of a chance.

NORTH MARSTON

NORTH MARSTON: SCHORNE WELL

Stuff that. It seems Angela Rippon is advocating a campaign for the over 55s to indulge in more exercise. Well, Ms. Rippon, as one who has spent the best part of 60 years studiously avoiding any forms of unnecessary exertion, I'm certainly passing on that one.

And anyway, I get quite enough recreation already, by regularly taking a half day's leave from the drudge of daily employment, and, 35mm camera to hand, heading off into the local countryside, to investigate some more fascinating aspects of the surrounding heritage.

But of course with the advancing years this has to be done at a leisurely pace, and therefore a pilgrimage is essential en route to one of those quintessential embodiments of rural England, a village tea room.

Those in Stewkley and Swanbourne can be highly recommended, and perhaps there were also teashops for pilgrims in medieval times, especially for those travelling to the Holy Well at North Marston.

Having been the rector of Monks Risborough, Master John Schorne first came to that village in 1290, and one of his many miraculous deeds was to supposedly 'conjure the devil into a boot.'

Having been called to 'exorcise' an epileptic woman he proceeded to cast out the devil and imprison him in a boot, and thereafter the superstitious villagers were quite happy to believe that she was no longer possessed.

Indeed, this incident is thought to have been the origin of the Jack in the Box, and news of John's miraculous ability soon lead to his widespread renown. In fact in further emphasis of his remarkable powers, when during a severe drought he tapped the ground with his staff a spring bubbled forth, and the resulting well gained such a repute for its curative properties, being especially 'moch sowght for the agow,' that multitudes of medieval pilgrims came to visit the village.

Their offerings soon enabled the parish church to be much enhanced, both architecturally and decoratively, and quite possibly those half timbered dwellings in Church Street were built as guest housing. Indeed, having been probably lost by one of the pilgrims a tiny pewter badge, depicting Sir John holding the boot (in which he imprisoned the devil) is to be seen in the County Museum at Aylesbury.

As decreed by his will, Sir John Schorne was buried in 1314 in the north chancel of North Marston church (where his 'knees became horny' through so much prayer) but his legend travelled far beyond the confines of North Marston since, due to the many miracles that were said to occur at his tomb, it became a revered shrine for pilgrims.

Jealous of this increasing fame, in 1478 the Bishop of Salisbury then obtained a licence from the Pope to have the shrine moved to the rebuilt St. Georges Chapel, Windsor to be placed in John Schorne's Tower.

Nevertheless, North Marston still had the Holy Well (sometimes known as the Town Well) and for centuries physicians from Winslow and Aylesbury would include the water in their medicines.

Those seeking a watery benefit drank from a chained gold cup, and - perhaps in evidence of the remarkable properties - although in 1835 several villages in the neighbourhood suffered from a cholera epidemic, North Marston escaped without a single fatality.

Yet despite the magical properties of this concoction they proved insufficient to save Jane Watson, who tragically slipped into the well and drowned one morning in July 1861. Her 3 year old daughter, Sarah, rushed for help, but nothing could be done. After this the authorities declared the well unsafe, and a wall to enclose the original basin was built.

A hinged trap door partly covered the depths, but even until the 1930s the

well remained a principal source of water for the village, drawn by a pump. In an extensive project in 2004/2005 a complete remodelling then took place. Ideal perhaps for a cycle ride.

OLNEY

'BROTHER WILLIAM' - THE POET COWPER

Many of the surrounding towns have thankfully escaped being swallowed up by the black holes of urban development, and Olney, which from 1767 until 1786 became the home of the famous poet William Cowper, is one that still retains an individual identity.

A gentle if rather depressed soul, William Cowper died in 1800 at East Dereham, in Norfolk, but he began his troubled life on November 26th 1731 at the parsonage of Great Berkhamstead, where his father John was the rector. In view of his later achievements, it is perhaps significant that his mother was descended from the poet John Donne, and William would be deeply affected when she died in 1737.

He was sent to school at Market Street in Hertfordshire, but his prospects were severely hampered by the attentions of a 15-year-old bully, at whom he "never dared to look higher up than his knees".

As a result of an eye inflammation, caused by his constant tears, William was returned to the sanctuary of his home, and the bully was kicked out of the school.

After being entrusted to the care of an eminent oculist, William resumed his education two years later, and remained at Westminster school until the age of 18.

He then began a legal career but, being deficient in academic diligence, he instead indulged in "three years misspent", "making giggle" in the company of his cousins Harriet and Theodora. It was now that William began "to ramble from the thorny paths of jurisprudence into the primrose paths of literature and poetry".

Further distractions were provided by his affections for Theodora, which far surpassed any passion for the law. But with marriage expressly forbidden by her mother, William's departure in 1752 from the attorney's office, for chambers at

William Cowper's house at Olney, now the Cowper Museum.

the Middle Temple, seemed to coincide with the beginning of a depression which would afflict him for the rest of his life.

Soon William transferred to the Inner Temple as 'a commissioner of bankrupts', and at the age of 31 he was presented with an opportunity to take up a position "with excellent pay and not much work" as Reading Clerk in the House of Lords.

But the prospect of public life completely unsettled his troubled mind, so he resigned and opted instead for the lesser appointment of Clerk of the Journals in the House of Lords.

However, realising that to prove his efficiency he would have to appear at the Bar of the House of Lords he fell into a second derangement, and was entrusted to the care of Dr. Cotton in St. Albans. His stay was financed by his relatives, and eventually in June 1765 he left for lodgings in Huntingdon, to be near his brother John, a don at Cambridge.

Intrigued by the arrival of this quiet and studious young man, whom they often saw walking the streets, or attending chuch, the Unwin family soon found William an object of benevolent fascination, and at the end of one service the Unwins' son William began to engage their unsuspecting quarry in conversation.

Thus commenced William Cowper's acquaintance with Unwin family, "the most cheerful and engaging family it is possible to conceive", and by November 11th 1765 he had moved in as their lodger.

The head of this Christian family was the Rev. Morley Unwin, rector of Grimston, but after a taste of village life the family swiftly returned to the comforts of town.

While setting out for his church on horseback one Sunday morning in July 1767, the Reverend suffered a serious fall, and died four days later. Now the bereaved family urgently needed a house elsewhere.

It was during this quest that retiring William Cowper would make the acquaintance of the adventurous, reformed slave trader John Newton. For it was due to a friend of their son that the Unwins were visited by Newton, who suggested they should move either to a house in the village of Emberton, or in the nearby town of Olney.

Thus the Unwins and William Cowper came to Olney on September 14th 1767. Not that this seemed an ideal choice, being "inhabited chiefly by the half-starved and ragged of the earth".

Nevertheless after an initial stay with the Reverend Newton, on December 7th 1767 they finally moved into their house, Orchard Side, "deep in the abyss of Silver End". Separated by only an orchard, their garden almost adjoined that of the Vicarage and, to avoid having to walk through the town, Cowper and Newton readily paid a guinea for the connecting right of way.

Following her wedding, the Unwins' daughter left Olney and, although speculation became rife that William might marry Mrs. Unwin, such a prospect was soon dispelled by an abrupt recurrence of William's mental malaise.

It was as a possible remedy for his depression that William was presented with a leveret by a neighbour, whose children had proved less than diligent in caring for it. And when the news of this gift became known, William soon found himself the potential recipient of many more such hares!

Eventually he accepted just three - Bess, Puss and Tiney - and their therapeutic value would soon be apparent, for: "Management of such an animal was just the sort of employment my case required", especially surly Tiney:

I kept him for his humour's sake,
For he would oft beguile
My heart of thought that made it ache,
And force me to a smile.

During the day, William would often sit at a window from which he could watch the goings-on in uneventful Olney, where "occurrences here are as rare as cucumbers at Christmas".

It was from this vantage point that one July day in 1781 he spotted an aristocratic lady shopping at a drapers in the Market Place. Accompanying her was Martha Jones, the wife of the rector of Clifton Reynes.

With uncharacteristic boldness, William immediately asked Mrs. Unwin to invite the couple in.

This would herald the beginning of an intense, if platonic, relationship with Lady Anne Austen, the widow of a baronet.

As Martha's sister she was staying at the rectory of nearby Clifton Reynes, and William found that in her presence he could feel calm and at ease, for she was one "who laughed and made laugh, and could keep up a conversation without seeming to labour at it". To William she soon became 'Sister Anne', whilst for Anne he became 'Brother William.'

In time, such a relaxed companionship would bear due reward, for it was following being told the outline of a story by Lady Austen that, alone in his room, William the same night penned the framework for John Gilpin, perfecting the work over the next few days in the solitude of his summerhouse.

Published in The Public Advertiser in November 1782, the story brought widespread acclaim and - again with the encouragement of Lady Austen - Cowper then wrote The Task, which met with similar success.

Now Lady Austen made plans to rent a property in Olney, and this intention was much accelerated when, during the absence of the Rev. Jones, armed thieves tried to break into the Clifton Reynes rectory.

In panic, the two sisters fled to Orchard Side, and, while Martha would eventually return to the rectory, Lady Anne stayed on, occupying the other half of the house.

However, no doubt discouraged by William's lack of marital interest, she eventually left Olney in 1784 and married a Frenchman, Baron Tardiff.

But fate as usual decreed that William would not be denied female company for long, for in June 1786 his cousin Harriet - the Lady Hesketh by marriage - came to live in the town.

Her initial opinions were unfavourable. On seeing William's abode she was appalled by the "tottering" house, and the thieving disposition of the servants, and swiftly arranged more suitable accommodation in the nearby village of Weston Underwood.

Here William and Mrs. Unwin began a new life on November 15th 1786, and William was far from saddened by this move, for now he could be near his friends the Throckmortons - or "Mr. and Mrs. Frog", as he affectionately called

A painting of William Cowper with Mrs Unwin and Lady Austen.

them - of Weston Hall.

He seemed little perturbed by leaving Orchard Side, for it had been "no attachment to the place that binds me here, but an unfitness for every other".

CIVIL WAR SKIRMISH

Throughout the centuries this district has borne tragic witness to various military encounters and skirmishes, and not infrequently a poignant reminder has been unearthed in the form of the skeletons of those warriors who perished.

Near the site of the Roman encampment of Magiovinium, Fenny Stratford, was found buried on the river bank the skeleton of a headless adult.

This was within an area where Belgic artefacts have been found – the Belgae being a warlike Celtic tribe – and since they normally cremated their dead the lone burial points to the aftermath of a brief skirmish.

Following the Roman withdrawal from Britain the country became vulnerable to other invasions and such evidence has past come to light at Passenham.

By 876 A.D. they had fought and pillaged their way across much of the English countryside and it was this rampage that King Edward, the son of Alfred the Great, resolved to end.

Intending to recover all the lands still occupied by the Danes he began to fortify Towcester and Buckingham and by this foresight when the Danes launched an attack against Towcester they were successfully repulsed.

Edward and his army then returned to their camp at Passenham while the Towcester defences were repaired.

Eventually Edward and his forces would leave their Passenham stronghold, but for a long while the evidence for their stay remained in the form of a square entrenchment, which had been built to guard the crossing of the river ford.

In fact for such a military camp the additional evidence is predictably gruesome and on many occasions broken bones have been unearthed and six skeletons were discovered beneath the rectory floor during restorations of 1874 and in 1916 two further skeletons were revealed.

Three more skeletons then came to light during drainage work of 1947.

In the 17th century the Civil War also saw the local area ravaged, with many towns and villages plundered and the crops destroyed.

In November 1643, for use as a possible Parliamentarian outpost Colonel Harvey marched into Olney at the head of three cavalry units.

However, scathed by recent Royalist defeats the dashing, if impetuous, Prince Rupert saw this as an opportunity to restore the standing of his army and consequently on the morning of Saturday, November 4th he advanced towards the unsuspecting town with a force composed of 'several troops of horses, four hundred dragoons, and two hundred musketeers carried on horseback behind the cavalry.'

Approaching from the Yardley road at 7am he led the charge and the defenders fled until rallied at the narrow bridge of the millstream by Colonel Harvey and his officers.

For several minutes a fierce engagement flared but eventually the firepower of the Royalist musketeers sealed the rout and leaving 'sixty killed, forty prisoners, besides one hundred and twenty horses and two stands of colours', after two hundred volleys the Roundheads fled for safety.

With revenge achieved Prince Rupert then marched from the town, to leave the shaken garrison to return the following day.

The graves of those who perished in the engagement lay near Emberton Bridge and in more recent times the Cowper and Newton Museum became the repository for some of the swords and skulls that were found.

However, at Little Brickhill during 20th century improvements 'to facilitate the improvement of the highway' a sealed lead coffin was among those disturbed, which when opened was found to contain the body of a Cavalier clad in the full dress of velvet tunic and plumes.

Even the locks of red hair were preserved and indeed the church registers contain an entry of August 27, 1644 which reads; 'Mr. Williams, souldyer of the King's Army, was slayne by the Parlimant souldyers and buried the same daye.' The coffin was later reburied.

Milton Keynes Citizen, June 14, 2012

COWPER'S HARES

Emerging from the realms of slumber, there's perhaps no deeper bliss than to sense the encroaching warmth of one's beloved, snuggling up with expectant longing. Yep, that flippin' dog's sneaked back on the bed again. But the hierarchy must be maintained, and so it's no to pooch power, and definitely no to walkies, since not only is it pouring with rain, but the temperature is such that even brass monkeys are applying to emigrate. In fact for a moment it's debateable whether dogs really are man's best friend, but then of course they are, and no where was this more locally apparent than for William Cowper, the inspired but melancholic poet of Olney. Having arrived in the town in 1767, as a therapy for his malaise he found the keeping of animals, and the building of their hutches, of great value, and at various times at his home at Orchard Side he would accommodate a veritable menagerie, to include a tortoise shell kitten called Mungo, squirrels, canaries, guinea pigs, jackdaws, doves, gold finches and - of especial affection - a spaniel named Beau, whom he immortalised in the poem 'The dog and the water lily.' Towards the end of one depressive bout, William had been given a leveret (a young hare) by a neighbour, whose children had been less than diligent in the animal's welfare, and soon William became the potential recipient of many more baby hares! However, he accepted just three - Bess, Puss and Tiney - and indeed their antics would prove extremely beneficial, for 'Management of such an animal was just the sort of employment my case required.' Especially the surly Tiney, for 'I kept him for his humour's sake, For he would oft beguile, My heart of thought that made it ache, And force me to a smile.' Yet on one occasion Tiney made a bid for freedom, and, having lead his pursuers a merry chase, had to be rescued from a local tan yard pit - by his ears! Eventually William and his long term companion, Mrs. Unwin, would move to Weston Lodge, in the village of Weston Underwood, and here one of their favourite walks would be in a secluded, overgrown spot known as the Wilderness. This lay within the Park, attached to the Manor Grounds, and upon an ornamental urn would be inscribed the following verse, composed by William at the request of his friend, Lady Throckmorton, in memory of her spaniel, Fop;

'Ye squirrels, rabbits, leverets rejoice,

Your haunts no longer echo to his voice

This record of his fate exalting view,

He died, worn out with vain pursuit of you.'

In view of his affinity for animals, no doubt William would have been pleased that in a later century the area was to become part of the Flamingo Gardens and Zoological Park, which, established around 1960 by Christopher Marler, included several rare breeds amongst the two hundred or so species, and sub species. Sadly this no longer exists, although supposedly a legacy still remains in the form of several escaped wallabies, who, it seems, are glimpsed quite regularly in the local countryside. So if anyone says that they've seen a wannabe kangaroo bouncing about, don't tell them to hop off, for it might just be true.

COWPER'S SUMMERHOUSE RETREATS

It seems women are adept at 'multi tasking,' which is certainly an attribute that I could do with, for in my little writing 'den,' at the bottom of the garden, several jobs have acquired an increasing urgency, and not least the need to fix a leaking roof. Oh well, true to gender, perhaps for now I'll just make a list. In fact blokes and 'dens' seem to be synonymous, and this would certainly be so for the poet William Cowper, whose home from 1767 until 1786 would be Orchard Side, at Olney. A gentle, if rather depressed soul, William would seek inspiration for many of his famous works in a summer house in the garden, but when on April 26th 1900 Orchard Side was presented to the town by Mr. W. Collingridge, to become the

Cowper and Newton Museum, the garden, in which the summer house was situated, was separately owned. Thus when the Museum trustees were offered first option to purchase the freehold, following a meeting in November 1918 they decided to try and raise the necessary £325, and, with this being successful, the opening ceremony for the garden and summer house was performed on Friday, September 19th 1919 by the Marquis of Lincoln, the Lord Lieutenant. Many notables were present, and in the afternoon a procession of 300 schoolchildren from Olney and the local villages marched along the High Street to Orchard Side, lead by the Town Band. William Cowper's acquaintance with Orchard Side came to an end in June 1786, when his cousin, the Lady Hesketh by marriage, arrived to live in the town. Appalled by the 'tottering' condition of the house, and the thieving disposition of the servants, she swiftly arranged for more

Cowper's summerhouse at Olney.

suitable accommodation in the nearby village of Weston Underwood, and here William, and his companion, Mrs. Unwin, would begin a new life on November 15th 1786. Yet William seemed far from saddened by this move, for he would now be near his friends the Throckmortons - or 'Mr. and Mrs. Frog,' as he affectionately called them - of Weston Hall. Finding inspiration in the surrounding countryside, William would often indulge in rural walks, and sometimes it would be during these that within the tranquil embrace of the 'Alcove' he would retire to write. Of hexagonal shape, with three sides open, this had been built by John Higgins in 1753 as a woodland summerhouse for Sir Robert Throckmorton, and, enhanced by views across an extensive sweep of ground, laid out by the renowned 'Capability Brown,' it was of little surprise that his poetic abilities were greatly heightened by this situation. However, recently a bank of wind turbines has been plonked right in the middle distance of these inspirational views, and although William had an interest in many innovations (from hot air balloons to medical 'electrical machines') it remains conjecture as to whether he would have found the present sight of the flailing arms revolutionary, or whether it would just have given him another depressive turn.

LACE INDUSTRY - OLNEY

For many years the making of pillow lace provided a major source of income for 'the poorer class of females' in the town, and no. 22 High Street was just one of several buildings that accommodated a lace making dame school.

However, with the beginnings of industrialisation the home based industry began a general decline, and in December 1777 came the comment that 'A machine has been introduced for making point lace, which threatens the destruction of the pillow lace trade, in which so many hands are now employed in Buckinghamshire.'

Not surprisingly the introduction of machine made lace caused a widespread recession for the traditional cottage industry, and this was not the only problem, for in May 1803 a public meeting was called at the Bull to consider the implications of a Parliamentary Bill 'for consolidating the Customs, as to its probable operation on the Thread Lace – Manufactory of this Country.'

In consequence the local manufacturers decided to set up a committee and petition the Minister, but nevertheless by 1826 the trade was in complete stagnation.

Workers who had previously earned 10s, 15s, or £1 a week could now expect only 2s or 3s, although in the following year the outlook seemed a little less bleak, for 'The staple trade of Buckinghamshire – lace-making – has partaken of the improvement that has been noticed in other branches of manufactures. Not only is there a ready sale for Buckinghamshire lace, but the price has advanced.'

However, such were the fluctuations of commerce that by 1830 fortunes had again declined, and it would not be until the arrival of Henry (Harry) Hillier Armstrong that the industry enjoyed a significant revival. A native of Stoke Goldington, there at the age of 23 he began as a lace buyer, and in 1906 he established the 'Bucks Cottage Workers Association.'

With the necessary materials furnished to the remaining lace makers, their finished products, fully examined for quality, would be purchased by travelling lace buyers, and in 1909 the success of the venture prompted a move to Olney, as more convenient for transport.

The lace was even purchased by Royalty, being in 1911 awarded the gold medal at the Festival of Empire and International Exhibition at Crystal Palace.

In 1919 Mr. Armstrong collaborated with Thomas Wright in writing a history of lace making in the district, whilst in other ventures he advertised for classical music pupils – '2s 6d an hour' – with persons interested to apply to 'Harry Armstrong, Silk Manufacturer, Olney.' Yet others in the town were also engaged in the lace trade, including George Smith.

An expert in his field, he designed the lace worn by the Queen of Spain on her wedding dress, and at one time he had 3,000 Bucks cottage dwellers working for him. As for Mrs. Whinnett, of the Market Place, she was in the market for pillow lace, for which she offered a postal order by return.

Then in 1928 came the construction of Mr. Armstrong's 'Bucks Lace Industry' factory in the High Street, Olney, although this was actually a warehouse. Unfortunately the construction coincided with the final decline of the industry, but nevertheless it was here that even in 1940 all kinds of pillow lace were bought, and parchments and threads supplied.

Harry died in 1943, whilst as for the building, in the 1960s this accommodated Schwinner's lampshade factory.

When this closed proposals were made to convert the premises into residential flats, but a reminder of the former craft may still be seen on the façade of the building, where a lace maker is represented with her traditional equipment – a wheel, pillow and globe.

OLNEY: MALICIOUS FIRES

Following a spate of nocturnal robberies, an outbreak of malicious fires plagued the town of Olney from the last days of 1852 until the early weeks of 1853, and to this day there has never been a satisfactory explanation. The first incident was discovered on Christmas Eve 1852 at about 10.30p.m., when, situated on the side of the road leading from Olney to Bedford, a large barley stack belonging to Mr. Whitmee was found ablaze. By the valiant efforts of the townspeople about a third was saved, but on the following Monday at about 7p.m. an attempt was made to fire the premises of Miss Raban, 'a harmless Miss,' who was the tenant of a farm belonging to Lord Dartmouth. Fortunately this blaze was tackled early, but on New Year's Eve at 7p.m. another mysterious blaze broke out in the centre of the town, in a large yard behind the house of Mr. Thomas Soul, a butcher. Soon a mass of flames enveloped the buildings, and 'Here the scene was most awfully grand and heartrending in the extreme, language being wanting to depict the awful sight - that of seeing nine fat and store beasts, chained to the rack, surrounded by an impregnable mass of fire - to hear their mournful cries, and see them fall one by one and consumed by the devouring element.' Then on January 2nd 1853 an attempt was made to set fire to the thatch of a cow barn. Fortunately this failed, and with fire watchers having been appointed to all the vulnerable farms and buildings of the area, the next night passed without incident. Then at about 6p.m. on the following day another arson attempt was made on the cow barn, and before the fire engines could reach the blaze the fire had spread not only to a neighbouring bake house, but also to several other thatched properties, including the premises of Mr. Killingsworth, a watchmaker. Now there was a real danger that the flames might reach the front of the street, but, despite a strong south westerly wind, by 8p.m. the blaze had been brought under control. Yet not without sacrifice, for a part of a burning building had collapsed on a party of men, among whom Jacob Clifton sustained terrible injuries. On regaining consciousness he then frantically asked after John Marson, the local rat catcher. He had been working with him at the time, and after a frenzied search Marson's body was recovered, albeit unrecognisable due to the burns and bruises. The rest of the night passed without incident, but the following morning the bellman went around the town to announce that William Scott, a farmer, was still missing. He had last been seen fighting the flames, and eventually his body was discovered in the same cellar as John Marson. News of the fires had now attracted a national attention, and - with three officers having been sent to investigate from Scotland Yard - a reward of £200 was offered, plus the promise of a free pardon from Her Majesty. In fact by their initial enquiries the officers were lead to suspect parties 'not of the labouring class,' and a month later a man from the town, 'of previous good character,' was brought before the magistrates. In fact a detective from the metropolitan force was even sent to begin proceedings, but the man's guilt seemed in doubt when on January 29th a further outbreak occurred. This was in the manger of a stable on Lodge Farm, but fortunately the fire was quickly discovered and put out. Yet still the fire-raising continued, and another outbreak occurred on March 23rd, again at Lodge Farm. This was discovered at about 6p.m., and despite gallant efforts the wheat hovel was completely destroyed. However, this seems to have brought an end to the local arsons. But to this day there has never been an explanation for the mysterious fires of Olney, which without doubt were the most traumatic events to ever befall 'this hitherto undisturbed little town.'

OLNEY: PANCAKE RACE

It's one of the puzzles of modern life, as to how society ever managed before the recent phenomena of 'non jobs,' of which - strangely - there appears to be a proliferation in those sectors where vast amounts of public money are spent, with seemingly scant regard for accountability. However, who would have wanted to be a 'Risk Assessor' in 19th century Olney, for on Guy Fawkes night the town annually succumbed to the ancient custom of booting a ball of blazing rags around the town - on one occasion through a draper's shop window. In fact on November 5th 1886, following the close of the commercial day small gatherings of people began to saunter up and down the High Street, and before long two fiery balls were being kicked about. When these were periodically extinguished by the puddles, they would then be kicked into a large fire in the middle of the highway, to re-emerge in a triumphant blaze of flaming glory. Yet despite frightening a few horses, little harm was done, and one participant, who became rather too exuberant, was even 'allowed' to be rescued from the police by his companions! As if balls of fire weren't enough, there was also another custom guaranteed to give a jobsworth a fit of the vapours, for Olney is famed for the Shrove Tuesday 'pancake race.' This is thought to have origins from 1445, and by tradition the race began as a final celebration before the long fast of Lent. Then with the outbreak of World War Two the tradition came to an end, until in 1948 the vicar chanced upon some old photographs, and the custom was recommenced. Yet not only was a national interest rekindled, for in America curiosity was aroused in the town of Liberty, which in consequence issued a challenge to Olney. Thus began the competition for the 'Transatlantic Pancake Trophy,' with the sound of the town crier's bell sending the competitors off along a 415 yard course, from Olney Market Place to the churchyard gate. In fact a similar race was even begun at Seeley's Bay, Ontario! Of course, today the danger of tripping over a pothole, or smacking one's self in the face with a frying pan - not to mention the risk of being struck by a piece of falling space debris - is too horrendous to contemplate, and so, in keeping with modern thinking, perhaps it might now be best to instead stage a 'virtual' race, via a computer link. However, since this would involve sitting down, it couldn't possibly be considered without a prior assessment by a Posture Awareness Co-ordinator, although it's doubtful if one could ever be found for less than £35k a year.

Passenham Mill.

PASSENHAM

GHOSTLY SECRET OF PASSENHAM

Gravel workings excepted, Passenham, with its mill, old rectory, manor house, and tithe barn, is one of the most picturesque of the local villages, and upon such an unspoilt scene the imagination finds little effort in conjuring up the happenings of an eventful past.

Yet hopefully these will only be imaginary, for the village has long been associated with the supernatural, not least with the tale of Nancy Lee, who drowned herself in the mill pond. Indeed, in despair her spirit is still said to haunt the area.

That the area has such a reputation is not surprising, for its history dates back to before the Norman Conquest.

By 876 AD the Danes had fought and pillaged their way across much of the English countryside, and it was this rampage that King Edward, the son of Alfred the Great, was determined to stop.

With his intention being to recover all the lands still occupied by the Danes, he began to fortify Towcester and Buckingham, and due to this foresight when the Danes launched an attack against Towcester they were successfully repulsed.

While the Towcester defences underwent repair, Edward then returned with his army to their camp at Passenham, and for a while the local Danes were subdued.

Indeed Edward and his army would eventually leave their Passenham stronghold, although as evidence of their stay a square entrenchment, which had been built to guard the crossing of the river ford, would long remain.

Not surprisingly, for such a military camp the further evidence is particularly gruesome, and with broken bones having been unearthed on many occasions, six skeletons were discovered beneath the rectory floor during restorations of 1874.

Then in 1916 two further skeletons were revealed, entwined within the roots of a tree blown over in a gale, and apart from three more skeletons, found during drainage work of 1947, burials have also been found in the old Tithe Barn.

Yet of all the supernatural tales told of the village the strangest is that of Sir Robert Banastre, a 17th century lord of the manor.

He died in 1649, yet even death could not curtail his dealings with the village.

Even as she prepared his body for the grave, an old woman sensed that all would not be well, and hardly had she finished her task than a ghostly wraith appeared at her bedside, bathed in the stench of brimstone and fire.

In the church at night the altar window blazed with unnatural light, and strange figures were seen to walk the ground. Then on the day of the funeral as the coffin was borne towards the church a ghastly cry was heard from within, 'Steady! Steady! I am not ready.'

But when the coffin was opened, only the corpse was found. The procession hurried on, but no sooner had it entered the church than a raven was seen to settle upon the porch, and once again was heard the eerie cry, 'Steady! Steady! I am not ready.'

In urgent haste the bearers made towards the chancel, but even as they drew near the screen crashed down, and dashed the coffin to the ground.

Without further delay Sir Robert's body was laid to rest, and in the chancel the covering slab may still be seen. Then events began in earnest.

At night, behind locked doors the villagers trembled as a phantom coach thundered past, skeleton footmen to guide the way.

A ghostly form appeared to many. Children screamed, servants fled the rectory, and even the rector would have fled, had not the sanity of his wife prevailed.

By her advice the Bishop was swiftly summoned, and, as the appointed hour drew near, in the darkness he waited with his attendants by the village mill.

Suddenly the Bishop dropped his book in startled fright as Sir Robert's apparition rose up. Mercy, it craved, promising to trouble them no more, and in the name of the Lord the Bishop bade the spirit go, and seek Redemption whilst it might still be found.

So ended the events at Passenham, but for those who venture near, when night or mist enshrouds, beware whose unseen eyes may be upon you!

In the wake of Sir Roberts Banestre's death, his widow, in the aftermath of the supernatural happenings, wisely left the district, and eventually the manor came to Lord Maynard.

However, although his family would hold the estate for many generations, they never chose to actually live at the place!

Nevertheless, their connection is still recalled in the village by the initial 'M', which may be seen on several examples of the estate housing.

In 1911 the Maynard association then came to an end when the interest was purchased by Francis Evelyn, the Countess of Warwick, and her main claim to popular fame is through having been 'Daisy', the well known mistress of Edward VII.

One can only conjecture what the local rector might have thought of such an association, although for the Reverend Loraine Smith, a rector of the village in the early 19th century, he was hardly above scandal himself, for he actively encouraged illegal prizefights.

However, no doubt having found this rather difficult to reconcile with his position as a JP, on one occasion he proved his 'concern' by arranging for an illicit contest to be broken up by the police.

Not that this proved a total success, for one of the contestants took great exception and laid out the constables.

Thereupon it was left to the Reverend to 'apprehend' the villain, and administer a 'stern' talking to!

Of more constructive pursuits was a later rector of the village, the Reverend George Capell. He patented some 30 specifications between 1882 and 1914, mainly for types and designs of mine and tunnel ventilation equipment, and many of the prototypes were made by the local blacksmith at Deanshanger.

In fact several of the Reverend's ideas would gain a worldwide renown, being noted especially for their contributions to safety.

As for one of his earliest inventions, this had been a pedal or hand operated fan 'for exhausting hot air from crops in stack', and since his design involved air being blown through a central column, no doubt to the delight of on looking children 'clouds of steam came out of the top.'

RAVENSTONE

GRAMMATICAL MISTAKES

It just beggars belief. Only a few days after the recent comments in the Citizen, regarding present standards of spelling and grammar, up pops a Government website extolling the need for accuracy in spelling and grammar - and littered with innumerable mistakes in spelling and grammar. And the alleged response from some woman supposedly in charge of this farce? Apparently she's not "bothered," because mistakes can be put right later. Could be rather interesting if a job hopeful with an iffy C.V. came up with that during an interview. But there's one field of literature where no doubt most of us wouldn't have a clue if there were grammatical mistakes, and that's the Latin inscriptions on church memorials. Locally, at Ravenstone in fairly recent times such an inscription, much weathered, could be read on a tombstone of the eastern churchyard commemorating the Reverend Thomas Seaton, and in 1932 the inscription was transcribed onto a wall mounted tablet in the south aisle of the church. Thomas was born in 1684 at Stamford, Lincolnshire, and in 1701 he entered Clare College, Cambridge as a 'sizar,' that is a poor student who, by acting as a servant to a Master or Fellow of the College, paid a reduced fee. In 1705 he then gained a B.A., and the following year became a Freeman Fellow. Ordained as a deacon in 1707, this was also the year that he gained an M.A., and in 1708 he became a priest. Following a period as chaplain to the Earl of Nottingham in 1713 he was appointed as vicar of Madingley, near Cambridge, and then in 1721 as vicar of Ravenstone. However, since this was a position worth more than £26 13s 4d a year, he had to resign his Fellowship. By the terms of his will Thomas bequeathed an estate at Kislingbury, Northamptonshire, to the University of Cambridge, and with the rents to be applied towards a prize for a poem on a sacred subject, this is still in existence. In fact the Times recently carried the obituary of the Hebrew scholar Professor Raphael Loewe, in which was mentioned that during his career he had been awarded the 'Seatonian Prize for Sacred Poetry' at Cambridge University, annually offered for a poem "conducive to the honour of the Supreme Being and the recommendation of virtue." With a seeming resurgence in the study of Latin, its perhaps opportune to also mention some other inscriptions to be seen regarding the local heritage, such as at North Crawley where the church of St. Firmin (this dedication being shared with only one other church in the country) has beneath the eastern window the weathered wording;

'Petrus cancellum tibi dat firmin
Ut cum lauderis Deo, Petri memoreris'
This translates as;
'Peter gives to thee, oh Firmin, a new little
Chancel in order that when you praise God
You may remember Peter'.

Then at Calverton, the almshouses near to the church bear their original inscription 'Deo ac Pauperibus' (To God and the Paupers), these having been built by Lord Arden, who financed much of the rebuilding of Calverton church. Yet perhaps the most poignant inscription is to be seen in Ampthill church, where the memorial to Richard Nicholls, born in 1625, incorporates the very cannon ball which killed him during a naval battle against the Dutch off Southwold. The wording reads 'instrumentum mortis et immortalitatis' - the instrument of his mortality and immortality. And for a certain individual perhaps another cannon ball could be in order where the sun don't shine, to buck their ideas up regarding a farcical website on grammatical correctness.

RIDGMONT

RIDGMONT - NINA CECILIA BENTINCK

With the present interest in the forthcoming royal wedding, perhaps now is a good time to recall the 'royal' role of Ridgmont, as being the birthplace of Nina Cecilia Cavendish Bentinck, the mother of Prince William's great grandmother, the late Queen Mother. The story begins with the Reverend Charles Cavendish Bentinck, a younger son of the 4th Duke of Portland, who, after a tragic first marriage to a Romany princess, married Caroline Louisa Burnaby, of Bedford, in 1850, the year following his appointment as the vicar of the parishes of Husborne Crawley and Ridgmont. Three daughters were duly born to the couple, and the Ridgmont registers record the baptism of Nina Cecilia, the eldest, on October 19th 1862. After the death of the Reverend Cavendish Bentinck in 1870 his widow married Henry Warren Scott, the third son of Sir William Scott of Ancrum, and the family would make their home at Forbes House, on the fringe of Ham Common, near Richmond. Being an officer in the Lifeguards, when not on duty at Windsor Castle, Claud George Bowes-Lyon, Lord Glamis, the son of the 13th Earl of Strathmore, would be a frequent visitor, and although the object of his affections would be Nina Cecilia, any thoughts of marriage were precluded by his army pay. Even when his grandmother died in January 1881 his financial prospects were not enhanced, for by a later codicil to her will she had amended the original inheritance - of estate valued at nearly £40,000, plus a house at St. Paul's Walden Bury (which had passed to the Strathmores via their Bowes ancestors) - such that all of this now passed to Claud's father for life. Thus Claud was left with only £400 a year, until his father allowed him not only the tenancy but also the income of St. Paul's and the original annuity. With their finances now secure, Claud and Nina were married in July 1881, and shortly after their honeymoon Claud, with few regrets, left the army. At St. Paul's Walden Bury the couple would now raise a large family, and as their ninth child, on Saturday, August 4th 1900 Elizabeth Angela Marguerite was born at London. Yet apart from a canny old gypsy woman, few could know that this infant would successively become Duchess of York, Queen Consort and then Queen Mother. In due course, on the death of the 13th Earl in 1904 Claud and Nina became the Earl and Countess of Strathmore and Kinghorne, and their inheritance included not only the sum of £250,000 but also Glamis Castle, where during World War One Elizabeth and her mother would devote their attention to the care of wounded soldiers. However, when one of Elizabeth's brothers, Fergus, was killed in action, Lady Strathmore fell seriously ill, and she would not fully recover until 1922. Matured by her wartime experience, Elizabeth now had little interest in the usual aristocratic pursuits, although it would be at a dance in 1920 that she made the acquaintance of 'Bertie,' Prince Albert. The story of their romance belongs elsewhere, but suffice to say that in the opinion of Lady Strathmore 'she was torn between her longing to make Bertie happy and her reluctance to take on the responsibilities which this marriage must bring.' But love duly triumphed, and when the drama of the Abdication propelled Bertie to the role of King, Elizabeth became his Queen. However, a few days before the Royal couple were to embark on a State Visit to France, Lady Strathmore suffered a heart attack, and died on June 23rd 1938. Her body was conveyed by the Royal Train to Scotland, and with the funeral being held at Glamis Castle, there she was interred in the private burial ground - the last resting place of Ridgmont's most famous daughter.

SHENLEY

ALAN TURING

Born in Paddington on June 23rd 1912, Alan Mathison Turing displayed early powers of deduction by planting his toy soldiers in the ground to make them grow.

Educated at Sherborne, he studied maths at King's College Cambridge and his paper 'On Computable Numbers' would prove fundamental to the development of modern computing.

His work took him to America but with the prospect of war he returned to Britain and was recruited for code breaking. In consequence he reported for duty at Bletchley Park on September 4th 1939, and for much of the war would be accommodated at the Crown Inn at Shenley Brook End, the story of which was told in 'The Way We Were,' March 10th 2011.

In 1940 Britain faced imminent invasion and Alan, aware that in World War One only silver had appreciably increased in value, converted his savings into two silver bars (of a combined value of some £250) loaded them onto an old pram and set off to hide his treasure in the countryside.

Choosing a wood in which to bury one of the bars he next proceeded to a nearby bridge, to sink the other in the muddy bed of the stream. Writing the

Alan Turing.

locations down in code, he then resumed his wartime work, being known at Bletchley Park as 'the Prof,' 'wild as to hair and clothes and conventions.'

Continuing the progress pioneered by the Poles he would be instrumental in developing the 'bombe,' which from late 1940 enabled all the messages sent by the Enigma machines of the Luftwaffe to be decoded, and it was also greatly due to his work, initially conducted alone in Hut 8 at Bletchley Park, that by mid 1941 the German navy signals were being unravelled.

After the war, not surprisingly Alan tried to retrieve his hidden silver bars and after one failed excursion in 1946 he and a friend began another search, now equipped with a home made metal detector.

However, instead of a third of any proceeds his friend had opted for a flat payment of £5 and this would prove a wise decision since yet again the search was disappointing.

Then in later years while Alan was visiting a friend and his wife at Woburn Sands another excursion was made, for which a commercial metal detector had been acquired.

With their investigations commencing at the bridge, despite remarking that 'It looks a bit different now' Alan paddled into the mud but found that the bed of the stream had been concreted over.

They then proceeded to the wood and although the pram was found there was no evidence of the bar.

With the war at an end, and no mention of his wartime achievements allowed, drawing on his recent experience Alan turned his attention to the creation of an electronic computer and in 1950 wrote his famous paper 'Computing Machinery and Intelligence in Mind,' in which he proposed the Turing Test to see whether a computer could be 'intelligent.'

As for his private life, despite having once proposed marriage to a female colleague his sexual preference lay elsewhere and in February 1952 he was arrested for 'misconduct' with a Manchester man.

As an alternative to prison he opted for a course of oestrogen injections and continued his scientific work, only to die in June 1954 from poisoning by potassium cyanide, found on a half eaten apple beside him.

Supposedly this was suicide but with shades of the recent past perhaps the real truth will never be known.

Mr. Turing received an official apology from former Prime Minister Gordon Brown in 2009, but he has still not received a pardon for his 'crime' of 'gross indecency'.

A petition calling for Mr. Turing to be pardoned has already been signed by more than 30,000 people.

Lord McNally recently rejected the call in the House of Lords, but the national campaign continues and the Citizen is asking people to back it.

ALAN TURING'S TREASURE

I was considering recently how useful - and interesting - it would be if we could travel backwards in time to revisit significant events and places. One local event particularly worth revisiting would be where the dickens Mr. Turing buried his stash of silver ingots.

As one of Bletchley Park's indispensable eccentrics in 1940, alarmed by the prospect of an imminent invasion, Alan Turing converted his financial assets into silver bars, loaded them aboard on an old pram and trundled off into the Shenley countryside.

There he buried them, until the time came to retrieve his hoard, which was somewhat difficult since he'd completely forgotten their whereabouts!

In fact there they may still quite possibly lie, unless with all the current housing developments, some fortunate labourer has made a happy discovery and disappeared hot foot to sunnier climes. One labourer who did make a lucky strike was part of a gang during World War Two putting in a new water service pipe at 35, Bletchley Road, a house then owned by the Bletchley Co-op.

Digging inside the pantry floor, he removed about six tiles when he chanced upon a tin box which, when opened, was found to contain around £300 in gold and silver coins.

At the consequent Treasure Trove, held at Bletchley police station, the coins were sent for examination by Mr. Eldred, a jeweller of Leon Avenue, who declared that they dated back from 1816 to 1881.

They were then sent on for further investigation at Hendon Police Laboratory and since no relatives of the previous house owner could be traced, it was decided that the finder should be entitled to 80 per cent of the value.

In the event he received £647 which he duly shared with his workmate, further donating £10 to the tenant of the house. Perhaps his financial sense was that possessed by one of Bletchley's earlier labourers who, having amassed quite a mint through several hours of arduous overtime, spent the lot in the hostelries of Little Brickhill.

Totally paralytic, he then secured himself a homewards lift in a police vehicle - a wheelbarrow commandeered by the local Pc, who dutifully trundled him all the way to a cell at Fenny Stratford police station!

Sunday Citizen September 8, 2002

'BOMBES' AND BOMBS - ALAN TURING, & SHENLEY BROOK END

As recently reported in the Citizen, the Alan Turing papers have now been secured for the nation, to be rightfully housed at Bletchley Park. With the outbreak of war, Alan had reported for duty at Bletchley Park on September 4th 1939, and there he became instrumental in decoding the German messages, a feat greatly assisted by the development of the cryptographic 'bombe,' the first British designed version of which had become available by the end of May 1940.

For much of the war he was accommodated at the Crown Inn, at Shenley Brook End, and there he would sometimes be found helping out behind the bar.

However, having left for Cambridge the day before, he had a lucky escape on October 28th 1940 when German bombs fell on the village, disrupting the village water main, blocking the road with debris, and damaging 11 houses.

In fact with the ceilings of their cottage blown in, the elderly Mr. and Mrs. Roberts had to seek temporary accommodation at the inn, where at the time Mr. and Mrs. Bourn had been having a drink.

Alarmingly a bomb had dropped not a hundred yards away, but for them the experience was nothing new, for they had already experienced bomb blasts not only in that war, but even earlier, for whilst living in Hackney, where Mr. Bourne had an upholstery business, they had been bombed during the First World War.

Then on the night of September 19th 1940 their home and business were totally destroyed in the Blitz. Fortunately they had taken refuge in a shelter, and the next day set off for Bletchley with their married daughter, the school of whose children had been evacuated to the town.

Providing them with assistance, a friend of the daughter met them in Bletchley, and from there they then moved to a cottage at Shenley - which was damaged by the bombs.

Yet it seems this was not the only bombing of the village, for during September a high explosive bomb had fallen in a local field. Fortunately it failed to explode, and with the area quickly roped off, danger boards were erected and the livestock removed, with the police mounting guard until 6a.m.

Subsequently from the Bomb Disposal Section at Reading, Second Lieutenant How-White arrived to inspect the area, and following his investigation he stated that no further action should be taken until September 8th.

The former Crown Inn.

However, he didn't turn up on that date, although he perhaps made an appearance in late October 1940 when, having landed 100 yards from Dovecote Farm, another high explosive bomb fell, damaging the windows.

Again the area was roped off, with danger boards erected. Yet despite such dangers Alan remained at the Crown, from where he would cycle each day to Bletchley Park whatever the weather, even spurning the use of an official car.

His achievements in breaking the German codes would be vital, but inevitably the strain proved immense and Mrs. Ramshaw, his landlady, became so concerned at his mumblings, alone in his upstairs room, that she contacted the medical authorities.

Nevertheless, towards the end of the war Alan became involved in another secret project, and for two days a week for six months would cycle to Hanslope Park, moving to the Officers Mess in 1944.

As for the Crown, this had been a pub since at least 1820. In 1853 the licence had been transferred from John Gregory to George Emerson, of the prominent farming family (hence Emerson Valley) but it closed in February 1959, since the brewery did not consider the £300 needed to modernise the toilets to be a justified expense.

Indeed, even the landlord, Stanley Ball, said 'the trade is a dead loss,' but having lived in the village for 35 years, and been the licensee for 15 years, he decided not to leave the premises, which he then continued to occupy privately.

SHENLEY: VILLAGE CURIOS

A Christmas Story: The Glastonbury Thorn

At the Crucifixion, Christ is said to have been helped to carry the Cross to Calvary by Joseph of Aramithea, who, according to legend, came to England bearing the Holy Grail. At Glastonbury he planted his staff in the ground, which grew into a hawthorn bush and supposedly flowers every Christmas Eve.

It seems someone planted a cutting at Shenley, and a row of village dwellings were named Glastonbury Cottages.

With the arrival of the new city the bush has achieved even greater prominence, for not only has the name been taken for a nearby road, but protection is now afforded by a railed enclosure.

Accommodating A Need: The Stafford Almshouses

Dating from 1614, the Stafford Almshouses, of Shenley Church End were built for people who did not indulge in 'riotous living', although now a much weathered plaque records:

> 'THIS ALMSHOUSE WAS CAUSED TO BE ERECTED BY
> THOMAS STAFFORD ESQ,
> DECEASED, AND WAS BUILT BY THOMAS STAFFORD HIS
> SON, ANNO DOMINI 1614'.

Sir Thomas had died in 1607 and his will left instructions for the almshouses to be built for the accommodation of four unmarried, impoverished men and two women, all of whom had not only to regularly attend Shenley church, but to refrain from any 'riotous living.'

A daily payment of 3d was to be made to each of the men, and 2d to the women. By the provisions of the will the trustees would purchase 70 acres of land at Great Linford, and with this being rented to William Hopkins the income, of £30 per annum, was to be expended on 'The Poor People of Stafford's Hospital in Shenley', thereby providing not only the necessary finance to maintain the building, but also to pay the pensions.

However, since the passage of time devalued the worth of the rent, in 1882 the Charity Commissioners agreed that three of the tenements could be let, with the income applied to the benefit of the three remaining occupants.

Today, the almshouses have been converted into private accommodation. Their founder is commemorated in the church by an impressive monument.

SIMPSON

REVEREND WILLIAM RICE: VICAR CHARGED FOR CAUSING 'BODLEY' HARM

At the age of around 73 the rector of Simpson, the Reverend William Rice, died after a short illness in February 1919.

But during his life many of his parishioners lost their reverence for him; and in fact he provoked many an unholy row.

DAUGHTER OF THE LATE LORD SEAFIELD MARRIED.

Lady Sydney Montague Ogilvie-Grant and the Rev. William Rice, rector of Sympson (Bucks), leaving St. George's, Hanover-square, after their wedding yesterday. The bride is a daughter of the late Earl of Seafield and of the Dowager Countess of Seafield.—("Daily Mirror" photograph.)

Reverend William Rice and his bride at their wedding in 1912.

Educated at St. David's College, Lampeter, he had taken his BA degree in 1875, and being ordained a deacon in the same year, proceeded to priest's orders in the diocese of Worcester in 1876.

After positions as curate of St. Paul's, Birmingham, 1875 to 77, Ashover, near Matlock, 1877 to 1879, Melbourne 1879 to 1888, Derbyshire, and Hodnet

1889 to 1890, he then became rector of Simpson in 1891, by the patronage of Sir William B. Hanmer.

However, when he came to the village his predecessor had been ill for four years, and during that time the parish had suffered accordingly.

Adding to the burdens of the new rector, he was unable to let the glebe, of some 225 acres, and because he had to therefore farm it himself, it was perhaps because of these combined pressures that, almost from the beginning of his appointment, he seems to have habitually antagonised certain of the parishioners.

In fact in 1896 he was fined £3 for assaulting a boy named Bodley. Yet having raised the funds, it would be under his auspices and direction that the parish church was restored in 1904, and it was also due to his efforts that a new bell was added to the belfry. In fact, he even offered to finance the building of a mission hall, for those of his parishioners who lived in Fenny Stratford.

It might have been thought that his marriage, on April 9th 1912 to Lady Sydney Grant, daughter of the 10th Earl of Seafield, would have tempered his entanglements, both with the authorities and parishioners, but sadly this was not to be.

He was fined for driving without a light, and for allowing heifers to stray on the road and was also in trouble in 1915, when a drunk parishioner hit him on the head with a stick.

The next day the man's wife then also hit him with a stick, but when she charged him with assault, he promptly issued a counter summons. In the event the couple called a witness, and the Reverend was fined £2.

As for other appearances before the magistrates, these included a summons for having a collie dog on the loose, which Special Constable Badger had managed to trace, by its barking, to a barn.

Yet despite these blights on his character, at the school board elections on two occasions the Reverend Rice had been returned as head of the poll and, having "the look of an open air man, with a sunburned clean shaven face and plentiful grey hair," many parishioners held a certain affection for him.

Others, however, held a different view, and alleged that for some years the church not been conducted satisfactorily and relayed their concerns to the Bishop of Oxford, who, as a consequence in early 1917 appointed the Bishop of Buckingham to preside over a commission into the supposed inadequacies.

The claims included that Sunday morning congregations had dwindled to an average of 17, including the choir, that early Communion was held at irregular intervals, and that no candidate for confirmation had been presented for many years.

Also, that there were no systematic visits to the sick, although there had been no case of actual refusal.

Occasionally, Reverend Rice had apparently been seen to walk through the village with his sheep on Sunday evenings, en route to the station to London, while regarding the church services it was said that the prayers were so gabbled as to be difficult for the congregation to join in.

The conclusion of the commission was that the rector no longer had any influence over his flock, because as a keen agriculturalist - having some 500 sheep and 33 beasts - he had neglected his church duties.

Therefore on receiving the reports the Bishop of Oxford, under the Clerical Discipline Act Parliament, inhibited the Reverend Rice from performing his clerical duties at St. Thomas's Church.

At this, the Reverend Rice appealed to the High Court of Justice, and - as the first to be held under the Benefices Act of 1898 - the case would be subsequently heard in the King's Bench.

During the trial, a solicitor said when he attended Simpson church in August 1914 not only was the congregation less than 10, but also the service began 10 minutes late, with the rector seeming to have just come in from a field.

In fact he looked as if he had not washed for a week, and it was alleged that he had been incoherent during the service.

However, another view was put that the rector had been known to leave his meal to pay a visit to those who were sick, and statements were additionally made that he had always conducted the service in a reverential and impressive manner.

Not that this seemed a unanimous view, for an old naval pensioner, who being a regular churchgoer, had lived in the village since 1905, had kept a diary of the rector's sayings and doings, and these included an entry that "the whole address, lasting 10 or 15 minutes, was most outrageous, especially from a Church of England pulpit on the Lord's Day."

"Many people left the church during the rector's abuse."

In fact because of this he had written to the Bishop.

As for the sermons, when asked "is he as good as other clergymen?", one parishioner replied "I have heard worse."

During the course of his questioning, the Reverend Rice denied having said to the mother of the churchwarden's wife "hold your tongue, woman, or I'll have you up for brawling," although as evidence of his alleged temper one man recalled that having asked him not to trespass on his land, the rector flew into "an absolutely disgusting exhibition of temper, so that he was quite incoherent and literally foamed at the mouth."

Another woman cited an instance where he had threatened her with a clothes prop, while another alleged he shook a stick at her, and called her a liar.

More alarmingly, a one-armed man alleged when he had 'touched' the rector with his stick, the Reverend knocked him down and stamped on him.

As for one tenant who, following the death of her brother, who had been killed in action, owed him rent, she was three times called a hussy, and she had even heard him use bad language to his sheep!

Therefore at the conclusion of the proceedings even the defence had to acknowledge that he had an "over virile temperament," and it was perhaps inevitable that the appeal failed.

Nevertheless, although he was debarred from exercising any clerical functions in his parish, the Reverend Rice still remained the rector, and now having more time for agricultural matters, he continued to farm the glebe land, plus the other land he had acquired from time to time.

SOULBURY

LOVETT FAMILY OF 'LYCHESCUMBE'

Accompanied by his two sons, Richard de Louet was amongst the army that crossed with William of Normandy in 1066, and following the Conquest his

The church at Soulbury.

eldest son, William, would be appointed Master of the Wolf Hounds 'over all England.'

For more than 20 generations William's descendants would be associated with Soulbury and Liscombe, and to remind of this long acquaintance the three wolves of the Lovett arms may be seen in the eastern window of the village church.

As well as other local interests, by the 14th century 'Lychescumbe' manor lay in the possession of Robert Lovett, and by his marriage he also acquired Biddlesden Abbey, where in the Turville chapel a brass, inscribed with two shields, an inscription, and the figure of a knight in armour, would be placed to commemorate Thomas Lovett, who died in 1491.

(Following the demolition of the Abbey in 1704 this brass was placed on the north chancel wall of Soulbury church.) Excepting the chapel, the manor house at Soulbury was pulled down in the early 16th century, and a new manor house would then be built. However, in 1626 the grounds were witness to a tragic incident when, on October 17th, highwaymen murdered Thomas Adams who, with his brother, had purchased the overlordship of lands at Swanbourne.

In fact on the north side of the chancel in Soulbury church, incorporating the shield of arms for the Butchers Company of London, of which he was a member, the inscribed figures of himself and his wife, Elizabeth, plus suitably poignant verse, a brass was placed to his memory, although in time this would be reset into the floor.

(Interestingly, at his former manor house in Swanbourne many sightings of a 'green lady' were said to have been made, supposedly the ghost of his wife.) As for Soulbury, in view of the Lovett's long possession of the manor the church contains several family memorials, including 'A filial offering to maternal worth.'

This, in remembrance of his mother, was placed on the south side of the chancel by Sir Jonathan Lovett, and the impressive monument is fashioned from Coade stone which, as a material immensely popular at the time, was a product of the 'Coade Artificial Stone Manufactory.'

With the death of Sir John Lovett, by whom the family mansion was much altered, in the absence of a male heir the inheritance passed to his daughter, and then after her death in 1855 to a cousin, by a son of whom the family's long association came to an end with the sale of the estate to Ernest Robinson, in 1907.

In fact Ernest was the son of John Peter Robinson, of the London firm of Messrs. Peter Robinson Ltd., but, as always, that's another story.

STEWKLEY

IVY LANE

14, Ivy Lane. Oops! Is it safe to crawl out of the bunker yet. Following my mini rant in the article regarding Broughton (09-09-10) a certain amount of flak has certainly been flying over the parapet, not to mention a certain degree of earache from a certain lady colleague at work.

And of course Sandra Glazebook (readers' letters) was fully justified in taking uppance that no mention was made of the married man.

However, this was because the story - as told to me by an 'old timer,' several years ago - made no such mention, which seems to confirm the 'ignorant age' which then existed.

Thus to hopefully redress the balance, this article deals with the local story of those women who were prominent in achieving the rights enjoyed by their gender today.

In a male dominated political sphere, the emergence of the Suffragette movement began to cause much concern, and in August 1909 when the Prime Minister, Herbert Asquith, arrived at Bletchley Park, to speak in support of a parliamentary candidate, substantial efforts were made to prevent the precursors of women's lib from disrupting the meeting. Nevertheless, one determined member still managed to chain herself to a tree, and others were temporarily locked up.

The Pankhursts were the most prominent of the Suffragettes, and from 1912 until 1914 it became a national mystery as to the whereabouts of Mrs. Emmeline Pankhurst, and her daughter, Sylvia.

In fact following her disappearance from London, Mrs. Pankhurst had retreated to Stewkley, where in the cosy confines of No. 14, Ivy Lane she took up residence. In fact locally there was much support for her aims, and when at the beginning of March 1914 Miss Mason, of the Women's Suffrage Society, spoke at a meeting of the Bletchley branch of the N.U.R., a resolution was passed supporting votes for women.

However, it would be the role of women during the First World War which provided the main incentive for extending the franchise, for it became increasingly apparent that they were well able to do the jobs performed by the men who were now on military service.

Indeed, as stated at a meeting staged by the National Union of Women's Suffrage Societies, held in Wolverton's Science and Art Institute, the aim was 'to secure the franchise for women by reasonable and fair agreement and by the overwhelming evidence which the war has produced that women have shown themselves admirably adapted to take their share in work of national importance.'

As for their local efforts, although being an experienced tailoress a young lady from Newport Pagnell became a conductor on the Luton Corporation tram service, to thereby release a man for the Forces, whilst regarding others their farm employment remained essential to the nation's food production.

Therefore in 1918 all women aged over 30 were enfranchised, with this age being lowered in 1928 to 21, the same age as men.

And so, as exemplified by their role during World War Two, no one could nowadays begrudge women their hard earned freedoms - as long as they can still find the time to do the housework of course - ONLY JOKING!

STEWKLEY: ST. MICHAEL'S CHURCH

For most people, it might seem preferable to French kiss a puff adder than to undertake a study of church architecture, although - in moderation - the subject can be quite fascinating, since, as with cars, or fashion, different styles are indicative of different eras.

In fact in our region we have several fine examples from various ages, but perhaps the most notable is that of St. Michael's at Stewkley, built around 1150.

After the Conquest, the Normans began a programme to provide every English parish with a stone built centre of worship, but of all the 6,000 churches thereby begun, only three now retain any abundant evidence of the Norman style - those of Studland, in Dorset, Iffley, in Oxfordshire, and Stewkley, which is the finest and least altered. In fact the characteristics of Norman architecture are amply displayed in the thickness of the walls, the low, squat tower, the round headed doors and windows, and the copious carvings of the typically bold and regular designs. Indeed, even the Norman font remains.

Externally, amongst the most discernible of the architectural features is the triple arched west door, where in the space between the top of the door and the upper archway may be seen a 'tympanum,' carved with dragons.

Externally, the length of simple ornamented carving running below the window line is known as a 'stringcourse', and another, which maintains continuity by arching above the doorways, is to be seen inside the building.

However, perhaps the most notable of the internal features is the chancel arch. This spans some fourteen feet, and here, as approached from the nave, no less than thirty seven 'beak head' carvings gaze bemusedly down, including a trinity of monkey faces!

Typically Norman, the name arose because of the distinctive shape, and as applied to the chancel arch their purpose is to deliberately draw a visual attention from the nave (as the preserve of the congregation) towards the more holy confines of the sanctuary.

For a similar reason the windows of the nave have a single row of chevron moulding, whilst those of the choir and sanctuary are endowed with two. As an indication of imitation being the sincerest form of flattery, in the early 19th century the building began of churches in a 'neo Norman' style, and one example is to be seen at Holy Trinity Church, Old Wolverton. The site had accommodated a place of worship since at least the 13th century, but in 1815 a dramatic rebuilding in the Norman style took place by order of the Radcliffe trustees.

The architect was Henry Hakewell, and his designs so altered the original plan that the central tower now formed the western extremity of a new cruciform shaped church, an impressive feature of which is the east window, a beautiful example of the rose type.

STOKE BRUERNE

DIGGING BLISWORTH TUNNEL

When the Grand Junction Canal Act was set out, in 1793, it was decreed that 'adjoining to the said Village of Stoke Bruern,' nothing in the wording should allow the proprietors 'to cause any of the aforesaid Earths, Stone, Gravel, or other Materials, which may be dug to make the said Canal, to be carried or laid on any of the Homesteads and small Mowing Grounds.' However, for the canal diggers their immediate concern was the geological strata, and by 1796 the Canal Company was having to deal not only with despondent contractors, but also the possibility of the excavations being flooded by hill water. In fact following consultations it was wisely decided to re-route the proposed Blisworth tunnel to a point just east of the original line at the northern end, and so cause the termination at the south to be some 130 yards west of the projected intention. Yet to carry off the hill water it would be necessary to dig a small pilot tunnel, beneath the proposed main excavation, and because of this delay the Canal Company decided that other projects elsewhere needed priority. Therefore only six men were left to continue the tunnel excavations, and as an interim measure a road would be laid over the course of the route. However, this soon proved unsuitable for heavy loads, and in March 1799 it was proposed to use a cast iron railway instead. Then with the Blisworth Tunnel as the only unfinished stretch of the canal, plans were introduced to hasten it's completion, and for the excavation 19 shafts were sunk to the required depth, after which the digging commenced in either direction. Horse drawn cranes winched out the spoil in baskets, and the mounds formed by this dumping may still be seen. After the completion of their section all the shafts were back filled except four, which - with brick chimneys erected on the surface, to prevent objects from falling or being thrown down the opening - were left to provide ventilation. As for the tunnel being haunted, this seems of little surprise, for two men crashed to their doom in October 1803, when a shaft bucket slipped off the hook of the crane. As for another tragedy, a story is told from the later stages of the work, when the navvies were allowed only 20 minutes for lunch. Supposedly, when his wife arrived late with his dinner one Irishman, possessed of a rather hot temper, became so enraged that he grabbed his pickaxe and took off her head in one swipe. However, so as not to cause any delay the incident was hushed up, and, with the body being buried somewhere in the tunnel, the woman's spirit is still said to haunt the watery confines. Eventually, with all the constructional difficulties overcome the tunnel was formally opened on Monday, March 25th 1805, and the first boat, carrying an assortment of local worthies, completed the 3,075 yard length in an hour and two minutes. Now the way was clear for commercial traffic, and to great excitement in May 1806 the first such vessel - laden with 100 sheep for the London market - set off from Northamptonshire, completing the 95 mile journey in 53 hours. But soon the railways, and later the roads, would siphon off the commercial trade, although the present popularity of leisure boating has ensured that the canal still remains in regular use today.

STONY STRATFORD

DANCING WITH WORDS (CITIZEN FIRST) - STONY STRATFORD

Graced with inspiration, the poet gilds words into works which soar to the heights of eloquence and passion, and thus it might seem that words are at one with the notes of music. For to be consummate with the joys of literature is to know the sensual intimacy of dance - on which subject the proprietor of a Stony Stratford dancing and deportment academy, Mr. Joseph Hambling, became the inspiration for the character of Mr. Turveydrop in a Charles Dickens novel, Bleak House. From around 1840 to 1870 Mr. Hambling ran his academy in a house at the corner of the Market Square and Mill Lane, and in the novel a description of him is to be found in chapter 14. The house was demolished around the end

The market square at Stony Stratford as it appeared in 1819.

of the 19th century, but the Cock Hotel still survives, where, with music by local musicians, the dancing lessons took place. Apart from Charles Dickens, this region has many past links with other well known writers and poets - to include William Cowper, John Mason, and Thomas Seaton - but more recently John Betjeman voiced his poetic eloquence when, in their successful fight against London's third airport at Cublington, he gave evidence for the 'Resistance Committee.' However, for the purpose of this article it seems appropriate to continue and conclude with Stony Stratford, and a man who, although possessed of poetic talent, might have had some difficulty with dancing. He was Sam Ashton, the one legged, tee total town crier, and here follows his flowing lines addressed to a Mr. Kightley, on the business of selling peas.

My dear Mr. Kightley, look out and be sprightly,
You are wanted down here, I assure you;
The people want peas, so make haste, if you please,
Or others will be here before you.

We've had none here yet, but, fine weather or wet,
I'm expecting them here every morning,
Old Langley or Odell, from Malden will toddle,
Remember, I've given you warning.

I know very well, if you come you will sell
A cart load of peas, just like winking;
Our ladies will flock, to purchase your stock,
You'll have no time for eating or drinking.

If by chance you or I, get a drop by the sly,
To discourse long we should not be able,
Ere Robbins politely, would say, Mr. Kightley,
Our dinner is now on the table.

Your maw for to stuff, you go ready enough,
As you doubtless are tired and weary;
I cut off to work, like a Negro or Turk,
Until night, then return to my deary.

So pray my good man, come as soon as you can,
For I am sure it will give me great pleasure,
The first time this year, I cry peas, cheap or dear,
To bawl round the town, heap'd up measure.

And if you intend, an answer to send,
Don't forget to address me – Esquire;
Until we meet again, I hope to remain,
Your's, as ever, the Stratford Town Crier.

STONY STRATFORD: WESLEY'S ELM AND RELIGIOUS OBSERVANCE

In Stony Stratford, until recently in the Market Square could be seen the stunted remains of an aged elm tree, beneath the branches of which John Wesley, the founder of Methodism, is supposed to have preached on at least one occasion.

Having been ravaged by not only Dutch elm disease but also two fires, the remains of the tree have now been removed, but a plaque, placed alongside the recently planted oak sapling, notes the significance of the site.

As recalled by a previous plaque, John Wesley came to Stony Stratford on five occasions, including July 30th 1777, when even the large and commodious barn prepared by Mr. Canham could not accommodate all those who had gathered to witness his preaching.

"However, all without, as well as within, except one fine lady, were serious and attentive."

In fact, his words seemed to have been well received, for he again found an attentive audience on a return visit on November 27th, at which he noted that those attending "need no repentance".

Despite the inadequacy of the barn, which was situated off the High Street, it would remain as the Wesleyan Chapel until 1844, when new premises were built in Silver Street.

Ordained in 1725, John Wesley was descended from a long fine of gentry and clergy, but he became increasingly convinced that the Christian faith was not "a mere acceptance of orthodox opinions but a habit of soul by which man enters into living union with Christ".

He therefore dispensed with tradition and, dismayed by the ungodliness of contemporary England, took to open-air preaching, as a means to circumvent the ban which barred him from most pulpits.

During 50 years, he would travel some 250,000 miles throughout the country, and preach 40,000 sermons.

As for traditional religion, at the time of the Norman Conquest, Stony Stratford as such did not exist, but since the increasing numbers of travellers passing along the Watling Street offered obvious opportunities for trade, the location attracted commercial enterprise from the nearby manors of Calverton to the west, and Wolverton to the east.

So began the origins of the town and, to provide a spiritual influence, chapels of ease to the mother churches of Calverton and Wolverton were soon built.

From these chapels would develop the churches of St. Giles, on the west, and St. Mary Magdalene, to the east, but both were severely damaged by a fire in 1742. Scorch marks can still be seen on the church tower. Despite some remedial attention by the noted 18th century antiquarian Browne Willis, this brought about the disuse of St. Mary Magdalene, and only the tower is now apparent, with scorch marks still to be seen on the upper stonework.

However, many aged tombstones remained in the churchyard, including one to commemorate the wife of a London architect, which reads: "Reader, beneath this awful tomb Lies Virtue cropt in early bloom."

As for the original church of St. Giles, having become a "too small and ancient and decayed building", an extensive rebuilding took place in 1776, for the purpose of providing accommodation for the combined congregations.

Since then much further work has of course taken place - but that is another story.

SWANBOURNE

DEBORAH KERR & ANTHONY BARTLEY

The story of Thomas Beecham (of Beecham's Powder fame) has been told in the Mursley section, but the village of Mursley has another claim to fame, as having been the home of David Tomlinson, the late film star.

However, the nearby village of Swanbourne also has connections with a famous film star, for Deborah Kerr had married one of the village sons, Anthony Bartley.

Anthony had been born in India where, having been a barrister of the Irish High Court, his father, Charles Bartley, was a High Court judge. In fact Charles would be knighted for his service, and thus on their return to England it would be as Sir Charles and Lady Bartley that they made their home at The Cottage, Swanbourne.

As a boy, Anthony was often out and about in the village with his air gun, and one day on seeing two aircraft flying over the Swan he raised his rifle and fired at the inviting, if distant, target.

Suddenly one of the planes developed engine trouble, and losing altitude had to make a forced landing in the fields between Swanbourne and Mursley. Circling a while to confirm the safety of the crew, the companion aircraft then flew off, and so did young Bartley who, convinced that his shot had been the cause of the descent, fled into hiding. However, having been on a training mission the aircraft had developed engine trouble long before reaching the hostile airspace of Swanbourne!

Anthony would soon be shooting down aircraft for real, for following the outbreak of World War Two he became a fighter pilot in the Battle of Britain, downing eight enemy machines.

Indeed, much to the delight of the more youthful villagers he would sometimes 'beat up' Swanbourne in his Hurricane. Later in the war Anthony was sent to lecture in America, and, having made the acquaintance of several film personalities, it would be when stationed in Brussels that, through an introduction by Stewart Granger, in 1945 he made the acquaintance of Deborah Kerr.

The two stars, and the rest of the cast of the E.N.S.A. production of 'Gaslight', were invited to the Officers' Club. Before the entertainers left Brussels, Deborah and Tony would be dining together, and when Deborah was filming in Ireland Tony proposed by telegram; 'Have been posted to the South Pacific Stop Will you marry me.' She replied; 'Yes Stop', Where and when'.

Since Tony was allowed only 48 hours of compassionate leave, before the wedding Deborah travelled alone to Swanbourne to make the acquaintance of her prospective in laws, and amidst great publicity the couple were married at St. George's Church, Hanover Square, in London.

Then in 1948 the couple's first child was christened in St. Swithun's Church, Swanbourne.

After the war Anthony become a test pilot and foreign representative for the Vickers aircraft company, but when Deborah's career took them to Hollywood this posed a dilemma, since, having been born in India, under American law Anthony was officially barred from working in that country. However, Congress resolved the situation by passing a private bill, 'for the relief of Anthony Charles Bartley, in recognition of one of our greatest Allies' greatest heroes.'

Sadly the marriage didn't last, but even until her final years Deborah retained an affection for Swanbourne, as also an interest in the activities in the village.

Deborah Kerr.

THORNBOROUGH

THE BURIAL BARROWS AT THORNBOROUGH

At Thornborough may be seen two of the most famous and spectacular Roman 'barrows' in England, about which in olden times 'the Vulgar have several odd Traditions about their being inhabited by Fairies.' However, the only association with the little people today seems to be a fairy ring of toadstools, set before the westernmost barrow. In 1839 the Duke of Buckingham, from Stowe, had excavations made of one of the mounds, and this revealed evidence of a cremation with, preserved to varying degrees, several ornaments of pottery and bronze. In fact one was a bronze lamp which was quite different from any previously known, and even the wick remained intact. Also found was an ornament of pure gold, elaborately chased with the figure of Cupid, but when this later disappeared there was allegedly some suspicion that the British Museum had acquired possession! All the finds were dated at the late 2nd century, with many being sent to the University Museum of Archaeology and Anthropology in Downing Street, Cambridge. Having been robbed at an earlier date, when investigated the second barrow proved more disappointing, but nevertheless both examples are still prominent features of the local landscape, being probably indicative of a settlement that developed at this important crossing of the Ouse tributary. In fact as an indication that the Thornborough settlement would flourish, evidence has been discovered of a temple built on a nearby riverside prominence. Constructed around 265A.D., this was possibly a shrine to a local river god, and in the course of the excavations the site revealed over 300 coins. Most dated from the period 333 to 350A.D, although an unsurprising decline in the quantities was apparent towards the early 5th century, at the time of the Roman withdrawal. Today, the setting provides a picturesque location for picnics, and as well as the barrows the adjacent 14th century stone built packhorse bridge is also well worth a peruse. However, that's a story for another time.

TYRINGHAM

BELGIAN REFUGEES AT THE LODGES OF TYRINGHAM HOUSE

The popularity of such television series as 'Downton Abbey' is perhaps not entirely unexpected, for in an age when modern communications have allowed the prolificacy of so called 'social networking,' it conversely seems that for many people human interaction has become increasingly isolated. Hours spent talking to an image on a screen, or communicating on a mobile phone in messages of clipped, and barely intelligible, English, seems hardly natural, and it's therefore perhaps unsurprising that the psyche yearns for an age when social interaction involved fluent and articulate conversation, a sense of close knit community, and the close, perhaps flirtatious, subtleties of body language. Anyway, OMG that's my two pennyworth, innit, LOL. And so to the upstairs downstairs world of Downton Abbey, where everybody was far from equal, and the 'lower orders' would have certainly not had the leisure time to spend on Facebook, or follow the banal 'twitterings' of some non entity. But if the 'Edwardian summer' seemed to be the culmination of this class divide, then for the social climate the gathering clouds of global conflict would soon instigate an irreversible change, and after the First World War for the aristocracy their fortunes would never be quite the same again. Yet locally, at the outset of the war the social order was still well entrenched, and not least for the Farrars at Chicheley Hall, the Carlisles at Gayhurst House, and the Boswells at Crawley Grange. As for Tyringham House, the fact that the dome of the mansion had been designed by the Kaiser's architect, and that the Kaiser himself had been planning a visit, did not perhaps bode well for the Konigs. But there could be no questioning the loyalty of Frederick 'Fritz' Konig, for as the owner of Tyringham House he had by September 1914 offered the Government the use of the new wing for sick and wounded soldiers. However, the War Office had already made preparations for a considerable number of wounded, and it was therefore hoped to obviate the need for four months or so. In this time of national danger many men from Tyringham and Filgrave readily volunteered for military service, and before leaving for Oxford each was presented with a sovereign by Mr. Konig, from whose own staff several members would also heed the call. Throughout the country, the prevailing patriotism had been stirred not least by the harrowing story of German atrocities in Belgium, and witness to this was well borne by Henri Vandenberg and his wife and four children. As an impoverished labouring class family, they had fled from Ashot, near Louvain, when their humble cottage was burnt down by the Germans, and having via Antwerp escaped to Holland, there their plight came to the notice of the Belgian Refugee Committee in England. Subsequently, on the evening of Monday, December 19th 1914 they arrived at Tyringham, and through the courtesy of Mr. and Mrs. Konig would there be accommodated rent free in the lodges of Tyringham House. As for the furniture, this was supplied through the kindness of Miss McFerran, of Tyringham cottage, and Mrs. Carlile, of Gayhurst House, who also did much to make the family feel at home. Indeed, locally there were numerous examples of how in this time of national crisis everyone, regardless of social standing, united in the common cause, and so if the producers of Downton Abbey are seeking material for a sequel, then for the period 1914 to 1918 there is no need for fiction. Just consult the annals of the local past, for there will be found a ready made cast of real people, facing real life events. Not a Facebook generation, but a generation who knew how to communicate face to face.

THE EAST LONDON MATERNITY HOSPITAL, AT TYRINGHAM HOUSE

Following the outbreak of World War Two, the East London Maternity Hospital, founded in 1884, was moved from its premises in Commercial Road, Stepney, to Hill Hall, in Essex. However, during the Battle of Britain this was destroyed by a land mine, with the 'Waiting House' receiving a direct hit by high explosives. Fortunately all the staff, patients and equipment were saved, as the mine did not explode immediately, and the Hospital was then transferred to Tyringham House, in Buckinghamshire. Being instructed in their own care, and that of their babies, the patients came from bombed out areas, and many received a month's rest before going home. An important part of the Hospital's work was the training of pupil midwives, whilst as for local help, in March 1941 a number of members of the Nursing Division of the Newport Pagnell St. John Ambulance Brigade volunteered for service as blood donors for the Hospital, with three having been called by May 1942. Through conducting various functions, in 1941 the villages of Tyringham and Filgrave played their part in the Newport Pagnell and District War Weapons Week, and towards the funds the Matron of the Hospital contributed £10. For entertainment, of an evening the nurses would often visit the cinema at Newport Pagnell, but on Tuesday, October 14th 1941 two were tragically involved in an accident, whilst walking back from watching 'Target for Tonight.' They were Nurse Pauriosent, aged 30, and a pupil midwife, Miss Margaret Ward, 21, who, whilst walking abreast a short distance behind their two companions, at about 10.30p.m. between Lathbury and Tyringham were run into by a motor cyclist and pillion rider. Nurse Pauriosent suffered concussion and severe bruises, and Miss Ward a fractured leg, and although they were taken to the Tyringham Hospital, since this did not have the necessary facilities they had to be taken to Northampton General by the Newport Pagnell ambulance. The motor cyclist and pillion rider were unhurt. At Tyringham Church, on Saturday, January 3rd 1942 a member of the domestic staff at the Hospital, Miss Dorothy Williams, the younger daughter of Mr. and Mrs. Williams, of Keeper's Cottage, Tyringham, married Frederick Clarke, who was serving in the Royal Artillery. He was the son of Mr. and Mrs. Harry Clarke, of Mill Street, Newport Pagnell, and about 100 friends of the bride and groom attended a reception, held at the Tyringham House Club by permission of Mr. and Mrs. Marcus Konig. The couple then left in the evening for a honeymoon at Bridgenorth, and on their return Mrs. Clarke, her father being the head keeper on the Tyringham Estate, would continue her employment at the Hospital. (In fact she and her parents had been lucky to escape serious injury the previous year, when, during a short but intense thunderstorm, their home was struck by lightning one Saturday evening in July. Mr. and Mrs. Williams had been standing by the sink in the kitchen, and the flash knocked Mrs. Williams unconscious, and threw her husband against a table.

As for their daughter, who had been in an adjoining room, she was so traumatised that for awhile she was unable to speak. When the smoke and sulphur fumes finally cleared, it was then seen that the sink had been cracked in half, the bolt having passed between Mr. and Mrs. Williams.) In January 1943, the 1,000th baby to be born at the Hospital was a girl, the daughter of Mrs. Margaret Devlin, from Dagenham. Mr. Devlin was employed at Millwall Docks, and Janet would be the name chosen for the new arrival. After the war, for awhile Tyringham House continued to accommodate the Hospital, which with the inception of the N.H.S. in 1948 joined the Stepney Group of Hospitals. Later it merged to become part of the East London Group, and finally closed in 1968.

TYRINGHAM HOUSE IN WWI

Following the outbreak of the First World War, by September 1914 Mr. Frederick Konig, as the owner of Tyringham House, had offered the Government the use of the new wing for about 40 sick and wounded soldiers.

However, with this offer having been accepted some time ago by the St. John Ambulance Association, Mrs. Konig had been informed that, since they had already made preparations for a considerable number of wounded, it was hoped to obviate the need for four months or so.

In fact for hospital use they could only accept premises on a much larger scale, but nevertheless they shortly afterwards asked if the accommodation could instead be used as a convalescent centre.

This was agreed, and in May 1915 Colonel Cree, as the representative of the Surgeon General of Southern Command, inspected the property in the company of Mr. and Mrs. Konig, and Dr. Wickham, from Newport Pagnell.

Thus by mid July 1915 Tyringham House had been taken over by the military authorities, and after the few days necessary to put the finishing touches to the fittings, as required to complete the equipment, the House was ready to accept 100 convalescent soldiers.

These would be those who had fallen victim to enteric fever, but only if their condition had sufficiently improved such that no threat was presented to the local district.

In fact the medical authorities would ensure that before being sent to Tyringham House the patients were completely rid of the 'fever germs,' with it being considered that the delightful surroundings of their new home, and the healthy air, would be conducive to their full recovery.

Having for some time been in the Addington Park War Hospital, Croydon, where they had been nursed back to convalescence, the first draft of patients arrived at Tyringham House on Monday afternoon, September 4th 1915, being 20 'bronzed and seasoned warriors' who, including those from the King's Own Royal

Interior of Tyringham's Temple of Music.

Lancasters, the Norfolks, the Durhams, and Northumberland Fusiliers, had all seen action in Flanders and France. Travelling under the charge of Sergeant Major Guy King, of the 5th King's Liverpool Regiment, they had arrived at Newport Pagnell by the 4.30p.m. train, and were taken to Tyringham in a fleet of motor cars supplied by Messrs. Salmons and Sons.

Officially known as the Military Convalescent Hospital under the Eastern Command, the medical facility, which comprised the whole of Tyringham House, came under the charge of Captain Norman W. Stevens, of the R.A.M.C., and whilst he had the use of a furnished suite of rooms, five other rooms were provided for his staff of six N.C.O.s and 18 men.

In fact Mr. Konig had not only fitted up a wing containing 32 beds, but had also ensured a modern system of electric light and a pure and ample supply of water, all of which was to be under the charge of his own employees.

Then in March 1916 the Military Authorities found it advisable, for the purpose of administrative convenience, to discontinue the hospital at Tyringham House, and, with arrangements consequently made to transfer the patients elsewhere, Mr. Konig was sent a letter of appreciation from the Director General of the Army Medical Service, thanking him for having generously placed the premises at the disposal of the military authorities. Including free seats at the Electra Cinema, Newport Pagnell, during their stay at Tyringham House the patients had been afforded much local entertainment to aid their recovery - to include sports, outings, concerts, and even a playet written by Mrs. Konig - and in fact all they lacked were the comforts of wine and women. However, even this a minority had sought to redress.

The complete story of Tyringham House during the First World War is told in the forthcoming book *Home Fires*,[2] which, with this being very much an 'upstairs, downstairs' era, will also recount the story of other local country houses, to

2 Home Fires: North Bucks During the First World War. ISBN: 978-1-909054-20-2

include Chicheley Hall and Lathbury Park, of the 'Lathbury Gents' fame.

WALTON

DR. EDWARD VAUGHAN BERKELEY HARLEY

The Harley family in front of Walton Hall in 1906.

In 1907, as his country residence Dr. Edward Vaughan Berkeley Harley purchased Walton Hall, including the estate.

As an eminent surgeon he practised at no. 25, Harley Street, London, and the fact that the names were the same was no coincidence, for he claimed descent from the Earls of Oxford, who had been the family responsible for developing that part of the city.

In fact as a heart specialist his father had practised in Harley Street and born on December 28th 1864 (some authorities say 1863) Edward decided from an early age to pursue a career in medicine.

Having studied at Edinburgh University he took the opportunity to travel around the world in 1887/8 and then for the following four years he studied at various foreign universities. In 1890 he was admitted to the Royal College of Physicians and having been invited by Sir Victor Horsley to organise the first department of pathological chemistry in England, when Horsley retired in 1896 Edward then became Professor of Pathological Chemistry, remaining in this appointment until 1919.

In 1905 he had married a renowned beauty, Mary, the eldest daughter of the Reverend Canon Blagden, and two years later the couple moved into Walton Hall.

However, possibly due to his continual travels to London, Dr. Harley would afterwards make preparations to sell the premises but these plans were never realised and in emphasis of his decision to retain the Walton estate he established a farm. This utilised all the latest methods and his prize 'Notlaw' herd of pedigree beef shorthorn cattle gained such renown that many specimens would be shipped to the Argentine.

In fact examples from the herd won numerous prizes at all the major shows with one animal, later sold for £1,000, gaining the Champion Bull of England prize. Thereupon the proud doctor awarded every man on the estate £1 and every boy 10s.

Continuing this success, in 1918 he then won the championship, reserve championship and Maclennan Cup at Birmingham, with his two exhibits making £2,000 and £1,600 in the sale ring. That year he was made President of the Shorthorn Society and perhaps of little surprise he enjoyed a close friendship with Lord Luke of Pavenham, the head of the Bovril concern.

Apart from cattle, the Oxford Downs sheep of the farm were also successful in the show ring and further bred at Walton were fine shire horses and large black pigs. Indeed, the estate provided work for many employees but it would be to his chauffeur, Bayford, to whom Dr. Harley could 'talk better than his own brother.'

Of Dr. Harley's two children, Diana, 'Dido,' was the eldest. She was born in 1907 but of twins born later only one, Primrose, survived, being named in commemoration of her date of birth, Primrose Day, April 19th. As for her mother, she was invariably referred to as 'Ming,' since, having a passion for all things Chinese, she even decorated the walls of the morning room with black wallpaper embellished with a gold Chinese pattern.

On Whit Monday, 1923, Dr. Harley spent much of the morning on the estate, shooting rooks in the company of his guest Sir John Macfadyen, President of the Royal Veterinary College, and after lunch he then retired to his room for his usual rest.

This was due not least through having suffered from an aneurysm of the heart for the previous seven years but despite this condition, and the knowledge that he could collapse at any moment, he had kept up with his medical and agricultural work.

Later in the afternoon Mrs. Harley went to see him but on suddenly being taken ill he died in her arms. At the funeral his coffin was carried from Walton Hall to the church on an estate wagon drawn by four fine farm bred shire horses and in addition to family and friends among the mourners were many members of staff.

Farm employees then carried the coffin from the church gates to the church, where it was met by the rector of Walton. After Dr. Harley's death the farm at Walton was discontinued, the farm equipment laid out for auction, and a part of the estate sold off.

But that, and the later coming of the Open University, is a story for another day

Milton Keynes Citizen, October 25, 2012

WESTON UNDERWOOD

GEORGE EDWARD WENTWORTH BOWYER

So for this week's picture - although it would doubtless enhance the prospects of Parliamentary selection - it's perhaps best to withhold the photo of my unclothed form draped in a bed sheet.

And so to more worthy role models, and a person who commanded the real respect of authority; George Edward Wentworth Bowyer. Born on January 16th 1886 he was the eldest son of Lt. Col. W.G. Bowyer of Weston Manor, Weston Underwood, and after an education at Eton and New College, Oxford, was called to the Bar by the Inner Temple in 1909.

In 1910 he joined the Buckingham Battalion of the Oxon and Bucks Light Infantry (Territorials) and as a Captain fought on the Western Front, being awarded the Military Cross for gallantry on the field.

On the evening of Thursday May 6th 1915, whilst in the trenches he was hit in the shoulder by a piece of rifle grenade, but fortunately the fragment missed the bone, and, after hospital treatment in England, he returned to France in 1916 as Adjutant of the 2nd Battalion of the county regiment.

He then remained in that capacity until recalled for special service at the Admiralty in 1918, the year before his marriage to the Hon. Daphne Mitford.

Entering politics, he was returned with a clear majority as the Coalition Conservative Member for North Bucks, and, being conscientious in his duties, gained much respect, not least from taking a great interest in the welfare of ex servicemen.

Knighted in 1929, in 1935 he was appointed as Comptroller of His Majesty's Household, and by 1937 had contested and won seven elections, all with substantial majorities.

Following the outbreak of World War Two he joined the Home Guard

1st Baron Denham - George E. Wentworth Bowyer

Directorate at the War Office, and there he would be engaged until the end of the conflict. Keen on hunting, he was also a keen cricketer, and during the summer would play for the Weston Underwood and other local clubs.

Of his three children, whilst serving in the R.A.F. his eldest son was killed in action during World War Two, and so his younger son, the Hon. Bertram Stanley Mitford Bowyer, born in 1927, would succeed to the barony in 1948 at the death of his father, which, at the age of 62, occurred on the morning of Tuesday, November 30th 1948, after an operation in a London nursing home.

Drawn by two horses, the coffin was borne from The Manor in a farm cart, and with many notables present the funeral took place at Weston Underwood Church on Friday, December 3rd 1948, the two standards of the Olney branch of the British Legion, of which he had been president, being held aloft at the entrance.

Writing in the Times on Monday, December 6th 1948, 'J' would pen this fitting tribute to Lord Denman - the Rt. Hon. Sir George Edward Wentworth Bowyer M.C., first Baron Denham of Weston Underwood and first baronet; "The motto of George Bowyer - the name I think, by which his old friends will still remember him best - should have been "I serve."

Whether it was an intimate friend, a constituent, or just an acquaintance that needed his help he was always available, and there must indeed be many who, on looking back, will gratefully remember the leg up which they owe to his kindness.

In politics, in his business, and in sport, he will be greatly missed by his friends in all walks of life, and not least by some of the humblest."

Pleasing credentials, and credentials which expose scantily clad antics as mere attention seeking silliness, through which the naked truth can be quite easily discerned by a far from silly electorate.

WHADDON

WHADDON - SECRETS OF WINDY RIDGE

Just before the outbreak of World War Two, Richard Gambier-Parry, sales manager for the Philco Company, had been tasked by the Secret Service to take on a new role in the overseeing and improvement of their radio communications equipment.

This would include providing transmitters for the propaganda operations, as required by the head of that department, Campbell Stuart, who in the early days of the War made his headquarters at Paris House, in the grounds of Woburn Abbey.

From there he paid several visits to Gambier-Parry now resident at Whaddon Hall, which had been taken over by the War Office. At the Hall, Gambier-Parry's wife, formerly his secretary, made the early propaganda broadcasts onto disc, working from a small outbuilding that had seen previous use as a gun room. Transmissions were then made from a radio station at Gawcott, near to Buckingham.

Very soon the propaganda elements were transferred to larger premises at Wavendon Towers, and Whaddon Hall thereon became a secret radio communications centre, more exactly the headquarters of the Special Operations Group of the Special Communications Units.

This entailed, among other operations, responsibility for the transmission to commanders in the field of the decrypted German intelligence from Bletchley Park whose initial radio station - Station X - had been originally housed in the converted water tower of the Park mansion.

In a field adjoining Whaddon church, two huts were especially built on Windy Ridge for the purpose, complete with receiving aerials in the neighbouring acreage. Of low brick walls, roofed by sheets of corrugated iron, one of the huts contained teleprinters, receiving decrypted information direct from Hut 3, at Bletchley Park, whilst the other was a radio transmission centre, broadcasting the information overseas to the various military commands.

For security reasons, the actual transmission aerials were sited many miles away, probably at Creslow but nevertheless the Germans still paid Whaddon occasional attention and indeed a local house was destroyed during one such bombing raid.

Personnel to operate the Windy Ridge station were initially accommodated in the village hall but as the Whaddon requirements grew, so Nissen huts had additionally to be erected in the field at the rear. Apart from the needs of Bletchley Park, Whaddon Hall - staffed by a mix of intelligence and army personnel - from outposts in the nearby fields also provided communication with agents in Occupied Europe and from purpose-built workshops manufactured the compact radio sets used by them.

On a larger scale, prior to D Day the special radio vans to be employed by the army in the Invasion were also fitted out there. To ensure the security of the transmitted information, provided by the codebreakers of Bletchley Park, special units were attached to each military command in the field.

These were known as SLUs, ie Special Liaison Units, and in simplistic terms comprised a radio truck manned by selected personnel, whose task was to maintain communications with Whaddon and thereby supply the military commander with the information gleaned by the codebreakers. SCUs were Special Communications Units, Whaddon being SCU1 and several were dotted around Britain.

Their job was to provide the personnel, equipment and training for the SLUs although the Training Wing for Whaddon was in fact situated a few miles away at Manor Farm, Little Horwood.

After the war, the activities of Whaddon Hall were transferred to Hanslope Park and following a variety of private uses, the Hall has today seen conversion into a number of flats. As for Windy Ridge, the huts were eventually given over to a local farmer, but later suffered the attention of arsonists.

Little now remains except the concrete foundations and there is nothing else to recall that once this site was among the most secret and important of locations, in wartime Britain.

WICKEN

WICKEN: THE REVEREND HUGH NELSON-WARD

Having little desire to voyage beyond the bounds of North Bucks, at school the enforced study of French always seemed rather pointless.

Although a brief interest had once been aroused, when it was revealed that a mademoiselle on the teaching staff had been entertaining the Head Boy to some extra curricular 'French lessons.'

However, when rumbled her secondment sadly came to an end, and she was swiftly packed off back across 'la Manche,' tres vite. As for other French advances, in days gone by these had been chiefly of the Napoleonic kind, and the local villages of Cosgrove and Swanbourne would be the home of two of the Admirals who commanded warships at the Battle of Trafalgar.

As for Wicken, from 1909 until 1928 the rectory became the home of the Reverend Hugh Nelson-Ward, who was the grandson of Horatia, the illegitimate - not that he ever acknowledged this fact - daughter of Admiral Lord Nelson.

In great secrecy Horatia had been born at 23, Piccadily, London, in January 1801, and in the early days of the following month her mother, Lady Hamilton, took her to a Mrs. Gibson, 'a lady without a husband,' in Little Titchfield Street.

There, in return for a monetary sum, Lady Hamilton asked Mrs. Gibson to look after the child, and with this agreed she quickly drove away in a waiting

Wicken Rectory.

carriage.

In time Horatia would marry Philip Ward, a Norfolk clergyman, and although a 'large and sturdy' family would be the result, more sturdy would be the sensitivities of other members of the family, since for many years the true parentage of Horatia would cause them great embarrassment.

Horatia's eldest son became the rector of Radstock, in Somerset, and it would be there that his son, Hugh, the future rector of Wicken, was born in 1863.

Before attending Salisbury Theological College, Hugh had begun his education at King's School, Bruton, and Brasenose College, Oxford, and after various incumbencies he became rector of Wicken in 1909.

There he would keep a large collection of 'Nelsonia,' including a death mask that no one but himself was allowed to touch, and although some of the memorabilia had descended through the family via Horatia, many of the other items Hugh had purchased at auction.

In 1928, on the advice of his doctors Hugh retired, and at a farewell presentation, held in the schoolroom one Tuesday evening in April, he received a cheque for £106 15s 6d, as an appreciation from his parishioners and friends.

Giving a suitable reply, he said that he would be sad to leave, and that he sometimes wondered if he had grown too fond of the church that he loved, of the parish that he loved, and of the garden that he loved.

Taking his collection of relics, he moved to 32, Marlborough Buildings, Bath, and there few would know that he had taken holy orders, since he preferred to be known simply as Mr. Nelson-Ward.

As for his collection of 'Nelsonia,' this he presented to the National Maritime Museum, where in 1939 a special gallery for their display was opened.

Early during World War Two the Reverend's Georgian home at Marlborough Buildings was severely damaged by enemy action, and in consequence, especially in view of his failing health, he decided to move to a private nursing home and guest house at 7, The Circus, Bath.

Retaining only a few possessions, he arranged for the rest to be auctioned, and the impending sale aroused such interest that in November 1942 even Queen Mary came to view the items.

At the age of 90, the Reverend Hugh Nelson-Ward, a lifelong bachelor, died on Saturday, March 21st 1953, and with his funeral being held at Bath Abbey, there he lies buried in the Abbey Cemetery.

WINSLOW

BENJAMIN KEACH AT WINSLOW

As a word, 'history' is probably a right turn off for many people, with connotations of boring dates and stuffy Kings and Queens. Therefore the word 'past' is probably a better option, since it conjures up a more 'how we used to live' feel. And there's no better way to sense the past than whilst in the ambience of some isolated country church, little changed for hundreds of years, perhaps such as Battlesden. And playing mind games, from the pulpit one could pretend to be a time traveller, addressing a medieval congregation of the wonders of things to come. Of a time when men shall ride to the moon in fiery chariots, and people, a thousand at a time, shall cross the oceans in horseless carriages high above the clouds, and faster than a speeding arrow. Guaranteed of course to have the yokels brandishing pitchforks and flaming torches. But yesterday's myth and magic is today's science and technology, and the church of medieval times is no longer the only religion, for just as soothsayers were once regarded as heretics so too were those who dared to branch from the established order. Locally of these 'Non Conformists' the most well known is Benjamin Keach. Born at Stoke Hammond on February 29th 1640, at an early age he was apprenticed to be a tailor but in his youth he had 'come to hold dissenting beliefs on the subject of infant baptism,' and even as a child attended the General Baptist Chapel, situated on the village green. In later years the building would become a village shop, whilst as for the house of his birth, just a few minutes walk from the Chapel, this was demolished around 1900. By the age of 20 Benjamin had become a preacher, and on moving to Winslow in 1660 he married a local girl. However, as a minister of the General Baptists the marital bliss would often be disrupted, such as the occasion when troopers were sent to suppress unauthorised assemblies. On finding a meeting being held by Keach they fell 'with great rage and violence upon the assembly, and swore they would kill the preacher.' Indeed, Keach was seized, bound and laid upon the ground and four troopers declared they would trample him to death with their horses, until an officer intervened. Keach was instead tied across one of the horses and ridden off to jail, there to endure many hardships before his eventual release. Yet despite his harsh treatment he continued his religious conviction, and in 1664 wrote 'The Child's Instructor; or a new and easie Primer,' a book in which 'he forthwith and without apology rejected the official Church teaching on Baptism, as taught in the Catechism.' Not surprisingly the Establishment was hardly pleased and although copies were clandestinely printed in London some were found at his Winslow home. Thereupon he was ordered to appear on October 8th 1664, at Aylesbury Assizes and when one of the jurors asked to speak to his lordship on a matter of doubt, during this converse the judge was seen to vigorously shake him by the shoulders! Soon afterwards the jury returned a verdict of guilty! Judgement was then pronounced; to go to jail for two weeks and then stand in the pillory at Aylesbury for two hours and then at Winslow, where 'your book shall be openly burnt, before your face, by the common hangman, in disgrace of you and your doctrine; and you shall forfeit to the King's Majesty the sum of twenty pounds; and shall remain in gaol until you find sureties for your good behaviour and appearance at the next assizes ...' Even this didn't deter his religious views, and his influence is today apparent at Winslow with 'Keach's Chapel,' built in 1625 within an area then known as Pillar's Ditch. Situated in Bell Alley the building is perhaps the oldest Non Conformist chapel in the country and whilst the internal wooden benches and table are undoubtedly original, beneath the gallery the hinged desk tops, complete with lead inkwells, are a legacy of a Sunday School which was commenced in 1824 for 14 pupils.

Milton Keynes Citizen February 16, 2012

POOR LAW & UNION WORKHOUSES

Gosh, I was excited but not that excited. For apparently in a couple of weeks I qualify for a free 'bus pass.'

Phew. And seemingly this is a reward from the State, for having throughout the past 42 years financially contributed to countless mismanaged government projects, cosseted the lifestyle of all manner of scroungers and chancers, and enhanced some MP's pond with a very nice duck house.

But I'm not one to be cynical, and I'm proud to have done my bit. And of course for we aged and impoverished we may also be thankful that the prospect of the Workhouse no longer looms.

On the subject of which, the foundation of a national scheme of poor relief had been laid in 1601 by the Elizabethan Poor Law, whereby overseers from each parish were required to raise money by taxation to fund the welfare of the unemployed, the relief of the aged and infirm, the apprenticing of pauper children, and the building of poor houses.

However, although welcome, this system was not only somewhat inadequate but also much abused. Nevertheless, the basic principle would continue until 1834 when, by the Poor Law Amendment Act, parishes were grouped together under elected 'Boards of Guardians.'

Guardians of the Winslow Poor Law Union c. 1930.

Whilst each parish continued to be responsible for the finance of its poor, the able bodied could now only receive relief if they moved into the Union workhouse, and since these became notorious for their dirty and disease ridden state, this was often a dreaded step.

Yet this reflected no discredit on the commendable motives behind the Act, and after 1834 the necessary building programme began.

As Sir Christopher Wren had designed Winslow Hall, so another architect of national renown would be responsible for the appearance of the Winslow workhouse - Sir George Gilbert Scott. Born at Gawcott parsonage on July 13,1811, he had been responsible for the design of the local church, and in view of this his father encouraged him to become an architect.

Heeding the paternal wish, George gained an early experience by assisting the architect of the Poor Law Commissioners in the designs for the new Union

Workhouses, and during 1835 he then set up in private practice.

By 'strenuous canvas' of the Guardians he duly received commissions for the workhouses of Buckingham, Towcester and Winslow, and at the latter the sale of the old poorhouse, plus a few parish owned cottages, would raise a part of the necessary £5,250.

With the Master's quarters situated in a rectangular central block, the inmates, segregated by gender, would be housed in radiating wings, and in fact some 280 persons could thus be accommodated.

Yet despite being undoubtedly grim, life in the workhouse could still be enlivened by the occasional unexpected incident, such as in July 1908 when, having sought a personal audience with the Guardians, James Rhodes, a 60-year-old inmate, proceeded to ask for a black coat, waistcoat, light trousers, bowler hat, pair of boots, and a trowel.

The clothes he supposedly needed to find work as a jobbing gardener, but there was perhaps an ulterior motive, for in a cottage near to the workhouse lived an eligible female. Being sympathetic to Jim's 'needs' the Guardians, although they could do nothing officially, duly raised the necessary sum, and respectably attired Jim won the affections of his lady.

With the beginnings of the Welfare State the last of the local workhouses closed in 1925.

WINSLOW HALL

Now this seems an interesting wheeze. Apparently, the family of one of the nation's favourite, if departed, children's authors has launched an appeal to move and preserve the great one's writing 'shed.'

Not withstanding that the principal exponent allegedly earns more in a year than the plebs being canvassed could hope to amass in a lifetime. And that the family are plugged into a fortune reputed to be well into seven figures. Still, what better way to preserve personal wealth than to spend as little of one's own filthy lucre as possible.

And on the subject of thrift, a well known saying has local origins, for whilst overseeing the attempts of a young clerk to tot up an accounts list, William Lowndes, Secretary to the Treasury, pointed out a slight error. "Oh, it's only a few pence," said the clerk, to which William replied "if you take care of the pence, the pounds will take care of themselves."

Born in Winslow on November 1st 1652, after an education at Eton and Oxford William was made Secretary to the Treasury during the reign of Queen Anne, and, being 'as able and honest a servant as ever the Crown had,' for many years held the position of Chairman of Ways and Means in the House of

Commons.

He thereby gained unofficial reverence as 'Ways and Means' Lowndes, and 'Ways and Means' would eventually became a part of the family motto.

In 1697 William purchased the manor of Winslow, and in 1699 instigated the building of Winslow Hall at the southern end of the town, which is still much apparent with its prominent chimneys and three storeys.

In fact it's no tall story that Christopher Wren was the architect, since William was a great friend of the eminent designer. In fact Wren would not only design the new building, but also personally check many of the building accounts.

Of the Lowndes previous residence, Thomas Deely, a bricklayer from a long established family in the town, agreed to take down, clean and stack the 60,000 bricks and 12,000 tiles for the sum of £7 4s, and with £8 10s 6d 'paid for digging the foundation of ye new House,' construction duly began.

Having worked under Wren's supervision on St. Paul's Cathedral, the King's carpenter had responsibility for all the woodwork, and indeed Wren's influence is apparent with the oak panelling (fashioned from some of the 111 oak trees used in the Hall's construction, many of which were brought from Stowe Park) as also the thin brass cased locks, manufactured by His Majesty's locksmith.

The final cost of the building totalled £6,686 10s 2½d, and above the entrance door may be seen the inscribed stone documented in the original accounts; 'Paid for cutting the Letters of Mr. Lowndes name and date of the year (1700) - 5/-'. William then lived at his new home until his death in 1724, after which although his descendants retained possession they would often be resident elsewhere.

But back to the preservation of writing dens, and of course there's no doubt that my own little haven needs conserving for the awe of future generations. So any donations of mid oak wood preserver would be much appreciated, thereby not only obviating the need to launch a public appeal, but also of having to break into this handy 50 quid win on the Premium Bonds.

WOBURN

BUILDING THE 'MODEL HOSPITAL'

No doubt we've all come across some wastes of space in our time, ranging from the usual suspects of politicians and 'managerial' types, whose extent of self delusion greatly exceeds ability, to that other perennial favourite the 'consultant.'

A quick glance through the 'sits vac' of the local press confirms that the gravy train is still firmly on the tracks, for in the local health service we appear to have a need for 'Non Executive Directors.'

But then who is going to apply at only £12,000 for up to four days per month?

Surely that can't be four full days; the little lambs would freak out with stress.

Still, they'll have plenty of time to chill, by helping out on the wards. But in the days before state funding there was little money around, and the poor had little recourse to any sort of medical treatment. In fact even at the turn of the 20th century hospitals in Britain were only supported by voluntary contributions, endowments, and patients' payments, and in many towns 'Hospital Week' was an annual feature to raise money for the purpose.

But the district of Woburn was more fortunate, for Mary, the wife of the 11th Duke of Bedford, not only set up her own cottage hospital but devoted herself to the actual nursing.

It had been in India during his service as aide-de-camp to the Viceroy that she had first made the acquaintance of her future husband, and after their marriage in 1888 on their return to England she set up a cottage hospital in Woburn.

Indeed, such was her devotion that by taking a course of lectures at London Hospital she would qualify as a nurse and operations sister, and later even acquire the skills of a radiologist and radiographer.

Then as a replacement for her earlier centre, during 1902-3 she had a 'model hospital' built to her own design, which, with accommodation for 14 patients, would be subsequently run by her private physician Dr. Glendining, who, having purchased the property in 1903, she installed at 'Woodcote', at Aspley Guise.

With the outbreak of World War One the facility became a military hospital – as also the converted Riding School and indoor tennis court at Woburn Abbey did – and in tending the casualties Mary would regularly work 16 hours a day.

In 1917 the hospital was then designated as a special surgical military hospital, and to here in a fleet of ambulances the wounded would be brought from the ambulance trains arriving at Bletchley station, direct from France. Some 2,453 NCOs and men were destined to pass through the Woburn facility, and in due course the Duchess would erect a plaque in the local church to commemorate the 60 NCOs and men who, between 1914 and 1920, died at the hospital.

Also commemorated would be Johannes Zacherias Truter FRCS of Wellington, South Africa, who until his death on December 15th 1918 had been the assistant surgeon at the hospital.

Apart from nursing, the Duchess also developed a passion for flying, but on a flight from her airstrip at Woburn she went missing in 1937, and parts of the wreckage would later be washed up at Yarmouth.

Following her death the Woburn hospital closed, and during World War Two became a printing centre for propaganda literature.

After the war, the premises, known as Maryland, became a hostel for Cranfield College, and then in more recent years an adult education centre.

However, this recently closed and the building is now being converted into

The hospital at Woburn.

apartments

Back to perusing the 'sits vac,' and as one who can only forlornly gaze at the heights of 'Non Executive Director,' on the same page my attention was drawn to becoming an extra in 'Adult films,' which one naturally assumed to be some part in a gardening or home cooking documentary. So imagine the fit of the vapours when informed au contraire.

Oh well, back to the day job, for it seems both careers are best avoided, unless you're happy to display more than seems decent of bare faced cheek.

TALES FROM THE WWI WOBURN POW CAMP

If you go down to the woods today you're in for a big surprise.

Or at least you will be in a few months, for it seems that we're going to have a Centre Parcs plonked in the local woodlands. Still, I suppose voluntary incarceration is better than the converse, which was the lot of German prisoners during World War One when, around August 1916, a POW camp was set up in Crawley Road, at or near Husborne Crawley, 'outside the park.'

Under the control of a guard, from here the inmates were sent to work in the local woodlands felling and cutting timber which, drawn on small trolleys running on rails, was then taken to the engine shed and saw bench for cutting up.

Yet despite being out of the war some of the inmates tried to break out, and one day just before dusk it was found that two had escaped.

The guard was swiftly turned out and together with the special constables remained on duty all night and up to the following mid day, when a message arrived that the fugitives had been taken into custody at Luton.

Soon after their escape they had apparently been seen at Eversholt, and reached Luton after walking through the night.

Special constables were sent from Leighton Buzzard to relieve the tired Woburn men, but in the event they were not required. As for the recaptured prisoners, they were respectively sentenced to 129 days and 168 days, with their sentence to be served at Aldershot.

Not that this deterred others from trying, for halfway between Soulbury and Linslade an escaped inmate was apprehended whilst in conversation with a man travelling to work at Linslade.

In limited English he asked the way to another camp in Surrey and it was just his luck that he had stopped a special constable. At the subsequent arrival of Police Inspector Walker he meekly enquired "Are you police? I go quietly," and was promptly handcuffed.

Following the arrival of a military escort from Woburn his adventure then came to an end with a brisk walk back to the camp. But the camp was not only associated with the conflict between nations but also between that of the sexes, in a case which involved a soldier who married a Woburn girl.

She was 18 and although after the marriage ceremony he went back to Woburn camp they later went to live with his parents in Birmingham, following his discharge from the Army on a pension.

However, it seemed he wouldn't find work nor provide her with any money, and so the means for their rooms and keep had to be earned by the girl's labours in a munitions factory.

Then she found a post card from another woman and when challenged he allegedly twisted and nearly broke her wrist. On another occasion violence was seemingly threatened if she didn't keep quiet, with an emphasis that if she failed to leave the house he would 'stick her.'

Not surprisingly, having given a week's notice at the factory she left him in July 1918, and went straight from night work by train to Woburn. Subsequently in a letter he said it was a pity that he hadn't the money to divorce her, for "I should very much like £15 from someone to do so, instead, I am giving you your freedom.

You can from now consider yourself single and marry whoever you wish. In return, I want an agreement from you. No one need ever know you have been married. I will do the same, as it is impossible for us to agree and come together again."

Following this the woman, who was now in domestic service, travelled to Birmingham and in consequence sent him a letter c/o 'the other woman' asking what amount of maintenance he was going to pay.

Now resident at 24, Bedford Street, Woburn, eventually she applied for an order under the Summary Jurisdiction (Married Women) Act but in court since the episode had happened some while ago, and there was no proof that he was still 'carrying on,' the Bench decided not to uphold the claim of desertion.

Not least since the woman had broken off the matrimonial relationship. Oh dear. And so for any sensible male, the moral of this article appears to be that in time of peace or war it's always best not to mess around with guns or women.

Milton Keynes Citizen, April 26, 2012

WOBURN SANDS

WILLIAM SWAIN

I just don't believe it.

Apparently some salacious tome entitled 'Fifty Shades of Grey' has become a publishing sensation, while that equally riveting read, 'The Aspley Guise and Woburn Sands Gasworks, The Early Years,' has shifted barely a copy.

So to introduce readers to some of the titillation they've been missing here follows a much condensed extract.

In 1878 William Swain travelled from Birmingham to Woburn Sands to be interviewed for the position of gas works manager. Successful in his application he was engaged to start in mid September, but despite being vouched for as 'thoroughly honest, steady and trustworthy, the truth would soon prove different.

Indeed he shortly rendered his resignation and in fact 'William Swain' was just one of several aliases used by William Milner Barratt, who was born at Swinefleet around 1848. It seems it was in 1876 that he first strayed from the straight and narrow, for during that year he was charged with fraud at Wakefield.

From Woburn Sands, William found employment at Swindon but soon lapsed into his old ways by obtaining the original plate for printing his employer's shares, taking it to London, having more shares printed, forging the names of several managers, and then disposing of the shares as his own property.

During the trial in his defence it was stated that he had excellent testimonials although that for 15 years' good service turned out to have been written by his father. Concluding the matter he was given a five years sentence and three years later sought a new life in Australia, arriving at Victoria on January 4th 1888 with his wife and children. A daughter was born in July in Port Fairy (earlier known as Belfast) and from 40 applicants it was here that he got a job as gasworks stoker.

Yet he soon tendered his resignation and in consequence appeared in court the following month for fraud. This misdemeanour had involved placing an advert for a 'Clerk and Bookkeeper' asking for a £50 cash security - 'On the £50 deposit we pay five per cent interest and the agreement is terminable and deposit returned on month's notice either side.'

Of course this was pure baloney and one of those conned swiftly issued a warrant for Barratt's arrest. He received a sentence of three months' hard labour but after his release successfully applied for the position of gas manager of the Borough of Sale gasworks.

However, this didn't last long because he was soon arrested for obtaining money by false pretences, albeit having still collected the gas rates without authority after he resigned.

After more colourful pursuits he successfully applied for the role of foreman of the Dandenong Shire Gas and Coke Company but during this employ on July 1st 1894 the supply of gas was suddenly cut off in the middle of the church services. In typical 'it weren't me Guv' fashion he blamed this on the poor state of the works, writing in the local press 'permit me to state that had my advice been followed, the company could never have appeared in the ridiculous light (or darkness) they have appeared in during the last month.'

Not surprisingly his employment with the gas company soon ended. During his time at Dandenong, William became involved with the Wesleyan church. He even aspired to become a local preacher but his behaviour, aggravated not least by drinking, soon led to his removal.

More colourful episodes then followed, including a spell in jail in 1899 for having conned a group of Geelong businessmen into financing a successful gold mine - which didn't exist.

By the time they realised, he was long gone. However he was eventually arrested - at a jail where he had just finished a separate sentence for fraud. Barratt died of pneumonia in Geelong five months after his release in 1906, but perhaps this was another confidence trick, for his grave in the Eastern Cemetery is unmarked.

Altogether quite a story, so regarding the secrets of publishing success perhaps I should get in touch with E.L. James. But then judging by her recent output I expect she's rather tied up at the moment...

Milton Keynes Citizen, July 19, 2012

WOLVERTON

OLD WOLVERTON: BOUVERIE WALTER ST. JOHN MILDMAY - A DARING PILOT DIVED TO HIS DEATH

On the 18th April, 1918 the RAF Board dispatched a telegram containing the sad news that 19 year old 2nd Lieutenant Bouverie Walter St. John Mildmay had been killed.

Born February 25th, 1899, he was the only child of the Reverend Arundell St. John Mildmay and Mrs. Mildmay of Old Wolverton Vicarage, and from the fellow members of their son's squadron Number 70 they received this fitting tribute; "He was a remarkably daring pilot, and he was trying a very steep dive over the aerodrome when something appeared to break in his machine.

Holy Trinity Rectory and Church. St. John Mildmay grew up here.

"He pulled out of the dive with difficulty, but almost immediately afterwards, while turning to land, his machine went out of control and he dived again into the ground. He was killed instantly.

"We have so far been unable to discover the cause of the accident because the machine was so badly broken on reaching the ground.

"Your son was so young and such a plucky fellow that we all took to him at once, and we looked upon him with a little more experience as likely to prove one of the best pilots we have ever had in the squadron."

Of his generation, Bouverie was the eldest male representative of the Hazelgrove Mildmay's of Somerset and in fact it would be by dint of his birth that he could, had he chosen, have claimed the position of a count of the Holy Roman Empire.

Educated at Mr. Churchill's School at Stonehouse, Broadstairs, and then at Winchester, it was through his headmaster's nomination that from Winchester Officer Training Corps he joined the Royal Flying Corps, as a cadet, in April 1917, and since he passed all his exams with high marks, it was of little surprise that he gained promotion to 2nd Lieutenant.

As a pilot he quickly showed great pluck and daring, and indeed within the first 40 minutes of his first solo flight he had looped the loop!

During December he was then appointed as a test pilot with the Service Test Squadron, although when this made known in the mess at South Carlton, where he was then based, his compatriots were initially somewhat sceptical; "Come, 'Cherub' (his nickname in the RFC), there must be some mistake: they would never appoint one with so little experience as you have had."

Yet there was no mistake, and it would whilst subsequently serving at Castle Bromwich that he began to perform a lot of test work.

However, his method could hardly be said to be orthodox, for on one occasion whilst chasing a fox over some down land the animal became momentarily caught up in his skid.

Then during another escapade a shepherd, who had been asleep, fled in terror with his dog when the aeroplane dived straight at them.

As for a later episode, he began flying in and out amongst people digging potatoes in Lincolnshire, but "when they began to pelt me with potatoes I flew off".

Unfortunately for his aunt, her house lay not far from Castle Bromwich, and deciding to literally pay her a flying visit he took great delight in chasing the butler and servants around the house, whereupon - as he later recalled - "the dear old cook fell flat on her back."

It was therefore of little surprise that his aunt, who was not in the best of health, became rather upset when he flew straight at her bedroom window, before zooming up among the chimneys.

Bouverie then concluded his visit by flying low between the houses along the village, to the great amusement of the many onlookers.

On March 9th, 1918, he joined 70 Squadron, and having apparently been wounded the previous day, it would be whilst flying a Sopwith Camel, D1782, that on April 16th, 1918, he was killed.

A plaque to his memory may now be seen in Holy Trinity Church, Old Wolverton.

As for another of Wolverton's associations with early aviation, one late Wednesday afternoon in July, 1919, whilst engaged in distributing Victory War leaflets a Government aeroplane came down heavily in the Recreation Ground.

The pilot, Captain Pomfret, suffered a severe gash over his right eye, and although Sergeant Hare escaped uninjured, both men were severely shaken.

During the landing a piece of the fence that divided Stacey Hill Farm from the Secondary School playing ground was carried away, and eventually the machine came to rest on the Recreation Ground fence, just behind a seat.

With the propellers smashed to splinters, the machine was badly damaged, and although there were thankfully no casualties, having endured such a narrow escape a little girl, named Muriel Lines, fainted from fright!

RECOLLECTIONS OF WOLVERTON WORKS

Not so long ago 'a job for life' was considered the norm, and nowhere was this more apparent than on the railway. In fact shortly after leaving school, whilst testing the waters for meaningful employment I found this most evident at Wolverton Works, where, having opted for incarceration in some enormous railway office, it seemed instead that an early appointment had been booked with God's waiting room. In fact for a select cadre the average age was a mind boggling 50, and with most of these having seemingly been fixtures before the Second World War, it appeared that when duty called they had all joined up together and then mostly all came back together. But of course their bravery was unquestioned, and some would bear a permanent disability as a result. So having seen off the Boche it was back on life's sedentary track, to await a post pension arrival at that great railway terminus in the sky. But ye gods, nine months of paper shuffling, interspersed with the long apparently mandatory stares into the middle distance, was more than 19 year old flesh could bear, and there was little option but to pull the communication cord, and seek life's adventures elsewhere. After all these years the site accommodates part of a Tesco complex, but no doubt upon this many of the railway warriors are still gazing down from on high with long, mandatory stares. Yet after 40 years their faces begin to reappear, for as one ages it seems that events from the past become clearer, whilst those of more recent days are merely a blur. So what became of pipe puffing 'Taffy' Maycock, a genial, fatherly figure, whom I sometimes drove during the lunch breaks to the little cemetery along the Newport Pagnell road, there to visit the grave of his son, who, whilst in the R.A.F., had been killed in a motorcycling accident. And the chap who sat at the next desk and made periodic 'choo choo' train noises, quite to the bemusement of Mrs. Barnett, who, through heavily rimmed bifocals, transfixed him with her unique glare of scorn crossed with pity. As for titillation amidst the tedium, every so often a long legged lovely from the typing pool would sweep through, and in fact it really was a typing pool, for there were no desktop computers in those days. And then there was the 'Works Manager,' a hallowed being whose presence was often rumoured but, at least for us minions, yet to be proved, for as with the Himalayan Yeti no firm evidence seemed to exist. However, legend told that he drove a high powered exotic red sports car, which had once been owned by the comedian Max Wall. This seemed to be confirmed by the chap who sat next to me, who, apart from the repertoire of 'choo choo' train noises, would sometimes burst forth with 'GT 88, cannot wait, cannot wait,' an apparent reference to the personalised registration, and the alleged impatient manner in which the vehicle was driven. Indeed, I found this quite plausible, for whilst ambling home of an evening in my customised Minivan (go fast stripe, and no hubcaps) my musings would often be startled by the sudden 'whoosh' of a red streak. But since our relative velocities differed by a magnitude of Warp Factor Six, in the ensuing blur it was quite impossible to confirm a positive sighting. Thus, for those deemed unworthy an exalted acquaintance could never be made, and not having transcended my clerical bounds I left British Rail quite deferent to my place in life's firmament. But in recent years came a life changing moment, for during a visit to the National Railway Museum, at York, my unbelieving eyes chanced upon a sign which - oh, may the Heavens be praised - read 'Works Manager's Office, Wolverton Works.' For as I gazed in knee trembling reverence I realised that this wood panelled splendour had indeed once been that forbidden Shrine, which, as with all that is great and is good, was now preserved as a permanent exhibit. However, as to whether this will ever apply to the elusive Works Manager, that I have yet to discover.

Wolverton Works General Office.

THE IRON TRUNK

With the advent of the Industrial Revolution, as an alternative to the rough and potholed roads of the time, which were frequently impassable in bad weather, canals were seen as a smooth and efficient means of transport for conveying raw materials, as well as the increasing quantities of manufactured goods, around the country.

The Grand Junction Canal (later known as the Grand Union Canal) is perhaps one of the best known of such waterways and, after Parliamentary approval of the relevant Act, in 1795, the original intention was to cross the River Ouse at the level near Wolverton.

However, to carry the canal into and out of the river valley would have required four locks on either side of the river. So the resident engineer, James Barnes, who had made the initial canal survey, submitted a report to the canal company proposing an aqueduct.

The canal company, mindful of the potential chaos that could be caused by the not infrequent flooding of the river, authorised an immediate start and, after consultations with the various landowners, plans were agreed in principle. The cost was estimated at £25,000 and the principal engineer, William Jessop, reported that the construction should not take more than two years.

So as to permit the passage of canal traffic, it was proposed for the interim that a temporary canal, using unelaborate locks, should be dug as originally planned, and when the aqueduct was complete the redundant locks could then be transferred to the proposed flight at Stoke Bruerne. By September 1800 the river had been crossed by this makeshift series of locks, but it would not be until May 1802 that Jessop was instructed to prepare the plans and estimate for the aqueduct.

In June his report was duly approved, and the scheme was submitted to tender. By the end of November a bid from Major Mansel Thomas Harrison, of Wolverton, and Thomas and Joseph Kitchen, from Castlethorpe, had been accepted.

Work began in early 1803 and Harrison, as chief of the syndicate, pledged to complete the project within two years.

By June, two thirds of the embankment and one half of the aqueduct had been completed, and it seems that the structure consisted of three semicircular arches, being built on dry land, with the river diverted to flow beneath it. By mid-August 1805, so advanced were the proceedings that a partial channel along the course opened on the 26th of that month.

However, progress came to a halt in January 1806 when a section of the embankment, near Cosgrove, collapsed. The canal company alleged poor workmanship, but in retaliation Harrison said that the work had been carried out as per the contract.

But this paled into insignificance when, on the night of February 18th 1808, the aqueduct collapsed, causing panic in Stony Stratford which would have been flooded to a depth of several feet had the rubble dammed the river. Fortunately, the northern arch still remained, allowing the water to escape, albeit slowly.

Since the old line of the canal and the makeshift locks were still in situ, to a certain extent canal traffic could continue, though only at a loss of revenue of £400 a month.

In the aftermath, Harrison offered to make an out-of-court settlement, but on July 18th 1808 the case came before the Court of King's Bench and the company was awarded £9,262, plus costs, mainly to finance the construction of a temporary wooden trough, and the manufacture of bricks for a new aqueduct.

In retrospect, however, it seemed that much of the trouble had been due to the malpractice of some of those engaged in the project. Nevertheless, when Harrison died in March 1809, his instalments were taken over and settled by his son.

As a temporary solution, at a cost of £2,500, a wooden trough, made by an experienced carpenter, allowed the canal section to re-open in June 1808, and plans for a more permanent remedy could now be made.

Of the two ironwork firms that were approached the bid of Reynolds and Co, of Ketley Iron Works, proved successful, and for a total sum of £3,667 they provided an 'iron trunk' 101ft in length, centrally supported by a pier of stone, brought from the Hornton quarries in Warwickshire. The work was guaranteed for two years.

The 'Iron Trunk' - wide enough for two boats to pass - was officially opened on January 21st 1811. Even today it remains little altered from the original appearance, apart from a rebuilding of the abutments between 1919 and 1921.

A repainting took place in 1931, and in a more recent revamp some 700 litres of paint were used, at a cost of £15,000.

Originally, the British Waterways Board had considered applying black paint on the grounds of cost. But fortunately, a donation of an extra £1,000 by the Milton Keynes branch of the Inland Waterways Association allowed a more decorative grey, red, and white scheme to be applied.

WOLVERTON: UNCOVERING A WWI SPYRING

It's the accepted wisdom that just prior to the outbreak of World War One all the German spies in Britain were rounded up, in an operation masterminded by Vernon Kell whose retirement to the village of Emberton was the subject of a previous article.

However this may not be strictly true, for many years after the war a well known resident of Newport Pagnell recounted how he had played a prime role in the detection of a previously unknown enemy spy ring.

Sworn to secrecy at the time it was only many years later that he revealed the details and the following are extracts told in his own words; "I was in a gentleman's house not many miles from Wolverton discussing a matter of business with the owner. As I was preparing to leave the daughter of the house came running up to me and said, "Can you tell us, if there are any anti-aircraft guns kept at Wolverton?"

I replied I did not know, but, I said, "You need not be afraid, the enemy airships won't come to an isolated place like this." They said, "Oh, we are not afraid in the least but we do so want to know."

I then thought they knew some young aircraft gunner. I said, "If you will tell me his name I will try and find out." "We don't know anyone at all in it, but we promised to find out if there are any aircraft guns kept there."

"I said I had some friends in Wolverton, and I would enquire. Then, to my surprise, they said, "What we promised particularly to find out was, are there any soldiers guarding the bridge that crosses the river." I said, "Do you mean the viaducts?" "Yes," was the reply; "do find out and let us know how many in the day time and how many at night."

I said, "Before I go to all that trouble you must tell me why you want this information." The reply was, "We promised not to tell any one." I said, "Then if you don't tell me I shall not make enquiries." "Well, if I tell you, you won't know who it is - a particular friend of ours up in London."

I said, "Ask your father; he can find out." "Oh, we promised not to mention it to him." I thought there was something very unusual and suspicious about these enquiries and I thought I would report it. Then I thought after all it is perhaps only a mare's nest.

However, I saw the housekeeper, who did not know anything of our conversation, and asked her if she could tell me where the young ladies had been staying. She readily gave me the address. I then thought I would go up to London and see if I could find anything out intending to go and ask the trades people and shopkeepers if they could give me any information about the people at that particular address.

But when I got there it was a residential neighbourhood, with good, large expensive houses. For a minute I was nonplussed. Then suddenly I thought I could go to the rating office and ask the rateable value of this particular house. This I did.

The official turned over the papers and said it was rated so much gross and so much nett. I thanked him and, in an off-hand way, said, "Can you tell me anything about the people living in it?"

He replied, "I cannot, but perhaps the rate collector could give you some information." I said, "You can tell me if they have been there long?" "Oh, yes!" and he turned back in the book; "They have been there four or five years, and by-the-by, they are Germans."

Reporting this to the authorities the resident then returned to Newport Pagnell where two days later a special messenger arrived and swore him to secrecy. Within two hours of the report the house had been entered and in the wake of arrests evidence was found that the persons were in communication with the enemy.

Further, a chain of espionage was discovered of which the authorities knew nothing. Evidently the Germans were intent on sending aircraft to not only blow up Wolverton Works but also the bridge over the viaducts spanning the Ouse and with this being one of the vital points on the L.M.S. railway it would, with no possibility of a loop line or a detour being made, have taken longer to repair or reinstate than any other section of the line.

Milton Keynes Citizen, March 22, 2012

WOUGHTON

GUNFIGHT AT WOUGHTON

A 23, Windsor Street, Bugs Bunny must have thought birthday time had arrived rather early, for having won second prize in a rabbit show at Watford, his owner had now decided to offer him up for stud.

Indeed, a fate far more deserving than that which befell many of his furry brethren, scampering around the local fields, for with rationing firmly established as a way of everyday life, rabbits were becoming an important supplement to the available food.

Classed as vermin, from the damage they caused to essential crops, unskinned examples could fetch 7/2d (3p per lb), while the skinned variety commanded an extra tuppence.

Bullets

However, it was not only gun-toting farmers stalking the local hedgerows, for on mobile patrol between Newport Pagnell and Bletchley, the local copper also became a mite perturbed when bullets started winging in his direction.

Some days previous, the police had circulated the details of a wanted man, and the police constable on duty near Woughton-on-the-Green, Pc Snarey, noticed a man resembling the description crouching in a field.

Immediately he attempted an arrest, but a gunshot suggested perhaps the suspect was none too keen on the idea and a chase then ensued.

During the pursuit Pc Snarey exchanged several shots with the fugitive, but after a mile or so the man then crossed the River Ouzel and escaped.

However, a war reservist constable had raised the alarm and with the entire North Bucks police force now mobilised, the search resumed, assisted by the Home Guard and military units armed with machine guns.

Reportedly aged between 35 and 40 and 5ft 8ins tall, the man was said to be wearing the uniform of a Scottish officer and all lorries travelling along the main road were stopped and searched.

At Simpson bridge, drivers found themselves confronted with fixed bayonets but even so one driver unwisely took uppance and had his attitude problem then corrected at the police station, where his credentials were checked.

Also at the police station, on the Sunday the Chief Constable of Bucks held a long conference with Superintendent Bryant and Inspector Merry and with an armed guard placed at the gate, prolonged telephone conversations took place with the authorities in London.

Yet this was not the only instance of gun law, for a young lady was wounded when the car in which she was travelling came under fire from the Home Guard, having ignored an order to stop. No doubt these were jittery times. In conclusion it would perhaps be best not to dwell upon the consequent laundry bill when several Bletchley residents were suddenly startled by the stately progress of an old crock proceeding along Bletchley Road in a series of loud backfires!

Sunday Citizen August 18, 2002

BV - #0055 - 131023 - C0 - 234/156/24 - PB - 9781909054905 - Matt Lamination